T0319830

The Strictures of Inheritance

THE PRINCETON ECONOMIC HISTORY OF THE WESTERN WORLD

edited by Joel Mokyr

Growth in a Traditional Society: The French Countryside, 1450–1815,
by Philip T. Hoffman

*The Vanishing Irish: Households, Migration, and the Rural Economy in Ireland,
1850–1914,* by Timothy W. Guinnane

Black '47 and Beyond: The Great Irish Famine in History, Economy, and Memory,
by Cormac Ó Gráda

*The Great Divergence: China, Europe, and the Making of the Modern World
Economy,* by Kenneth Pomeranz

The Big Problem of Small Change, by Thomas J. Sargent and Francois R. Velde

Farm to Factory: A Reinterpretation of the Soviet Industrial Revolution,
by Robert C. Allen

*Quarter Notes and Bank Notes: The Economics of Music Composition in the
Eighteenth and Nineteenth Centuries,* by F. M. Scherer

The Strictures of Inheritance: The Dutch Economy in the Nineteenth Century,
by Jan Luiten van Zanden and Arthur van Riel

The Strictures of Inheritance

THE DUTCH ECONOMY IN
THE NINETEENTH CENTURY

Jan Luiten van Zanden and Arthur van Riel

Translated by Ian Cressie

PRINCETON UNIVERSITY PRESS

PRINCETON AND OXFORD

First published in the Netherlands as *Nederland, 1780–1914: Staat, instituties en economishe ontwikkeling*
copyright © Uitgeverij Balans 2000

Translation copyright © 2004 by Princeton University Press
Published by Princeton University Press, 41 William Street, Princeton, New Jersey 08540
In the United Kingdom: Princeton University Press, 3 Market Place, Woodstock, Oxfordshire OX20 1SY
All Rights Reserved

Library of Congress Cataloging-in-Publication Data
Zanden, J. L. van.
[Nederland 1780–1914. English]
The strictures of inheritance : the Dutch economy in the nineteenth century / Jan Luiten van Zanden and Arthur van Riel ; translated by Ian Cressie.
p. cm.—(The Princeton economic history of the Western world)
Includes bibliographical references and index.
ISBN 0-691-11438-2 (cl : alk. paper)
1. Netherlands—Economic policy.   2. Netherlands—Economic conditions.
I. Riel, Arthur van. II. Title. III. Series.

HC325.Z36613 2004
330.9492'06—dc21   2003056328

British Library Cataloging-in-Publication Data is available

This book has been composed in Times Roman
Printed on acid-free paper. ∞
www.pupress.princeton.edu

Printed in the United States of America

10 9 8 7 6 5 4 3 2 1

Contents

Figures

Tables

Preface

IN 2000 we published the Dutch version of this book: *Nederland 1780–1914. Staat, instituties en economische ontwikkeling* (The Netherlands 1780–1914. State, institutions and economic development). It was the product of a research project focused on the reconstruction of the national accounts of the Netherlands for the period 1800–1940 that had been organized by one of the authors and carried out at the Free University of Amsterdam and the universities of Utrecht and Groningen between 1987 and 2000. The project was set up to address one of Dutch economic history's major issues: the slow pace of industrialization in the Netherlands during the nineteenth century. The first aim of the project was to create a historical database of the national accounts for the period. A number of Ph.D. students, each covering a certain sector and/or period, formed the backbone of the project. Research by Ronald Albers (investment), Ronald van de Bie (1914–21), Ary Burger (international comparisons), Alain Callewaert (industry 1850–1914), Michael Jansen (industry 1800–50), Peter Groote (investment in infrastructure), Edwin Horlings (services 1800–50), Merijn Knibbe (agriculture), Joost Jonker (money and banking), Gert Pons (fisheries), Arthur van Riel (prices), Jan Pieter Smits (services 1850–1914), Wybren Verstegen (capital income), Annelies Vermaas (wages and salaries), and René van der Voort (government) all contributed to the database on which this book is based, and their studies helped us to understand the development of these parts of the economy. The database was molded into its definitive form by Jan Pieter Smits and Edwin Horlings. The results are also available on the Internet at **http://nationalaccounts. niwi.knaw.nl.**

From the very beginning the project was embedded in the close international network of researchers working on historical national accounting. Regular seminars organized together with the research group of Herman van der Wee and his successor, Erik Buyst, of the University of Leuven (Belgium) did much to improve the results. We also profited greatly from contributions by the regular participants of these and similar workshops: Bart van Ark, Steven Broadberry, Albert Carreras, Nick Crafts, Rainer Fremdling (who also headed the Groningen section of the project), Riitta Hjerppe, Herman de Jong, Olle Krantz, Pedro Lains, Jonas Ljungberg, Michelangelo van Meerten, Leandro Prados de la Escosura, Peter Solar, and, of course, the "godfather" of the network, Angus Maddison. Also, Richard Griffiths played a major role during the first stage of the project: not only did his research (and that of Jan de Meere) put the debate on the slow industrialization of the Netherlands back on the agenda, but he also prepared the way for setting up the project at the Free University of Amsterdam in 1987. The second stage of the project was the interpretation of the long-term development of the Dutch economy during the nineteenth century, the synthesis of a coherent perspective of the development process, and the writing of the Dutch manuscript. We tested our ideas on the link between state, institutions, and economic development on a number of audiences, in particular participants in seminars organized by Charles Feinstein at All Souls College Oxford and Joel Mokyr at Northwestern University. Maarten Prak read the whole manuscript of the Dutch version; his comments were, as always, thoughtful and critical, and helped to sharpen our ideas. Joost Jonker and Thomas Lindblad commented on parts of the manuscript and helped us to avoid a number of mistakes. Ian Cressie translated large parts of the manuscript and corrected those parts that had been rewritten in English, and by raising all kinds of questions contributed to the quality of the manuscript.

We have made a number of changes to adapt the book for an international public. These include incorporating more explicit international comparisons of Dutch economic growth (in particular in chapter 8), recalculating some of the tables to correct a few mistakes made in the Dutch version, adding more information on typical Dutch institutions and terminology, and shortening certain parts of the book that may have been less interesting to an international audience.

December 2002
Arthur van Riel
Jan Luiten van Zanden

Institutional Change, Nineteenth-Century Growth, and the Early Modern Legacy

WHEN THE ENGLISH STATISTICIAN Gregory King drew up the first comparative statement of per capita income within England, France, and the Dutch Republic at the end of the seventeenth century, the economic achievements and derived political leverage of the United Provinces had already been distinctive for several decades.[1] Since the 1580s, their technical prowess, financial strength, and commercial preponderance had baffled and worried foreign observers from Thomas Mun to Jean-Baptiste Colbert. Productivity, per capita income, and investment had experienced a structural increase—a process which, as King acknowledged, had made Holland by far the most prosperous region within Europe by the end of the seventeenth century. Rooted in a long history of agricultural development related to early urbanization and in ecological changes that made arable agriculture on increasingly marginal (peat) lands difficult to practice, farming in the provinces of the western and northern part of the country over the course of the fifteenth, sixteenth, and early seventeenth centuries became geared to specific parts of market demand, with an emphasis on raising livestock and dairy produce. Even more famously spectacular were changes at the other end of the reallocation process, that is, in services. Substitution of imported grain for homegrown cereals linked agrarian change to an original expansion in commerce and shipping. Yet it was only with the exploitation of the wider complementarity of especially Baltic and southern European supply and demand patterns, and the organization of "rich trades" based on colonial expansion, that Dutch overseas commerce evolved into the active entrepôt system that would serve as the hub of world trade and finance for over a century and a half. Based on a mixture of geographic advantage, shipbuilding innovations, financial instruments that lowered transaction costs, naval power, and an unrivaled stock of low-cost merchant shipping, Dutch merchants were able to extend their traditional dominance in Baltic bulk cargoes to include items such as spices, sugar, and textiles, all requiring close links with a wide range of processing industries.[2] Backward linkages between naval transport and ancillary industries, a human capital windfall from the skilled hands of immigrants fleeing the Habsburg provinces, reliable access to imported inputs, and a spate of technical change also helped foster the export-based growth of a labor-intensive industrial sector. By applying improved methods of using wind and peat energy and by modifying processing technologies in sectors such as textiles, paper-making, oil pressing, distilling, sawing, and ceramics, the productivity of labor and competitiveness in manufacturing soared. As a consequence, foreign and domestic labor was attracted to cities such as Leiden, Gouda, and Haarlem, where specialized branches of industry grew up.

From a wider perspective, Dutch primacy in international trade revolutionized the *économies mondes* inherited from the late sixteenth century. It transformed European colonial settlement in the Far East and the New World and established patterns of trade based on comparative efficiency by reducing risk and information asymmetry.[3] At the domestic level, it linked Dutch regional grain prices to the international market (thus dampening the variability of food prices), fostered an unparalleled division of labor, and established the role of formal factor and commodity markets.

The political and fiscal institutions underpinning these development characteristics were affected only to a limited extent by the economic changes after 1580. Rooted in resistance against the executive centralization, fiscal reforms, and religious strains of Habsburg rule, the Dutch Revolt that started in the 1570s served to consolidate "traditional" regional and urban privileges within a loose confederate alliance, rather than transforming the structure of politics. By limiting the leverage of central policy-making institutions and leaving sovereign power in the hands of the provincial states, the Dutch polity functioned on the basis of subsidiarity that acknowledged earlier prerogatives and the need for negotiated compromise over common interests. Because its decentralized structure was composed of a hierarchy of urban particularism and representation at the provincial level, the mechanics of the Republic's political system were defined only in part by its constitutional aspects. To a perhaps larger extent, they were forged by a changeable equilibrium in the allotment of powers, ruled over by the seemingly contradictory principles of provincial sovereignty and that of the union between the provinces, which was dominated by Holland. With the constitution of government specifying the sovereignty of the seven provinces, the provincial states were, in turn, mostly dominated by largely independent towns. But even in the more rural inland provinces, political opinion in the states typically balanced out. Moreover, while delegations of each of the "allies" held a single vote in the States General, and unanimity was prescribed in decisions of federal importance, that—contrary to the provincial states—it was in permanent session, dependent on the fiscal leverage of Holland, and physically close to the meeting place of the states of Holland and the quarters of its *stadtholder*, made monitoring costs over the inland delegates high, the distribution of power asymmetric, and the qualification of issues open to dispute.[4] With the effectively depoliticized Council of State left to preside over annual budget proposals and a reinterpreted position of what (except for the two northern provinces) was typically a joint *stadtholder* wielding power over numerous local appointments and the armed forces, the Dutch early modern system of executive rule functioned by an elaborate complex of largely informal checks and balances. Yet in defiance of forces pushing toward centralization, notably debt accumulation that placed pressure on the existing fiscal fragmentation and the recurrently changing political prominence of successive *stadtholders,* the Republic would continue to abide by this form of government for the duration of its existence. Indeed, as especially J. L. Price has propounded, it was only through such a limited set of central institutions that the context could be provided for formulating joint policy objectives while at the same time balancing the economic and political dominance of Holland against the political independence of the other sovereign provinces for more than two centuries.[5]

In contrast to its "anachronistic exceptionality" in political structure, the Habsburg Netherlands and the ensuing Dutch Republic, finally, are also held to have pioneered a revolution in public finance. Fueled initially by the wartime fiscal demands of Charles V, the regular imposition of province-wide excise and property taxes, formally earmarked as service annuities transferable on the open market, underwrote a smoothing of tax returns, the creation of long-term public debt, and the emergence of a market in negotiable securities.[6] After 1572 the rebellious provinces were increasingly able to command large sums with a high risk profile for relatively low rates of interest. The reverse implication was, of course, a comparatively unparalleled incidence of taxation and the introduction of fiscal redistribution as a principal bone of distributive contention between the various provinces. Given the commercial and financial preponderance of Holland, this "capital-intensive path of state formation" (in the terminology of Charles Tilly) provided an efficient way of raising funds beyond taxation by implying the strongest possible nonreneging commitment to bondholders, but at the same time was rooted in the fact that the underlying reform of public finance did not inaugurate the emergence of a nation-state.[7]

Despite being built upon a longer history of political and economic change, the Dutch economic and political ascendancy of the late sixteenth and early seventeenth centuries was nevertheless swift, hegemonic, and threatening to vested commercial interests. The Republic not only achieved dominance in trade, transport, and finance but also acquired the international leverage to promote and protect its adjoining policy objectives. But, at the time when its macroeconomic performance was assessed as part of King's exercise in political arithmetic, a change in its advanced path of development occurred, and the essential phenomenon of the period subsequent to King's inquiries was to be one of relative decline. While there has been largely unresolved debate over the precise pace and chronology, it is widely agreed that between the last quarter of the seventeenth century and the commercial disruptions of the Napoleonic era, the economy of Holland—and, by force of numbers, that of the Republic—

experienced a long-term standstill in productivity, a loss of international market share in commodity trade, and a decline in manufacturing output.[8] In parallel fashion, by the end of the eighteenth century Holland's international political stature had been reduced to little more than that set down in John Adams's famous metaphor of a squeaking frog caught between the legs of the two bulls engaged in the Anglo-French conflict.[9] Starting with the commercial disruption, aggravated fiscal imbalance, and rekindled political turbulence engendered by the Fourth Anglo-Dutch War of 1780–84, the years prior to the 1814–15 Treaty of Vienna saw not only overseas blockades and international monetary policies distorting commodity and capital flows but also Prussian and attempted British and French military invasions, fiscal exigencies, and finally the default of the state. Accordingly, it is a basic yet only rarely emphasized fact that the history of the early modern Dutch state is delimited not only by the events that occasioned its independence from Habsburg rule and, at the other end of the spectrum, a subordination to Napoleonic policy objectives after 1795, but simultaneously also by the rise and decline of its economic viability.

Such a conclusion is further enhanced by the evolution of scholarly exchange in the debate on the chronology and sectoral aspects of nineteenth-century industrialization. Few hypotheses in Dutch economic history have attracted as much scholarly discussion as that about the nation's late, or "retarded," transition to industrialized modernity, reflected in a piecemeal process of mechanization until the 1890s. From the first works addressing the issue—most famous is I. J. Brugmans's 1925 dissertation—to the authoritative 1968 work by De Jonge on industrial growth after 1850, the tendency is to associate this apparent lack of industrial dynamism with macroeconomic stagnation.[10] Yet in more recent years the historiography of nineteenth-century development has moved away from conflating a paucity of changes in mechanization and firm size with a lack of income growth. Starting with a range of books and papers by Griffiths, Bos, and De Meere published between 1979 and 1982, the notion of backwardness became questioned, and the focus of debate on industrial performance shifted from alleged entrepreneurial inertia and capital market failings to combined cost penalties resulting from transport and input costs related to natural resource endowments and from high wage levels, the result of early modern wage developments.[11] Moreover, modest growth in sectoral output and productivity was identified for the years after 1830. Instead of "backward" or "late," as Griffiths's 1980 inaugural lecture termed the issue, the Dutch development transition had been "different," its sectoral pattern having been marked by "balanced growth."[12] Finally, a recent succession of quantitative analyses of economic performance during this period have posited a drawn-out transition in the structure and causes of productivity change coming to full fruition after 1850. This new range of sectoral studies measuring changes in value added and factor-input combinations have argued for a modified chronology and broadened interpretational framework of Dutch economic development.[13]

In consequence, evaluated from either side of the turbulent 1795 to 1813 revolutionary period and within the context of disjointed historiographical debates, the present general consensus may be said to identify a chronological concurrence between a transition in the structure of economic performance and a realignment of executive government and fiscal accountability. Straddling the political turbulence and commercial disruption triggered by the Fourth Anglo-Dutch War and the institutional changes of the years after 1840, this phase saw the mechanisms of Dutch politics altered in a way seemingly at odds with all that had gone before, while simultaneously witnessing a transition in the structure of economic performance. A central message of this book is that this concurrence was not just chronological. Rather, it was deterministic. Far from being part of the separate realms of enlightened intellectualism and economic change that have been featured in the literature so far, both processes—the reorganization of the state and the observed pattern of economic development—were strongly interrelated. We will argue that a specific constellation of political power adapted from the early modern legacy and the post-Napoleonic settlement, shortsighted fiscal policy, tax distortions, and institutionalized failings in product markets together shaped the features of Dutch development in the early nineteenth century. The 1840 political crisis over public finance that ushered in debt conversion and constitutional reform was in the long run linked to another restructuring of the process of growth. As a result, after 1860 we witness the emergence of sectoral and distributive characteristics that fitted the typology formulated by Kuznets in the 1960s: that is, shifting sectoral output and employment shares, urban labor absorption, increasing real wages, an enhanced integration of markets through deregulation, and infrastructural change.[14]

These interrelationships were not limited to the phase between 1780 and 1848. Liberal democracy and emerging industrialization (after 1860) caused the emergence of new problems, such as the "social question," which required solution. This induced, after 1870, a series of developments into the direction of a new institutional structure that would have a great effect on the state (i.e., the emergence of the welfare state in the course of the twentieth century) and would shape the direction of economic change in the twentieth century. In this complex way, we establish indirect links between the dramatic changes that began after 1780, which demolished the old structure of the Republic, and the new sociopolitical and economic structures that would arise in the Netherlands in the twentieth century.

The theoretical basis for our assertion that reforms in the political sphere and in the institutional framework of economic life in general affected the development of the economy can be found in the extensive literature on institutional economics in the broadest sense. In this context, institutions are defined as the rules, laws, and customs that facilitate transactions. These vary from unwritten customs on a specific market (e.g., is bargaining permitted? how is the sales price determined?) to the laws of a country that regulate the property rights of market participants. One of the concerns of institutional economists is where these institutions come from and how specific institutions determine the structure of incentives that affect the behavior of the state, of entrepreneurs, and of workers. For example, Douglass North, perhaps the most influential theoretician in this area, defines the economic problem as the question of how cooperation between individuals can come about: How do market transactions develop that lead to division of labor and specialization? Which formal institutions—in the sense of laws implemented by the state and enforced by a judicial apparatus—and, at least as important, informal rules and customs guarantee the property rights of agents? And how do these institutions, these rules of the game of the market economy, change over time?[15] It is clear that the state—the organization that creates the statutory framework for market transactions—plays a fundamental role in this process of change. From this point of view, politics can be interpreted as the game to continuously modify these rules. The rules of this "meta-game" are, ultimately, determined by the constitution of the state. This document establishes the formal rules that determine how political relationships are defined and how changes can be made in these relationships.

Economics and politics, the economy and the state, are from this point of view closely linked to each other. The development of an economy is ultimately self-determined by the constitution of a country, which, after all, defines how the political game will be played. For example, it defines how the monarch and the parliament can affect the outcome of the political process and, consequently, how changes in institutions can come about.[16] Our book will investigate how close these relationships were. One central theme is the influence of the various constitutions of the Netherlands on economic development. This concerns the following stages of constitutional development:

- the decentralized state structure of the Republic, based on the Treaty of Utrecht of 1579;
- the establishment of a unified state in 1798;
- the formation of the Kingdom of the Netherlands between 1813 and 1815;
- the breakthrough of liberal democracy in 1840–48;
- fundamental reforms aimed at the extension of the franchise of 1887 and 1917

We will attempt to show that these sequential constitutions had a major influence on economic development during these periods in order to test and refine part of the program of the institutional economics. Moreover, this approach links up with another closely related school of economic thought: political economy. Economists from the generation of Tinbergen and Kuznets viewed the state as an independent umpire striving for the maximization of welfare, "the formulator of rules under which economic activity was to be carried out; as a referee . . . and as provider of infrastructure."[17] The essence of the new political economy (public choice) that has unraveled such myths is that the behavior of political actors is analyzed in an identical fashion to that of the participants in markets, assuming that they strive for the maximization of a specific public utility function, for power, prestige, budgets, or votes. During this process, they are also confronted with constraints, with scarcity. In the view of economists such as Downs, political entrepreneurs strive to be elected or reelected; to achieve this aim, they attempt to accommodate the preferences of the average voter (and in this way acquire the support of 50 percent of the electorate plus one). A change in the voting system, such as an extension of the franchise, can therefore have major consequences for the behavior of political entrepreneurs and, consequently, for the result of the political process. As a larger part of the population gains the right to vote, politicians who promote the interests of less prosperous population groups can count on greater support.[18] This mechanism will turn out to be very important for understanding political dynamics after 1870.

The state can be seen as the first layer of the institutional framework of an economy. The second institutional layer is the arena of collective action, of groups that have organized themselves with the aim of promoting their specific interests. In their rent-seeking they often require the support of the state; exerting influence on the political process is therefore one of the most important aims of these interest groups. In a stable society, Olson (in his classic work on political economy) expected a continuing increase in the number of interest groups that were able to organize themselves. This ultimately results in a process of institutional sclerosis, where the economic surplus will no longer be invested in growth and development but is completely consumed by the distributive coalitions that control the state apparatus.[19] This thought plays a role in our analysis of the decentralized state structure of the Republic, which is rooted in a relatively closely knit corporatist structure in which many interest groups had entered coalitions with the urban oligarchy (or parts thereof). The destruction of this corporatist society was one of the most important goals of the Batavian revolutionaries. Under the slogan "Freedom, Equality, and Brotherhood," they attempted to eliminate these corporatist structures; the abolishment of the guilds is an example of this process. As we will see, these reforms were only partly successful. The liberal reformers after 1840 still had to complete the process. The acceleration of economic development that began in the second half of the nineteenth century is, in our view, related to the liberalization of economic life that began after 1798 and was finally completed in the 1840s and 1850s. However, it is striking that this process was barely completed when the construction of new corporatist institutions—trade unions, farmers' organizations, employers' organizations—began. A phase of spontaneous, bottom-up, institutional renewal, which began after 1870, formed the basis for the corporatist structures that would characterize economic development in the twentieth century. While in the eighteenth century institutional sclerosis and economic inertia went hand in hand—which is in accordance with Olson's expectations—the growing corporatism of the first quarter of the twentieth century was in fact linked to an acceleration in economic growth, which does not agree with Olson's predictions.[20] Also at odds with his model is the fact that the emergence of new interest groups did not appear to be a continuous process—inherent to a stable society—but was concentrated in a relatively brief period (between 1890 and 1920). This, too, requires an explanation.

The third layer of analysis in the present book concerns the issue of how economic change was steered by these institutional changes and how it was in turn the cause of new institutional experiments. This analysis concentrates on the transition from a "stationary state" (characteristic of the eighteenth century) to the process of "modern economic growth" (beginning in the 1860s and 1870s). The first term, which refers to a stationary economy, was coined by the founder of economics, Adam Smith, who in his famous *Wealth of Nations* (1776) typified the economic development of Holland in this way. This raises the question of how it was possible for this relatively modern market economy to achieve a virtually constant level of production and income during a period of approximately 150 years (between 1670 and 1820). Why was there no growth, based on technological and organizational progress, during this extended period? The second term, "modern economic growth," originates from the founder of long-term economic growth analysis, Simon Kuznets.[21] He showed how long-term growth in per capita income, the most important characteristic of modern economic growth, is closely related to processes of structural transformation of the economy, especially those characterized by the relative decline of agriculture and the expansion of industry and the services sector. These changes were also linked to the process of urbanization. The economic development after 1860 will be analyzed within this framework.

Focusing on these two concepts—a stationary state until 1820 and modern economic growth after 1860—introduces a risk of disregarding the intervening period. It is therefore important to pay a great deal of attention to explaining the deviating development of the Netherlands during the first half of the nineteenth century. The explanation, as one could expect on the basis of the preceding, can primarily be sought in the specific institutional development of the Netherlands during this period.

Although this book concentrates on the endogenous forces that gave shape to the processes of economic and institutional change, we certainly cannot ignore the external influences that affected this small country. The decline of the Republic after 1780 was initially the result of the dramatic end to the naval war with the British (1780–84), the Prussian intervention (1787), and the French occupation (1794–95). In other words, it was the result of the incapacity of the

Republic to sustain itself within the European state system, which, as Tilly has pointed out, was characterized by warfare and preparation for war.[22] This relative decline undermined the legitimacy of its form of government and led to attempts to implement drastic reforms, first by the Patriots and later by the Batavian revolutionaries. Between 1814 and 1815, the major European powers intervened in another way by expanding the state to include the southern provinces of the Low Countries. The relatively independent position that the Republic was still able to occupy as a "great power" was lost after 1815, and the kingdom realized at important moments that it was especially dependent on its "most natural ally," Great Britain (which, for example, returned some of the colonies after 1815 and also continued to supervise how the Netherlands exercised this colonial authority).[23] To a certain extent, the Netherlands became a "client" of the powerful Albion and had to explicitly adapt important aspects of its international policy to the demands of this power on the other side of the North Sea. But like every client, the Netherlands attempted to optimally utilize the latitude it was given by this complex relationship.

Of a somewhat different order were the economic forces of the world economy that acted on a small, open economy. These included not only changes in relative prices—the result of industrialization elsewhere—or the growing demand for agricultural products in these newly industrialized regions but also the waves of cyclically increasing and decreasing protectionism. One of the causes of the relative decline of the Republic after 1670 was the emergence of mercantilism, especially in the England of Cromwell and the Stuarts and in the France of Colbert and Louis XIV. This protectionism, in varying disguises, would thrive until the mid–nineteenth century, only to make way for free trade after 1846, when the Corn Laws were abolished. Free trade would again come under pressure due to the agricultural depression after 1873. Here as well, the question arises of how the institutions called into life by the government—in the form of import and export duties and other measures focusing on promoting domestic industry—affected economic development in this small, open economy.

Despite these important exogenous influences, institutional developments in the Netherlands during the period 1780–1914 displayed a high degree of "path dependency," which brings us to another fundamental aim of the analysis that follows.[24] The generations of politicians who shaped the development of this state, from the Patriots of the 1780s to the radical liberals of the 1890s, responded to the specific economic, political, and institutional problems with which they were confronted. The solutions they found for their problems often determined constraints and problems that then confronted the next generation of politicians. With some exaggeration, one could even state that parts of the Republic's economic inheritance, such as its capital wealth, its very productive agricultural sector, or its rich colonial possessions, would continue to dominate the evolution of the economy until deep into the twentieth century. Similarly, it took three generations of reformers—from the 1780s to the 1840s—to free the economy of the institutional sclerosis that was the sociopolitical inheritance of the Republic. The fact that the Dutch economy took its own path between 1780 and 1914 was to a large extent due to this specific inheritance. In this book, we will attempt to reconstruct this path in its depth and breadth.

An important aim of this book is to show the extent to which the economic history of the Netherlands can be rewritten based on the new insights offered by the new institutional economics. We are convinced that the most important characteristics of the specific path taken by the Dutch economy between 1780 and 1914—a path that has been debated by historians for generations—cannot be understood without these new insights. In addition, we provide a great deal of new information about the growth of incomes, production, employment, prices, wages, and other economic indicators. This information is essential to analyze the long-term development of the economy. We can do this because the present book is the final result of a major study into the national accounts of the period 1807–1913. This study, in the tradition of scholars such as Gregory King and Simon Kuznets, has been conducted during the past ten years at the universities of Amsterdam (Vrije Universiteit), Utrecht, and Groningen. It has resulted in a unique and consistent database concerning the national income and various aspects thereof, and is the quantitative basis for this book.[25] In this regard, we have not aimed at making an exhaustive quantitative analysis of this database; other publications are being prepared with this aim. An important objective of our book is to make the information about the economic developments during the nineteenth century accessible to a relatively broad readership, since this historical-quantitative research has led to many new insights about the exact course of economic modernization. During the process of researching and reconstructing the national accounts, however, we gradually realized that the ultimate determinants of economic development cannot be found in the growth accounts themselves but must be sought in the complex interaction between markets and institutions.

CHAPTER ONE

The End of the Republic

ADAM SMITH'S "STATIONARY STATE" AND

THE ENLIGHTENED REVOLUTION

THE "STATIONARY STATE" AND HISTORIOGRAPHICAL DEBATE

One of the original ways of typifying the development of the economy of the Dutch Republic during the eighteenth century involves viewing it as having reached a stationary equilibrium. Adam Smith and David Ricardo, classical economists of the late eighteenth and early nineteenth centuries, were both of the opinion that economic development by means of trade, the extension of markets, the division of labor, and the accumulation of capital would in due course result in a "stationary state," although each held a different view of the mechanisms responsible for this eventual stagnation.[1] It was Smith who, in the 1770s, first wrote of Holland in these terms. In his view the accumulation of capital—"the increase of stock"—was the most characteristic aspect of the process of economic development taking place. Smith attempted to demonstrate that while "the increase of stock . . . raises wages, [it] tends to lower profit." This decrease in profitability would in time lead to a structural decrease in interest rates. He described the stationary state that was held to be the outcome of this process as follows: "In a country which had acquired its full complement of riches, where in every particular branch of business there was the greatest quantity of stock that could be employed in it, as the ordinary rate of clear profit would be very small, the usual market rate of interest which could be afforded out of it, would be so low as to render it impossible for any of the wealthiest people to live upon the interest of their money. . . . It would be necessary that almost every man should be a man of business, or engage in some sort of trade," subsequently adding that "the province of Holland seems to be approaching near to this state. . . . The government there borrow at two percent, and private people of good credit at three. The wages of labour are said to be higher in Holland than in England, and the Dutch, it is well known, trade upon lower profits than any people in Europe." Despite high wages, which Smith associated with indirect taxation and the public debt it supported, Holland's merchants continued to be able to compete in world markets because of the advantages of low real interest rates to which they had access at home. Or, as

Smith put it, "In reality, high profits tend much more to raise the price of work than high wages."[2]

Some two centuries later, Smith's ideas were incorporated by economic historian Peter Klein in his historiographical review of the economic development of the Republic. In addition, he associated the stationary state with patterns of specialization and the division of labor, both of which occupy a pivotal role in Smith's work. In his view, the growth of towns as a market for agricultural produce played a key role in initiating the division of labor. Because the division of labor was determined by the extent of the market, progressive urbanization had been required to continue the process of specialization.[3] Under these circumstances and given the limited potential of the domestic market, the cities and towns of Holland, according to Klein, were to an important degree dependent on the capture of an increasing share of a world trade volume. When, as a result of the rise in mercantilism and competition from neighboring countries, this share could no longer be increased, economic performance began to falter.

In this fashion, Klein elegantly connects both elements of Smith's stationary state: his ideas on the limitations to the degree of specialization and the surmised fall in the profit rate through capital accumulation. After all, if we assume that the process of specialization attracts investment, then both processes would run parallel to each other. The well-known paucity of investment opportunities in the economy of Holland in the eighteenth century has been attributed to the process of specialization, on the one hand, and to the accumulation of capital that occurred in previous decades, on the other, so that the existing opportunities for investment were exhausted. As we shall emphasize later, these processes in turn were related to the growth of the public debt (and the institutional commitment to the associated interest payments) and the increasing extent to which monied interests invested in loans to foreign governments and stocks.[4] This same mechanism was also emphasized in the 1995 textbook on the economy of the Dutch Republic by De Vries and Van der Woude, although their work offers no clear explanation as to why the Republic ultimately reached a state of stationary equilibrium.[5]

A remarkable precursor to this set of views can be found in the contemporary work of W. M. Keuchenius, the Schiedam civil servant who in 1803, shortly before his departure for the East Indies, published a book inspired by the English "political arithmetic" that contains the first macroeconomic analysis of the Republic.[6] Based on his broad knowledge of the topic, he attempted to reconstruct the "national balance"—that is, the balance of income and expenditure of the Batavian Republic. For our purposes, it is particularly interesting that this quantitative description was related to a sectoral analysis of economic development in the previous century and a half. What is special about the analysis is that it is based on what we today would refer to as a sectoral model: agriculture, trade, and, in the words of Keuchenius, *"Fabrieken en Trafieken,"* due to their distinct economic characteristics, are seen to exhibit different patterns of development. Agriculture, which, in line with the popular physiocratic ideals of Batavian administrators, Keuchenius typified as "mild mother of Nature" and the "foundation of all trade," was considered to be of fundamental importance as a source of wealth and exports. Moreover, Keuchenius believed that this sector had made a great deal of progress: earlier (in the seventeenth century) it had not been able to feed the population without additional grain imports, whereas at the end of the eighteenth century it could do so. The grains imported from the Baltic region, according to Keuchenius, largely served processing industries (Trafieken) such as distilleries and breweries, a significant portion of the production of which was again exported. Second, trade was considered "the station that offers a people the most services and the greatest advantages. It supports agriculture by promoting greater demand and higher prices for their produce." As such it "encourages industry . . . and bestows on all peoples the most essential of benefits by fulfilling the needs of one through alleviating the excess of the other."[7]

It need hardly be cause for surprise that this representative of Holland's economic thought was a staunch defender of the interests of trade. Remarkable in the light of the existing historiographical debate, however, is his consideration of the "Fabrieken en Trafieken," which were believed to have undergone considerable decline: "As flourishing as manufacturing or weaving once was in our fatherland, it languishes today and the same can be said of several other Trafieken and branches of business." The proximate cause of this industrial decline, Keuchenius asserted, consisted of the fact that "for two hundred years foodstuffs were two-thirds cheaper, taxes lower and thus wages not as expensive; international trade, shipping, and agriculture were then not as extensive as now, and therefore required fewer people, all of whom could be employed in the weaving industry; and the third and most important reason was that other peoples did not enjoy freedom and could not establish factories; on the contrary, as a result of religious persecution, craftsmen and businessmen fled Brabant and France to come here or go to other regions and set up a number of factories in our country."[8] This situation changed under the influence of an increase in foreign competition and the protection of export markets, but also as a result of endogenous developments: due to the increase in wealth in the Republic, the growth of international trade and shipping, and the influence of growing government expenditures, prices and taxation rose steeply in Holland, leading to an important increase in nominal wages (see chapter 2 for a more detailed discussion). The growing demand for labor itself also contributed to this increase in wages. All these factors were detrimental to the Fabrieken "because in general, given the conditions under which factories operate, even weavers of the best quality of sheets are such that they cannot support high wages . . . on account of the many hands needed to carry out the numerous operations, such as preparing wool, spinning, weaving, fulling, and finishing." In modern terms, Keuchenius propounded that because of the relatively low productivity of labor in industry, at least in domestic terms, this sector could only decline, as the demand for labor in sectors able to pay higher wages—trade, shipping, and agriculture—increased.

From this point of view there was of course no valid reason to stimulate industry by means of protective measures, as several earlier eighteenth-century authors and an increasing number of contemporaries had advocated. Keuchenius was strongly opposed to plans in this direction. In his stationary state, Holland's economy, in full agreement with comparative factor endowments, had become specialized in highly productive activities in the agricultural and service sectors while profiting from cheap imports of grains and industrial inputs from low-wage regions. Given this process of specialization, the policy choices underwriting the economic development of the Republic were in close accordance with Ricardian (or indeed Heckscher-Ohlin) trade theory: labor and capital had been actively withdrawn from the sector in which they experienced a comparative disadvantage, that is, industry. The inability of the Republic to reform its trade policies and adopt a stance more attuned to the needs of industry from this point of view was perfectly understandable. Given the system of political representation, trade policies, in the euphemistic term coined by Johan de Vries, were and remained "staple market friendly"; that is, first and foremost oriented towards a prolonged effort to strengthen the position of Holland's international trade, thereby accentuating the trend signaled by Keuchenius.[9]

Insofar as it can be reconstructed, the actual development of the economy of Holland, between the 1670s and 1795, appears by and large to have been consistent with the views expressed by both Smith and Keuchenius, stressing different aspects of the process leading up to the stationary state. What information at the macroeconomic level there is, indicates that in the wake of the spectacular process of economic growth between 1580 and the 1670s, a long period of stagnation set in, during which output per capita failed to increase and, in the years between 1670 and 1740, possibly even declined (table 1.1)[10]

Following the swift increase between 1500 and 1670, population growth, too, came to a standstill (table 1.2). In the century after 1650, the number of inhabitants of the Republic hardly changed. Only during the second half of the eighteenth century did it once again increase slightly, albeit in the outer provinces. Between 1680 and 1750, Holland's population decreased by approximately 11 percent; real growth would only occur again after 1815. Elsewhere, in part under the influence of the dynamics of agricultural development, some natural growth did take place. As part of this process, de-urbanization and a relative growth of agricultural employment occurred between 1680 and the beginning of the nineteenth century.

Although, due to margins of uncertainty and the long time between reliable counts of the urban population (1622 and 1795), the exact chronology of this development is somewhat unclear. It is likely that the number of inhabitants of the industrial towns of Holland (Leiden, Haarlem, Gouda, and Delft) fell by

TABLE 1.1.
Estimates of Gross Production in Holland, 1650–1805.

				Years			
	Weight	1650/59	1670/79	1700/1709	1740/49	1760/69	1800/1805
Textiles	0.30	100	109	63	52	49	30
Construction	0.20	100	81	63	74	81	67
Shipbuilding	0.08	100	107	105	85	65	45
Brewing	0.08	100	85	75	55	50	25
Paper	0.02	100	180	355	470	480	480
Soap	0.02	100	78	57	53	61	67
Other	0.30	100	100	100	100	100	90
Total manufacturing	0.36	100	99	84	82	81	66
Agriculture	0.16	100	105	85	75	85	100
Fishing, herring	0.02	100	95	87	40	25	11
Fishing, whale	0.02	100	238	241	222	125	2
Domestic services	0.05	100	127	120	115	115	130
Trade	0.37	100	99	100	115	121	113
Transport (barge)	0.02	100	155	118	78	83	92
Total	1.00	100	105	95.5	96.5	98	90.5
Idem per capita		100	97	91	96.5	98	90.5

Source: Van Zanden, "Economie van Holland."

roughly a third in the second quarter of the eighteenth century, followed by a somewhat less steep decline of some 17 percent in the next forty-five years up to the Batavian revolution. Towns oriented toward international trade (particularly those suited to accommodate the increasing volume of Rhine trade) experienced a more moderate decline and, at least up to 1795, boasted stable population numbers (Amsterdam) or even expanded (Rotterdam). It was Johan de Vries who, in the 1950s, first interpreted this continuing relative prosperity of the capital as a demonstration of what he referred to as a process of "internal

TABLE 1.2.
Demographic and Urban Development, 1622–1795.

	Holland				Republic			
	1622	1680	1750	1795	1622	1680	1750	1795
	Population (thousands)							
Total population	672	883	783	783	1,685	1,810	1,925	2,079
Towns ≥ 2,500	381	540	475	469	622	815	755	781
30 largest towns	348	463	449	457	522	671	650	669
Amsterdam	105	191	205	217	105	191	205	217
	Urban shares (percent)							
Towns ≥ 2,500	56.7	61.1	60.7	59.9	36.9	43.2	39.2	37.6
30 largest towns	51.0	52.4	57.3	58.4	31.0	37.1	33.8	32.2
Amsterdam	15.6	21.7	26.2	27.7	6.2	10.6	10.6	10.4

Sources: Nusteling, "Periods"; J. De Vries and Van der Woude, Nederland, 74–84; Horlings, Economic Development, 323. Estimates of urbanization according to Nusteling, using adapted data by Horlings.

contraction."[11] To sum up, insofar as the chronology of the development of the most essential variables can be retraced, the economy of the Republic as of the last quarter of the seventeenth century conformed to the characteristics of the stationary state, albeit with a large degree of regional variation.

Surveying the literature, it might thus be stated that the various authors discussed here have suggested some broad answers to the question of how Holland's stationary state should be interpreted. Yet, a number of essential analytical questions remain unanswered. In essence, these relate to the macroeconomic working of the process: What mechanisms can explain how a small, open economy that is exposed to continuous movements in relative prices and other external stimuli, and which, moreover, steadfastly adopts a trade policy that makes little attempt to filter out such influences, underwent such a prolonged period of economic stagnation? Which were the forces that helped maintain the high, stable income level of the economy of Holland, or indeed that of the Republic as a whole? Economic theory here suggests three equilibriums in need of attention when attempting to explain Holland's "stationary state":

- The internal equilibrium between savings and investment and its effect upon the allocation and accumulation of capital: What were the forces structuring this equilibrium? What was the role of investors and entrepreneurs in the reinvestment of their incomes? Was it saving or investment that was elastic with respect to output and income growth, and thus decisive in determining the adjusted equilibrium?

- The external equilibrium: How can a stationary economy maintain equilibrium in its balance of payments under the condition of an international economy with changing trade and capital flows and an associated reshuffling of the pattern of balance of payments settlements? And which were the structural changes in the balance of trade and the allocation of capital upon which the revised equilibrium was based?

- Labor market equilibrium: Was unemployment in the cities and towns high, and did pressure on social support increase, as argued by contemporaries and studies on social welfare? Or were the endogenous response in labor supply and the ability of the labor market to cope with regressive structural change such that a long-term equilibrium was reached, as, for example, Keuchenius argued? Or do both hypotheses describe different aspects of the same historical reality?[12]

Focusing on the first of these questions, the transition from a dynamic economy to a stationary state in the second half of the seventeenth century was undoubtedly accompanied by a significant decline in the investment share. Indeed, there is evidence that after about 1670 the growth of the mercantile fleet and the housing stock decelerated sharply. Thus, capital goods industries—shipbuilding and construction—were confronted with a fall in sales. As a result, the domestic demand for savings declined markedly. In order to maintain equilibrium, this development could theoretically have been compensated for by three alternative responses: (1) an increase in consumption and a commensurate decrease in the savings quota, (2) a dissavings of the public sector, and (3) the export of capital. And while the change in investment has been obvious to all participants in the debate, it is the relative weight of these mechanisms that has been the largely implicit focus of discussion.

It is perhaps most difficult to determine with any degree of certainty whether consumption patterns underwent any systematic change. Research on the socioeconomic history of the *regenten* (urban ruling class) suggests, however, that durable luxury goods became more accepted and widespread in the eighteenth century than they had been before, providing a contrast with the rather sober lifestyle for which the regenten of Holland in the first half of the seventeenth century were known.[13] Wealthy citizens in the seventeenth century may, for example, have maintained a modest country house in one of the large reclaimed polders; their eighteenth-century descendants had stately houses built for them along the river Vecht or owned one of the mansions strewn along the dunes of North Holland. The turning point for this reversal is often dated in the last quarter of the seventeenth century, which would coincide with the fall in the investment share after 1670.[14] Simultaneously, the amount of durable consumer goods, such as clocks, furniture, and jewelry, registered in probate inventories increased.[15] In the same manner, the revenues from duties on luxury foodstuffs such as tea, coffee, sugar, and tobacco point to a strong rise in consumption.[16] The propensity of the elite to save, therefore, in all probability decreased. Indeed, it might even be argued that this apparent propensity for greater luxury was simply a rational reaction to falling real interest rates (causing saving to become a less attractive option).[17] However, even if these observations are correct, it should be noted that the rate of savings, even at the end of the eighteenth century, cannot possibly be characterized as low in an absolute sense. Intimately familiar with the financial market, Henry Hope, as late as 1791, still observed, "Though we have many in this Country who spend their incomes, I believe the people taken in a body do not consume more than five-eigths, or at most three-quarters of their Revenues."[18]

Much more evident, however, is the fact that the government made an important contribution to the mobilization of large surpluses of savings. This was especially true between 1672 and 1713, the period overshadowed by war, bounded as it was by the *rampjaar* (year of disasters or catastrophes) of French and German invasion, on the one hand, and the Treaty of Utrecht ending the War of the Spanish Succession, on the other. During these years, Holland's debt rose from around 130 million guilders (fl 130 million) to over fl 300 million. The macroeconomic importance of this increase should not be underestimated; these were very large amounts to be mobilized in a period when the normal functioning of the economy was crippled or at the very least hindered by war on land and at sea. The sudden rise in government expenditure and the concomitant growth of public debt in times of war must have had a stabilizing effect on the economy. Still, a substantial part of this money was used to subsidize the Republic's foreign allies, paid off to perform its military duties abroad. The impact of this type of early modern, war-imputed built-in stabilizers therefore must nevertheless have been of limited importance.

In the initial years after the War of the Spanish Succession, the public debt increased at a much more leisurely pace. However, given the fact that the reform of public finance as proposed by Raadpensionaris Van Slingelandt and others was frustrated by the resistance of the individual provinces seeking to maintain their fiscal autonomy, the Republic after 1713 was nevertheless forced to abandon its role as a broker of international power and henceforth sought to stay out of major international conflicts. At midcentury, the War of the Austrian Secession, however, once again forced repeated deficits, thereby increasing Holland's debt from fl 300 million in 1742 to fl 362 million in 1752 (table 1.3).

Regardless of the chronology of wartime deficits, the predicament of Dutch public finance consisted of the fact that in years of peace and relative prosperity no remotely sufficient measures were taken to reduce the debt burden, so that each new international conflict—widening in scale and cost as the tax base of the larger European nations expanded—caused a further accumulation of

TABLE 1.3.
Estimated Development of the Public Debt, Participation in British Funds, and Estimates of the Sum Invested in Foreign Bonds, 1670–1795 (in millions of guilders).

Year	Debt in Holland	Debt in Generaliteit	British 3% Consols	All British Funds	Riley Foreign	"Best-Guess" Domestic	"Best-Guess" Total
1670	128.4	15.5	—	—	—	222	222
1680	161.5	15.5	—	—	—	279	279
1690	159.5	19.5	—	—	—	280	280
1700	193.3	27.5	—	—	—	354	354
1710	265.7	46.5	—	—	—	478	478
1720	307.5	65.4	—	—	—	545	573
1730	297.9	68.7	—	—	—	531	599
1740	295.3	64.5	—	—	—	519	627
1750	347.6	59.1	—	62	—	579	727
1760	350.8	45.0	—	—	—	558	746
1762	347.9	42.8	53.6	152	200	551	751
1769	337.9	35.3	79.9	—	250	531	781
1776	325.5	29.7	71.0	177	—	510	820
1780	321.0	26.5	—	—	350	509	859
1782	332.4	24.3	89.8	202	—	534	929
1788	383.3	20.1	102.4	—	—	628	1,158
1790	405.9	19.5	—	—	575	666	1,241
1792	403.6	18.7	63.0	—	610	678	1,288
1795[a]	455.0	17.5	67.1	164	650	760	1,410

Sources: J. De Vries and Van der Woude, *Nederland*, 150, 177; Dormans, "Economie," 474; Neal, *Rise*, 207; J. F Wright, "Contribution," 657–74; Riley, *International Government Finance*, 15–16, 84; *Gedenkstukken* 4, bk. 2, 471–73.

debt. The reason for this behavioral stance lay in the fact that the ruling elite had no alternative domestic destination for its funds once redeemed and therefore resisted any government attempts to pay off its loans. In fact this very mechanism had been distinguished as early as 1673 by the British ambassador Sir William Temple, who dramatized the reaction of those holding government paper to suggestions of having their deposits returned to them as follows:

"When they pay off any part of the principal those it belongs to receive it with tears, not knowing how to dispose of it to interest with such safety and ease."[19] In a similar manner, a century later one of Gouda's mayors remarked that "continued repayment by the government and the reinvestment of these monies is causing investors considerable embarrassment."[20] In this situation, the perpetually extensive amount of savings, on the one hand, and the almost monopsonistic position of the government on the capital market, on the other, eventually made it possible to lower interest rates on the public debt to a mere 2.5 percent.

After 1713, investment in the debts of foreign governments began to exert a similarly absorbing effect. During periods in which the domestic public debt did not rise—between 1713 and 1740 and between 1752 and 1773—surplus domestic savings left the country in the form of capital exports (see table 1.3). Investment in foreign securities increased from next to nothing at the beginning of the eighteenth century to fl 250 million around 1770 and an estimated total of some fl 600 million in 1790—a sum that, since it was in large part invested in British funds, has been at the heart of an extensive discussion on the role of Dutch money in propping up the capital market that supported the British industrial revolution and on the effects of its withdrawal in the years leading up to the Batavian revolution.[21] Under the stationary state, the sizable savings surpluses of the private sector flowed to domestic public debt and to an increasing extent to foreign countries. Conversely, the share of the interest payments based on such foreign loans in national income increased steadily (table 1.4).

Nevertheless, the impression remains that these destinations for excess savings still lacked sufficient absorbing capacity. From inventories of the possessions of wealthy Amsterdammers in the second half of the eighteenth century, it appears that many maintained enormous amounts of cash or deposits at the Wisselbank, money that was simply hoarded in want of a profitable economic use. This constituted a problem that increased in prominence and visibility after 1780, when the credibility of the Wisselbank fell and it became clear that the ability of Holland to continue interest payments on its public debt did in fact have limits. Indeed, it seems likely that this hoarding process contributed in large measure to the economic decline.[22]

The manner in which the external equilibrium was maintained—again, until about 1780—was slightly more complex. Traditionally, the Republic was heavily dependent on a large export of services: the mercantile fleet and international trade contributed considerably to the balance of payments. In absolute terms the Netherlands was probably able to roughly maintain this level of service exports, an outcome that was the net result of two opposing forces. On the one hand, from the mid–seventeenth century onward its market share in international trade was in continuous decline, primarily due to rising mercantilism among its neighbors: the English Navigation Act (1651) and French protec-

TABLE 1.4.
Annual Interest Paid on Domestic and Foreign Bonds according to De Vries and Van der Woude in Relation to Estimates of GDP, 1690–1810.

Years	Holland	Generaliteit/ Provinces	Total Domestic	Foreign	Overall Total	Estimated GDP	%
1690–1713	10.90	5.26	16.16	—	16.16	324	5.0
1714–39	13.75	6.70	20.45	2.00	22.45	301	7.5
1740–51	14.00	6.42	20.42	4.00	24.42	307	8.0
1752–62	14.80	6.00	20.80	6.00	26.80	314	8.5
1763–79	13.70	5.40	19.10	11.00	30.10	349	8.6
1780–95	17.50	5.17	22.67	22.50	45.17	370	12.2
1795–1804	—	—	28.60	21.50	50.10	403	12.4
1805–10	—	—	34.00	17.20	51.20	397	13.9

Sources: De Vries and Van der Woude, *Nederland,* 150.
Note: The estimates of domestic product are based on a combination of the earliest 1807–9 level estimates by the National Accounts Project with the average of two projections of income per head (by J. De Vries and Van der Woude, *Nederland,* 814) and an index of price development based on Posthumus, *Nederlandsche Prijsgeschiedenis.* Obviously, these estimates are of a tentative nature.

tionism, which, under the influence of Louis XIV and his first minister, Colbert, steadily increased in prominence from 1667 onward, were both by and large intended to bring an end to Holland's primacy in trade and shipping. After having lost several decisive confrontations and having otherwise been unable to stem the tide of mercantilist trade policy measures, the Republic after 1713 had to accept the role of underdog among the great political powers of Europe. Its military vulnerability, which after 1713 became increasingly apparent, meant that in an age in which war and international trade were so closely intertwined, the Republic was forced into a position of defensive neutrality. The large trading companies lost several of their outposts to competitors, which, in combination with a lack of powerful maritime support, made the position of Holland's traders in foreign ports increasingly difficult. In short, international competition increased—backed up by larger states, by now harboring a broader tax base than the wealthy yet small Republic.[23] On the other hand, the loss of market share was compensated for by a vigorous expansion in absolute terms of international trade. In the case of the Republic, the combination of these two trends resulted in a more or less constant level of international trade and shipping, as is, for instance, clearly expressed in its share in the size of the European mercantile fleet: from an approximate 40 percent share around 1670 it fell to a mere 12 percent in 1780, while remaining constant in absolute terms.[24]

The largest contrasting element in this story is constituted by the fact that financial services continued to grow in importance. The pivotal role of Amsterdam in international finance increasingly fed on the capital surpluses of the Republic itself. The insurance and financing of international trade and the complexity of the international pattern of settlements increased most rapidly and in so doing created highly profitable markets. Closely related to the growth of these financial services was the export of capital. The consequences of this development for the balance of payments are, however, not immediately clear: during the eighteenth century capital exports appeared to consist mainly of the reinvested net interest payments from previous investments, with a neutral effect on the balance of payments. However, when capital exports came to a standstill in the 1790s, the continuing income from abroad lent significant support to the Republic's external position.

The weak element in the external position of the Republic was made up by the export of industrial products, especially textiles. Although the latter had been an extremely important industry in the seventeenth century, from 1670 onward it witnessed a dramatic decline as the result of protectionist measures in neighboring countries and a significant loss of competitiveness.[25] Contemporaries and later historians alike have related this general deterioration to the high level of wages in Holland, which in turn was considered the result of the local high cost of living. Simultaneously, the imports of industrial goods probably increased (but a lack of trade statistics has meant that this is not a very well-documented supposition). The background to this was that described by Keuchenius: because of an increase in wealth, growth in agriculture, trade, and shipping, rising prices on the housing market that followed a growing urbanization, and increasing government outlays, prices and taxation in Holland rose sharply, pushing up nominal wages in their course. By 1720 real taxation per inhabitant as expressed in hectoliters of wheat, for instance, was about two-and-a-half times that of the United Kingdom and more than six times that of France.[26]

At the same time, the process of technical innovation came to a halt (see table 1.5). By contrast, elsewhere—especially in England—technical progress was achieved at a rapid pace, which to an important extent contributed to the decline of Dutch competitiveness. Through this combination of factors, industrial production in the Republic shrank. Several branches of industry, particularly the capital-intensive ones in the large ports (papermaking, distilling, sugar refining), managed to avoid the general slump. However another driving sector in the sixteenth and seventeenth centuries, herring fishing, shows a trend comparable to that of the industrial sector as a whole: production, which was to a large extent directed toward exports, fell perceptibly (see chapter 4 for a description of the institutional foundations of this failure).

As Keuchenius also noted, the decline in the industrial balance of trade was partially compensated for by the success of the agricultural sector. In the sixteenth and seventeenth centuries, the Netherlands had imported agricultural produce on an extremely large scale—particularly grain from the Baltic. Yet toward the end of the eighteenth century a slightly positive export balance had emerged, resulting from extensive exports of animal products, especially to England. The reduction in grain imports due to greater domestic production and the replacement of bread by potatoes also contributed to a positive balance in the trade flows of agricultural produce.[27]

Two important developments therefore were behind the maintenance of external equilibrium. The decline in the international market share of industry and international services was partially compensated for by absolute growth in these markets, as a result of which exports of services remained more or less stable. In addition, an almost covert growth of the financial sector and the export of livestock products and other forms of agricultural produce (i.e., industrial crops such as madder) played an important role. Remarkably, this sector was spared the technological stagnation of the industrial sector. Agriculture developed in the seventeenth and eighteenth centuries from a relatively weaker sector—or at least a sector that was unable to sufficiently feed the population—to one of the mainstays of the economy, a process that was to continue throughout the nineteenth century. The stability of the Dutch economy was ultimately based on the success with which its farmers were able to adjust their costs to international competition, where industrial entrepreneurs and, at least to some extent merchants, had conspicuously failed to accomplish the same result.

To the extent that a labor market equilibrium held sway, it was the result of endogenous changes in supply. The falling demand for labor in industry and construction after circa 1670 brought about a change in demographic propensities, thereby realizing a fall in the population of Holland as such. A new equilibrium was reached through various mechanisms. To begin with, there was an outward component. In the seventeenth and eighteenth centuries the Republic was a favored destination for migrants: the high death rates in the towns of Holland and Zeeland had to be perpetually compensated by immigrants from the other provinces, but labor migrants flowed in even from Germany and Scandinavia. In fact, as we know since Jan Lucassen's revealing 1984 dissertation, seasonal migration was an important factor in the Dutch labor market. As the demand for labor in the western provinces declined, it became less attractive to seek work there, causing the flow of immigrants to slacken. Laborers in the large industrial centers who lost their jobs had to find other work, a fact that often resulted in their leaving for other cities or towns, or indeed for other countries. Signing up as a crew member on the mercantile fleet and the ships of the Dutch East India Company (VOC) in particular provided another escape option for unemployed laborers. In periods of economic decline—the years after 1670—the share of laborers recruited by the VOC that were of Dutch origin increased. Since only a minority (one-third to one-half) of the crews that sailed to the East ever returned, and payment was poor, this was probably one of the last resorts to which people turned. Nevertheless, from a purely demographic point of view, this was one mechanism through which a new equilibrium was established.[28]

More important, however, Malthusian preventive checks played a role. As elaborate studies on the features of Dutch early modern demographic and marital behavior have shown, the decision to marry was by and large made by both spouses, and marriage took place only when the intended couple was able to set up and maintain a common household. This not only represented a substantial investment, but it also had to be clear that both partners were able to provide for a reasonable existence for themselves: fixed employment or, in the countryside, a farm, according to this "European marriage pattern," was a prerequisite for setting up a family.[29] Correspondingly, the average age at first marriage of Dutch men and women at the time was already high, usually twenty-five years or more. Following the downturn of the economy, the age at marriage after 1670 rose even further, leading to a reduction in births and in the long term to a reduction in the supply of labor.[30]

All of this did not, however, prevent the existence of "open" unemployment that resulted from the decline of industry. Due to enhanced seasonal fluctuations in the economy and concomitant variations in labor demand, unemployment and poverty increased markedly during the winter period. Poor relief was only able to make a modest contribution to lightening the burden of those affected. Poverty was especially acute when food prices were high and in times of war or economic crisis—particularly when these coincided—and death rates increased. Characteristically, as already emphasized in Faber's 1976 inaugural address, this relation between food prices and death rates, which is usually associated with "traditional" agricultural societies, was not apparent in seventeenth-century Holland but did emerge in the eighteenth century.[31] In this respect, too, things appear to have regressed.

In brief, there are two ways of looking at the stationary state of the eighteenth century. To a certain extent it was a story of success: the Republic was able—in spite of losing its position as a technological leader—to maintain its place as one of the wealthiest regions in Europe. The most recent estimates at any rate suggest that it was only sometime between 1780 and 1800 that the United Kingdom caught up with the Netherlands in terms of income per head.[32] This relative performance in absolute terms should be accredited to the Republic's great capital wealth and its high savings ratio, to the stability in the international services sector, and to the dynamism in agriculture. However, this aspect covers only one part of the story: what prevented this highly developed economy, which appeared to be in such a favorable position, from pursuing its further development? What prevented entrepreneurs in domestic industries and in the service sector from introducing new technologies, allowing them to keep up with the competitiveness of their British, French, Belgian, and German colleagues? This question is even more pressing, given the fact that Holland's entrepreneurs were indisputably innovative during the seventeenth century. To answer this question, profitable use may be made of the historiographical record of another nation that, since it established itself as the "workshop of the world" and dominated both the international economy and the adjoining political network, has undergone a long process of relative decline. The economic history of Great Britain from the late nineteenth century onward shares various debates with the economic history of the Netherlands in the eighteenth and early nineteenth centuries that sharpen existing ideas on the latter's development.

TECHNOLOGY AND INSTITUTIONS

The technologies used by society to produce goods and services are not isolated artifacts but instead are strongly interconnected and linked to the prevailing socioeconomic and cultural environment.[33] Thus, the most important innovations of the British industrial revolution of the eighteenth century—the steam engine, the use of coke in the iron-smelting industry, and new techniques in the spinning and weaving of textiles—display a process of mutual reinforcement. Through improvements in iron technology, the quality of the iron produced increased, allowing the construction of better, more efficient steam engines. These made it possible to mine coal at lower cost (the first generation of steam engines was used predominantly in mining) and in turn stimulated improvements in quality in the iron industry. Due to the falling price of coal and an increasing efficiency of steam engines, the market for steam engines continued to expand. In due course, waterwheels and human strength—in the textile industry as elsewhere—were replaced by steam power.[34] Seen from this vantage point, one can identify a coherent technological system that, as a result of these interdependent processes, during the eighteenth and nineteenth centuries was able to establish an unprecedented technological dynamism. However, this same process also had its limits. Beyond a given point of development, the potential to further raise the capacity or efficiency of the steam engine petered out, just as efforts to streamline the production of pig iron failed to generate large systematic advances in the productivity or the organizational structure of industry: the technological system of the first industrial revolution had reached a situation where further technological change along the same lines began to exhibit distinctly diminishing returns.

As emphasized in a broad range of studies, British industrialization after 1780 followed this stylized technological life cycle. By contrast, after 1870, especially in Germany and the United States, a new technological paradigm came to fruition that was characterized by the use of new sources of energy (crude oil and electricity instead of coal), new instruments of propulsion (the combustion engine instead of the steam engine), and breakthroughs in, for example, the chemical and electrotechnical industries. This process is commonly referred to as the second industrial revolution.[35] The British economy, until 1870 the dominant force in international economic relations, was unsuccessful in profiting adequately from these new opportunities. The transition from the first to the second industrial revolution proved troublesome, resulting in British productivity being overtaken in the new industrial sectors that were to dominate economic development in the twentieth century: the automotive, electrotechnical, and chemical industries. The problem of the relative decline of Great Britain in the period after 1870, therefore, can be seen as one of an evidently difficult transition from one system of productivity frontier technology to the next.[36]

This approach to the issue of British economic stagnation appears to hold important insights for the interpretation of the economic history of the Netherlands in the eighteenth century. After all, during the seventeenth century a new technological system had emerged in the western Netherlands that was characterized by the use of wind and peat as the most important sources of energy and by mills as the foremost source of industrial power. In industries such as papermaking, shipbuilding, tobacco processing, and chemicals, significant technological breakthroughs had been achieved. In fact, technological diffusion ranged far beyond industrial development, as in sectors such as fishing, domestic transport (barge shipping), and of course international trade and finance Dutch techniques also set the standard of productivity advance. As a result, Dutch craftsmen were frequently recruited by other European countries to introduce their new techniques, just as foreigners traveled the country gathering information. The high levels of production per capita in Holland were based on this technological lead (and the higher level of structural transformation of the economy).[37]

Yet as of the late seventeenth century the dynamics of Holland's technological system began to falter. The only data source available that allows us to form an idea of this process is that on the number of patents awarded by the States General and the provincial estates, numbers that may offer an impression of this declining pace of technological progress.[38] Because the Republic possessed a fairly modern form of patent legislation, the data presumably are suitable to fulfill this purpose. As collated in table 1.5, the data show that up to the 1630s the number of patents increased sharply, after which they fell to a much lower level.[39] Moreover, inspection of the patents themselves shows that over time their contents change from being dominated by fundamentally new findings, especially in machinery, industrial processing, and waterworks, to limited refinements in each of these. Parallel research has also indicated that

TABLE 1.5.
Patents Issued by the States General and the Provincial States, 1575–1794.

Years	States-General	Holland	Other Provinces
1575–94	30	13	1
1595–1614	116	24	6
1615–34	252	6	4
1635–54	87	29	5
1655–74	68	61	9
1675–94	37	52	24
1695–1714	15	38	9
1715–34	5	10	1
1735–54	1	9	3
1755–74	4	14	8
1775–94	8	26	5

Source: Doorman, *Octrooien,* 82–329.

decelerating technological progress can be observed for the later part of the seventeenth century and at any rate for the eighteenth century.[40]

By the late eighteenth century the Netherlands, therefore, availed of a comparatively sophisticated but stagnating technological system. Even so, the transition to the production methods of the British industrial revolution was hampered by that to which we, following Edward Ames, Nathan Rosenberg, and Jan de Vries, will refer as the "penalties of the pioneer."[41] There are in fact two such penalties to be distinguished. First, the advantages of the transition to newer production techniques were less significant because of the relatively high productivity level already achieved. Jan de Vries, for example, noted that the construction of railways in the mid–nineteenth century offered Holland comparatively lesser advantages because the country possessed a still relatively efficient transport system for a "mass market"—its canals and barges.[42] In general terms, therefore, investment in new production techniques tended to yield higher returns the greater the difference in productivity levels between the old and new techniques. In Holland this difference was generally smaller than in Belgium or Germany, since, due to the technological lead that had been established in the course of the seventeenth century, initially prevailing production methods were more advanced than they were elsewhere.

While the potential returns to technological transition in the case of the Dutch economy thus were limited, at the same time the costs were probably comparatively high—the second penalty. The technological system that had emerged in the seventeenth and eighteenth centuries had been characterized by an already high comparative level of capital intensity, a feat afforded by the financial wealth of the Republic. Transition to new technologies inevitably meant that existing, expensive capital goods (the industrial windmills of the Zaanstreek, for example) had to be written off. Even if a better technique could be made available, it therefore may have been quite rational to continue using the old one. Only when the losses thus incurred could be compensated by the expected higher profit that a new installation would bring, the adoption of machinery-embodied new technology was rational.[43] Yet the stretch of this argument is obviously limited. For while its macroeconomic relevance may account for a lack of technological dynamics in existing industry, it does nothing to explain the evident paucity of newcomers at the micro-level (especially given the relative abundance of venture capital seeking for higher rates of return), nor does it explain why the equally evident competitive pressure of foreign imports did not lead to different cost strategies in tradables.

In explaining the underlying behavioral stance, two types of mechanisms can be advanced. First, as has been the central argument of the literature on Dutch nineteenth-century industrial development that emerged in the late 1970s, the new technological system of the British industrial revolution did not fit with prevailing natural endowments and comparative cost structures.[44] The Netherlands, for example, did not have its own coal reserves (making coal vastly more expensive than in England or Belgium and subject to trade regimes), nor did it have any natural minerals to speak of, and it lacked a heavy iron industry. As a result, expertise in iron technology was imperfectly developed, and early progress in this field was hardly exploited. Dutch technological know-how was to an important extent concentrated in water management and the construction of wooden machinery and equipment, with an emphasis on windmills and ships. In practice this meant that the introduction of new techniques was often achieved only by relying on foreign expertise, which again was expensive. Foreign workers—engineers, metalworkers—played a key role in the dissemination of these techniques throughout a large part of the nineteenth century, but recruiting and maintaining them was a costly affair. In addition, there is the effect of wage costs—to which Keuchenius referred in terms of sectoral specialization and marginal productivity differences—and which was made the pivot of a model of strained development and capital-intensive technology choice by Mokyr in 1976.[45]

Yet undisputedly relevant as it is, the static comparative cost argument alone cannot account for the pattern of events surrounding the Dutch nineteenth-century growth transition. First, as already pointed out at an early stage of the debate, the effect of costs and endowments was subject to geographic differentiation: high wages in the west, distant ports (providing coal, raw materials, and export outlets), parsimonious access by water, and poor roads in the east and south. Even more important, however, is the fact that a systematic transition in the pattern of development did take place (contrary to the claim that Dutch development would simply have been "different"), and policy choices can be shown to have governed the chronology of this process. This, in turn, leads to the general conclusion that the resilience of political and economic institutions in upholding traditional distributional interests was essential to the time path of the Dutch economic change under the conditions defined by the technological system of the first industrial revolution.

While acknowledging the influence of such traditionally identified factors as endowments, the limitations of the domestic market, and the role of larger European nations in placing the fiscal and economic system of the eighteenth-century Republic under pressure, the core of our leading argument thus is formed by the resilience of early modern mechanisms of governance on the one hand and the political catch-up process taking place after 1795 on the other. Whereas modern-day economists have adopted income convergence as the pivot of comparative growth performance, the effects that the stumbling efforts to reform the Dutch state can be shown to have exerted on the structure of economic performance reveal the assumptions on the institutional structure of policy choice that are implicit in this approach. That which set the Dutch situation apart and defined its institutional resilience is hidden in the extent to which the Republic's political and fiscal structure underwrote the very emergence of the Dutch state. The definition of fiscal and executive autonomy at the level of the *gewesten* (provinces) and cities formed the cornerstone of the pragmatic federal alliance that supported the successful revolt against Habsburg fiscal and religious obtrusion. In addition, just as the Republic developed its own technological system, an institutional framework for the regulation of economic life was developed in the seventeenth century. This framework played a prominent role in ossifying the technological system: it influenced the relative prices to which entrepreneurs responded and more generally determined the structure of incentives to which they reacted. Just as the Republic's technological system followed a particular course, so economic regulation followed its own life cycle, spanning the late Middle Ages (from which some of the institutions of the Republic dated) to the first half of the nineteenth century, when attempts were made to break their rigidity. In some cases, these efforts even took until the 1850s before meeting with success.

Moreover, the story line does not simply break off there. As already referred to in the introduction, the interaction between the institutional framework of politics, taxes and production and the performance of the economy did not end with the removal of those corporatist relations which the Patriots had idealized. In the second half of the nineteenth century, it led to a new and equally fascinating process: the emergence of the institutional framework that has dominated twentieth-century politico-economic relations. Our emphasis on this same sequence of events is also testimony to the fact that we do not see the early modern system of institutional relations as inherently inefficient. Indeed, the economic success and self-established political independence of the Republic defy such a characterization. Stronger still, as emphasized earlier with respect to seventeenth-century commercial policy by Israel and in relation to the precarious equilibrium of particularistic forces at all levels of governance by Price, the pragmatic choices made at the time probably provided the only way of positioning Dutch economic interests and creating a viable political federation.[46] Moreover, as we will emphasize as a critical factor in the nineteenth-century legacy analyzed here, the fiscal system of the Dutch Republic long remained very successful in supporting an exceedingly large public debt. Rather than one of absolute judgment, our view therefore is that of an emerging mismatch between distributional interests and incentives for economic change. In between stands the role of institutions and mechanisms of economic and fiscal policy choice. It is in the lack of possibilities for adjusting the "rules of the game" that we see the institutional deficiency of the Republic and the fundamental change realized during the period under consideration.

This type of interaction between economic change and institutions was also brought forward in the debate on the relative decline of the British economy after 1870. According to Elbaum and Lazonick, the restricted transition to a new technological system in Britain at this time can be attributed to the rigidity of the structure of firms and labor markets there.[47] In his magnum opus, *Scale and Scope,* Alfred Chandler reaches a similar judgment, albeit by means of a different approach. In Great Britain, in his opinion, family capitalism did not make way quickly enough for the managerial enterprise of the twentieth century. As a result, Britain remained weak in those economic sectors that were to dominate the twentieth century.[48] To the most ardent theoretician of "institutional rigidities," Mancur Olson, Britain in the twentieth century is the outstanding example of a country afflicted by institutional sclerosis.[49]

Returning to the eighteenth-century Republic, it is possible to distinguish institutional rigidities at a number of complementary levels. In the following we will examine the relation between the decentralized, corporatist government of the Republic, the process of economic stagnation in the eighteenth century, and the crisis in which the state found itself after 1780. In our assessment two problems receive particular attention. The first is the issue of public finance and the closely related problem of the national debt. In the decentralized political structure of the Republic, the influence of centrifugal forces led to a gradual erosion of public finance and ultimately to a loss of confidence on the part of the financial elite in the ability of the state to continue to guarantee servicing its future financial obligations. The Republic's military decline in the century after 1672 should also be viewed in this light: due to its financial problems, the state was increasingly less able to arm itself against neighboring countries and therefore lost commercial leverage. The second, related institutional problem to receive attention is made up by the gradually emerging chasm between the political and economic elite of the Republic, which even to contemporaries was particularly evident in the withdrawal of city regents from economic life. In the sixteenth and seventeenth centuries both elites were to a large degree intertwined, and reapers of commercial or industrial fortune had access to the ranks of the political elite—the regents. In the eighteenth century, however, a widening gap emerged between citizens and the regent oligarchy, which became all too apparent after 1780. These two problems especially would play an important role in the political and financial denouement of the Republic in these years.

Apart from this, it should not be overlooked that the ossification of institutional structures was not restricted to the political system but could be found in numerous branches of industry as well. Export industries, such as those dealing in woolens, madder, and herring, which had blossomed in the seventeenth century, were heavily regulated by regional or city bylaws. These had originally been intended to guarantee a consistently high quality of export products (whether it be *lakens* [woolens] from Leiden or madder from Zeeland), which was a definite interest of the traders who exported these products. Unfortunately, this system of bylaws and regulations stood in the way of further technological development of industry. Experiments with new techniques and forms of organization were prohibited; to introduce new techniques, entrepreneurs were forced to move to other regions or indeed different countries.[50] Criticism of this institutional ossification was as old as the phenomenon itself and can, for instance, already be found in Pieter de la Court's *Het welvaren van Leiden* (1660).[51]

The organization of those parts of industry that served only local markets was possibly even stricter. The levying of excises and the underlying fiscal autonomy of the cities played a critical role in this issue; many industries were regulated in minute detail to prevent the loss of tax revenues and preempt fiscal competition. For this reason, the buying and selling of flour and bread, for example, were strictly regulated, outlawing the private possession of grinding instruments while rendering the use of a specific mill compulsory for any given part of the city and allowing local millers and bakers to form cartels. In addition, local authorities fixed the price of a given quantity and type of bread on the basis of market quotations and a fixed markup for baking and milling, thus offering such institutionalized forms of collusion almost complete protection from competition. As a result, rye bread, an important staple of the working class, was 40 to 60 percent more expensive in the cities and towns of Holland than it was in the eastern Netherlands or in neighboring countries.[52] Such cartels were additionally supported by municipal authorities as part of efforts to regulate labor markets and—through protection of urban employment—maintain a level of social stability.[53] Apart from this, the fact that cities additionally exercised their staple rights so as to restrict the potential reconstruction and rerouting of roads and canals (for which scarcely any public funds were available throughout the eighteenth century) would continue to hinder infrastructural change until the 1851 Municipal Law. To top things off, the fiscal autonomy of the gewesten did lead to fiscal competition (e.g., by forcing the skill-extensive parts of textile making to the outer provinces due to wage costs), and even internal tariffs were not officially abolished until after the 1795 Batavian revolution.[54]

It is undoubtedly true that similar—if less strict and less pervasive—institutional arrangements can be found elsewhere in early modern Europe, and the relevant questions therefore are, How extensive? and For how long? This book argues that the remarkable economic development and idiosyncratic political structure of the Dutch Republic combined to yield a situation in which these questions might be responded to with adjectives such as "systematic" and chronological demarcations such as "far into the nineteenth century." Specifically, the influence of institutional restrictions on the development of industry and the chronology of their erosion will be demonstrated in several case studies. For instance, developments in herring fishing (typical as a tightly regulated export industry) and in milling and baking (highly regulated in connection with the local excise on milling) are described in chapter 4. Similarly, the direct effect of institutional reform on technology, firm size, the currency system, and infrastructure (and through this on, for instance, coal prices and communications) is shown in chapter 6. From these stories it emerges that institutions and production and transport technology were to a large extent intertwined. The common element in all these phenomena, in turn, is the troublesome reform of administrative structure and fiscal accountability within the newly unitary Dutch state taking place between 1795 and 1848.

The Institutional Deficiency of the Republic

Rather than devising our own, it is more convincing to base our efforts in describing the institutional structure of the Republic on a broadly accepted typology of socioeconomic and political relations developed elsewhere. One such characterization is that developed by Maarten Prak in his recent research into social change in Den Bosch between 1770 and 1820. In it, the Republic is typified as a corporatist system of more or less independent, parallel functioning bodies: provinces with their own form of representation; *waterschappen* (drainage boards) and trading companies with their separate authorities; cities and towns with their autonomous civil laws and administrative jurisdiction;

civil guards, guilds, and charities, all governed by specific rules and procedures rooted in a distant past. Outside the cities and towns the situation was no different: it was primarily the nobility, organized by province, that represented and governed most of the countryside. Similarly, economic life was to some extent regulated by guilds, just as the exploitation of common fields was in the hands of *markegenootschappen,* independent bodies of freeholders in a certain village. In particular, the middle class of small businessmen in the towns, independent farmers in the countryside, and groups of prominent citizens (nobles, regents) were organized in specific bodies that promoted the economic, social, and political interests of their group, which at one point had acquired the privilege to do so. To a large extent, these institutions were a local affair: each guild was regulated according to its own *keuren* (ordinances), and each charitable institution of a specific denomination had its own rules and practices, just as each city had its own method of administration, appointment, and selection.[55]

Large parts of the Republic's international trade were completely run or regulated by similar independent bodies. The largest one, the VOC, was such a corporation, wielding the monopoly of trade with the East Indies and exhibiting a characteristic structure. The company was made up of six more or less independent chambers, each of which was established in the large trading centers of the western part of the country. A supervisory board, the Heren Zeventien, coordinated the chambers' activities. In some ways, the VOC even constituted a state within a state: it maintained diplomatic relations with Asian royalty, possessed its own army and fleet, and was empowered to declare war, sign treaties, and pass legislation in its own possessions. The Dutch West India Company, which controlled large portions of the trade with Africa and the Americas, was in many ways like the VOC, although its authority did not extend quite as far. Other trading bodies, such as the Levant and the Northern Companies, regulated trade in the Mediterranean and with Norway, respectively.

From a wider, European perspective this corporatistic system was characteristic of the zone of urbanization that ran from the Low Countries, via Germany and Switzerland, to northern Italy—a territory in which especially the cities had resisted the rise of the centralized autocratic states. From the start of the early modern period, centralized states had evolved in France, Spain, Prussia, and England that had been successful in stripping such "medieval" corporatism of its power and influence. By contrast, the Dutch Revolt of 1572 had its roots in resistance against similar ambitions of the Habsburg Empire, which implied that acknowledgment of the privileges of the provinces and the cities had been a central feature of the "constitution" that bound the provinces together since the Treaty of Utrecht of 1579.

The state, the Republic of the United Provinces, was rooted in this structure: the provinces, each with its own system of public administration, taxation, and representation, were in principle sovereign. The autonomy of the provinces, in turn, was ultimately based on the autonomy of the cities and the colleges of nobles (or, as was the case in the north of the country, other organizations that represented the countryside). The power of the Estates General in The Hague, the central college of civil administration that consisted of representatives of the provinces, was derived from and in practice limited by the interests of the cities, towns, and provinces. The authority of the stadtholder, by the same token, was a derived one: the provinces were responsible for appointing the stadtholder, who was primarily the first military officer of the Estates. In practice, however, the stadtholder wielded extensive powers and through an extensive system of patronage and local appointments was able to influence almost all political and semipolitical positions. In this way, the regents of the cities and towns were to a large extent dependent on the favors of the stadtholder, allowing him to bring his influence to bear upon the process of political rule. Whenever the stadtholder was a powerful figure—Willem III is probably the best example in this respect—political decision making was quite centralized, even though especially cities in the western part of the country continued to have access to methods to oppose his policies. An almost stealthy process of political centralization by the stadtholders continued into the second half of the eighteenth century, although the last stadtholder, Willem V, was notoriously less proficient at pulling the strings of power.[56]

Simultaneously, some centralization of political decision making took place, albeit within the confines of the system of autonomous provinces. Such increasing efficiency and purposefulness had, however, all the appearances of a continuation of a development path that was in fact a dead end, because outside the Republic the process of state formation continued, resulting in states that were much more successful in mobilizing means for warfare than the Republic. The relative advantage that the Republic enjoyed in this respect in the seventeenth century disappeared as a result of its small size and inertia, particularly as the problems inherent to its decentralized political structure became more urgent, as we shall see. Calls for fundamental change—for example, centralizing taxation—met so much resistance that they stood no chance. There was no central authority able to carry out reforms that ran counter to the perceived interests of elites of provinces and cities. Because the regents had invested almost all their wealth in the public debt, they had every reason to ensure its continuation, even if the income from interest on that debt fell and taxation increased. Of greater importance was perhaps the lack of an innovative approach by which the state and the corporatistic society in which it was rooted could be reformed. There was no clear alternative for the form of government of the Republic, at least up until the 1790s. In ideological terms, too, the Republic was a prisoner of the situation that existed: before the 1790s the major proposals for reform aimed at recasting its original decentralized constitution.

These problems and the differences of opinion they created among the political elite are clearly visible upon further analysis of the main problems arising from the public finances of the Republic. Without much exaggeration one can state that the national debt had a key role in the *contract social* upon which the Republic was founded. Besides the precarious equilibrium between central authority and provincial autonomy that served as a political foundation, the ruling elite had completely committed itself to ensuring that interest on the national debt continued to be paid. They had to a large extent invested their personal wealth in public debt, a situation that dated back to the sixteenth century and one that in some ways was at the heart of long-standing success of Holland's financial policy.[57] In surrounding countries the ruling monarchs sometimes went bankrupt, after which a reform of the public debt had to follow, to the detriment of the creditors. Such risk meant that investors were likely to demand higher rates of interest when making new loans, which could aggravate the monarch's financial problems. The low interest rates and the extensive, but solid, public debt of the Republic were by contrast based on the steady conviction that the Estates General or the Estates of Holland would never turn to such measures, since they would themselves be the biggest victim of such a step. Moreover, as the regents withdrew from trade and industry, they became more dependent on the solid financing of the public debt.[58]

The financing of public expenditure in the Republic was based on the quota system, under which each province was responsible for a certain proportion of the expenses. Holland, by far the richest and most populous province, had, according to a quota dating back to 1616, to carry approximately 58 percent of collective expenditure; the quotas of the other provinces were much smaller (see table 1.5). In practice, however, the system worked differently. The contribution of the other provinces to the war expenditures by the Estates General was in fact so modest that they could permit themselves the luxury of continually postponing payment until the last minute. They neglected their contribution to the States of War, the central budget for warfare of the Dutch Republic, from which the actual expenditures for troops and war materials were paid. They were, moreover, able to continue to do so with impunity because these matters were subject to strict secrecy.[59]

The consequence of these hidden obstructions (with all the qualities of a public secret) was that when worst came to worst Holland would have to come to the rescue and make up the shortfall. It was only there that it was possible to borrow on the capital market the enormous sums of money needed; use was made of this potential in times of war, leading to a drastic rise of the burden of debt in Holland under such circumstances. As the largest province, which to a large degree determined the political course of the Republic, it was in Holland's interests to maintain the strength of the army and navy; indeed, many international conflicts were fought to defend the commercial interests of this province. Aware of this situation, the other provinces could persist in their unofficial politics of obstruction in the knowledge that Holland would defend the "general interest." In other words, to a certain extent the behavior of the other provinces was a rational choice, one of paying as little as possible and of reducing their contributions to the States of War as much a possible, given that capital-rich Holland would foot the bill anyway, a classic example of free riding.

Comparable problems occurred with the financing of the navy. This had to be done by separate semi-independent bodies, the admiralties, which received the incomes from tariffs on international trade for that purpose. There were five admiralties, in Amsterdam, Rotterdam, Middelburg, West Frisia, and Frisia, which to a certain extent could follow their own policies. The result was that different cities tried to get a competitive advantage by levying the tariffs in a way that was favorable for their merchants. This implied, for example, a very friendly assessment of the tariffs on goods imported by the merchants of the city itself, whereas goods of "foreign" merchants were treated more formally. This meant that most merchants paid only a fraction of the official tariff, a practice that was known as "the spirit of the law of 1725" (after the latest renewal of the systems of tariffs in that year). This obviously undermined the financing of the navy. The Admiralty of Amsterdam had to make large debts to keep the navy intact. The other admiralties could free ride on Amsterdam's efforts; the Admiralty of Middelburg became, for example, notorious for the degree of evasion of tariffs that occurred there.

From the point of view of the inland provinces, this situation appeared rather different. There it was emphasized that the wars served in particular Holland's interests and that in the perspective of Holland's politicians the landed provinces were nothing more than extended lines of defense, useful for keeping the enemy far from Holland's borders.[60] The practical effectiveness of such a strategy had already been demonstrated in 1672, when the French and troops from Münster conquered large parts of the south and northeast of the Republic; they got as far as Utrecht but did not reach Holland. Essentially it all boiled down to lack of agreement on who really profited from the collective defense efforts of the state. Due to the specifically decentralized structure of government, it was possible for provinces other than Holland to exploit the situation and "free ride" at Holland's expense, so that the possibilities of the Republic maintaining an army and navy of sufficient strength were undermined.[61]

The consequences of this institutional problem, the result of the specific structure of the quota system, were complex. Because Holland was forced to pay an extremely large proportion of the war expenditures, this province had to finance a disproportionate amount of the public debt (table 1.6). Of the total debt of the provinces in 1795, fl 605 million, Holland bore as much as fl 455 million, or 75 percent. Interest payments on this debt accounted for nearly 70 percent of the province's taxation revenues, whereas in provinces such as Overijssel, Gelderland, and Groningen this was less than 35 percent.[62]

Through the disproportionate burden of the war expenditures, the divergence in the taxation systems of the provinces grew: Holland was forced to increase duties and direct taxation, yet this was much less so in the other provinces. In

TABLE 1.6.
The *Quotenstelsel* and the Regional Distribution of the Public Debt and of Tax Revenues in Relation to the Distribution of the Population, 1616–1808.

	Holland	Utrecht, Zeeland, Friesland	Eastern Republic	Groningen	Republic outside Holland
Shares (in percent)					
Quote, 1616–1792	58.1	26.5	9.7	5.7	41.9
Quote, 1792–1806	64.9	18.5	11.0	5.6	35.1
Tax revenues, 1807–8	60.5	24.2	10.0	5.3	39.5
Total public debt, 1792	75.0	21.0	3.3	1.6	25.0
Population, 1622/1680/1750	40 47 41	—	—	—	60 53 59
Population, 1795	48.0	21.0	24.0	7.0	52.0
Indices per head					
Quote, 1622/1680/1750	145 124 142	—	—	—	70 79 71
Quote, 1792–1806	135	88	46	80	68
Tax revenues, 1807–8	126	115	42	76	76
Total public debt, 1792	156	100	14	23	48

Sources: calculated from J. De Vries and Van der Woude, *Nederland,* 129; Van der Woude, "Demografische ontwikkeling."

Overijssel milling duties in the second half of the eighteenth century were no higher than in 1675, that is, fl 12 per 30 hectoliters rye (and this was even lower between 1700 and 1750). In Holland these important duties were raised in 1723 from fl 15.90 to fl 30.80, and later in 1749 to fl 42.50.[63] As a result, the differences in economic structure were further accentuated, leading to higher prices and higher nominal wages in Holland, and lower prices and wages in provinces with much milder taxation, as in Overijssel and Gelderland. The autonomy of the provinces made it virtually impossible, moreover, to change the situation. The quotas had not been adjusted since 1616 because of the resistance to do so by provinces that feared they would have to pay more. The political autonomy of the provinces hinged increasingly on this privilege of being able to levy taxes and to resist any reform of the system.

The institutional structure described led ultimately to progressive neglect of the country's defenses: the official figures presented in the States of War no longer corresponded to the actual capacity of the army.[64] The undermining of the military prowess of the state ultimately played an important role in the definitive crisis the Republic had to face: the navy in 1780–84 no longer was a match for the British fleet; in 1787 Willem V had to make use of Prussian troops to ensure his position and to suppress the opposition; and French troops encountered hardly any organized opposition in 1794–95. A state that was unable to defend itself, as was the case for the Republic after 1780, was doomed to be conquered.[65]

The institutional impotence of the state and the resulting problem that it was no longer capable of defending itself became obvious in the 1780s. This was clearly demonstrated in the Fourth Anglo-Dutch War (1780–84), which was a disaster for the Republic. The navy could not counter the British navy, which was able to continuously blockade Amsterdam and to capture various overseas trading posts. The VOC in particular suffered from the loss of many richly laden ships to the English. Important VOC trading posts, such as the settlement at Cape Town, could be maintained only with French support. Political crisis and economic depression (to be discussed later) were the result, together stimulating opposition to the prevailing regime, in particular the stadtholder, Willem V.

Ironically the Patriots, the opposition against the stadtholder and his regime between 1781 and 1787, formulated as their main aim the restoration of the autonomy of the cities to resist the centralizing tendencies that the stadtholder personified. For want of new ideas, they were to a large degree in favor of the *reestablishment* of corporatist structures in society. The military weakness of the Republic was attributed to a lack of commitment among citizens to the defense of the cities, which had resulted in the decline of the *schutterijen* (civil guard). Reestablishment of the original function of this semimilitary body, whose role had been reduced to that of an enforcer of public order in the cities and towns, was one of the main points in the Patriots' reforms. This would also make an expensive professional army unnecessary, and so lead to a reduction of government expenditure and taxation. Another main theme of the Patriots was resistance to the reestablishment of the "old constitution," the old "freedoms" of the various corporatist bodies, which was seen as the panacea for the political and economic problems. Their ideas sometimes went further than this; the more radical Patriots wanted to involve a greater proportion of the populace in the government of the cities and nation. Such an undercurrent of democracy was one of the innovative elements in the Patriot movement. As this "revolution" progressed, the idea of the nation as a sociopolitical unit grew, and debate sprang up about reform at the national level. Nevertheless, no important reforms were carried out, partly because no one had a clear alternative for the prevailing system; the most obvious alternative was an advanced form of centralization of political power, but this was the very thing the Patriots opposed, and in any case many contemporaries considered the prevailing central powers to be incompetent.[66]

During the rather chaotic Patriot Revolt (1781–87), there was no more than speculation about the possibility of salvaging public finances from the mess it was in. It did nothing to halt the gradual erosion of trust in the creditworthiness of the state (figure 1.1). After the Prussian invasion of 1787, when the Orangists again tried to take control of the reins, it was in particular Grand Pensionary Van Spiegel who pled for more careful financial management and an increase in government income. Willem V bogged down, however, the reforms he proposed as a result of lack of understanding or plain opposition. He was successful, however, in enlarging the state's grip on the West India Company (WIC) and the VOC—the former was in fact taken over by the government—and in reforming the quota system, although this was of minor significance.[67] Holland's continual budget deficits, which in this period increased to approximately fl 10 million annually, could only continue to be financed by compulsory loans and the taxation of wealth, which exposed the desperate state of the public finances (which had been an official secret).[68] The example of the new Negotiatie op het Gemeene Land (a loan for Holland) of 4 percent in January

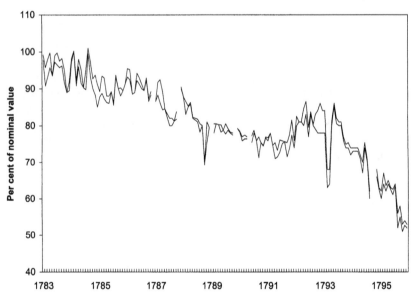

FIGURE 1.1 Highest and lowest prices of Holland 2.5 percent bonds, January 1783 until December 1795 (in percent of nominal value). Recorded prices of 2.5 percent bonds issued by Holland (mostly blank, Amsterdam) from *Maandelijksche Nederlandsche Mercurius,* 1783–96. Data for 1783–92 are of actual transactions, of which the highest and lowest prices were recorded (last of the month); data for 1792–96 are quotes of market prices.

1793 typifies the situation: the price of other (2.5 percent) bonds immediately plummeted from 80 to 65 percent, after which the price only recovered with great difficulty (see figure 1.1). After a brief recovery in April and May 1793—probably due to the Liberale Gifte—the confidence of the capital market in the government's solvency began to fall rapidly from mid-1793 onward, a fall that occurred simultaneously with progress by the French army in the southern (and later the northern) Netherlands. It was virtually impossible, as the new comptroller and auditor-general Hiëronymous van Alphen was quickly forced to admit, to raise funds to pay the army and navy: "Without credit, no money; without money, no army, no navy; no national defenses, neither on land nor at sea."[69] The falling creditworthiness of the Republic left it defenseless, so that French troops, almost without resistance, but with the assistance of the freezing over of the rivers, brought the Republic to its knees.

UNITED AND INDIVISIBLE: CENTRALIZATION AND POLITICAL REFORM

After the failure of the Patriot Revolt and the Orangist Restoration, with its associated Prussian invasion, it was the French army's turn to break the political stalemate in which the Netherlands found itself. With an unusually hard winter having frozen over the main rivers, French generals Jourdan and Pichécru encountered little opposition when satisfying Napoleon's anxiety to lift the pressure from domestic fiscal policy antagonisms by sweeping north.[70] Yet this time foreign intervention to the Dutch came with a flavor that resonated in policy debate as it had established itself since the Patriot Revolt. In the period following the 1789 Revolution, a concept of government had been developed in France that reflected the centralist traditions of the royalist state and the rationalist, egalitarian thinking of the Enlightenment. The reform of the French civil service by Abbé Sièyes, which included such items as the introduction of a uniform system of departments that could be tightly controlled, is an enlightening example of this process.[71]

Variants of such measures, aimed at bringing about reform in the Republic, were already popular in the first half of the 1790s among Patriot émigrés having fled to France. It was these ideas that were introduced in the Netherlands from 1795 onward by coalitions of Patriots and French army officers and civil servants. The key concept in all this was that the state was an autonomous power that was bestowed with the task to create a society that would increase the wealth and happiness of its citizens. The state fulfilled this role—in theory at least—in the name of the sovereign people (i.e., its citizens), who in principle were each other's equal. This implied not only that discrimination against Catholics and Jews had to come to an end but also that those institutions based on certain historically rooted privileges, such as the guilds or the aristocracy, should be abolished.

The new model of the state was also centralist in making: to allow the state to intervene for the benefit of national welfare, the wide variety of rules, regulations, and practices in such areas as poor relief or education had to be harmonized. Instead of the diversity of institutions that was characteristic of the ancien régime, unity needed to be created, and the state had to develop transparent instruments to the benefit of all its citizens. Such a centralist system would inevitably bring an end to local autonomy. In a nutshell, the new ideal conceived of the state as the most important vehicle of progress in bringing about the ideals of the Enlightenment as perceived by the French Revolution. However, although in the first phase of the Revolution the democratic legitimacy of the new order played an important role, the dynamics of the revolutionary process caused the new state to increasingly become an instrument wielded by a revolutionary elite. Under Napoleon, the new system of governance, finally, even became an instrument of a regime bent on territorial expansion and financial exploitation. For a country such as the Netherlands, the two faces of the revolutionary regime were apparent from the beginning: for the Patriots it offered a way of breaking the Republic's stalemate. Yet its price was cooperation with the French, whose aim it was to strip the country of its wealth.

This painful dilemma had already become apparent during the preparation of the Treaty of The Hague between the new Batavian state and France, in which not only an enormous war contribution of fl 100 million was levied, but the new Republic also pledged to permanently ally itself with France and took it upon itself to maintain an occupying army of twenty-five thousand troops.[72] In a way, the French-Batavian period—from the velvet revolution in early 1795 until the departure of French troops and officials in November 1813—was one long experiment in the implementation of this new conception of the state. The conductors of this experiment were a group of officials whose ideal it was to build a state capable of overcoming the large financial and economic problems currently faced, notably the enormous and nevertheless still waxing national debt, the French demands for transfers, and economic decline. At decisive moments, however, the experiment was disrupted by interventions on the part of the French polity. In practice, the room for maneuver declined on a permanent basis until 1810, when Napoleon annexed the then Kingdom of Holland to become a formal part of his empire.

The first three years of the new regime were taken up with fairly futile debates in the National Assembly (newly elected through universal suffrage for all adult males) between two opposing parties. With their consistent pleas for the formation of a decentralized state, the federalists—who to a certain extent dominated the assembly—could broadly be seen as successors to the Patriot ideals. The opposition of the federalists against the proposal put forward by the other group—the Unitarians—for a single state was influenced by the fear of the inland provinces for the financial consequences of an amalgamation of all public debts.[73] In fact, even under the new situation, the federalists wanted to play the "game" as it had been before 1795, when the burden of war expenditures and the national debt were largely borne on Holland's shoulders. For the unitarians, particularly supported by Holland, this was unacceptable: their aim of a unified and indivisible state was expressly meant to straighten out the problem of the public debt, through centralizing decision making and the streamlining of public finances. In their view this was the only possibility of securing the public debt: only by spreading the burden more evenly over the other parts of the country was there hope of solving this enormous financial problem.

The result was that the discussion about the most desirable form of government was from the very beginning dominated by the differences of political opinion on financial matters, and attempts to design a transparent new form of government were unsuccessful. The decision in January 1797 of the National Assembly to take over the old debts of the provinces and amalgamate them was a major step forward. Despite this defeat of the federalists, the struggle over the form of government continued. The National Assembly finally produced the Dikke Boek, a proposed constitution that was perhaps an acceptable compromise for the federalists, but it contained so many contradictions that it was rejected in the referendum that was held in August 1797.[74]

The bankruptcy of the federalist proposal, through which the creation of the Batavian state was in danger of stalling, provoked intervention by the French. In 1798 a small group of radicals took power after a coup d'état, which had been planned with French assistance. The radicals, in cooperation with the French envoy Delacroix, drew up a new, unitarian constitution that could count on the support of the populace (even though the most outspoken federalists had to be removed from the electorate to achieve this result). This ushered in a period of important reforms that was to last three years; a new coup d'état in June 1798 furthermore brought a more moderate provisional government to power that set itself the task of implementing the many changes brought about by the new constitution.

An important component of the task was creating a modern bureaucracy. The radicals had already begun instituting a new organization of government along lines that had been discussed previously. Several new ministries were to be set up: war, finance, foreign affairs, education, national police, national economy, justice, and the navy; these were under the charge of an agent, ranking somewhere between today's minister and the administrative head of a department.[75] In particular the establishment of ministries for completely new tasks of the state, such as education and economy, implied a program: the government was in these matters expected to assume a great deal of authority. Completely new powers were created in the areas of water management, poor relief, and public health, for example.

The constitution of 1798, similar to its French equivalent, abolished all "guilds and colleges," which despite opposition from various sides almost immediately led to their disbanding and the management of their legacies.

However, this component of the French Revolution had little or no relation to domestic developments and encountered rather strong opposition. Amsterdam, in particular, was a staunch supporter of the guild system, partly because of the guilds' regulatory functions: for example, the supervision of the practicing of medicine, and the collection of all sorts of duties. Furthermore, the guilds provided a certain degree of social security for their members: widows' pensions, sickness benefits, and the burial of members were paid from central funds. An estimated 30 percent of the male working population in the urban sector belonged to guilds, indicative of their importance.[76] Ultimately, the guilds were sociopolitical instruments wielded by the municipal authorities of the towns and cities; they regulated the labor market of craftsmen, so as to stabilize labor relations.

The radical abolition of the old sociopolitical structures brought with it the need for new social foundations; in many ways the radicals were more skillful in the former activities than they were at the latter. Attempts were made at the national level to come to grips with the problems confronting the country. How could the quality of education be improved? How could poor relief be incorporated into the governmental system and its implementation in different towns and cities be harmonized? How could water management be improved? What should be done about stagnating industry? How can agriculture be improved? How should the colonies be governed now that the possessions of the VOC and WIC had been transferred to the state? The most competent agents studied the situation carefully: Johannes Goldberg, agent for the national economy, and Jan Kops, commissioner of agriculture, traveled throughout the country to hold the first "national inquiry" into the economy.[77] They compiled the first statistical tables of import and export, employment and production in various parts of the country. Through correspondence and personal conversation they set out to discover ways to stimulate the economy. The first national legislation for education, water management, poor relief, and public health was established, in spite of opposition from towns, charitable institutions, and educational bodies. Much was insufficiently thought through, and after the more federalist and conservative regime assumed power in 1801, a great deal of the legislation was forgotten or rescinded. For example, the new administrative organization of the Netherlands into eight departments, which—as a replica of the French system—were given new names and had no relationship to the old provinces, was immediately dissolved in 1801. The opportunities for reform were furthermore greatly limited by the continual financial problems that had to be faced. This resulted in repeated reductions in the budgets of the ministries; because of the dire financial straits, any plan that required an increase in expenditure was doomed in advance.

To cite Simon Schama, the 1795 Treaty of The Hague simultaneously constituted the birth and death certificate of the Batavian Republic.[78] It burdened the new state with enormous financial obligations and established indissolvable bonds with revolutionary France that exacerbated the financial problems of the state considerably. Furthermore, the attempts of the Batavian state to attain legitimacy were also dependent on its being able to find a political solution to the issue of public debt. As we have already described, the old Republic lost its legitimacy under influence of financial and political crises of the period 1780–95; it now remained to be seen whether this new institutional structure—the indivisible state, which came into being only after much effort and delay—was able to provide the solutions for such obstacles. The unitarian reformers among the Batavians were of the opinion that through rational administration and centralization of taxation, income could be significantly increased, so that the public debt could be secured. Moreover, according to Isaac Gogel, agent for finance during 1798–1801 and the most important Batavian financial expert, these reforms would in addition to removing inequalities in the fiscal system simultaneously stimulate trade and industry.[79] In addition to the practical side of these reforms, there was also an issue of principle involved. Prior to 1795 the cities and towns could with some justification claim certain privileges for their inhabitants because they paid considerably more taxes than rural inhabitants. The new egalitarianism of the French Revolution rejected such inequalities on principle, implying that the taxation system had to be universally consistent.

Yet, especially as Wantje Fritschy made clear in her 1988 dissertation, the margins in which these reforms were to be realized were extremely small.[80] The continually increasing expenditures for war and the navy had as a result of the suffocating alliance with France become unavoidable; an increasing amount of the energy of the Batavian politicians, and subsequently of Louis Napoleon, was spent in attempts to convince authorities in Paris that the Netherlands had exhausted its means and could not contribute anymore to the financing of France's war with the United Kingdom. They were nevertheless, and certainly after Napoleon assumed power on 9 November 1799, unsuccessful. As White has demonstrated from his reconstructions of French government finances, the compulsory foreign contributions were the financial foundation upon which the stability of Napoleon's political system was built; Napoleon could maintain his power base only as long as he was able to press conquered states to fill the coffers of the French treasury.[81] War expenditures in these years soared to historically high levels, reaching more than fl 30 million annually (table 1.7). In comparison, the reforms planned shortly after the Orangist Restoration of 1787 were estimated to cost fl 15 million annually, an amount that was higher than actual expenditures on these items before 1795. The alliance with France and the almost continual state of war (only in 1802, after the Treaty of Amiens, could a modest "peace dividend" be enjoyed) meant an annual increase in defense expenditures of fl 20 million, approximately 5 percent of estimated GDP. Only under Louis Napoleon, when the state was really in danger of going bankrupt, were the expenditures reduced (see table 1.7).

TABLE 1.7.
Outlays and Income of the Batavian Republic up to the Treaty of Amiens, 1795–1802 (in millions of guilders).

Year	Expenditures				Income	Deficit	Debt	Debt /GDP
	Interest	Defense	Other	Total				
1795	—	—	—	—	—	—	766	1.62
1798	36.2	27.3		63.5	25.6	38.0	794	2.32
1799	29.3	37.9	17.4	84.6	33.8	50.8	832	2.15
1800	28.0	37.7	12.3	78.0	33.8	44.2	882	2.01
1801	32.7	35.2	4.8	72.7	33.8	38.9	927	2.14
1802	32.9	24.4	8.7	66.0	33.8	32.2	959	2.31

Source: Pfeil, "Tot redding," 169, 473; the tentative GDP series used is that of table 1.4.

If at all possible, even more pressing was the second large item on the budget: interest payments on the public debt. The argument against cutting the interest to be paid on the public debt was in 1804 put in no uncertain terms by Van de Kasteele, a leading financial expert: "Our Republic bankrupt! What shame for the name of the Netherlands, what betrayal! With our industry in ruins, living off interest payments has become a necessity for thousands. Widows, orphans and poor relief, all cry in protest. If our Republic goes bankrupt what can be expected of the English, the Russians, the Austrians and others? How would they, always in need, raise money? As a trading nation we cannot depend on conscription; in times of war we need money, and thus credit."[82] Furthermore, the credit of merchants, in the view of the financial elite the mainstay of the economy, was closely linked to the solidarity of the public debt. After all, many had invested a great deal of their wealth in public debt, and their creditworthiness would suffer seriously should the state go bankrupt. In short, the security of the national debt was one of the most important aims of the financial reforms of the Batavians, indeed, one that was not a matter for discussion.

The remaining items of expenditure were much smaller; usually they amounted to no more than 20 percent of total government expenditure. In the first few years following centralization of government finances, in 1798, some reductions in expenditure were realized in these items. On the other hand, the Batavian revolution was launched with the aim of creating a state that would reform Dutch society in every facet. The creation of a centralized taxation system and the establishment of an independent bureaucracy were cherished objectives. Moreover, the creation of a unified state was a learning process: the composition of necessary routines and regulations, the appointment of the right people to the many new positions; it all cost time and money, both of which were structurally lacking for the Batavian politicians. Therefore, the remaining items of expenditure, which exhibited a decline shortly after 1798, began to rise again, exacerbating the financial problems.

Nevertheless, with all these problems hanging over their heads, the Batavians were able to realize some significant successes in modernizing government finances. The provinces' debts were amalgamated in 1798, and a year later the first *Algemene Begrooting der Staatshehoeften voor de Bataafsch Republiek*— a summary of expenditures planned for 1799—was accepted by the National Assembly. The submission of this budget was such a leap forward, and everybody was so impressed, that it was printed and distributed among the population. To meet the large deficits, Gogel was soon forced to introduce the first compulsory national income and wealth taxes, a significant breakthrough in the relations between the former provinces and the central authorities (table 1.8). The final facet of these reforms, a system of national taxation, was prepared and submitted by Gogel himself, but the decision-making process for this was so slow that it was completed only in 1801, by which time the political balance had changed.

Perhaps the best indication of the success of the reforms of 1798–1801 is the development of public confidence in the solidity of the public debt. Earlier, beginning with the financial crisis of 1793–94, the price of government bonds had fallen. In February and March 1798, immediately after the coup d'état on 22 January 1798 that resulted in the formation of the radical regime, bond prices reached a temporary nadir, only to creep up a little in the months that followed. In the ensuing years until 1803, when Napoleon resumed war with England, prices remained conspicuously stable. In the period that Gogel was at the financial helm, from the end of February 1798 until September 1801, bond prices rose by 10 percent (figure 1.2). In this respect, at least, the Batavian reforms were successful.

In the hope that it would enable him to squeeze more money out of the Netherlands, the during summer of 1801 Napoleon decided that reconciliation between Batavians and Orangists was desirable, which resulted in the introduction of the constitution of 1801. This was accompanied by the repeal of a number of important reforms that had been accepted between 1798 and 1800. The old provinces were again given a greater say in affairs, temporarily sealing the fate of plans for a national system of taxation. Gogel had to step aside for less radical financial experts (e.g., J. A. de Vos van Steenwijk), who with the advantage of Napoleon's politics of peace, which in the year after the Treaty of Amiens remained intact attempted to meet government deficits through more conventional approaches. At first this led to further offerings of government bonds at high rates of interest, for which subscriptions were rapidly filled. When it became clear that in the long term the problems would only worsen, De Vos van Steenwijk was forced to issue new, compulsory loans, so that in the course

TABLE 1.8.
Survey of the Moneys Raised by Means of Forced Levies on Property and Income until 1803 (in millions of guilders and percents).

	Tax (%)	Total Receipt	Taxed Wealth	Tax (%)	Total Receipt	Taxed Income	Best-guess GDP
Holland							
		Property					
1795	6	50.4	840	—	—	—	474
1796	6	44.7	745	—	—	—	402
1797–98	2.5	16.8	670	—	—	—	339
Batavian Republic							
		Property			*Income*		
1797[a]	—	—	—	8	7.17	89.6	335
1798–99[b]	5	57.1	1,141	10	7.17	71.7	365
1800[c]	3	32.6	1,086	3	2.49	83.0	439
1801[d]	2	20.6	1,032	4	3.15	78.6	433
1802[e]	0.5	5.3	1,060	5	3.94	78.8	416
1802[f]	—	—	—	2	1.58	79.0	416
1803[g]	0.5	4.5	900	5	3.50	70.0	415
1803[h]	2	18.0	900	2	1.40	70.0	415

Sources: Gedenkstukken 4, bk. 2, 472, report by Van Stralen to Schimmelpenninck on the basis of a survey by Canneman; otherwise as in table 1.4.

[a] Income: interest-bearing.

[b] Property: interest-bearing.

[c] Income: "don gratuit"; property: interest-bearing; income: lasts for twenty-five years, raised in 1801 and 1802 by 1%.

[d] Property: interest-bearing over 17 million; income: second of twenty-five-year levy, "don gratuit."

[e] Property: "don gratuit," lasts another seven years; income: third of twenty-five-year levy.

[f] Income: "don gratuit," lasts eight years.

[g] Property: "don gratuit" from the second until the eighth year; income: fourth of the twenty-five-year levy.

[h] Property: "don gratuit"; income: second of the eighth-year levy.

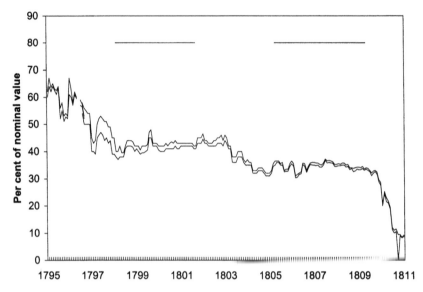

FIGURE 1.2. Highest and lowest prices of Holland 2.5 percent bonds, January 1795 until March 1811 (in percent of nominal value). The two horizontal lines indicate the periods during which Gogel was in charge of finance. Data from Prijscourant der Effecten, augustus 1796–januari 1811; 1795/96: see figure 1.1.

of time this government, too, lost all credibility among investors (see table 1.7). Resistance on the part of provinces, which had regained some of their influence, to further budget cuts and new taxation led in the long run to chaos. The failure of the financial policies of the Staatsbewind of 1801 was clearly reflected in the decline in the price of Holland's bonds between the beginning of 1803 and the end of 1805: the experiment with a neofederal infrastructure was unsuccessful in winning confidence in the government's finances (see figure 1.2).[83]

Again Napoleon intervened, this time in favor of a by and large centralist state, based on the French model, in which the direct role of provinces in decision making had no place. After 1805, under Schimmelpenninck, the National Assembly, which had been an important force in the period 1796–1801, lost any influence it had. The government of the country lay in the hands of a small group of bureaucrats among which Gogel was the most important. The pain of the financial crisis was so keenly felt that once again new reforms were implemented, the most important of which was without a doubt the national system of taxation that was introduced in 1806 and, with the exception of a few details, was a replica of proposals made by Gogel in 1799. It was modeled on the system in Holland, with only a few adjustments to take into account the situation in other provinces; its introduction therefore increased tensions. This had been foreseen by Gogel, who upon submitting his proposal under the government led by Schimmelpenninck stated that among the inhabitants of the land provinces, who were "used to paying lower taxes and who had less means at their disposal," heavy opposition and, as a result, evasion could be expected.[84] Resistance to the sharp increase in land taxes and the introduction of duties on staples (e.g., bread, and meat) was particularly strong in the land provinces, where production for the market was far less important than in the west, leading to all sorts of problems.[85]

In addition to formal protest, evasion occurred on a large scale, and local civil servants (who had difficulty identifying their work with the national interest) often came to some agreement with the local population to prevent the taxes from increasing too quickly. Consequently, the yield of the new system was disappointing. Despite the significant increase in income, the financial difficulties continued as expenditures also increased (table 1.9). In his study of government finances from 1795 to 1810, Pfeil referred to this as the "paradox of reform": it was necessary to significantly increase the expenditures of the centralized bureaucracy if the fruits of the modernized national system of taxation were to be enjoyed.[86]

The new tax system that was introduced in 1806 failed to meet the expectations of the Batavian revolutionaries. When plans had first been put on paper,

TABLE 1.9.
Expenditure and Income of the Batavian Republic and Its Successors, 1803–1814 (in millions of guilders).

Year	Expenditures				Income	Deficit	Debt	Debt /GDP
	Interest	Defense	Other	Total				
1803	33.9	32.6	7.0	73.5	35.0	38.5	997	2.40
1804	35.0	32.0	5.9	72.9	35.0	37.9	1,035	2.67
1805	33.9	31.8	6.5	72.2	35.0	37.2	1,072	2.58
1806	34.3	35.9	11.8	82.0	42.7	39.3	1,112	2.71
1807	34.8	27.8	15.5	78.1	46.6	31.5	1,143	2.93
1808	38.8	17.6	23.6	80.0	44.0	36.0	1,179	3.03
1809	38.9	15.8	15.3	70.0	48.3	21.7	1,201	3.07
1810	41.5	32.5		74.0	42.8	31.2	1,232	3.11
1814	20.8	27.5	11.3	59.6	45.0	14.6	(1,726)[a]	4.72

Sources: As in table 1.7 and Horlings and Van Zanden, "Exploitatie en Afscheiding."
[a] Exempt of Napoleonic default (reduction to a third, the so-called tiërcering), otherwise as table 1.7.

after 1795, it had been expected that a direct taxation of income, which was to replace the excises on the necessities of life, would be a great improvement. These excises not only hit the pockets of the poorest groups in the population but also stood in the way of the development trade and industry. However, the experiments with centrally imposed income taxation demonstrated how unstable this alternative source of income still was.[87] It was virtually impossible to check the tax returns of citizens, particularly in cases of collusion between citizens, local politicians, and tax officials in their common opposition to Holland. As a result of evasion of these centrally imposed taxes, whose foundations were difficult to objectivize, the old differences between Holland and the other provinces, which were at the heart of the Republic's financial crisis, reared their head in a new form. This forced Gogel to replace direct taxation of income and wealth by taxation of "means" that were indirectly related to income: number of servants; rent paid for dwelling; the value of furniture, and so forth. In addition, Holland's *verponding,* the most important form of direct taxation on the value of real estate, was introduced throughout the country. Nevertheless, income from direct taxation was completely insufficient and had to be supplemented by heavy duties on milling, salt, soap, *jenever* (Dutch gin), peat, and several other necessities of life. The harmonization of these duties was a vast improvement over the old system, under which duties differed greatly from province to province, but their continuation and the actual increase of their rates (in the provinces outside Holland) represented a defeat for the original efforts at reform by the Batavians. To some extent this was the price to be paid for the fact that taxation of interest paid by the state was considered off limits. Despite passionate pleas to implement such taxation by the land provinces, Gogel and other experts (in particular Canneman and Goldberg) refused to implement such a tax, arguing that this would be interpreted as indicating the bankruptcy of the state (because it would be arbitrarily cutting the interest paid on its own debt). The issue of public debt continued to dominate the political landscape.

Gogel's system of taxation endured. Except for a brief period in 1812–13, it would remain in place for almost the entire nineteenth century. It was only in the 1890s that major reforms were again instituted. Other reforms introduced in the early years of the century, such as the first publication of the accounts of government expenditure and income for 1806 and the introduction of the National Debt Register in 1809, were further significant steps in the rationalization of government finance. Once more, the capital market's response to these reforms was markedly positive; the price of Holland's bonds, which shortly earlier had reached new depths, rose conspicuously after Schimmelpenninck and Gogel took office at the beginning of March 1805. This ended the downward trend in bond prices that had begun in 1803 and led to a fall in the minimum price of 2.5 percent bonds from 44 percent in January 1803 to 31 percent in January 1805. Between March 1805 and May 1809 (with the exception of the relapse between March and July 1806, when it appeared that the new head of state, Louis Napoleon, might announce partial default), the minimum price fluctuated between 33 and 36 percent, indicating a stabilization of the market's confidence—or, rather, the lack of it (see figure 1.2). The drastic cuts in the defense budgets which Louis Napoleon as the new head of the Kingdom of Holland dared to announce (duly blocked by his brother), contributed to a slight improvement in public finances. Ultimately the deficits were so large, however, that even Gogel's new system could not help. In the course of 1809 Napoleon lost confidence in his brother, whom he considered far too accommodating in favor of Holland's interests in instituting the Continental System, aimed at blocking trade with the United Kingdom and cutting off its means to finance the continental war (by disrupting the flow of bills of exchange that linked soldiers' pay to the credibility of the British Crown). Ultimately, in mid-1810, this led to the liquidation of the Kingdom of Holland and the formal integration of the Netherlands into the French Empire, almost immediately followed by a *tiërcering* (cutting by two-thirds) of interest payments on the public debt. The capital market had been expecting just such a development: not only the clear signal of deferred interest payments in 1808 but also the dismissal of Gogel as chief financial adviser to Louis Napoleon in May 1809 led to a decrease in the price listings of 2.5 percent bonds. In a little more than a year they lost some two-thirds of their value in anticipation of the tiërcering, which was announced by decree in July 1810 (see figure 1.2).

We may be brief about the period in which the Netherlands formed an annexed part of the French Empire. Napoleon appears to have had no problem with temporarily maintaining the old system of taxation with its higher revenues, while outlays had already been reduced as a result of the tiërcering. It took Gogel, establishing himself as one of the most loyal servants of the French revolutionary regime, some time to convince Paris that for the sake of unity within the empire, it was necessary to introduce the French system of taxation in the Netherlands. This was finally achieved in 1812 under Gogel's direction and, as a result, was short-lived.[88] French rule came to an end in November 1813. In the months that followed, a new and even more daunting task would have to be dealt with: to design a tax system suitable for the United Kingdom of the Netherlands formed under Willem I.

CHAPTER TWO

A Complex Legacy Tossed

THE DUTCH ECONOMY DURING WAR
AND REVOLUTION, 1780–1813

THE LEGACY: SPECIALIZATION AND STRUCTURAL CHANGE

In historiography the period from 1780 to 1813 has acquired a bad name. For example, Johan de Vries, in his classic study of "the economic decline of the Republic in the eighteenth century," published in 1959, declared that up to 1780 per capita income at best remained stationary, but thereafter in almost every sector of the economy signs of economic decline were unmistakable.[1] More than thirty-five years later (in 1995), in their classic book on the economic development of the Netherlands between 1500 and 1815, Jan de Vries and Ad van der Woude were even more critical: they typified the years following 1780 as "the terminal phase" and "a lengthy crisis" in which the sick patient—the Republic's economy—comes to an impoverished end, thus implying a structural discontinuity in development from 1813 onward.[2] Nor were Erik Buyst and Joel Mokyr less critical in the overview they published in 1990 on developments in trade and industry between 1795 and 1814. They state that a sharp decline in national income must have occurred.[3]

The unqualified criticism of both publications is particularly noteworthy because other research that touches on aspects of this period, which has been published since De Vries and Van der Woude's work appeared in 1995, suggests that at least Holland's economy showed various signs of resilience, so that up until the period of the Continental System at least the decline appears to have remained limited.[4] Instead of positioning the economic changes that occurred through obvious medical metaphors, it is likely to be more useful to analyze the economic developments of the period in detail. The primary task, then, is to determine interrelationships between the political-economic changes analyzed in the previous chapter and developments in production and income in the major sectors of the economy as reflected in available data. In doing so, particular attention will be paid to the resilience of the economy in relation to its openness. To what extent were the various sectors able to accommodate the largely external forces that buffeted them between 1780 and 1813, especially events that disturbed trade, such as the maritime war, the introduction of the Continental System, emergency taxation measures, flight of capital, and monetary destabilization through loss of confidence about the public debt? In such an analysis, the sector model that Keuchenius found so useful could serve as a starting point: How did the services, industry, and agricultural sectors respond to these shocks? Did the trends he identified—marked decline in industry and fisheries, compensated for by stability in international trade and growth in financial services and agriculture—continue in this period, or was there a wider discontinuity in economic development?

Before trends between 1780 and 1813 are examined, we will first sketch the sectoral and spatial structure of the Dutch economy at the end of the eighteenth and the beginning of the nineteenth century. There were three clear concentric circles of activity in the Netherlands. The urban part of the Province of Holland was without doubt the heart of the economy. In the highly urbanized western part of the country, at least 80 percent of the population worked in industry and the services sector, while agriculture was a rather subordinate source of employment. Ten percent of the country's population lived behind Amsterdam's walls alone; the city not only was the undisputed center of the economy but also served an extensive area of the surrounding countryside. In addition to capital-intensive industries closely related to the city's trading activities (*trafieken* such as sugar refining, textile printing, gin distilling, and papermaking) and a diverse services industry, Holland was also home to an extremely specialized horticultural sector and a very productive dairying sector. In economic terms this region was especially dependent on international services (trade, shipping, and banking). Several industries (the Trafieken mentioned earlier) contributed to the strengthening of the economic foundations of this region, but they, too, were dependent on the flourishing of international trade. Traditionally Amsterdam was the most important center for the European grain trade, and a significant proportion of the European trade in tropical goods (from the West and East Indies) passed through Amsterdam and Rotterdam, while both cities played a significant role in the trade with and transit of goods to the primarily German hinterland. However, partly as a result of the United Kingdom becoming the largest importer of grain, Amsterdam began to lose its primary position in the trade of grain.

This economic heartland, Randstad Holland, was flanked by concentric circles of highly productive agricultural areas, producing specialized primary products. In these parts of the country, Friesland and Groningen, Zeeland and northwest Brabant, the economy was almost entirely dependent on agriculture (at that time flourishing), and there were few other activities (shipping in Friesland and Groningen being the exception) geared at international markets. Jan de Vries's thesis has demonstrated that agriculture had played an important role in the structural transformation of the economy of this region; the process of specialization that had begun in the sixteenth and seventeenth centuries laid the foundations for the high levels of productivity that were being achieved there.[5] A conspicuous feature of farming in these regions was its rather large-scale nature: an average farm in Zeeland or Groningen employed a considerable number of laborers, had a large number of animals, and cropped no less than twenty to thirty hectares of arable land.

The third region—outside Randstad Holland and the circle of specialized farming surrounding it—more or less coincided with the eastern and southern Netherlands, the provinces of Drenthe, Overijssel, Gelderland, North Brabant, and Limburg. In these areas, too, agriculture was relatively the most important activity, and significant agricultural surpluses for Holland (and to a lesser extent international markets) were produced there. Their agricultural productivity was, however, for a variety of reasons much lower: for example, in sandy parts of the country much more labor was needed to fertilize the land, yet yields remained behind those of clay and peat soils in the west and the north. Furthermore, the infrastructure was much less developed: the extensive network of waterways that connected farmers in, for example, Zeeland and Friesland with markets was missing in the "periphery" of the Netherlands. Financial markets were also less well developed, and the degree of specialization was lower than elsewhere in the country, which contributed further to the rather low levels of productivity. For example, farmers in Drenthe consumed a sizable portion of their rye harvests themselves. Gogel's introduction of duties on the milling of grain led not only to angry protest and molestation of civil servants who enforced the duties but also to an increase in the cultivation of buckwheat and potatoes, produce not subject to duties.[6] The farms in these parts of the country were much smaller than those in the heartland of the Netherlands: a farmer in Overijssel had no more than five to ten hectares in production and employed farm labor only at harvest; family labor dominated in this region. Typically, a farmer in Overijssel or Gelderland possessed four to five cows and perhaps a few horses; an "average" farmer in Holland, Utrecht, or Friesland owned fifteen cows and often four to six horses.

The high levels of agricultural production in Holland and Utrecht was to a large extent an inheritance of the Republic. Following the strong growth of the cities and towns in the sixteenth and seventeenth centuries, agricultural production in the coastal provinces concentrated on increasing production to meet demand from these nearby markets and profited from opportunities to specialize in producing a limited number of products—from butter and cheese to strawberries and flower bulbs. The cultivation of madder in Zeeland and on the islands of Zuid-Holland is a good example. A red dye was extracted in special stoves from the roots of the madder and exported to the most important textile-manufacturing centers around the North Sea: in the Middle Ages to Flanders, later to Holland (Leiden), and increasingly during the eighteenth century to England. The cultivation of madder required a great deal of skill, which had developed and been prized in this part of the country over the centuries. The processing of the roots was capital-intensive (the stoves required were often financed by the farmers themselves), a delicate activity that involved certification by several regional bodies, with the aim of achieving a standard level of quality. The foreign buyer had to be able to put blind faith in the certification of quality given by the manufacturers in Zeeland and Rotterdam's traders. This complicated and strictly regulated industry made an important contribution to the agricultural export surpluses of the day.[7] To some extent the situation was a paradox: one of the most urbanized and densely populated countries in Europe in the eighteenth century successfully produced more agricultural produce than it consumed. That was only possible through clever response to the opportunities created by international specialization. Large quantities of grain—particularly rye and to a lesser extent wheat—were imported from the Baltic States.[8] This was balanced by sizable exports of animal produce (butter, cheese, and meat) and produce from intensive arable farming (madder). In this, specialization had reached the degree that fattening of calves was based on the supply of calves from northern Germany and Denmark.[9] Further, the import of Baltic grain (rye) was limited due to the specialized cultivation of wheat (more of which was consumed in Holland) in Zeeland and West Brabant, something that clearly illustrates the separate regional structure and productivity of Dutch agriculture then.[10] The replacement of bread by potatoes in the daily diet of laborers, which became established after 1760, also contributed to the decline in grain imports.

Regional diversity can be clearly seen in data on agricultural yields per hectare and per laborer in the provinces (tables 2.1 and 2.2). The division

TABLE 2.1.
Grain and Milk Yields (in hectoliters) in Six Provinces, 1812–13.

	Coastal Provinces			Inland Provinces			
	Groningen	North Holland	Zeeland	Drenthe	Overijssel	Gelderland	Netherlands
Yield per hectare							
Wheat	21	21	21	12	15	11	20
Rye	22	22	21	13	12	11	15
Barley	31	27	40	13	17	15	27
Oats	38	32	41	18	19	16	25
Potatoes	180	146	170	—	120	150	170
Milk yield per cow	—	2.4	2.4	1.0	1.0	—	1.9

Source: Van Zanden, *Economische ontwikkeling,* 91, 105.

TABLE 2.2.
Key Productivity Data: Provincial Differences in Agricultural Development in the
Early Nineteenth Century.

	Labor Productivity (1812/13) (Netherlands = 100)	Land Productivity (1812/13) (Netherlands = 100)	Rent per Hectare (1820) (fl)	Wage per Day (1819) (fl)
Groningen	141	104	24.8	.65
Friesland	145	94	21.8	.82
Drenthe	76	58	9.0	.60
Overijssel	59	62	14.1	.54
Gelderland	77	81	18.8	.48
Utrecht	130	108	22.6	.75
North Holland	131	121	31.3	.80
South Holland	139	133	30.0	.88
Zeeland	159	137	30.6	.86
North Brabant	62	88	22.6	.57
Limburg	67	114	18.7	.49
Average	100	100	23.0	.65

Sources: Van Zanden, *Economische ontwikkeling,* 117–119; Van Zanden, "Regionale ver-schillen."

between the coastal provinces and their inland counterparts is evident from the estimates of the productivity of labor: in the coastal provinces the average pro-duction per laborer was approximately twice that of the inland provinces; rents on leaseholds and wages (related to the productivity of labor) showed the same pattern. The data also reflect the greater population pressures that existed south of the major rivers: in Brabant and Limburg farmers were able to raise their yields to levels greater than those in Friesland and Groningen, but this was out-weighed by the many more mouths that had to be fed.

A typical feature of the countryside of the periphery was that in the Middle Ages owners of agricultural land had been able to consolidate their rights to use the wastelands adjacent to their lands. In the eastern Netherlands the period of population growth before 1350 led to the formation of *marken,* communi-ties that collectively farmed the wastelands (and peat bogs, forests, and pastures). The rules for their management were derived largely from local traditions and practices; this meant that the local rural inhabitants acquired virtually unlimited rights to these *common lands:* they were allowed to graze their animals there, cut grass sods (to gather the manure), cut peat and gather wood, and in numerous other ways make use of this communal good (arable fields in these areas were privately owned by farmers). The management of these marken struggled with the problem of "the tragedy of the commons": the common lands were continually in danger of being overexploited. Forests disappeared—the result of continual demand for wood for fuel and building—to be replaced by extremely impoverished heaths, which were in turn so intensively exploited that large sand drifts developed.[11] Moreover, an "infield-outfield" system developed here, in which the available nutrients were taken from the commons (in the form of turf and fodder for livestock) and concentrated on the fields. The productivity of the crops gradually increased (the yield ratio rose from about 3 in the sixteenth century to 5 at the beginning of the nineteenth century) but remained relatively low. The marken attempted continuously to prevent the overexploitation of the common lands, for example, by introducing strict rules for their use and even stricter system of fines, but these were only partly successful.[12]

Farmers in the eastern Netherlands and to a lesser degree that on the sandy soils of the southern Netherlands, where comparable institutions *(gemeynten)* managed wastelands, were prisoners of a system of land use that led to continually increasing "polarization" of farming land: the wastelands became poorer and poorer and more difficult to use, whereas the arable fields gradually improved their yield capacity. Increasingly in the course of the eighteenth and nineteenth centuries, the existence of the wastelands in the eastern and southern parts of the country became a thorn in the side of the new group of "enlightened" gentlemen farmers, many of whom were rich owners of large areas of land. They were of the opinion that a densely populated country such as the Netherlands could not allow such large tracts of land to remain barely used or even unused.

In these peripheral areas, due to the meager productivity of the agricultural sector, rural industries sprang up, serving markets outside the region. In Twente and the Achterhoek an important linen industry arose, which was gradually displaced by the production of cotton textiles.[13] In Brabant the city of Tilburg was an important center for the woolen industry, with strong traditional ties with the laken industry in Leiden; the linen industry in Helmond (in the same province) had similar ties with Haarlem. In this way patterns of specialization occurred in which the most labor-intensive activities—first spinning of yarns and later weaving of coarse products—were performed in Brabant, and those phases of the production process requiring more capital and craftsmanship were carried out in the cities and towns of Holland. The gradual "emancipation" of the textile industry in Brabant and the decline of industry in Holland resulted in the displacement of the industrial center of gravity farther to the south.[14]

The concentric rings of economic activity around Randstad Holland were to a certain extent disturbed by a gradual increase in population density in a southward direction, especially in the countryside. Agriculture in Zeeland, for example, was far more labor-intensive than that in Groningen or Friesland; sowing in rows and regular weeding of crops was virtually unknown in the north at the turn of the century, but in Zeeland it was the rule rather than the exception. Similarly, agriculture in North Brabant, which was comparable to the famous "Flemish method," was far more labor-intensive than that of Drenthe (a province where the ratio of population to available agricultural land was very low). Overijssel and Gelderland exhibited gradations of these trends. Southern Limburg, with its fertile loess soil but lack of good communications and market centers, was a separate case in this matter.

In addition to a productive agricultural sector and, by international standards, weak industrial sector, the economy of the Netherlands at the beginning of the nineteenth century was characterized by a large and strong services sector. According to our estimates, one-third of the working population was employed in tertiary activities—only in Great Britain was the proportion probably as high[15]—and as much as approximately 44 percent of national income was earned in this manner. In reality the sector comprised a number of diverse activities:

- productive services, including trade, transport, and banking, in which the Netherlands had already occupied a strong position since the seventeenth century; at the turn of the nineteenth century this accounted for no less than one-sixth of the total employment in the coastal provinces.
- government services, which by the turn of the century were rather extensive (especially due to the role of the military).
- consumer services, such as education, religion, and law, as well as a large domestic service branch (in numbers of employed, by far the largest occupation of the entire economy); in the coastal provinces it provided employment for one in six members of the working population.[16]

In the Randstad the services sector was by far the largest source of employment, by rough estimates accounting for 40 to 50 percent of total employment (table 2.3). In the inland provinces, which by European standards displayed a more "normally" structured labor market, this sector accounted for only 18 percent of employment. The relatively large contribution of the services sector should not be attributed only to the great importance of international services, although it was there, particularly in trade and related banking services, that the highest incomes were earned. The merchant was traditionally the most prominent citizen of the Netherlands, and "since time immemorial" trade was seen

TABLE 2.3.
Occupational Composition (in percent) of the Working Population in Inland and
Coastal Provinces, 1807.

	All Provinces	Inland	Coastal		All Provinces	Inland	Coastal
Agriculture, fisheries	42.7	57.2	33.3	Total industry[a]	26.0	23.8	27.3
Total services	30.5	18.3	38.6	Construction	25.6	25.2	25.8
Domestic services	11.7	7.2	14.6	Clothing	15.3	9.7	18.5
Government, army	3.8	2.4	4.7	Textiles	17.4	25.9	12.4
Trade	7.1	3.6	9.4	Metal/shipbuilding	5.6	4.1	6.5
Shipping	3.1	1.4	4.2	Woodworking	5.5	4.9	5.8
Other transport	1.4	1.4	1.4	Pottery	4.0	2.9	4.6
Medical and education	1.1	0.6	1.5	Food industry	12.0	11.4	12.4
Other services	2.4	1.8	2.9	Chemicals	1.7	0.7	2.3
				Leather	9.8	13.1	7.9
Laborers (casual)	0.7	0.7	0.7	Printing, paper	1.8	1.7	2.0
				Other industry	1.3	0.4	1.8
Total agriculture	374.5	200.4	175.8	Total industry	227.7	83.5	144.2
Total services	267.6	64.1	203.5	Laborers	6.3	2.5	3.8
Total employed	876.2	350.5	527.3	Population	2163.1	861.9	1301.2

Source: Horlings, Economic Development, 333.
[a] Subsectors in percentages of total industrial employment

as the foundation of the nation's economic welfare. However, employment in this international services sector was rather modest; certainly with the increase in international competition throughout the eighteenth century, an increasing proportion of international trade was lost to the city (and Amsterdam's traders concentrated only on financing trade). The bankruptcy of the VOC led to a similarly marked reduction in employment in the sector.

A much more important source of employment was the broad spectrum of services focusing on the domestic market, varying from services for the extensive domestic trading sector—in part due to a relatively fragmented trading network—to the numerous servants at work in well-to-do households in Holland.

The demand for these services appears to have been related to the degree of urbanization and the level of income in the cities and towns of Holland. In other words, the larger and richer the town, the more extensive the services sector was as a source of employment.[17] Of course this employment was indirectly dependent on the blossoming of international trade; when this collapsed during the Napoleonic period, the entire town-based economy of western Netherlands felt its loss.

A large proportion of the services sector contributed to only a limited extent to economic growth, however. The retail trade was plagued by poor turnover and extremely low profits; comparisons with the "informal" economies of today's developing countries come to mind in this connection. The system of distribution of domestic markets was in part affected by protection of local markets and trade hindrances due to provincial and local taxes. The uncountable numbers of shops and stalls in the towns and cities were often the source of extra income for, for example, married women and widows. Large groups of peddlers were barely able to earn a living from their activities. This informal economy expanded and contracted in rhythm with the purchasing power of the population, similar to developments in industries focusing on the domestic market (see chapter 1).

The general picture emerging from reconstructions of the earliest employment figures by profession is presented in table 2.3. Differences between coastal provinces and inland provinces in relation to the contribution to employment of, on the one hand, agriculture and, on the other, specialized services can be clearly seen. The relative size of employment in industry is conspicuously comparable, but after a more detailed breakdown it appears that protoindustrial activities (textiles) dominated industrial employment in the land provinces, whereas in the west, port-related activities (trafieken) were very important.

ECONOMIC INTEGRATION AND REGIONAL PRICE GAPS

As has already been emphasized, the large regional differences in economic structure were rooted in disparities in the structure of agriculture in various parts of the country. In turn, those disparities were related to differences in quality of agricultural land (sand vs. clay), the degree of specialization, and the institutional framework of the countryside, which, for example, affected the speed with which systems of common lands were dismantled. In addition, the degree to which each region had been able to profit from the enormous expansion of the towns and cities in the sixteenth and seventeenth centuries played a determinant role.

The simultaneous existence of regions with extremely different economic structures was once again made possible by large differences in the cost of living between the heartland of Holland and the rest of the country. Housing rents in Amsterdam in particular were multiples of the amounts paid in Brabant or the Achterhoek. For example, Soltow calculated that the annual rent paid for an *average* house in North Holland was almost ten times that of a similar house in Drenthe (fl 112.51 vs. fl 12.48); the *median* house in North Holland cost roughly fl 45 as against fl 10 in Drenthe and Overijssel.[18] For a small amount, the poor in the eastern Netherlands were permitted to set up a cottage on common land. Moreover, these cottagers had the right to graze several head of cattle on common lands, to cut peat, and to cultivate a small patch of land to grow some food. In contrast, in the cities the cost of living was extremely high, as every scrap of food had to be imported and was subject to numerous taxes and duties. These taxes and the much higher costs of bakers meant that the price of rye bread, the staple diet of many households, was 30 to 45 percent higher in Holland than in Overijssel.[19]

Differences in the price of bread were paralleled by the enormous regional contrasts in the price of coal; in Middelburg or Leiden at the beginning of the nineteenth century, its price was four times as high as in Zuid-Limburg (see chapter 6). The market for potatoes, a product with relatively little value in proportion to its weight, was also subject to regional differences in price. In contrast, the market for grain and turf was characterized by large flows of goods, which for centuries had made use of the relatively efficient network of inland waterways. In the seventeenth and eighteenth centuries, grain market prices in Groningen, Arnhem, and Den Bosch closely followed prices on the Amsterdam market, which was a major international market in the grain trade. The continued existence of such large differences in the price of goods for consumption, despite an infrastructure that by international standards was relatively good, particularly in the coastal provinces, must have been the result of to politico-economic factors. Millers and bakers in Holland were protected by a complicated system of taxation and fixed pricing at regional (until 1806) and town (until 1864) levels. Import of bread into the larger cities and towns was therefore forbidden, so that rural bakers who were able to make their bread more cheaply were unable to compete with bakers in the cities and towns. In a similar manner the system of taxes and duties stimulated the use of turf so that the development of a market for coal was held back (see chapter 6). Gogel's reforms were to an important degree designed to remove these obstacles to domestic trade, although in many ways they did not go far enough. The most important reason for the partial failure was the poor state of government finances, which made it necessary to continue to levy duties on many consumer goods, such as bread and coal, and prevented the reform of the finances of the large towns and cities.

Such differences in the cost of living had a great influence on wages, as contemporaries such as Keuchenius emphasized. It is possible to analyze the close

TABLE 2.4.
Differences in Average Prices (guilders) at Provincial Markets, 1824–29.[a]

	Rye	Rye Bread	Butter	Potatoes	Beef	Pork	Candles	Peat
Groningen	4.26	5.62	7.30	3.04	59.7	1.23	57.7	36.4
Friesland	4.55	6.65	7.96	3.41	74.3	1.27	60.0	38.3
Drenthe	4.37	5.86	—	1.49	61.0	—	—	—
Overijssel	4.53	7.03	6.67	2.14	60.3	1.81	56.7	36.8
Gelderland	4.81	6.80	7.75	2.94	57.0	1.39	53.6	54.6
Utrecht	4.98	7.58	8.41	3.43	60.8	1.30	57.2	59.3
North Holland	4.82	6.56	8.58	3.76	78.1	1.61	60.0	50.0
South Holland	4.87	7.46	8.83	3.96	76.8	1.87	56.1	49.9
Zeeland	4.82	7.22	9.50	4.68	71.8	1.90	57.4	39.7
North Brabant	4.62	6.99	6.75	2.13	53.5	1.65	40.0	41.6
Limburg	4.79	7.06	6.56	1.77	53.8	1.19	52.6	34.1
Average	4.67	6.90	7.65	2.98	64.3	1.52	55.1	44.0

Sources: ARA, *Archief Binnenlandse Zaken, Binnenlands Bestuur B, 1814–1831*, 1365; *Provinciaal Blad van Noord-Braband* (1816–1850); *Provinciaal Blad van Zeeland* (1830–1855); RA Overijssel, *Provinciaal Bestuursarchief, 1813–1831*, 25E, 356–57; RA Limburg, *Archief Provinciaal Bestuur* (04.01) 8588–93.

[a] Prices in guilders per hectoliter (grains, potatoes, and peat) or in cents per kilo (others).

relationship between relative wages and relative prices for the period around 1820. Tables 2.4 and 2.5 give the results of comprehensive research into the regional differences in prices of consumer goods and wages at that time, showing how strong the correlation was. In North Holland, the province with the highest nominal wages, the cost of living was more than 25 percent higher than the national average, while in Drenthe and North Brabant the cost of living was 10 percent lower than the national average. Ultimately, approximately half the regional differences in wage levels can be attributed to these price differences. In fact, the highest real wages were to be earned not so much in the western Netherlands but in the relatively sparsely populated agricultural regions in the north, that is, in Friesland and Groningen. Why did laborers not migrate in large numbers from the low-wage regions to Holland and Friesland, to earn more money there? To some extent they did just that; Lucassen has shown that large groups of seasonal laborers traveled every year to the North Sea coast to

TABLE 2.5.
Regional Differences in Wages And Prices, 1819–1820.[a]

	Wages, Agriculture (cents)	Wages, Industry (cents)	Wages, Weighted Average	Cost of Living	Real Wages (average)
Groningen	79.0	92.9	99.4	83.7	118.8
Friesland	99.9	91.6	108.7	91.5	118.8
Drenthe	73.3	70.4	78.9	89.6	88.1
Overijssel	66.4	72.6	76.3	96.5	79.1
Gelderland	58.9	82.2	79.9	98.2	81.4
Utrecht	91.5	98.0	111.7	105.5	105.9
North Holland	97.8	124.0	148.7	127.4	116.7
South Holland	107.6	109.4	131.3	116.2	113.0
Zeeland	105.6	107.3	119.1	108.0	110.3
North Brabant	69.7	68.8	75.4	89.3	84.4
Limburg	59.9	69.7	70.6	94.3	74.9
Netherlands	82.7	89.7	100.0	100.0	100.0

Sources: De Meere, "Daglonen"; De Meere, Economische ontwikkeling, 72; Kint and Van der Voort, "Economische groei," 114–35; regional differences in the cost of living: database national accounts (research Arthur van Riel).

[a] All wages data used concern day wages for males.

take advantage of the high wages to be earned there in agriculture and industry.[20] The stream of permanent migrants from, for example, Overijssel to Amsterdam grew in the seventeenth century and continued in the eighteenth century at a high level. Such mobility did not, however, lead to equalization of wage levels. Indeed, the opposite was the case: available data show that the nominal differences in wages between the western and eastern Netherlands increased rather than decreased over the course of the eighteenth century.[21]

Migration from "low" to "high" wages was insufficient to cause the differences to disappear. One reason was that life in the urban west was more uncertain: on the one hand, high nominal wages, but on the other, a high chance of becoming unemployed. Informal networks that provided relief to the unemployed in the east and south of the country did not function as well in the large towns and cities of the Randstad. "Open" unemployment was prevalent there, especially in the winter months, and although there was a rather extensive network of poor relief institutions to support the poor unemployed in their need, this relief was not always accessible to newcomers, and payments were too small to live on. The economic decline of the large towns and cities of Holland and Zeeland, moreover, meant that it became less attractive to migrate to the west of the country. Migration came to an end after 1795.

Another cause of regional differentiation was, finally, the capital market. In Holland, particularly Amsterdam, an enormous amount of capital had been accumulated in the previous centuries, while the other regions were in this respect relatively poor. During the eighteenth century a growing proportion of the wealth of the rich was invested in government bonds; at the same time, Holland had been successful in lowering interest payments on its public debt considerably. This had probably also affected interest rates on the private market, both within Holland and in the rest of the country; data on the interest on mortgages, for example, show rates in Twente, Groningen, Beijerlanden, and Amsterdam had also reached similarly low levels, which as a result of inflation gradually increased somewhat in the second half of the eighteenth century (see chapter 4). The enormous amount of disposable capital and the high wages in Holland meant that the per capita income was much higher there than in the "periphery." This higher income did not, however, result in a higher standard of living; on the contrary, there is every indication that the deepest poverty was concentrated in the large cities of the Randstad. Life expectancy was much greater in the "high" parts of the Netherlands than in the "low" parts, which was also related to poor hygienic conditions in the urban areas and to inferior drinking water there. Conditions in the countryside were simply better: for example, the degree of literacy in Drenthe was much higher than in Holland, although in this matter there was a distinct difference between literacy in the Protestant north and the Catholic south of the country.[22]

An important reason for this paradox—that the standard of living in the "poor" periphery was higher than in the "rich" center—was the large difference in income inequality. In the urban west inequality was much greater than in the countryside of Brabant or Drenthe.[23] In addition, the cities of Holland were greatly affected by the industrial decline of the region, which was accompanied by falling employment and an increase in expenditure on poor relief. In contrast, there was a more or less continual upswing in the agricultural sector. Whereas households in the east or south had some income from small parcels of land and the cattle they possessed, workers in Holland and Zeeland were dependent solely on their wages, which contributed to their vulnerability. Behind the facade of the canal houses of the well-to-do in Amsterdam there was much poverty, in particular in times of poor harvests and high grain prices. To a certain extent, peasant farmers in their sod huts in the eastern Netherlands had, through the development of their small pieces of land, better prospects for a gradual improvement of their circumstances.

WAR AND REVOLUTION: BETWEEN STABILITY AND DECLINE

Particularly in French literature, much attention has been paid to the economic climate that was specific to the ancien régime, one characterized by large fluctuations in agricultural yields. Exogenous shocks—the result of bad weather, for example—caused economic fluctuations that were felt throughout the entire economy of the ancien régime. Crop failures led to high grain prices, which in turn meant that consumers had no money to purchase anything other than food, confronting industries with a disappearance of their markets. By contrast, during years of good harvests and low prices for agricultural produce, consumers were able to buy clothing, shoes, and household goods, causing a boom in industry. But little evidence could be found that such a "premodern" business cycle, which was typical for the French economy before 1789, existed in the Netherlands. One reason for this was that the Republic—and especially Holland—profited from crop failures and high grain prices. Amsterdam was, after all, the central grain market for northwest Europe, and shortages in, for example, France and Spain brought with them more work and profit for Amsterdam's traders and dockworkers. In other words, there was a compensatory economic cycle in the grain trade that brought about a certain stabilization of purchasing power.[24] This goes some of the way toward explaining why in the seventeenth century there was no relation between grain prices and demographic variables; high grain prices did not lead to an increase in the death rate.[25] The level of economic activity displayed a certain stability that would not look out of place in Adam Smith's "stationary state."

The question as to whether the Republic, in contrast, exhibited the features of a modern business cycle, which results from the interaction between investments, effective demand, and supply, has not been satisfactorily answered. Posthumus and Jan de Vries found evidence for this in various series (production in the textile industry of Leiden and passenger transport in Holland), but this was more obvious in the seventeenth century than in the second half of the eighteenth century.[26] It is to be expected that a modern business cycle would exist in an economy that is growing strongly, since in that case investment plays an important role and can cumulatively affect effective demand and supply. This is less likely in the case of the eighteenth-century economy, with its low levels of investment.

Political and military "exogenous shocks" were, on the other hand, most important after 1780: the Fourth Anglo-Dutch War (1780–84), the French occupation (1794–95), bringing confrontation with the British once more, and the introduction of the Continental System (beginning de facto with the Berlin Decrees of November 1806 and imposed by military force from 1809 on) were responsible for the most significant depressions. The Treaty of Amiens (1802), on the other hand, ushered in a short period of recovery in trade, which can be seen in the trade statistics of the day. We shall attempt to give an impression of developments in the Dutch economy between 1780 and 1813. Because of the wealth of material available, more attention will be paid to Holland, by far the most important province, where in 1795 approximately 44 percent of the Dutch lived and where by estimates more than half the national income of the Republic was generated.

It is perhaps rather traditional to begin this overview of economic forces by looking at the Republic's international trade. This sector was for centuries the foundation of the Republic's economic success, upon which the welfare of industry, agriculture, and banking was dependent. The close relations between the various sectors of the nation's economy grew weaker during the course of the eighteenth century, but in the eyes of many—among them Keuchenius—trade remained the most important source of welfare by far.

In the eighteenth century Amsterdam gradually lost its central role in European international trade for a broad spectrum of goods through the increasing amount of direct contact between countries of supply and countries of destination of the goods that Amsterdam had traditionally traded. Amsterdam also lost position as its traders' networks shrank; in absolute terms, trade with the Levant and large parts of Asia, Africa, and America probably even decreased. Increasingly the Netherlands' international services sector was largely dependent on its German neighbors and on the supply of a fairly small range of tropical products from its colonies (Surinam and the East Indies). Traditionally, Dutch trade policies were meant to encourage this flow of goods. Attempts were made to strengthen the strategic position of Holland's ports as much as possible by discouraging transit trade—duties on goods in transit were much higher than for imports and exports—and by channeling goods from the colonies through the mother country (through monopolies as the VOC and the WIC). The centuries-old blockade of Antwerp's port was a facet of this *stapelmarktpolitiek*. In this way the Republic attempted to stand up to the strong protectionist forces in the world economy of the late seventeenth and eighteenth centuries.[27] It repeatedly became apparent that economic success—improving market share in international trade—and military power were closely related. As the power of the Republic contracted and it became incapable of responding adequately to international threats to its position, the trade network of Dutch merchants also came under increasing pressure. During the Fourth Anglo-Dutch War, the Republic even had to appeal for help to the French fleet to prevent the loss of all its colonies to the British; the impotence of Dutch naval power contributed significantly to the decline of trade during this period.

The development of two important trade flows is shown in figure 2.1. The overseas trade of Amsterdam and of the other, much smaller trading cities on the Zuiderzee was reflected in the amount of *paalgeld* (a tax on shipping that entered the Zuiderzee from the North Sea). Rhine shipping, the second most

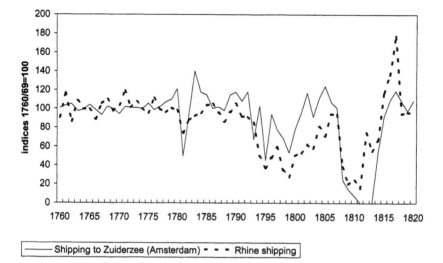

FIGURE 2.1. Development of the *paalgeld* and the toll at Schenkenschans, 1760–1820 (indices 1760/69 = 100). Data on Paalgeld from Heeres, "Paalgeld"; on Rhine shipping from Verheul, "Rijnvaart," in 1807 combined with data from Horlings, *Economic Development*, 409.

important trade flow, was required to pay a toll at Schenkenschans. The collected tolls are a matter of record. Both graphs show that before 1780 there appear to be few systematic trends in either flow of international trade. For example, the financial crises of 1763 and 1773 do not show any clear traces in these sets of figures. After 1780, very large fluctuations occurred, which were related to the previously discussed political-military actions. It is clear that following the crisis of 1780–81, both trade flows returned to the level they had reached before the Fourth Anglo-Dutch War, a recovery that was sustained until the beginning of the 1790s. The depression that began after 1794 was much more serious and lasted longer than that at the beginning of the 1780s, but once again the economy recovered and reached a high point between 1805 and 1806. Based on this information, the total magnitude of trade during these years was not much less than that in the best days before 1780. After 1807, however, there was a marked decline, which resulted in these trade flows contracting to less than one-fourth of the volume they had before 1780. After 1813 there was a rapid recovery, with international trade reaching an extremely high level of activity between 1816 and 1817. The Rhine trade surpassed even the best years of the eighteenth century.

To summarize, the level of international trade conducted by the Netherlands did not show a clearly declining trend during this period (contrary to frequent assumptions in the literature). Instead, there were strong fluctuations, with the lowest point being the sudden depression that began after 1806, reaching its nadir between 1809 and 1811. This was the result of the armed enforcement of the Continental System, which brought overseas trade to a virtual standstill. The Rhine trade appeared to recover after 1811, probably because this partially compensated for the closing down of overseas trade. During these years, a great deal of grain that usually reached Holland by sea was transported instead on inland waterways. Moreover, the depth of the depression remains unclear. Smuggling, which of course was not shown in these records, must have increased dramatically during this period. As a result, the actual decline of trade and shipping was probably less severe than suggested by these data.

Initially one would expect that the business cycle of shipping would be in step with that of international trade, with dips in years of war and political turbulence and peaks in years of peace. In practice, however, Dutch ship owners were able to continuously adapt themselves to the political and military developments of this period. Consequently, earnings were sometimes much higher in wartime than during periods of peace. A detailed analysis of the profits made by thirty-six Frisian *reders* (ship owners) illustrates this point nicely.[28] During the course of the eighteenth century, the Frisians had become the most important skippers in the Netherlands; they frequently worked on behalf of Amsterdam merchants, providing a large part of the overseas transport in northwest Europe. The analysis shows that in times of peace, freight rates were relatively low and not much was earned. But this changed when war broke out; cargo space was then immediately scarce, and reders from a neutral country could profit from this scarcity. The best years of the eighteenth century in financial terms were therefore the periods during which the Republic was able to remain neutral during major international conflicts: that is, the Seven Years' War (1756–63) and the American Revolution (1775–80). But many ship owners also prospered during the following period, during which the Netherlands was involved in international conflicts, by profiting from the tight market, in particular if it was possible to place one's ship under a neutral (Danish, Austrian, or Russian) flag by means of a fictitious sale. The sale of the ship to one of the involved parties (to France, for example) was sometimes a lucrative option as well, even though this of course meant the end of the company. Until well into the eighteenth century, however, reders were able to profit in all kinds of ways from the new opportunities offered by a virtually permanent state of war. To achieve these profits, they often took big risks; after all, the ship could be confiscated by the British or, if it evaded the Continental System after 1806, the French.

The risk for the reders was extremely high. The average profit earned by thirty-four ships that were outfitted between 1740 and 1814 was approximately 6 percent, but this figure hides an extreme range of profits and losses, ranging from a loss of more than 50 percent of the initial capital to an average annual profit of 64 percent. Moreover, of the thirty-four ships analyzed, ten lost money, the profit of five other ships was less than 5 percent, but the other nineteen made more than 5 percent profit. The *partenrederij,* where every ship was in fact owned by a large group of "shareholders," made it possible to spread the risks and, when the portfolio was large enough, to approach the average profit of approximately 6 percent—slightly more than the interest on a mortgage or a private loan.[29]

But as this case study also demonstrates, after 1780 many ships were eventually taken over by foreign owners, or the shipping companies moved abroad, where the conditions for their continuity were more beneficial. On balance, this meant that the Dutch fleet became much smaller. As will be shown in the following section, this trend was accompanied by a severe decline in shipbuilding and related industries.

Another picture of the business cycle appears when data about the development of industry in Holland are considered together. We have access to five sets of figures that provide a good impression of the development of various branches of industry: the development of beer brewing in Amsterdam; the production of the textile industry in Leiden; the trade in building materials, from which the development and construction industry can be derived; the production of soap; and the production of sailcloth in the most important center of this branch of industry, Krommenie. The latter series represents a number of industries related to trade and shipping, such as shipbuilding, anchor making, rope making, and copper founding. These five series have been combined into an index of the industrial production in Holland. These data have also been compared with an index of the actual wages in the west of the Netherlands during this period.[30]

As is strikingly apparent in figure 2.2, not only do both series show a strong decline—real wages fell almost continually, and industrial production shrank steadily—but also there is a close correlation between the two indices until about 1806. During years of high prices and low wages (in nominal terms, the wage level is almost constant), industrial production declined, while the high real wages led to an increase in industrial production. We therefore encounter the "premodern" business cycle, characteristic of agricultural societies. Further analysis of the underlying data shows that a strong link existed between the development of real wages and fluctuations in the production in the construction industry, soap manufacturing, textiles, and beer brewing, which indicates that these branches of industry primarily serve the domestic market and that a large percentage of their sales was made to the wage-earning population. No relationship between wage development and the production of sailcloth was found; the ups and downs of the latter branch were determined not only by the business cycle of international trade but also by the large purchases of sailcloth in times of war (probably by the navy), which appeared to affect the industry.

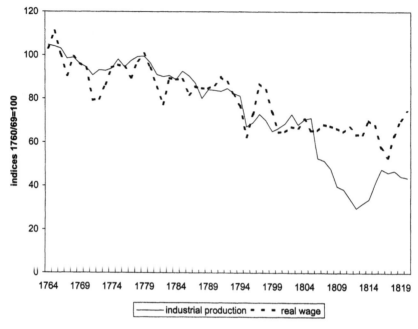

FIGURE 2.2. Indices of the production of industry in Holland and the real wages in the west of the Netherlands (1760/69 = 100). Data from ARA, *Financie van Holland,* no. 826-828 (excise tax on building materials and soap); Posthumus, *Geschiedenis,* 3:1096–97 (textile production); GA Amsterdam, Brouwerscollege, no. 1704-12 (water usage of brewers); Lootsma, *Historische studiën,* 2:43–55, 155 (production of sailcloth); cf. Van Zanden, "Economie."

This premodern business cycle fits closely with the development of the living standard during this period. Faber has already ascertained that periods with a high cost of living appear to occur more frequently during the course of the eighteenth century and are strongly reflected in data on marriages and deaths. This indicates that there were more years of famine, resulting in marriages being postponed and more people dying of starvation or illness.[31] The compensatory effect of the grain trade of Amsterdam, which was very strong during the seventeen century, was completely spent by the end of the eighteenth century. This is remarkable because the magnitude of this trade in absolute terms did not decline significantly, while its effects on the economy became much weaker.

The gradual contraction of industry until 1807 and its collapse thereafter were especially characteristic of the development of industry in Holland and other maritime regions. But there were certainly exceptions to this trend. The printing industry, for example, had a totally different business cycle, which was determined primarily by political developments; the Patriot movement led to

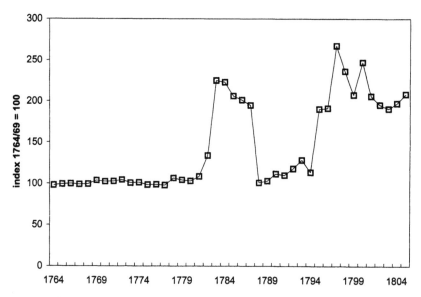

FIGURE 2.3. Revenue from excise tax on printed wares in Holland, 1764–1805 (1764/69 = 100). Data from ARA, *Financie van Holland,* 826–28.

an enormous increase in the use of the printing press, as shown in figure 2.3, after which this branch of industry was confronted with a sharp drop in turnover in 1788. After 1794, however, a golden age dawned for the printing industry: the new governmental structure had a virtually insatiable need for all kinds of printed matter, and the flowering of the free press contributed significantly to the growth of turnover. The printing industry was doubtless an exception, however. Generally speaking, industrial expansion took place far outside of Holland, in Twente, for example, where the textile industry experienced a successful period until approximately 1807, partly due to the weakening of the English competition on the domestic market.[32] For the textile industry in Brabant (the cities of Tilburg, Helmond, and Eindhoven), it was especially the French period (1810–13) that provided a strong impulse, although this did not apply to all cities and all parts of the industry.[33]

One of the reactions of workers to the rapid decline in actual wages after about 1770 was to switch to cheaper foods. During this period the potato in particular rapidly became more popular, a trend that would continue until the mid-1840s.[34] The growth of potato production is one of the signs that agriculture in these years was developing prosperously. The high and steadily increasing prices of agricultural products had possibly stimulated an increase in agricultural production that was expressed in increased shipments of dairy products on the most important markets (in North Holland and Friesland, for example), slowly increasing yields in arable agriculture in Groningen and

Limburg, and an increasing production of madder in Zeeland. But there was also a reduction in tobacco cultivation at the same time.[35] On balance, however, the Netherlands developed into an important net exporter of agricultural products during this period, partly due to a falling consumption of grain (caused by the popularity of the potato) and meat (caused by impoverishment). This trend did not escape observers of the time. Jan Kops, the first commissioner of agriculture after 1798, published an essay in which he includes calculations about the contribution of agriculture to the exports of the Batavian Republic.[36] The expansion of agriculture stood in stark contrast to the virtual collapse of the fishing industry in the years after 1797. This branch of industry, which was one of the pillars of the economy of Holland in the sixteenth and seventeenth centuries, had declined greatly in magnitude during the course of the eighteenth century. An important cause of this decline was increasing international competition. The 1770s and 1780s were, for that matter, not bad years at all; the number of sailings of herring boats (herring busses) even increased from 150 in 1771 to 200 in 1792–93. But during the following decades, the virtually permanent state of war with England prevented fishing almost entirely (between 1798 and 1801, not a single ship sailed, and the same occurred in 1803; in the latter years of the Napoleonic Wars, there were only a few dozen sailings; see chapter 4).

The economic decline that took place in a number of branches of industry reached an absolute low point between 1812 and 1813. International trade had been largely brought to a standstill by the strict monitoring of compliance with the Continental System (the economic blockade of Great Britain). Only shipping on the Rhine experienced a certain revival after 1811 because a great deal of grain was imported in this manner that had previously been shipped via the Baltic and the North Sea to the Lowlands. These grain imports were especially important in 1810 and 1811 because the grain harvests had remained far below their normal level, resulting in a sharp increase in agricultural prices in 1811 and 1812. On the most important market for domestic grain, that in Groningen, the price of wheat in 1812 reached fl 15.47 per hectoliter, a record that stood until 1914 (in previous years a price of around fl 8 was normal).[37] Luckily, there was a good harvest in 1812, and in 1813 there was even a bumper crop, causing grain prices to fall sharply. However, for the population of the large cities of Holland, this was a disastrous combination of developments; high prices (with nominal wages that stayed the same) and rapidly increasing unemployment resulted in a massive exodus from cities such as Amsterdam, where the population fell from 222,500 in 1795 to 183,500 in 1815.[38]

A third factor that contributed to the economic malaise during this period was the tiërcering of the national debt, implemented by Napoleon in 1810, which meant that only one-third of the interest would be paid out. The economy of Holland—and especially that of Amsterdam—had been kept going in former years by stimulating the circulation of money. Governmental expenditures—due to the virtually permanent state of war and the interest that had to be paid on the public debt—increased enormously, causing a sharp rise in the budget deficit (see chapter 1). The government was therefore forced to permanently borrow large amounts from the urban citizenry, who, as a result, were largely prevented from hoarding money. The revenues, acquired primarily by means of forced loans, were then put back in circulation as interest payments on the debt. This circulation of money, from which the financial sector primarily benefited, came to an end in 1810 (at that time, moreover, the government was already behind in interest payments on the debt; virtually no interest on debts had been paid since 1808). As a result, these powerful stimuli to purchasing power disappeared.

An equally important factor was the disappearance of trust in the government, which had definitively shown that it could no longer meet its obligations. The degree of uncertainty of transactions between businessmen must have also increased greatly. After all, many merchants had invested a significant part of their capital in the national debt, which suddenly was worth almost nothing. The "credit" of the merchant, of his family, and in a sense the basis of the system of international trade during this period was seriously eroded as a result. The logical effect was that people withdrew their deposited money from the cashiers, resulting in a large number of the latter going bankrupt.[39] The pyramid of mutual trust on which the multiplicity of mutual credit relationships between merchants, suppliers and buyers were based threatened to collapse during these years—and did indeed collapse for many cashiers and merchants. The wave of bankruptcies that passed through the economy of Holland then paralyzed economic life. In this context, it is understandable that Willem I, following his coronation at the end of 1813, attempted to alleviate this crisis of trust by restoring the public debt.

INSTITUTIONAL RIGIDITIES AND THE FALL OF THE VOC

It is quite possible that the picture of the international sector of the economy presented here is overly positive. The collapse of the VOC following the Fourth Anglo-Dutch War appears to have been taken insufficiently into account. During the eighteenth century, the VOC, with its trade with the Indies, had become one of the most important pillars of the economy of Holland. The international competition in the trade with Asia increased sharply, however, and the company failed, partially or completely, to reform itself sufficiently to meet this competition. Political and military factors also played a significant role in this process. The position of the VOC during the seventeenth century in parts of Asia was based partly on its military, especially naval, strength and was ultimately founded on the capacity of the Republic to conduct war even in this remote region of the world. As the military position of the Republic began to erode, the military-strategic strength also eroded. For virtually all major conflicts in which the Republic became involved after 1700, this ultimately resulted in the loss of trading posts and spheres of influence. During the years following 1780, when the Republic appeared to be entirely powerless, the VOC was able to maintain its position with respect to the British only due to the support of the French navy. This ally of the Netherlands attempted to prevent colonial possessions from falling entirely into British hands in 1780–84 and again after 1795.

Besides the decline of the Republic and the VOC as military powers, the institutional structure of the company also played an important role. The States General granted the monopoly for the VOC in 1602. Due to necessary political compromises during this process, a complex company structure was agreed upon: all large trading cities which at that time participated in trade with the Indies became involved with the new VOC. The result was that the VOC was composed of no fewer than six "subsidiaries": the chambers in Amsterdam (with a 50 percent share in the activities), Rotterdam, Zeeland, Delft, Hoorn, and Enkhuizen. The management of trade for these chambers was in the hands of the governors, who were appointed by the burgomasters of the cities just mentioned or, in the case of Zeeland, were nominated by the Provincial Estates, and were appointed for life by the Hoofdparticipanten, that is, the most important shareholders. To establish some unity in the leadership of the company, the charter of 1602 established a superior body, the Heren Zeventien (the seventeen directors of the VOC), who were recruited from the governors of the various chambers; Amsterdam had eight representatives on this board. During the various reforms of the VOC charter, this structure was sometimes slightly modified. For example, due to their political weight, cities such as Haarlem and Leiden acquired their own governors in the chamber of Amsterdam.

This structure, though the result of complex political decision making focused on making precarious compromises in the decentralized political structure of the Republic, was reasonably successful for a long period. It was also remarkably flexible. When after the political crisis of 1672 the VOC was suddenly placed under heavy pressure, and reforms became necessary, the management succeeded in implementing important cost-reduction measures and developing new, long-term commercial initiatives, thereby enabling the company to enter a second period of boom after 1680. Gaastra, who investigated the administration and policy of the VOC during this period, praises the quality of the leadership at the end of the seventeenth century.[40]

The impact on the VOC that resulted from the Fourth Anglo-Dutch War of 1780–84, following a long period during which the Republic had remained neutral, was still significantly stronger than the consequences of 1672. The British captured many ships, often loaded with costly return freight, causing a sudden lack of goods to be auctioned and therefore a shortage of cash. At the same time, a serious claim was made on the available shipping space and on qualified sailors. Initially, the governors continued to deny the situation: they believed that there would be only a temporary drop in income and that recovery would quickly follow the end of the war. Drastic reforms to turn the tide were therefore not considered.

Two detailed studies concerning the attempts of the VOC to reform itself arrive at fairly negative conclusions about the quality of the management, partly on the basis of the resistance of the governors to making any changes to the course of the company. The reformers, in contrast to the period after 1672, were primarily outsiders who had to convince the governors and the Heren Zeventien that reforms were necessary. According to Dillo, "The Heren Zeventien maintained a very reserved standpoint, and the discussions about cost reductions and reforms dragged on for years due to the lack of will and indecisiveness of the company. . . . The conservatism and indecisiveness of the governors often prevented energetic and flexible action by the VOC."[41] As a result, the decline of the VOC became inevitable. Steur states that "the Heren Zeventien . . . remained seriously in default during these years" and ascertains failing policy in both the Netherlands and Asia.[42] Such hard language from historians, who generally voice their understanding of the conditions under which entrepreneurs had to operate in the past, is very unusual.

For that matter, this resistance to drastic reform was not a recent development. As far back as 1740, various groups of participants had called for cost reductions and rationalization of the organization. But these plans almost always encountered indolence and lack of cooperation from the governors.[43] The high costs of operating the VOC were related, among other things, to its decentralized structure: the small chambers in Enkhuizen, Hoorn, Delft, and Zeeland had a more expensive overhead than that in Amsterdam. Consequently, it was very obvious that the activities should have been concentrated in Amsterdam and Rotterdam. However, this obvious—but drastic—cost-cutting measure was not negotiable due to the company's political dimension and the heavy dependence of the economies of the small cities on the activities of their chambers. In this way, the VOC was held prisoner by the same political-economic structure that also held the government finances of the Republic in its grasp.

The decline in the quality of its management therefore appears to have been an important factor in the demise of the VOC. This cannot be seen separately from the way in which the governors were recruited, that is, primarily from the political elite of the relevant cities, where the burgomasters controlled the nomination and selection of these officers. The function of governor was one of the most lucrative posts that could be granted in the eighteenth century by the regents. For example, a governor from the Amsterdam chamber earned fl 3,100 per year, comparable to the income of a relatively wealthy merchant. And this was often just the beginning. The governors could become involved in virtually all functions of the VOC and thereby support their political clientele or provide their family members with an income. They supervised, for example, the purchases of the VOC; by setting up their own rope manufacturing plant and selling its production for attractive prices to the VOC, a governor could acquire a substantial extra income.[44] Although this was formally forbidden, it still happened in practice; these forms of collusion probably occurred more often in the small cities than in Amsterdam, which contributed to overhead costs.

Similar practices undoubtedly took place in the seventeenth century as well. However, the fundamental problem was that a gap developed between the political elite (the groups of regents who dominated the politics of the cities of Holland) and the economic elite of merchants who were actively involved in trade. The regents increasingly began to passively invest their capital in public debt, resulting in the rejection of active economic activities. Moreover, they became increasingly closed to newcomers. Regarding the recruitment of governors for the VOC, this meant that it became more and more difficult to find experienced merchants in the ranks of the regents. In the seventeenth century virtually all governors of the VOC had been active merchants or had previously been active merchants; this changed rapidly in next century. In 1770, among the sixty-seven governors, there were only nine who had not been regents; in 1780 this number had declined to six.[43] The decline in the quality of the VOC management, which is shown in the studies by Steur and Dillo, can be explained in this way.

The analysis of the company's dividend policy makes it possible to acquire more understanding of these changes in the financial management. In his

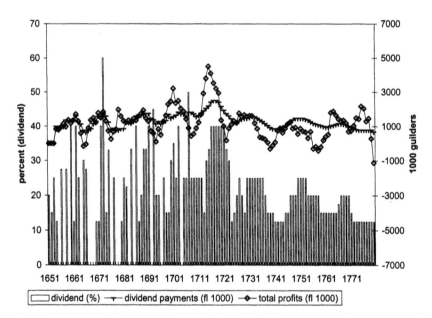

FIGURE 2.4. Dividend percentage (left-hand scale) and seven-year moving averages of dividends paid and the actual profits made (right-hand scale; in thousands of guilders), 1650–1780. Data from De Korte, *Verantwoording.*

detailed study of the bookkeeping of the VOC, De Korte showed that there appears to be no link between the company's profits and the dividends distributed to shareholders. During the thirty-two years between 1650 and 1780 when the financial result was negative, a dividend was almost always paid (twenty-five times).[46] Even more blatant was the dividend policy between 1780 and 1795, when the losses were becoming greater and greater, and the VOC nevertheless paid a dividend of 12.5 percent in eleven of those fifteen years.

Figures 2.4 and 2.5 combine important financial data, derived from De Korte's study, which provide insight into this criticism. In figure 2.4, the change in the dividend policy around 1710 is striking. During the seventeenth century, the level of the dividend changed almost annually, but after 1710 it became largely fixed. During the seventeenth century, it was fairly normal for no dividend to be paid. This occurred in fifteen of the sixty years between 1651 and 1710 (moreover, during another four years, no cash was paid; bonds from Holland and Zeeland were used instead), while between 1703 and 1783, dividends were always paid. As shown in the upper half of figure 2.4, in the longer term up to 1730 there was a reasonable link between the dividend and the actual profits; the seven-year moving average of the dividend follows the same average of the profit at some distance. After 1730, however, this changed. The sales of the VOC then show a decline (see figure 2.5), causing a drop in profit, but the dividend remains at a high level. The result is an explosive increase in debt, which had a negative long-term effect on profitability—after all interest had to

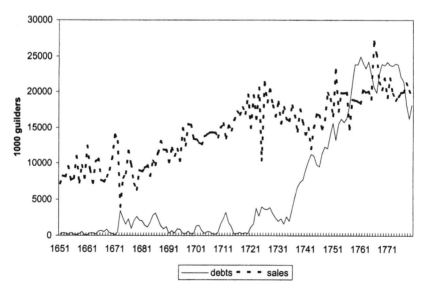

FIGURE 2.5. Sales and debts of the VOC, 1650–1780 (in thousands of guilders). Data from De Korte, *Verantwoording.*

be paid on the debts—and contributed significantly to the financial problems of the VOC after 1780. For that matter, the dividends on profits and the actual profits converged again around 1760, resulting in an end to the rapid increase in debt; at the end of the 1770s, some of the debt was even repaid.

An inspection of these graphs therefore shows an important shift in the dividend policy around 1710. Dividend policy after that year aimed at maintaining a stable dividend, which was an important cause of the increasing debt during the second half of the eighteenth century. On the eve of the Fourth Anglo-Dutch War, the VOC was already significantly weakened by the rising burden of debt. The lack of supply from Batavia led to acute problems in Holland; the losses climbed to more than fl 10 million in 1784—in total there were losses of more than fl 106 million between 1781 and 1796. Nevertheless, the Heeren XVII regularly paid a dividend of 12.5 percent; only during the disastrous years of 1783–85 and in 1788 and 1790 was no dividend paid. The debt of the VOC increased explosively as a result of this policy. Besides bonds against the company, this also concerned large private loans from the Amsterdamse Wisselbank. In 1790 the States General (under the influence of Van de Spiegel) tried to save the company by exerting greater political control, but this attempt failed. The losses continued to increase, partly due to the growing interest on obligations under which the VOC struggled. The company was ultimately nationalized in 1798 by the government, resulting in the assignment of the large debt to the state and thereby greatly increasing the public debt of the Batavian state. Trade and shipping with the colonies were opened up afterward, but this led to few initiatives to rejuvenate trade.[47]

According to this analysis, around 1710 there was a drastic change in the dividend policy; at least to a certain extent, the later financial problems can be attributed to this change. An obvious explanation, but one that is difficult to test, is that the governors of the VOC became increasingly interested in the effect the dividend had on the price of shares in the company. Strictly speaking, however, the VOC received no direct financial benefit from a high share price; after all, the company did not consider issuing shares, which would have enabled it to cash in on the price. Of course, the share price may have affected the company's creditworthiness, but this was never in doubt during the entire period up to 1780. Moreover, the question remains why the VOC allowed itself to skip paying dividends with a certain regularity in the seventeenth century—even then it must have had an eye for share prices and creditworthiness—while in the eighteenth century this was seemingly impossible.

We believe the shift in the dividend policy points to an important change in business behavior. In the seventeenth century, the governors dealt with the dividend as if the VOC was a "normal" trading firm, where big profits were made one year and losses the next. Every merchant was familiar with this pattern and could therefore justify such a policy arising from the ups and downs of the trade of the VOC. In the historiography of the VOC, it has almost become a cliché that the dynamic merchants who made the company successful in the seventeenth century were followed in the next century by pensioned regents who were primarily interested in the value of their share capital and in big dividends. The shift in the dividend policy around 1710 appears to confirm this assessment. The dividend policy no longer reflects the ups and downs of an early capitalistic trading firm but appears to focus especially on maintaining the income and capital of the shareholders, not the least of whom were the governors themselves.

THE FINANCIAL SECTOR: DEBT ACCUMULATION AND CAPITAL EXPORTS

The crisis situation in which the VOC found itself after 1780 also had consequences for the financial sector, especially the Amsterdamse Wisselbank. During the second half of the seventeenth century, Amsterdam had grown to become the most important financial center of Europe, where a large part of the international financial exchange took place, specifically through the Amsterdamse Wisselbank. Moreover, Amsterdam merchants were starting to play a larger role in financing international trade; during the course of the eighteenth century, a number of merchant houses had developed into banking firms, which were involved with placing international emissions of various European countries (Austria, Russia, France, and Sweden).[48] Without exaggerating, one can state that the *bankgulden*—the financial unit used by the Amsterdamse Wisselbank, which was related to the value of the Dutch guilder but had a premium of just under 5 percent with respect to it—was the most important international currency in the eighteenth century. In international trade it held a comparable role to that of the pound sterling in the nineteenth century or the American dollar after 1945. The trust enjoyed by the bankgulden was partly determined by the fact that the Wisselbank was not allowed to use the currency deposited there for providing credit, which meant that its value was always backed for nearly 100 percent by bullion.[49] During the previous financial crises—probably the most well known being the run on the bank during the crisis of 1672—the Wisselbank was therefore able to pay its depositors entirely in bullion, which made an enormous contribution to the reputation of the bankgulden.

The Wisselbank was a city institution and as such was under the control of the burgomasters of Amsterdam. Under their influence, the Wisselbank had already provided credit on a small scale to the VOC that was to be repaid when the auctions of the company had taken place. During the Fourth Anglo-Dutch War, however, the Wisselbank was pressured by the city government to provided credit on a much larger scale to the troubled VOC. This innovation, which in fact caused a great deal of hoarded money to be returned to circulation, was kept strictly secret because it could have eroded the trust in the bankgulden. But the debt of the VOC not only rose in an unprecedented sharp fashion, from fl 1.3 million at the end of 1779 to fl 7.7 million at the end of 1783; it also acquired a structural character. To this end, it was converted into a bond loan guaranteed by the states of Holland.[50] In addition, the debt of the city of Amsterdam to the Wisselbank increased during these years to fl 2.3 million at the end of 1783. The bullion reserves of the Wisselbank simultaneously decreased from nearly fl 22 million at the end of 1779 to fl 6 million at the end of 1784. Due to these developments, the backing of the currency fell to a low point of nearly 20 percent in 1788, after which the bank's directors attempted to reduce the amount of credit provided. The anxiously kept secret gradually trickled out, and the premium of the bankgulden, which was 4 to 5 percent at the beginning of the 1780s, fell to 2 to 3 percent between 1785 and 1789. After 1789, this premium quickly became negative, a development demonstrating the loss of trust in the Wisselbank.[51]

Among merchants, the distrust of the Wisselbank increased rapidly. In 1791 they insisted on exercising the right of withdrawing their deposits in precious metals, a right that was acknowledged by the statutes of the Wisselbank but that had been unused because people had become accustomed to giro transactions (transactions from one bank account to another). The burgomasters then limited the amount that could be withdrawn on a weekly basis, but they had to cancel this plan because there was a run on the bank, and fl 2 million guilders was withdrawn in a brief period.[52] During the course of 1791, a loan of fl 6 million was made by the city to the Wisselbank in an attempt to restore trust in the institution. This was initially successful: the premium rose to above parity. However, the advance of French troops at the end of 1794 caused a new run on the bank and a definite reduction of its activities.

The revolutionary government of 1795 began an investigation of the Wisselbank, which immediately showed how bad the financial situation was. The premium instantly fell far below parity, and people began to massively withdraw money, resulting in a very rapid decline in the bank's activities. As a local bank, the Wisselbank continued to function until 1820, but it lost the central position in the international financial system that it had held for nearly two centuries.

For that matter, the position of the Wisselbank had gradually become less important even before 1780. During the second half of the century, cashiers had been able to take over part of the financial transactions; the so-called cashier notes that clients received in exchange for depositing money with the cashier developed into paper money that, at least within Amsterdam, was widely accepted.[53] In addition, various large trading firms became more involved in providing financial services. These banking firms, of which Hope and Company was the most well known, were for the time being not confronted with a reduction in their activities. In fact, for this part of the financial sector, the business cycle reached its height after 1780. While foreign investments focused primarily on England before this year, after 1780 there was an actual boom in issuing large loans to royal houses, especially those of France, England, and Austria.[54]

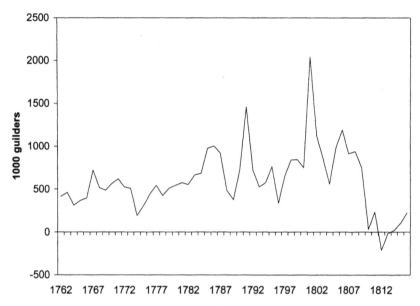

FIGURE 2.6. Profits of Hope & Co. in Amsterdam, 1762–1815 (in thousands of guilders). Data from Buist, *At spes non fracta*, 520–24.

The profit figures of Hope and Company reflect this boom quite well (figure 2.6). Of course, this firm was not representative of banks at the time—during this period it grew to become by far the largest and most successful bank—but other firms must also have profited from the boom. One factor that probably played a role was that a great deal of capital that was previously invested in financing international trade in Europe was invested in the 1780s in foreign government paper, which was thought to be solid. This money was seeking new investment possibilities due to the problems with the Wisselbank, the disturbed relations with England, and the increasing competition from London. Hope himself suggested a similar negative relationship between credit provision to international trade and the growth of foreign investments.[55] The declining trust in the public debt of Holland may also have played a role. The enormous capital export that took place between 1780 and 1793 did, however, cause problems in the balance of payments. During these years there were increasing complaints about the scarcity of currency, caused in part by the lack of trust in the Wisselbank, which resulted in a halt to the influx of precious metals. The crisis of trust that manifested itself in these years was expressed primarily in the development of bond prices on the Amsterdam exchange. From mid-1784, these prices began to fall, a decline that accelerated as the political crisis worsened. The arrival of Prussian troops at the end of 1787 resulted in a small and temporary recovery of trust, but the prices quickly began to decline at an even faster rate (see figure 1.2). In the autumn of 1788, they fell to below 80 percent, and in the spring of 1791, even the maximum prices did not rise above 75 percent. In 1792, there was a brief recovery of bond prices, but beginning in the spring of 1793, an accelerated decline began, which was accompanied by an almost total loss of trust in the finances of the Republic (see chapter 1). For that matter, during these same years the financial crisis in France, which formed the prelude to the French Revolution of 1789, made it clear that investment in foreign government paper was also subject to significant risks.

The flights of capital, especially to England, and the removal of money from circulation were the "logical" responses of the elite to the declining trust in the Wisselbank and the government debt. Both reactions certainly worsened the structural and cyclical problems of the economy. For example, currency was becoming increasingly scarce, and interest rates rose almost constantly. A percentage of the investments abroad were also lost after 1793 due to the bankruptcy of various monarchs and countries that resulted from the revolutionary and Napoleonic Wars, which was an extra blow to the middle classes of Holland.

In 1794, Henry Hope transferred the majority of his capital to London, in part because he was a prominent Orangist and therefore had a great deal to fear from the new regime.[56] Nevertheless, he succeeded in continuing the banking firm. Following the political change of course in 1801, the firm became increasingly involved with international credit on the Continent. For example, Hope & Co. played an important role in the sale of the French colony of Louisiana to the United States, a transaction that involved record amounts of international credit. Hope also provided new credit to Spain. Moreover, the firm was able to profit from the opportunities for arbitration that were created by the continuous political-economic and military developments during these years. In this regard, Hope & Co. was not an exception; without a doubt, the years following 1795 offered unlimited possibilities for speculators on the stock exchange. The amalgamation and continuous growth of the Dutch national debt due to periodic large bond emissions and the transfer of enormous amounts of war contributions from the Netherlands to France gave Dutch bankers turnover and income. However, this was accompanied by people removing more of their money from circulation due to their loss of trust in anything except gold bullion; the cashiers, whose companies were actually based on an expansion of trust in paper money, experienced increasing difficulties. During the deep depression of 1810–13, many cashiers went bankrupt, which dealt a powerful blow to this "progressive" part of the financial sector.[57]

After 1780, Amsterdam ultimately lost its lead in the international capital trade, and London easily assumed this position. Mismanagement of the Wisselbank in the 1780s, capital exports to England, and the loss of depth and breadth in the Amsterdam capital market due to the bankruptcy of the government, which resulted in many citizens losing a large part of their wealth, were the most important factors behind this relatively sudden decline. After 1815, interest rates on the money market and the capital market in Holland were generally higher than in England, and sometimes even higher than in France or Belgium, which eliminated the basis for the dominance of the Dutch in the international financial world.[58]

CONCLUSION

It is almost impossible to summarize the complex developments that took place in the period 1780–1813. Nevertheless, we will make a cautious attempt to do so. We have seen that the Republic, in the fifteen years after 1780, declined primarily due to its own institutional incapacity; the decentralized structure of the state obstructed the solution of the most fundamental financial problems and their related military-political concerns. This caused the state to become steadily weaker (in both relative and absolute terms), and in the long term it was no longer capable of defending itself adequately. During the Fourth Anglo-Dutch War, this situation led to a crisis in which the gap between the political elite (the regents) and the economic elite (the middle classes) became apparent. That crisis ultimately signaled the demise of the Republic through the "liberation" by French troops in 1794–95.

The institutional problems described here also played an important role in the decline of several strategic sectors, which were organized on a large scale—the VOC and the Wisselbank—and therefore were controlled by the political elite. Mismanagement, possibly caused in part by the previously cited gap between regents and the middle classes, played an important role in both cases. Moreover, the decline of the Wisselbank and later the bankruptcy of the Dutch state meant that the very important financial sector lost a great deal of significance. In the same way, the bankruptcy of the VOC meant the end of trade with Asia, which was still very important to the economy of Holland in the eighteenth century.

After 1795, the decentralized Republic made way for a unified state, but one caught in the stranglehold of the French liberator and occupier. The representatives of the Dutch middle classes who attempted to give shape to the new unified state were severely obstructed in this aim by the strong French grip. This was expressed in extremely heavy financial burdens placed on the shaky Batavian Republic and its successors, as well as in the frequent interference with the political process in the Netherlands. In some cases, such as in 1798 and again in 1805, this political interference actually broke existing stalemates. A goal that was at least as important was that of maintaining the value of the public debt, in which a large percentage of the nation's capital had been invested. Pfeil has emphasized that this "primacy of public finance" played an important role in the political dynamics of this period and that the pressure to increase the income of the state made a significant contribution to the many experiments focusing on the modernization of the state apparatus between 1798 and 1810.[59] Isaac Gogel was by far the most successful politician in this regard: in the period when he managed government finances, the value of government bonds stabilized, thereby serving the primary interest of the elite. He also was able to implement a strongly centralized taxation system, which can be seen as the most essential material support for the unified state. However, he could not prevent an explosive increase in the national debt over the long term, which made the tiërcering implemented by Napoleon in 1810 inevitable.

In many ways the development of the economy reflected the political and military turbulence of these years. As a consequence of the "stationary state" of the eighteenth century, the importance of agriculture in the national economy increased over the long term (also after 1780), the production and income from large parts of the services sector more or less stabilized, and industry experienced a virtually continuous decline that proceeded in step with the decline of real wages and the contraction of the domestic market. Due to problems with government finances, the decline of the Wisselbank, and the continuous expansion of London as a financial center, Amsterdam lost most of its status as a supplier of international financial services, while the bankruptcy of the VOC virtually eliminated colonial trade. Although the share of the Netherlands in the combined imports of Great Britain, France, Russia, and the United States was still 17 percent in 1798, after 1815 this declined to about 7 percent, which clearly indicates the marginalization of the Dutch economy.[60] The deurbanization that took place in Holland and Zeeland between 1795 and 1815 was one of the most visible results of the economic crisis resulting from this marginalization. In this way, the relative decline of the eighteenth century was transformed into a process of absolute decline, certainly after 1806.

The image of the Batavian and French period is therefore quite mixed; economic decline was accompanied by "progressive" institutional changes that were potentially very promising but had not yet borne any fruit or had benefited only the French conquerors. After 1813 the new monarch, Willem I, was left with the task of attempting to fulfill the promise of the unified state.

CHAPTER THREE

Unification and Secession

THE AUTOCRATIC EXPERIMENT OF WILLEM I, 1813–1840

THE NEW INSTITUTIONAL FRAMEWORK: THE CONSTITUTIONS OF 1814–15

The years between 1814 and 1840 form an exceptional period in Dutch history, especially so with respect to constitutional relations and economic policy. The reason for this special character lies first and foremost with the fact that it was dominated by the political activity of one particular person: Willem I, son of the previous stadtholder, Willem V, and crowned as the first king of the new United Kingdom of the Netherlands in March 1815. In mid-November 1813, with French administrators and remaining troops fleeing southward before the approaching allied armies, the provisional government headed by the former pensionary of Rotterdam, Gijsbert Karel van Hogendorp, faced the question of how the country should be governed in the future and in what way decision making over this issue was to proceed. In an attempt to place the increasingly divided allied governments before the established fact of a restored independence, this group of The Hague prominents—acting in the name of the prince of Orange, whose whereabouts had been hurriedly traced to London—proclaimed themselves as members of a provisional cabinet on 21 November. And although the proclamation issued four days earlier had declared an end to all political discord, the appointment of "all notable persons" in government, a renaissance of trade, and a return to past times, this by no means meant that an uncompromised restoration of former political and fiscal relations was an obvious or even feasible possibility. Not only did the same piece announce the proclamation of the prince as "High Authority"—a far cry from the ambiguous position of the stadtholder under the former political system—but many of the institutional changes introduced in recent years could not be restored to pre-1795 relations, even if such would have been the objective. The amalgamation of the public debt, fiscal unification, the tiërcering, the judicial reforms, and the reorganization and extension of the central government apparatus could not be simply undone.

The actual constitutional reform as formulated in the proposals of the committee appointed in December 1813 thus started from the reality of a centralized system of administration. Unified above-local taxation, the reorganization of civil law and the judiciary, and the centralization of both the executive and the legislative powers were maintained. In formulating its proposals, the Grond-wetscommissie, not least because of a lack of alternatives, largely based itself on a draft that Van Hogendorp had held in preparation since 1799 and which he had finished in 1812.[1] The ultimate result accorded by an Amsterdam meeting of provincial representatives on 29 March 1814 was characterized by the acceptance of the fiscal and administrative aspects of the unitary state founded in 1798, but above all by the bestowment of hereditary autocratic powers upon a new king.[2] And although the latter was not at liberty to disband the Parliament he was obliged to consult, the new constitution failed to complement the parliamentary right to audit the budget with a system of ministerial responsibility. In practice, this implied that every fiscal policy conflict could result in a confidence issue between the king and his self-appointed ministers on the one hand and Parliament on the other, which could not be resolved on the basis of formal procedures. Moreover, while the king was additionally obliged to submit policy proposals to the downgraded Council of State for evaluation, power relations here had been clearly demarcated. As the relevant article 73 ends: "Le Roi décide seul."[3]

After the allied powers, to some extent influenced by lobbying efforts on the part of Willem himself, had agreed to the integration of the former Habsburg provinces in a united kingdom, the constitution additionally became applicable to an enlarged national territory. Having already accepted executive authority over the new provinces on 31 July of the previous year, Willem I was crowned king of the Netherlands on 16 March 1815. Characteristic of the unitary state thus conceived was the fact that both parts—north and south—were equally represented in both chambers of parliament and shared the same financial obligations. The result of these various influences was a constitution that attempted to combine the "radical" British model, in which the power of the sovereign was greatly limited and ministers fell under the control of Parliament, with Continental practice, in which the legislative and executive powers of Restoration sovereigns were largely unlimited. At the same time, to use the words of Ernst Kossmann, the actual Dutch solution of this dilemma constituted more of a synthesis of traditional developments than a compromise between "old and new"—between "the British system and that of the middle European Restoration regimes."[4]

The new constitution changed Dutch politics in a fundamental way. An essential detail was that both the executive and the legislative powers became concentrated in the hands of the central government—that is, the king and his ministers. In contrast with the situation of the impervious quota system before 1795, the overall budget and the power to tax not only were essential instruments in the hands of the executive power (allowing for the evolution of the later activist policies instigated by Willem I) but also because of this developed into the essential vehicle of conflict between government and Parliament. The States General did acquire the right to audit the budget—doubtlessly the most fundamental instrument of power wielded by British Parliament—but this right, too, was amended by articles 123 and 126 of the 1815 constitution. Starting in 1819, there was to be a ten-year budget for recurrent expenditures, which, consequently, had to meet with the approval of Parliament only once every decade. Moreover, the consequences of a sustained rejection of the budget were unclear. Formally, ministers answered to the king only and were under no obligation to resign if their budget proposals were not carried. The king, by definition, could not abdicate without provoking a constitutional crisis, so that a fundamental conflict over the budget between Parliament and the government could be resolved only by a dissolution of the former assembly.

The most obvious implication of the compromise strived for by the 1815 constitution, therefore, was the enlarged power of the former stadtholderate lineage, now endowed with a hereditary position. Like no other ruler or statesman in Dutch history, Willem I would leave his mark on the development and institutional infrastructure of the economy during his twenty-five-year reign. Indeed, the success or failure of numerous branches of industry during this period can be directly related to the degree to which they were able to profit from Willem's experiments in economic policy. To be sure, the task he faced in 1814 was huge. In the preceding decades the economy of the northern Netherlands had undergone at least relative decline, had failed to keep up with British industrialization, and now was in danger of falling even further behind. Within the terms of the newly united economy, this decline was to some extent compensated for by the growth taking place in the other part of the kingdom. During the French occupation, the southern provinces had profited greatly from their proximity to the protected French market. Whereas the northern provinces had been excluded from the French free trade zone until October 1812 and had thus been confronted with both overseas and landward trade barriers, the southern provinces had enjoyed free access to Continental markets additionally cleared from British competition. In the southern Netherlands the new, prototypical branches of the industrial revolution had developed swiftly in the preceding two decades. Textile production in Flanders (Gent) and Limburg (Verviers) and coal mining and iron manufacturing in Wallonia (Liège and Namur) had become major industries.

In his own view, it was the task of the king to forge an economic unity from this new kingdom. From his political actions at least it is clear enough that the king thought in such terms, even though he rarely explicitly expressed himself on long-term policy goals, doubtlessly to avoid a further raking up of north-south controversies. During his post-1795 exile, the prodigal stadtholder-in-waiting had been forced to live off the profits generated by his German dominions.[5] In doing so, he had become impressed by the actions of bureaucrats and monarchs that had been influenced by the "Kameral-Wissenschaften," which advocated institutional reform in order to promote industry and improve general economic infrastructure. From 1802 onward, Willem, for instance, maintained contact with Karl, Freiherr vom Stein, the architect of the Prussian reform program of 1807–8, which laid the foundation for the revival of the Prussian economy in the nineteenth century.[6] Central to the philosophy of such reformers was the notion that in those countries having fallen behind the pace of British industrialization, the state held a responsibility to create conditions that would enable them to bridge the gap. Evidently, the stimulation of systematic improvement in education (especially technical training) and the guided construction of infrastructure were of major importance according to this viewpoint. Moreover, over and above the gestation of these general conditions, the state was also seen as responsible for the development of concrete initiatives in industry and trade, for financial support, and for commercial policies attuned to such strategic interests.[7] New enterprises had to be founded and old firms modernized in order to revive the economy as a whole. As the traditional political historiography in particular has emphasized, such an activist view of the state matched Willem I's personality remarkably well. Numerous annotations in the documents attest that he was a perfectionist, seeking to control any decision of importance and supervise its implementation. Being in the habit of working on Sundays and holidays, on Christmas Day 1822, for instance, he processed no fewer than 212 official documents. As a result, he was increasingly surrounded with ministers and civil servants who did little more than serve the king with limited advice.[8] Even so, it would be unjust for him to be seen as an enlightened despot in the traditional sense. After the unification with the former Habsburg provinces, he lost every interest in territorial issues, and the army and navy likewise had to make do with limited attention. Manufacturing, education, infrastructure, and trade: these were the issues to which his true interests went. In this respect, his multiple bynames of "canal king" and "merchant king" speak for themselves.

Yet the large financial and economic influence that he gained after 1813 was not simply the result of his personality and ambitions but first and foremost of the constitutions formulated in 1814 and 1815. Of additional importance in this respect was the fact that the king had a dominant, albeit indirect influence on the composition of Parliament, whose members were delegated from the provincial councils, in their turn elected by a taxpayers' elite of some 3.5 percent of the relevant age-group to represent the towns, the nobility, and freeholders. In this, especially, the nobility was relatively overrepresented. The first group of parliamentarians, which was to sit unchanged until 1817, had even been directly appointed by the king himself. Hence, any meaningful opposition against the monarch had been fettered in advance.[9] Since the actual appointment of the shortlist of candidates depended on the king's approval, political opposition was limited and slow in gathering momentum. If members overstretched their informal mandate by expressing systematically critical views on government policy, the king possessed the formal means to ensure that incumbents of this type would not be reselected to serve a new term. This, rather ironically, was in fact what happened to Van Hogendorp himself. Having evolved into an important critic of the king in the aftermath of the 1816 Commercial Tariff Act, he was strategically promoted to the Council of State in 1819.

The underlying concentration of power, strikingly at odds with Dutch political traditions, had important implications for the behavior of those subjects seeking to extract direct transfers or monopoly rents from the state—in short, for the prominence and effectiveness of collective action. Economists examining rent-seeking behavior have invariably approached this issue from the perspective of a balance between costs in decision making and persuasion and potential returns.[10] With the political system commanding extended resources and wielding legislative powers over a larger territory than, say, the former states of Holland, the concentration of the executive in the hands of the king resulted in a systematic change in the appeal of lobbying and informal pressure. The virtual explosion in the number of petitions that survive in the archives, for instance, is testimony to the fact that the role of interest groups became more prominent at the cost of the formerly dominant system of political patronage. From southern industrialists facing the postwar renewal of British competition and Groningen farmers protesting the low grain prices of the mid-1820s to groups rising up against the king's cultural and language policies seeking to forge a joint national identity, the subjects of the newly unified state eagerly plowed the hitherto largely uncultivated field of direct yet informal political influence.

From all this the argument may be construed that the constitution of 1815 did not establish an efficiently structured balance of power within the new kingdom: the combined executive and (shared) legislative position of the monarch was strong, whereas the formal leverage of Parliament was limited. In the absence of a ministerial responsibility at the individual level, its prime means of information and control lay in the ten-year budgets (given that these stated the bulk of government outlays of which those on debt service were the most strategic), while its shared legislative powers had been curtailed: Parliament could block government plans but not resolve the resultant policy dispute without provoking a constitutional crisis. The natural reaction thus was to shy away from such confrontations for as long as the political gravity of the issues involved did not reach this threshold value.[11] Obversely, what criticism there was above the level of individual policy proposals became duly focused in the 1819, 1829, and 1839 budget debates, although the intermediate changes in excises and trade policy did stir some rather powerless particularistic protests. Indeed, it might even be claimed that the emerging role of the newspapers in public debate—apart from the political lawsuits and financial scandals of the 1830s—found its prime catalyst in these debates. Moreover, it also seems likely that the earlier experience with parliamentary representation between 1795 and 1801, when decision making in the National Assembly had been notoriously inapt, discredited any early efforts to undermine the primacy of autocratic rule.

But whatever the reason, it is easily observed that public debate on constitutional relations was conspicuously absent until 1829, at which time it was still primarily conducted in the southern Netherlands.

Another legacy of the revolutionary period that proved of importance in strengthening the king's position was the rapidly growing power of the government bureaucracy, modeled after its French counterpart. The pre-1795 Republic might be described as a powerful state without a large bureaucracy, one in which the number of civil servants involved in preparing and implementing policy was uncommonly small. Actual departments began to be created during the Batavian and French periods. From 1799 onward, so-called agents, who in fact fulfilled the role of ministers, headed these departments. During this period, the number of people working for central government bodies increased from a staff of approximately 185 in 1795 to an estimated 1,050 in 1810.[12] Moreover, the overhaul of the tax system in 1805–6 also made a significant contribution to the creation of an enlarged and integrated bureaucracy. Finally, Willem himself was a fervent advocate of the philosophy of the state introduced by the Batavian revolution. Like no other Dutch statesman before or after him, he was successful in holding the reins of power over a rapidly expanding bureaucracy and launching numerous policy initiatives. Clearly, such strong centralism was decidedly at odds with the corporate structure of the Republic; in this respect, at least, Willem's form of government was just one more step along the path of political catch-up followed since the 1780s.[13]

PRECARIOUS CONSENSUS: TRADE POLICY AND PUBLIC FINANCE

When Willem I began his reign as the first king of the United Kingdom of the Netherlands, the coffers of the Dutch treasury were all but empty. However, since the new kingdom now contained almost twice as many citizens as the old Republic and boasted a stronger economy, it had every prospect of solving its financial problems. Moreover, in so doing, the credibility gap that had grown between the state and its moneyed elites—above all evident in the price of government bonds—could be dampened and the cost of servicing the outstanding debt reduced. However, as duly stressed in the presentation of the first budget by the new minister of finance, Six van Otterleek (an Amsterdam banker), a prerequisite for achieving all this was the introduction of a tax system that was acceptable to both the northern and the southern parts of the realm.

The essential problem here was the fact that the separate parts of the new kingdom had fiscal traditions that were fundamentally different. Not only had the northern Netherlands become accustomed to a high level of taxation (largely related to the vast public debt), but taxes as such were also levied in a way that imposed as little of the burden as possible on international trade. Import and export duties, known as *convooien* and *licenten,* were relatively low and assessed in a discriminating manner that was preferential to Dutch trade. Under the guidance of what was known as the "spirit of the Placcaat of 1725," duties were in fact to be "estimated" by customs officials, which in practice meant that the amount charged was considerably less than the tariff prescribed. Holland's merchants nevertheless charged foreign clients the full amount, so that foreign traders (through their agents in Holland) paid more than their local competitors. The fact that import and export duties were collected in this fashion also meant that evasion was widespread and the cost of inspection and surveillance was minimal. Moreover, as for instance expressed in the memoirs of the first minister of the interior, W. F. Röell, in this matter the former existence of the Republic's five regional admiralties had resulted in competition "to attract trade as much as possible to their respective location of origin." In doing so, Röell asserted, "abuse had not only been tolerated, but in fact openly encouraged."[14]

The burden of taxation in Holland, which as of 1806 Gogel had by and large introduced in the entire northern Netherlands, therefore was not borne by import and export duties but by excises on staple commodities and by several direct taxes on income from real estate and taxes on what was referred to as "external indicators of wealth." Income derived from capital (notably interest on government bonds) remained untaxed, although following the heavy criticism in the years after 1780, a very modest yet much resented and ineffective stamp duty on foreign stocks and bonds was introduced in 1814.

By contrast, in the southern provinces of the Low Countries, import and export duties traditionally provided the greatest source of revenue. The most important taxes were levied at the source and served the additional purpose of protecting domestic industry.[15] Duties on sugar and coffee, for example, were due at the moment of the commodities' actual landing, a practice that affected international trade but left domestic commerce unhampered. Indeed, as few duties as possible were imposed on finished products and end users, so as not to hamper the development of the domestic market. In more abstract terms, taxation is invariably accompanied by distortion effects and limitations to the free flow of factors and commodities. This in turn implies that choices over the selectivity and the extent to which markets are distorted and the way in which taxation is distributed over social or economic groups are contingent on the balance of political power. It is therefore the comparative structure of the system of formal and informal representation and the structure of the economy that are reflected in the balance and extent of taxation. Moreover, due to the comparative size of the public debt, the required total volume of redistribution in the north had been considerably larger than in the south, causing the economic impact of decision makers' fiscal policy choices to be of a much greater prominence.

Moreover, the rationale behind the differences in taxation went beyond clear-cut policy choices. Duties on the milling of grain were raised in but a few cities of the southern Netherlands. Elsewhere, especially in the countryside, the production of flour and bread had rarely even been commercialized, which in practice made it difficult to tax the consumption of bread. The same was true of some small parts of the northern Netherlands (most notably in Drenthe and parts of Overijssel). Yet in Holland the duty on milling had been one of the cornerstones of the tax system since the late sixteenth century. Accordingly, milling and baking were tightly regulated forms of industry. Moreover, the excise on milling led to an increase in the price of bread and therefore met with stiff opposition from industrialists from the south, who feared it would induce a call for higher nominal wage rates and corresponding production costs.[16] Equally important was the resistance to taxes on agricultural produce among large landowners, who feared that the higher price of grains that resulted from taxation would squeeze their incomes through lower demand. In fact, the elite of the southern provinces considered all new taxes—including those paid on "external indicators of wealth"—as unjust, since their main purpose was to finance the new kingdom's large public debt. This, in turn, for more than 95 percent was due to the legacy of public finance in the northern provinces. In the eighteenth century, the elite of Holland had still opted for a relatively high level of direct taxation (once it was clear that indirect taxation had been pushed to its limits), the reason being, of course, that it formed the only way of continuing to finance the public debt in which almost every regent had invested part of his wealth. The elite of the southern Netherlands, clearly, had no such motive.

The public debate on taxation that emerged after 1815 initially focused on trade policy. In 1813, the tariffs of the Placcaat of 1725 had been reintroduced in the north. However, the fiscal union that came into being necessitated a harmonization of the entire system of import and export duties, thereby forcing a political discussion over an issue that had been repeatedly sidestepped for over ninety years.[17] Under the new constellation, however, it was clear that a repositioning had to take place. Already in 1814, the new Council for Commerce and Colonies urged the king to speedily take up the issue of a harmonization of northern and southern duties, so as to avoid "that the recent blossoming of trade, as a consequence of the calculations of neighboring countries and other nations skilled in trade, would be diverted."[18] Initially Willem I was inclined to meet with at least some of the demands of the southern provinces: his position as their ruler was far from undisputed, and it undoubtedly was in his best interest to demonstrate that their interests would be respected. Moreover, by deciding not to default upon the outstanding debt and seeking to undo at least part of the tiërcering (see later discussion), the most crucial financial issue had already been settled in favor of northern interests.

By means of a secret instruction, the king "strongly advised" a commission headed by the former *agent* for economic affairs, Goldberg, to draft a detailed compromise proposal that would address the most urgent protectionist needs without raising the overall tariff burden on imports.[19] The resultant Commercial Tariff Act of October 1816 provided limited protection for a number of industries, particularly textiles and metal. Likewise, the import of coal from outside the Dutch kingdom (most notably England) was curtailed by means of a considerable tariff, thus serving the interests of the Walloon mining industry. Fierce criticism from both halves of the kingdom ensued. In the north, it duly focused on the incidentally high tariffs and on the stringent methods used to collect them; influenced by customs practice during the French period, the spirit of the Placcaat of 1725 was conspicuously absent from the actions of the now centralized service administrating import and export duties. The entrepôt system, under which goods for reshipment could be stored exempt from duty, was rejected by the Amsterdam trading community, since it was believed to undermine the function of the so-called second hand, constituted by the middle agents in the trading system, specialized in the distribution and processing of imported goods. In the south, on the other hand, the decline of industry in the years after 1816—at least partly due to restored British competition and the protectionist tariffs imposed by France—was attributed to a lack of adequate protectionist measures. In the end, the revenues generated by the new system of taxation were disappointing, in part because pressure from the southern Netherlands resulted in the milling and slaughtering excises being abolished. In the north, tax revenues fell from a near fl 40 million in 1815–16 to fl 31 and fl 32 million in subsequent years, a decrease that was especially attributable to the decline in excise revenues.

The immediate consequence of this decline in government revenue was the occurrence of a first financial crisis in 1818–19, reflected in rising budget deficits and an overt lack of confidence in the time consistency of government finance on the part of the Amsterdam capital markets. The last element is especially apparent in the stagnating quotations of public bonds during this period (figure 3.1). Parliament regularly appealed to the government to cut back on outlays, but for the most part these appeals had little effect (figure 3.2). In 1818 measures were proposed by the recently appointed inspector general of import and export duties, J. H. Appelius, to solve the crisis. Again, the interests of the southern Netherlands featured heavily in the proposals. As defended in April 1819 by Appelius and the minister of industry and colonies, A. R. Falck, the proposed measures included raised import duties on a number of strategic goods (most notably coffee and sugar), causing Appelius to even be confronted with physical assault upon a visit to Rotterdam. Even so, despite the opposition from representatives of the northern Netherlands, the proposed duties were carried.[20] This measure hit at the heart of commerce in the northern Netherlands, especially because these two colonial products had come to play a key role in Amsterdam's narrowing trade package, with the trade sector already struggling to adjust to the post-1813 situation. A new Tariff Act (still issued in 1819), which resulted in lower import and export duties, did little to appease the opposition. Parliamentary debate on the 1819 annual and ten-year budgets resulted in biting criticism of the government's policy. Led by Van Hogendorp—by now

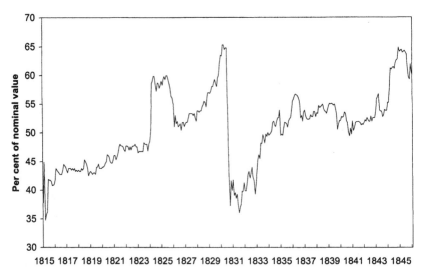

FIGURE 3.1. Price of NWS bonds (2.5 percent), monthly figures, 1815–45 (percent of nominal value). Data from the *Prijscourant der Effecten,* 1815–45. The figures relate to end-of-month quotations.

also expulsed from the Council of State and deprived of his honorary title as minister of state—the northern representatives rallied around the defense of trade interests, resulting in a repeated rejection of the budget. In reaction, Appelius, seeking to avoid a definitive deadlock over the complete budget, suggested the creation of a committee that was to draw up proposals for a revision of the entire tax system.[21]

The committee of 1820, in which the northern and southern Netherlands were equally represented, would eventually be used by the king and its chairman, Röell, to introduce a system of taxation that was more advantageous to the northern provinces. Gogel, who had steadfastly avoided taking part in the discussions, was asked to draw up proposals for a new system, proposals that revived the system he had introduced in 1806: duties on milling and slaughtering were to be included; those on coffee and sugar were to be dropped; and import and export duties were to be lowered considerably. After Gogel had declined to implement the system as the new minister, the king proceeded with a less radical plan, in which sugar, for instance, remained subject to import duties.[22] An important feature of this switch in policy was the formation of the Fonds voor de Nijverheid (Fund for Industry) as a compensation for the lowering of import tariffs. The fund, which would have an annual sum of fl 1.3 million at its disposal, was to distribute subsidies to "lend support to especially those sectors of national industry that can not be provided with adequate protection without raising tariffs to such levels that these could have a disadvanta-

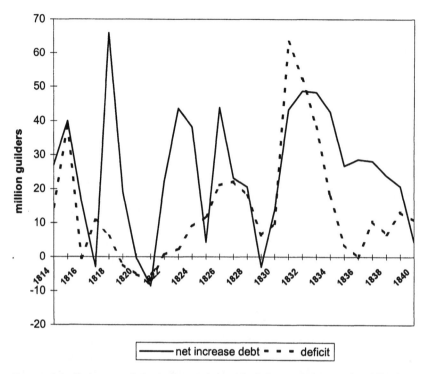

FIGURE 3.2. Estimates of the budget deficit and of the net increase of public debt, 1814–40 (in million guilders). Data from Van Zanden, "Development."

geous influence on commerce."[23] The draft for the Beginselen- or Stelselwet, which laid the foundations for the new tax system, was accepted by the committee only after extensive pressure by the king. Having turned it down once, Parliament in June 1821 also acquiesced, albeit this time with the sole support of its northern members. In 1822, efforts to find a new compromise also resulted in a new Tariff Act that incorporated the "liberal" sentiments of the Beginselenwet of 1821, albeit in a somewhat weaker form.

The public debate on taxation and trade policy between 1815 and 1822 shows a king who attempts to bring the various parties together and create harmony between the traditional points of view of the southern and northern Netherlands, in the face of the competing pulls of different industrial interests. Given this situation, it is remarkable that issues in the end became polarized along "national" lines rather than by the contrasting interests of, for instance, manufacturers, merchants, and landowners. Indeed, northern merchants were able to continue to dominate the political platforms of the northern Netherlands, which in view of the growing interests of other sectors of the economy— mainly agriculture and the industries of the land provinces—seems surprising.

Although nobles of the northern provinces, who were designated as the representatives of the countryside by the constitution of 1815, were able to play a far greater role in national politics than was the case before 1795, this did not result in a more balanced interest in the various sectors of the economy. As we will argue later, the prime reason for this continued imbalance lay in the prominence of the deadweight of fiscal policy over other issues.

In the early years of his reign, Willem I's efforts to integrate the former Habsburg provinces led to a tax system that met with southern demands. However, this generated too little revenue, partly as a result of a downswing in the economy in those years, and met resistance from the northern Netherlands. In the final analysis Willem was much more dependent on the northern provinces: they were the seat of power of the House of Orange; above all, it was only there that he could raise the money needed to finance his systematic deficits. The "compromise" finally reached in 1821 resulted in a system that almost entirely reflected the interests of the northern Netherlands, although import and export duties were to be applied much more rigorously than before 1795, and an excise on sugar was introduced (the resistance to which had decreased since manufacturers had learned to exploit these to their advantage). In addition, Amsterdam traders had learned how to work with the entrepôt system, thus removing one of the causes that had fueled opposition to what was first seen as excessive import tariffs. To appease the south, the large subsidizing body of the Fund for Industry was created, distributing its favors among southern industrialists. In what would turn out to be the last few years before the secession, the king developed other policy initiatives, attempting to be seen to honor southern interests and bind the new provinces to his crown.

COSTLY PRIORITIES: FISCAL POLICY AND PUBLIC DEBT

Obviously, fiscal policy in the early years of Willem I's reign was more than an elaborate juggling act, attempting to appease the economic interests of dominant political groups and with consequences only for northern traders and southern industrialists. Instead, choices on the level and sources of taxation, spending, and debt creation at the same time reflected Willem's implicit views on the welfare effects of economic activism relative to the comparative statics of the fiscal distortions maintained or enlarged. The appropriate historiographical task, therefore, is to weigh these respective effects.

The available literature is of two minds on this issue. First, the (nearly) contemporary view of the early 1840s is strictly negative in its judgment: large deficits, a once again growing national debt, and comparatively high interest rates were taken as the focal point of the liberal critique of autocratic rule. Indeed, this criticism has formed the basis for the hypothesis of a retarded industrialization that has dominated the historiographical debate ever since.

Stripped of their rhetorical embellishments, these same characteristics of public finance have reappeared as the stylized facts of the financial history of the Netherlands between 1814 and 1840, albeit in a style that has recently become dismissive of possible welfare effects and instead emphasizes the functional idiosyncrasy of Dutch financial institutions at the microeconomic level, given the structure of wealth ownership.[24] Contrary to the politically inspired inferences of contemporary debate, the focus of a more recent vein of literature has been chiefly with the effects of the king's activist program. The construction of roads and canals, the foundation of institutions such as the Dutch central bank and the Société Générale seeking to stimulate industrial development, and the derived trade in raw and processed goods are seen as dire initiatives facilitating a structural reform of the outmoded Dutch economy. Moreover, a subsidiary angle on both views is that which gained currency in the course of the 1820s and 1830s: the image of a dominant king who ruled not merely autocratically but also isolated from advice, who ingeniously manipulated his underlings as well as both personal and national funds and in doing so overstretched the credibility of the very institutions he himself had created. In sounding our position on this issue, we will begin by describing the actual policy choices and the evolution of political behavior itself. In the next chapter we then turn to the balance of their effects.

The perhaps most striking aspect of Willem's financial policy consisted of his attempts to reduce the influence of Parliament on fiscal policy and to suppress public debate in general on issues of government finance. This may have originated in the thought of this field as primarily belonging to the competence of the monarch—again, a view strengthened by the example of Prussia. Equally important, though, was that as a result of the politico-economic pressure described and his own activist ambitions, he unchangingly found himself in the situation where the creation of one financial hole was used to fill the next, leading to a situation that became more and more difficult to control. As a result, it became increasingly less attractive to be candid about the true state of government finance; attempts to suppress information or present things in a better light than was justified by the facts gained ever greater currency, until the parliamentary debate over the 1839 ten-year budget and the subsequent special inquiry blew things apart (see chapter 5). As of yet, however, Willem was successful in curbing the influence of Parliament on financial policy, so that by the 1830s it had become minimal. In some ways this was the logical destination of the path already chosen in the early twenties. Indeed, the strongest opposition to his policy was specifically directed at his often unconstitutional behavior.

Even so, in the early years of his reign there was a considerable degree of candor about the policies adopted. The first issue to be dealt with was the status of the national debt, following its tiërcering by Napoleon. To create the impression that this emergency measure could at the same time be rescinded without having to return to the draconian level of interest payments in 1810,

Willem I developed the shrewd idea of a conversion of the public debt, linked to a time-smoothed readoption of the funds defaulted upon. Indicative of his later more broadly applied prowess in financial scheming, the "law for restoration of the national debt and the attainment of funds needed to fortify the Exchequer" already adopted in 1814 (causing the south to be confronted by a fiscal fait accompli a year later) thus sought to win back traditional moneyed interests. The extremely obscure state of the debt, consisting of a huge variety of government paper in terms of maturity and rates of interest, provided an additional motive for these plans.

Through the reorganization, more than twenty different sorts of public debt (bearing rates of interest that ranged from 1.25 to 7 percent) were converted to Nieuwe Werkelijk Schuld (NWS), with an interest rate of 2.5 percent. In the conversion, allowances were made for the nominal interest rates of the various sorts of debt, so that government bonds bearing interest rates in excess of 2.5 percent were converted to proportionally larger values of NWS. In this manner, the total nominal value of the debt increased from what had been an original fl 1,222 million to fl 1,726 million. Under the new law, the government was willing (and initially able) to pay interest on just one-third of this sum. The remaining two-thirds were earmarked as so-called deferred debt, which was to be reconverted at a rate of fl 4 million per year. Accordingly, more than three hundred years would be needed to reverse Napoleon's decision.[25]

The conversion of 1814 was an enormous step toward the appeasement of the citizens of Holland. In 1815 the king even published an analysis seeking to demonstrate the extent to which citizens had profited from this measure. Through an increase in credibility the quotations of NWS bonds rose from 32 percent to more than 40 percent, representing an aggregate capital gain of some fl 46 million. Another, equally important part of the plan was the fact that the holders of government bonds were obliged to pay for the conversion, thus giving the operation the character of a compulsory loan. In this manner the king was able to collect fl 27 million, thus alleviating the acute financial strains of 1814–15, although the "loan" did of course add to the size of the public debt.[26]

The long-term consequences of the reform of the public debt in 1814 were decidedly negative. The existence of a very large "deferred debt" was a lasting obstacle to a structural reorganization of government finance. Each year, upon reconversion of "deferred debt," public debt grew automatically so that an annual fl 4 million had to be reserved for repayment of NWS. An added effect of the entire operation was to preempt the possibility of converting the high-interest-bearing debt of the French-Batavian period in such a way as to alleviate financial problems after the necessary restoration of confidence in the government's finances and a concomitant fall in interest rates. Hence, for the next decades the conversion of 1814 made it virtually impossible to structurally reduce the national debt and instead fixed its basic level. The scheduled repayments were counterbalanced by the reconversion of "deferred" to "real"

NWS, so that the burden of interest plus repayment did not fall and, due to further deficits, in fact increased. Accordingly, the 1814 decision would place public finance throughout the entire reign of Willem I under pressure.

The reorganization of debt in 1814 fixed one important item of expenditure: the burden of interest decreased spectacularly in comparison with the French-Batavian period (from fl 35 to 40 million between 1806 and 1810 to some fl 20 million in 1814–15), only to rise swiftly again shortly after the creation of the new kingdom (table 3.1).[27] In reducing the burden of expenditure, cuts in

TABLE 3.1.
Income and Expenditure of the Central Government during the Reign of Willem I, 1814–40 (in million guilders and percent).

	1814–20	1821–25	1826–30	1831–35	1836–40
Income					
Direct taxation	16.1	15.5	14.3	17.4	16.0
Indirect taxation	7.0	6.0	6.7	7.1	7.5
Excises	8.3	11.2	12.0	13.2	16.0
Tariffs	3.7	3.5	4.0	3.3	4.0
Other	6.6	6.9	8.0	5.6	6.5
Total	41.7	43.2	45.0	46.5	49.9
Expenditure					
Finance	21.3	35.0	43.6	43.6	57.4
Defense	28.0	20.9	21.9	38.4	22.8
Other	12.5	14.1	16.4	8.3	4.8
Total	61.8	70.0	81.8	90.3	85.0
As % GDP	14.3	18.9	19.8	20.9	16.3
Net transfers					
Belgium	11.8	25.3	28.8	—	—
Indonesia (Batig Slot)	—	—	—	10.5	28.4
As % expenditure	19.1	36.1	35.2	11.6	33.4
Deficit	8.3	1.5	8.0	33.2	6.7
As % expenditure	13.4	2.1	9.8	36.8	7.8

the budgets of the army and navy had of course also been possible, yet Willem I was strongly opposed to this. Great Britain, Russia, and Austria, after all, had allowed for the new kingdom as a powerful buffer against France, which meant that Willem I was expected to invest heavily in his military capacity. In the early years of the kingdom large sums were spent on fortifications in the southern Netherlands, to the construction of which the king had committed himself under the terms of the 1815 agreement. Military expenditure was by far the greatest item on the budget between 1814 and 1820, with the astonishing amount of fl 50 million being reserved in 1815 (see table 3.1). Thereafter, the amounts dropped to a little more than an annual fl 20 million, considerably less than, for instance, the approximately fl 30 million that had been budgeted by the Kingdom of Holland for this item in the years before 1808.[28]

However, other items of government expenditure such as large infrastructural projects and the reform of the currency and the judicial system, not to mention the cost of the monarchy itself, featured far more heavily in the budgets between 1815 and 1830 than had been the case during the years of the Batavian Republic. The monarch's active role in politics was demonstrated most clearly by the growth in the amounts reserved for these items; he sought to maintain at all cost his executive competence over these expenditures even against the explicit wishes of Parliament. At the high time of government infrastructural investment between 1826 and 1830, these items alone accounted for just over fl 10 million, of a total budget of some fl 90 million. Moreover, by this time expenditure on debt service, which had fallen sharply between 1810 and 1814, again started to increase (see table 3.1). Despite the relatively favorable conditions at the start—a tax base almost doubled in size, a sharp decrease in interest payments, and a politically stable Europe—Willem I had great difficulty in balancing his budget. Figure 3.2 presents available estimates of budget deficits and the increase in central-government debt in the Kingdom of the Netherlands (in 1814–15 and in 1831–40) and the United Kingdom of the Netherlands (1816–30), two series that indicate the seriousness of the financial problem faced by the state. For various technical reasons the two series do not always coincide, but the figure shows that the large deficits of 1814–15 (in part due to the Hundred Days of Napoleon) were followed by two years of relatively small deficits.[29] After the crisis of 1818–19, two years of relatively small deficits again followed. Parliament was able to bring enough political pressure to bear to enforce cuts in the defense budget and introduce new taxes.

However, these openly fought conflicts and public debates over financial policy did not continue into the twenties. Two developments provided Willem I with the opportunity to gain control of the treasury. The constitution of 1815 distinguished between two different budgets: a ten-year budget for "constant" items of expenditure, and an annual budget for varying budgetary items. In his first ten-year budget of 1819 (covering 1820–29), Willem I included virtually all controversial items, so that acceptance of the budget allowed him a free hand in the subsequent decade. The rejection of this budget—a rare occasion in which north and south were united in their opposition—that was the result of parliamentary resistance by Van Hogendorp and others should probably still be seen against the background of the debate on commercial policy and the tax system. Following resubmission, the ten-year budget, with a few minor alterations, was in fact carried. As with the still more controversial 1829 budget, for Parliament persistence resulting in a constitutional crisis was still too large a political risk to consider.[30]

Even more drastic than the decadal parliamentary bypass was Willem's plan for the foundation the Amortisatiesyndicaat in 1822. The primary purpose for such a separate fund was the purchase of "deferred" debt against low market prices, so that government finance could gradually be freed from the millstone around its neck. The proposal built upon a tradition of establishing separate funds for debt settlement: to this end the Amortisatiekas had been established in 1814, followed in 1816 by the Syndicaat der Nederlanden, each with its own revenues (a surcharge on taxes or fixed allocations from the treasury) to pay off specific debts. The Amortisatiesyndicaat was to subsume both of these funds and, simultaneously, administer other sources of income (among them the domains). Ultimately, taxation—according to the original bill—was to be reduced, which was translated into a reduction of the surcharge resting on several taxes. The Amortisatiesyndicaat was also to be given responsibility for the funding of the reorganization of the monetary system, the payment of pensions, and other executive tasks so that, at least cosmetically, these would no longer burden the treasury budget. To fulfill these responsibilities, the Syndicate was allowed to borrow as much as fl 68 million (later even fl 80 million) and placed under the minister of finance, who, similar to the overall budget, was obliged to seek parliamentary approval for the Syndicate's operations only every ten years.[31]

Opposition to this plan, which served to further marginalize the position of Parliament, was minimal, probably because it was expected to lead to lower taxation. The capital market was even remarkably positive about this "magic potion": NWS prices shot upward at the end of 1823 once it became clear that the Syndicate's borrowing was a success and that the announced tax cuts (in a period of rising deficits) would be implemented. In practice, the Syndicate quickly abandoned its efforts to buy all the "deferred" debt, partly because its price shot up as a result of these developments, so that it became impossible to achieve its original goal. The capital it had amassed instead was used for activities for which the king could find no other funds, such as the construction of canals, and projects undertaken by the Fund for Industry. In 1825, for instance, Parliament decided that the annual surcharge for the Fund for Industry included in the yearly budget was to be reduced to fl 800,000. Yet funds supplied by the Amortisatiesyndicaat, under pressure from Willem I, more than compensated for this cutback.[32] There was no legal foundation to justify such an act, only the notion that government finance was the privileged domain of the monarch. The fund (administered by only one civil servant, Netscher, who was of course in constant consultation with Willem I) and virtually any other activity that the Syndicate became involved with soon became shrouded in an atmosphere of secrecy, something that hindered Parliament's supervisory role.

Through these various ways, Willem I was able to further increase his leverage over fiscal policy. The annual confrontations that took place before 1822 between the king and his minister of finance on one side and Parliament on the other were replaced by a political cycle—and corresponding rate of time preference—of ten years, during which the king allocated funds at will. As a result, after 1822 deficits increased significantly (see figure 3.2). The fact that even during a period of political stability and, certainly by standards of past experience, rapid economic growth, Willem I and his government were unable to control the growth of the deficit, exposed the administration to criticism. Especially the activities of the Amortisatiesyndicaat in the 1820s led to a considerable increase in public debt. At close reading its first 1829 report clearly demonstrates that, contrary to its original purpose, the Syndicate itself was responsible for much of the increase in public debt, despite elaborate efforts in priming the ledgers. The debate that followed led to renewed opposition to Willem's financial policies.[33] In the southern Netherlands in particular these developments, one year before its actual secession, led to a loss of confidence that Willem would be unable to restore. As a compromise, Willem reduced the executive powers of the Syndicate, but the system of ten-year budgets remained essentially intact.

The fact that support especially from southern members of Parliament experienced a strong decline can be conveniently demonstrated using the assessment of partisanship in the Estates General by the French diplomat Boislecomte as reported in the *Gedenkstukken* (table 3.2). Starting from the original situation of a group appointed by the king himself (unchanged until 1817), is can be gleaned that during the decisive discussions in 1830, a majority of representatives from the northern Netherlands still supported Willem I, even though that support had fallen markedly since 1815. The number of opponents among the representatives of the southern Netherlands was much larger than those loyal to the government: there was almost no support left whatsoever from this part of the kingdom.

The criticism of the opposition in the southern Netherlands also focused on the net fiscal transfer flowing from the south to the north. As a result of the introduction of a "Holland-oriented" tax system, the southern tax burden rose significantly. Consequently, the contribution of the southern Netherlands accounted for a growing proportion of tax revenues, increasing from 41 percent in 1816 to 50 percent in 1829. By contrast, their share in government expenditures during the same period remained at a modest 20 percent.[34] Almost all the interest paid on the public debt, for example, found its way into the hands of the citizens of

TABLE 3.2.
The Composition of the Parliament according to the French Diplomat Boislecomte,
1815–40.

	Northern Representatives				Southern Representatives	
	1815	1830	1840[a]	1840[b]	1815	1830
Dévoués[c]	53	34	12	4	50	2
Indépendants[d]	2	14	27	10	5	11
Douteux[e]	—	4	11	32	—	31
Catholiques Exaltés	—	3	5	7	—	11
Séparatistes	—	—	—	2	—	—
(Calvinistes exaltés)						
Total	55	55	55	55	55	55

Source: Gedenkstukken 10, bk. 2, 545.
[a] Regular representatives.
[b] Extraordinary representatives for the constitutional changes, August 1840.
[c] Dedicated to the government.
[d] Independents.
[e] New representatives whose views are still unknown, and others who did not belong to a party.

Holland. Recent estimates have shown that the net flow of revenue from the south to the north increased from about fl 17 million in 1816 to fl 31.5 million in 1829, the latter amount representing no less than between 5 and 6 percent of the gross domestic product (GDP) of the Dutch (or the Belgian) economy.[35] This fiscal "exploitation" of the southern Netherlands played an important role in the rift that occurred in 1830; again, the fiscal policy stance and its parliamentary evaluation formed an important catalyst in the inception of fundamental political change. Accordingly, it was by no means a coincidence that both the Belgian secession and the political crisis that would involve the abdication of Willem I and a constitutional amendment ten years later occurred directly in the dislodging wake of the parliamentary presentation of the ten-year budget.

For the time being, however, voices calling for an overhaul of government finance fell silent directly after the Belgian secession. Due to the disappearance of income from the south and the large military expenditures needed to resist the secession by force, government debt soared (see figure 3.2), and the price of NWS plummeted (see figure 3.1). Yet although the future of the kingdom seemed to be at stake, no criticism was uttered. Tactically, it was by this time that the Amortisatiesyndicaat admitted it was no longer able to meet all its liabilities insofar as the redemption of government paper was concerned.[36] In the meantime, now that the Syndicate's mandate had been severely limited, the king had ventured to replace its sources of income: the Cultivation System in the East Indies gradually began to generate large surpluses, and pressure was brought to bear on the Nederlandsche Handelmaatschappij (NHM) for considerable payments in advance of the actual auction of produce in Amsterdam (out of which government remittances were paid). In addition, De Nederlandsche Bank was repeatedly brought under personal pressure to secretly provide the government with credit from its reserves.[37] Even more than government finance, the executive administration of the colonies fell under the direct competence of the king, so that he alone had access to these surpluses. With the notion of an extended war in mind, Parliament also approved several new issues of government bonds, the first of which had all the characteristics of a compulsory loan, the mere threat of which was necessary to ensure the success of subsequent offerings. It was in this manner that the king was able to finance the enormous deficits of the early thirties.

Willem's financial and political hubris finally unraveled in 1839–40. The second report of the Amortisatiesyndicaat, published in 1838, had made it abundantly clear that the Syndicate was all but officially bankrupt, which led to increasing pressure for its liquidation; insistence upon such a course of action was voiced repeatedly within the States General.[38] The gradual improvement in the quotations of NWS—an unfailing indicator of the Amsterdam capital market's confidence in the government's fiscal policy—came to a clear end after 1838 as the rate began to crumble. The Treaty of London of 1839, in which Willem, due to foreign pressure, finally was forced to accept the independence of Belgium, brought the preceding period of quasi war to an end, thereby also forcing the government's hand in having to put the financial position of the north before Parliament in the upcoming debate on the ten-year budget. Until then essentially uninformed on actual deficits and the net balance of the loss of the fiscal transfer from the south and the proceeds from the colonial reforms since 1829, Parliament went into the debate with the notion of having to stand its ground, lest a renewed acquiescence with the purpose of preserving a constitutional standoff would effectively render its own position obsolete. The new ten-year budget and the added proposal for a new loan of no less than fl 59 million, earmarked to cover the general deficit and a fl 39 million debt with the NHM (with total annual expenditure just under fl 60 million), was confronted with a unanimous rejection. Limited adjustments led to a renewed rejection the same year, as well as to urgent requests to liquidate the Amortisatiesyndicaat and revise the constitution.[39] The necessity of adjusting the constitution to accommodate the independence of Belgium created an opportunity for other modifications: a modest degree of ministerial responsibility was created, and two-year budgets replaced the ten-year ones. These severe limitations of Willem I's power are likely to have contributed to his abdication in 1840. The decision to liquidate the Amortisatiesyndicaat followed during the same year.

Under the influence of Willem I's fiscal policy, public debt had increased from fl 575 million in 1814 to around fl 900 million in 1830 and fl 1,200 million a decade later. In 1840 this sum amounted to more than 200 percent of GDP, comparable to the level of 1807, when the ratio stood at some 225 percent. Similarly, the burden of interest, some 6.9 percent of GDP in 1807, had again grown from 3.7 percent in 1814 to 6.5 percent in 1839 and would go on to reach a 7.9 percent value in 1844.[40] Because of the unchanging deficit and the capital market's lack of confidence in fiscal policy, interest rates on the public debt in the Netherlands were higher than those in surrounding countries (with the exception of newborn Belgium), whereas during the eighteenth century these rates, famously cited by Adam Smith in the 1770s to hover around an incredibly low 2 percent, had been lower than elsewhere.[41]

The ultimate cause of the failure of Willem I's fiscal policy must be sought in the institutional infrastructure, particularly so in the constitution of 1815. The system of government finance and the distribution of executive and legislative powers it introduced were highly ambivalent. Parliament's influence was limited (and as such was stripped even further), whereas that of the king was unrestricted up to the point of turning a financial conflict into a constitutional one. A similar financial policy would, for instance, not have been possible during the Republic, given the fact that for most of its existence the group that decided on government outlays and taxation was the same one that had invested its wealth in government paper—by and large the financial elite of Holland. This, however, had in turn led to inflexibility, given the fact that a lack of alternative investment opportunities of adequate size deprived the group of the incentive to institute redemption and a reduction of the tax burden. For this reason, eighteenth-century attempts to repay the debt were resisted, which in the long term led to a rise in the national debt and a commensurate increase in the tax burden. The British system of separating the government and the Crown, under which the king and his ministers annually submit their proposed budgets for the allocation of expenditure—and the taxes by which they will be financed—to Parliament for its approval, had been explicitly created to curb the monarch's power in this respect and enlarge the influence of taxpayers. In the version of this system introduced into the Netherlands in 1815, however, an equal balance of power between monarch and Parliament was absent, allowing Willem I ample opportunity to develop the tangled financial policies observed. The weakness of the opposition, in combination with Willem I's ambitions and personality, completes the explanation of the events.

The financial and political crisis of 1839 sealed the fate of Willem I's autocratic experiment. At decisive moments he had been unable to command sufficient loyalty from the citizens of Holland, despite several attempts to do so, for example, through the debt reform of 1814 (when the seed was planted for the financial problems he was to struggle with throughout his reign). In the 1830s he became entangled in the contradictions created by his own policies: to uphold his position he found it increasingly necessary to hold back information on the true extent of the problems, so that when the lid blew off and it finally became clear how he had contrived to maintain his policies, he lost almost all authority. The reform of the constitution in 1840 and Willem I's abdication partly solved the problems and also meant that his direct successors, Willem II and Willem III, were no longer able to adopt similar policies. Thus, the period after 1840 was to witness a search for a better way of formalizing political relations between monarch and Parliament (see chapter 5).

The Activist Experiment: Domestic Economic Policy, 1813–30

The main objective of economic policy during the short-lived existence of the United Kingdom of the Netherlands was to achieve a closer degree of integration between the different parts of the realm. One of the most obvious and least controversial ways of realizing this objective was to improve the transport infrastructure. Such plans entailed not only an improvement of infrastructure between the northern and southern Netherlands, which, due to the divergent developments that had taken place after 1585, had been neglected for over two centuries, but also improvement in the transport infrastructure between the various parts of the northern Netherlands. While much of the coastal provinces enjoyed access by water through the extensive, if somewhat outdated, barge system, connections to and within the inland provinces left much to be desired—as had been duly noted by Agent for Interior Affairs Goldberg on his famous investigative journey across the country in 1800.[42]

In the southern Netherlands great progress had been made in the construction of a network of paved roads over the course of the eighteenth century; in the northern provinces, where water transport was traditionally more important, the road system was relatively poorly developed. Even before 1813, several large projects had been started involving the construction of regional roads; Willem I promoted the continuation of these works from the very beginning of his reign. In 1815 funds were earmarked for that purpose, which was followed in 1816 by a plan for an integrated system of national roads. In subsequent years loans of fl 6 million were raised on the capital market to finance the system.[43] In the ten-year budget for 1820 the responsibility for maintenance of these roads was passed on to the provinces, which were allotted income from tolls for that purpose. This led to a boom in the construction of paved and unpaved regional roads in subsequent decades.[44]

After 1820, Willem I concentrated his efforts on constructing waterways. A recent study of this aspect of his policies shows how he encouraged existing activities and, sometimes without consulting Parliament, attempted to finance them.[45] According to Filarski, the total expenditure on waterways amounted to just over fl 50 million, of which 56 percent was spent on works in the north and the remainder in the south. Among the most important projects were the Noordhollandsch Kanaal, which in due course contributed to the recovery of Amsterdam as a port, and the Zuidwillemsvaart, a canal to connect industry around Liège via 's Hertogenbosch with Holland. Up until 1823 Willem I could generally count on the support of Parliament for these plans. With the establishment of the Amortisatiesyndicaat, however, Parliament was of the opinion that such works should fall under the Syndicate's responsibility, and, moreover, opposition to Willem's plans grew. In the latter half of the 1820s, however, when the Amortisatiesyndicaat began to run out of funds, the possibilities for starting new projects seemed to vanish rapidly. Almost all attempts to attract funds from the private sector failed, partly because implementation costs often exceeded the amounts budgeted. The financial consequences were by and large passed on to the Amortisatiesyndicaat (and the Société Générale, founded in Brussels in 1822).

The financial results of these projects varied considerably. Almost all canals laid out in Belgium to transport coal to cities and industrial centers were successful. The volume of traffic over these new waterways grew rapidly, and income from tolls was more or less sufficient to make the investments worthwhile. Projects in the northern Netherlands were less profitable because the volume of traffic did not meet expectations, as was the case with the Noordhollandsch Kanaal. In the early years the return—the relation between net income and construction costs—amounted to a meager 0.5 to 1.5 percent (while several Belgian canals generated more than 10 percent).[46] To make matters worse, because of the separation of Belgium and the Netherlands, the large canal between 's Hertogenbosch and Luik could not operate as was originally envisaged, with negative financial results.

Available data on the size of investments in infrastructure show a remarkable peak in the second half of the twenties, thanks to the policies of the Kanalen Koning.[47] The financial strictures of the thirties brought this first boom in investment in infrastructure to an abrupt end. The selection of projects to be implemented was subject to the influence, particularly in the northern Netherlands, of groups representing dominant (commercial) interests. The port cities especially, and in particular Amsterdam, profited from these initiatives, which paid too little attention to the integration of the various regional systems of waterways and through that to the creation of a domestic market.[48] Our view of the boom in new infrastructural works should also take into account the changes in government that had taken place after 1795. The political autonomy of the towns and regions before 1795 had to some extent retarded the development of an optimal system of transportation: it was to the advantage of some towns to ensure that transport flowed through them and to prevent the construction of more direct connections between competing centers. To achieve this, political influence was brought to bear. The route between Amsterdam and Rotterdam was far from straight in its course, meandering via the IJ, Haarlem,

Haarlemmermeer, Gouda, and the Hollandse IJssel. Lock charges were among the most important sources of income for Haarlem and Gouda, which stood to lose much should the route change. Both towns had in the past resisted efforts to shorten the route, for example, with a direct connection between Amsterdam and Haarlemmermeer (which would have cut Haarlem out of the route) or via Delft (at the cost of Gouda's position). Almost any proposal to improve the system of waterways met similar problems: again and again, an improvement would threaten the position of a particular town, and usually the opposition was so stifling that nothing came of the proposed improvement.[49]

Theoretically, the solution to the problem was to simply earmark part of the extra revenue that the improvement would generate for compensation of income lost by the town. Unfortunately, the complex negotiations necessary to reach an agreement for such measures among the different parties stood in the way of such a solution ever being put into effect. Consequently, prior to 1795 the construction of new waterways stagnated. However, the new form of government in place after 1795 in principle limited the power of the towns and effectively made it possible to force parties to compromise. This occurred in 1808 in connection with the construction of the Overtoom lock, which made direct connection between Amsterdam and the Haarlemmermeer possible. Louis Napoleon decided that one-third of the income from the toll for this lock would be paid to Haarlem and one-third to the Hoogheemraadschap Rijnland, joint owners of the lock at Spaarndam.[50] A similar compromise was reached in 1823 in connection with construction of the Amstel-Drecht-Aar link, which opened up a direct route from Amsterdam to the Hollandse IJssel (cutting Gouda and Haarlem out of the route). Only Gouda, which was directly involved in the negotiations, received any compensation, in part from the doubling of local lock charges (at the expense of those using the traditional route). Hardly by coincidence, both compromises were reached only after intervention from above: by Louis Napoleon in 1808 and by Willem I and his governor, Tets van Goudriaan, in 1822–23.[51]

These examples show that the intervention of the centralized state resulted in an important change in the rules of negotiation for infrastructural works, indeed, for any issue that affected the interests of towns. One immediate result was a reduction in transaction costs, which greatly stimulated the submission of initiatives for the construction and improvement of the waterway system, a considerable number of which were approved by Willem I. The scale of this development was, however, not very large because, as the estimates of Filarski have shown, the projected income was rarely realized. Even the Dedemsvaart, perhaps the most successful new project of the first half of the nineteenth century, could not support itself and had to be sponsored by the government. In addition, the compensation claims of towns lowered the profitability of these waterways: without a doubt the Overtoom lock would have been much more profitable had the town of Amsterdam not been compelled to pay two-thirds of the lock's income to Haarlem and Rijnland. In this way the "old" political structure was still able to stand in the way of progress through reform.

The foundation of the Fund for Industry, to support industry particularly in the southern Netherlands, was a feature of the compromise reached in 1821 during negotiations between the northern and the southern Netherlands on the structure of the taxation system. Between 1823 and 1830 the fund provided soft loans on a large scale to industry; on most loans three percent interest was demanded, well below market rates, and even interest-free loans were not unusual.[52] The fund was the manifestation of the active industrial policies that Willem I was so taken with. In the southern Netherlands, the iron industry in particular, and on a smaller scale textiles and mining, profited. "Model" entrepreneurs were selected by Willem I and his civil servants to take a leading role in the modernization of their respective industries. The best known of these was John Cockerill, who played an important role in the modernization of the iron industry, mining, and the machine industry in Belgium, receiving almost fl 3 million for that purpose.[53] G. M. Roentgen, a pioneer in the construction of steamships who worked in close cooperation with Cockerill, also enjoyed the support of the fund.

Already by the end of the 1820s, the Fund for Industry had become controversial. The northern Netherlands saw little advantage in its activities and as early as 1825 were able to ensure that the annual subsidy transfer reserved from the government budget was reduced from fl 1.3 million to fl 0.8 million. Nevertheless, through several ingenious constructions—the fund's finances were administered by the Amortisatiesyndicaat, which provided loans to the fund itself—Willem I was able to partially circumvent the cuts. Its expenditures grew rapidly between 1823 (when the fund began its activities) and 1826. The preserved administrative records (which are not wholly complete) indicate a peak in loans extended in 1826 amounting to a total of fl 1.4 million, of which only fl 200,000 was spent in the north. The cuts introduced by Parliament and the growing problems of the Amortisatiesyndicaat made further reductions inevitable, more or less halving the loans made in 1826–29. Remarkably, no reduction followed in loans extended to the northern Netherlands. After the secession of Belgium, the fund's activities decreased: in the thirties loans averaged a total of fl 100,000 annually.[54] Only a very small proportion of loans were repaid. Of the fl 2.5 million loaned to enterprises in the northern Netherlands, fl 629,000 was allocated to the textile industry (including carpet making), fl 663,000 to shipping companies, and fl 460,000 to the shipbuilding, iron, and machine manufacturing industries.[55] In addition to supporting existing businesses in Leiden, Tilburg, and Twente, the fund's activities in textiles included support for branches of enterprises formerly located in the southern

Netherlands that had established themselves in the north after 1830. The largest loans were extended to two new enterprises that were actively involved in both merchant shipping and the building of steamships: Roentgen's Nederlandsche Stoomboot Maatschappij and Van Vlissingen's Amsterdamsche Stoomboot Maatschappij.

Generally speaking, the Fund for Industry was relatively successful in picking "winners." The sectors in the southern Netherlands that received the most money were without a doubt the most dynamic, and its choice of entrepreneurs to receive extra support was not unjustified, as the examples of Cockerill and Roentgen show. Moreover, the growth of the iron and textile industries in the southern Netherlands was so turbulent that they could do with all the external capital they could get, especially given the fact that the elasticity of supply on the capital market in the southern part of the country was far less than that which prevailed in Holland.[56] It is doubtful, however, whether similar imperfections in the capital market in the northern Netherlands played a role in the relatively slow development of industry there. Jonker has recently shown that capital was rarely an obstacle for establishing new industries or expanding existing ones.[57] This is probably the case not only for wealthy Holland but also for the other regions of the country. As early as 1800 entrepreneurs in Twente, for instance, had accumulated so much venture capital that investment opportunities were systematically explored outside the textile industry.[58]

The fund never rose to being a significant force in the northern Netherlands. Roentgen and Van Vlissingen's enterprises profited from its activities, but for other sectors and businesses its support was modest, of little consequence, or even counterproductive. The bureaucratic capriciousness that is inherent to a system of camouflaged subsidies was exacerbated by the fact that the fund's administrator, Netscher, had little faith in the future of industry in the northern Netherlands. Moreover, Willem I more than occasionally ventured to use the fund for his political ends, more concretely to support cooperative entrepreneurs such as publishers who proved themselves loyal to the government.[59] As a means of currying favor with the elite of the southern Netherlands, the fund was, of course, undoubtedly useful. Another important gesture by Willem I to his southern subjects was his founding of the Algemeene Maatschappij voor de Volksvlijt, a bank that to a large extent he financed himself, and whose mission it was to promote the development of industry and infrastructure in the southern regions of the kingdom. However, just as with the Amortisatiesyndicaat, Willem used the Société Générale as an instrument for arranging certain "private" matters, so that it became more and more enmeshed in the financial manipulations of himself and his civil servants. Only after the secession of 1830 would the Algemeene Maatschappij begin to play the dynamic role in the development of the Belgian economy that Willem I originally had in mind.[60]

EAST INDIAN FRUSTRATION: COLONIAL POLICY, 1813–30

The new kingdom that came into existence in 1814 inherited large colonial possessions that were to play a crucial role in its economic development. Until its liquidation in 1799, the Dutch East India Company (VOC) was the effective owner of the Dutch East Indies, which exploited the local population through systems of forced labor (in particular in the east of Java) and feudal forms of taxation by which certain products were produced that had to be sold to the company. Although the company held a monopoly over international trade in the colony, with the rise of British and American trade in the area it became increasingly difficult to maintain. In addition, the VOC administration in Batavia had developed into an oligopoly that had virtually complete control over the archipelago, including the Dutch enclaves situated there. Under such circumstances VOC administrators were hardly willing to listen to the "mother country," particularly as the many wars and trading blockades made communication so difficult.

After 1795 debate grew as to the future administration of the colony: Should it be as liberal as practicable and encourage local peoples to develop export-oriented agriculture, or should a system of forced deliveries and the trade monopoly of the VOC be maintained?[61] Following the tradition of Batavian revolutionaries, Governor H. W. Daendels (1808–11) began to build up a centralized and unified system of government, to modernize its bureaucracy, and to invest in infrastructure.[62] Invasion by the British in 1811 accelerated the process: the old administrative oligopoly was marginalized, and Th. S. Raffles, the ambitious British lieutenant governor, introduced a system of land taxes that were meant to replace income from the monopoly trading. In introducing this system, however, Raffles faced a dilemma, namely, through which level of the local population was he to work? The VOC had worked through the local elite, but this group, which through forms of noneconomic exploitation had great influence over the local population, was expected by reformers to resist the planned changes. Raffles chose to maintain contact through the *dessas* (villages): taxes were levied by dessa and had to be paid by the dessa, for which the village head was held responsible; Raffles's original intention of individual taxation had to be quickly abandoned. Disappointing sales, due to lack of shipping, made it very difficult for him to find financing for his plans, and to a large degree he was forced to continue to use traditional sources of income.[63]

After the return of the Dutch East Indies in 1816 had been arranged by treaty—through which the Netherlands lost to Great Britain other possessions in South Africa and Ceylon—Willem I took control over this aspect of policy, too. According to the constitution of 1815 the administration of colonies was under his authority. As a gesture to the British—or rather as a sign of the dependence of the new kingdom on this ally—the colony was opened to ships and traders of all nations, a policy criticized by the Amsterdam Chamber of

Commerce, which favored the reintroduction of a monopoly. Through a number of royal decrees on import and export duties, however, this liberal stance was slowly but surely abandoned in favor of increasing protection of the Dutch flag and its trade. The first regulation on import and export duties stipulated that import duty on cargoes coming from the Netherlands on Dutch ships was to be 6 percent, while the same cargo carried on foreign ships was to attract 9 percent duty; cargoes not from the Netherlands that were carried on foreign ships were to attract 12 percent duty. From 1823 onward, the protection extended to Dutch textiles went even further by raising duty on foreign textiles from 25 to 35 percent. In short, in all sorts of little ways efforts were made to escape the grip of British supremacy.[64]

Up to 1823 this policy had only limited success. In the period 1811–14 the British had built up a strong presence in the archipelago and controlled the most important trading markets, including the cotton trade, which thanks to the superiority of their textile industry was completely in their hands. The trading company Maatschappij van Koophandel en Zeevaart, founded in 1817 to cater to trade between Amsterdam and the East Indies, suffered heavy losses and in 1823 was forced into liquidation.[65] If anything, this only stimulated the cries of Amsterdam merchants, who pleaded for the king to pay attention to the city's declining trade, encouraging him to launch new initiatives.

Following the Prussian example, the Nederlandsche Handelmaatschappij was formed in 1824. According to the king's original plan, in which he speaks of "the unfortunate course shipping and trade with our overseas possessions, particularly the East Indies, has taken," the newly formed enterprise was to concentrate on shipping and trade between the mother country and the East Indies, as well as "all other parts in the Indies and nearby regions, the tea trade with China, and fisheries in the waters surrounding the Indies."[66] The company was, moreover, to give trading preference to Dutch goods and to only use ships sailing under the Dutch flag, which preferably should have been built in the Netherlands. It was also meant to promote agriculture and fisheries. Deliberately, the NHM was not given a monopoly over trade with the colonies, nor was it given any administrative responsibilities, although the king did award it exclusive rights to the shipping and supply of all government goods between the colonies and the mother country. Finally, Willem I guaranteed an annual dividend of 4.5 percent on the company's share capital and was himself a significant investor, holding fl 4 million of the fl 12 million to perhaps fl 24 million of the enterprise's initial float.[67]

Interest in this project was enormous, in part due to the sovereign's guarantee on the dividend. Even on the very first day of issue, the share enjoyed subscription totaling fl 70 million, half of which originated from Amsterdam (including the king's fl 4 million), fl 14 million from Antwerp, a good fl 11 million from Rotterdam, and fl 8 million from Brussels. The great interest in the southern Netherlands is most unusual, as in general the supply of investment capital there was much lower than in the north, and investment from this part of the kingdom in government bonds was almost nil. Ultimately it was decided to increase the emission to fl 37 million (table 3.3), including the subscriptions

TABLE 3.3.
Distribution of the Share Capital of the NHM at the Emission.

	Number of Participants	Allocated Shares	Average per Participants	Number of Representatives in Board
Willem I	1	4.000	4.000	—
Northern Netherlands				
Amsterdam	706	13.739	19.5	11
Rotterdam	376	5.644	15.0	6
Middelburg	95	410	4.3	2
Leiden	52	338	6.5	2
Dordrecht	44	183	4.1	1
Schiedam	25	120	4.8	1
Gouda	4	80	20.0	—
Total	1,302	20.514	15.8	23
Southern Netherlands				
Antwerpen	415	7.104	17.1	7
Brussel	330	4.023	12.9	4
Gent	104	894	8.6	3
Brugge	16	167	10.4	1
Ostende	28	165	5.9	1
Doornik	18	38	2.1	1
Total	911	12.391	13.6	17
Total	2,214	36.905	16.7	40

Source: Mansvelt, *Geschiedenis,* 1:73.

of small investors and the king, whose subscriptions were honored for the full amount.

The large number of shareholders, among them many with one or two shares (fl 1,000 each), is reminiscent of the foundation of the VOC in 1602, when more than sixteen hundred shareholders subscribed to share capital totaling fl 6.5 million.[68] In all other respects the situations were radically different, however: the VOC was created to put an end to excessive competition between various Dutch shipping companies trading with the East Indies, whereas the NHM was founded because of the lack of sufficient shipping and trade with the Indies. The former was born out of an excess of entrepreneurship and profit seeking, while the latter was born out of their lack. Willem I's guaranteed dividend contributed significantly to the success of the issue, which came at a time when the effective return on government bonds had dropped sharply to below 4.5 percent (see figure 3.1). The VOC had no such guarantee, and the success of its issue was entirely dependent on the expected profitability of the company. The NHM's mission was to promote Dutch industry, fisheries, and agriculture, while these matters were only side effects of the VOC's main activities.

In the years following its inception, the NHM's activities expanded to numerous fields. It attempted to resuscitate trade with South America, the West Indies, China, and the Mediterranean, but the results were in general negative, and after a few years the decision was made to concentrate on trading with the East Indies.[69] Trade only with this colony was profitable, not the least because of the privileges the enterprise enjoyed there. Thanks to a contract with the Indies government, the NHM was given sole access to the coffee crops in Priangan, the western part of Java where large-scale forced deliveries of this crop were levied as taxes; the prices agreed to in the contract were also lower than those in the markets of Batavia. Nevertheless, no great profits were made through the contract, primarily due to unfavorable developments in coffee prices in the second half of the 1820s, which meant that the expected profits from sales in the Netherlands could not be achieved.[70] It is likely that the relative inefficiency of the company also played a role in this: the freight charges it had to pay Dutch ships were much too high, and it was in general obliged to sell Dutch produce, which was often more expensive than similar produce of British origin. The most important exception was the successful export of cotton goods. Partly due to protective tariffs of 1823 and 1824, the export of calicoes to Java leaped dramatically (see figure 4.3) at the commensurate cost to British exports. This export trade, which was profitable due to the relatively low prices of Flemish cotton manufacturers, made an important contribution toward improving the balance between outward and return cargoes.[71]

In the course of the twenties the relations between the NHM and the Indies government became closer and closer. In 1827 the NHM became the sole leaseholder of the opium tax on Java, which for the following four years was by far the most lucrative source of income for the company. In the years that followed, the policy of the Indies government changed noticeably, and in directions that were to be extremely profitable for the NHM.

The experiment in the liberalization of the Javanese economy, begun by Raffles and continued in other forms by Governor-General Van der Capellen (1816–26), by the mid-1820s had come to be considered a failure. Public revenues, despite a definite increase due to the land taxes introduced by Raffles, were still largely dependent on products cultivated by means of forced labor. Attempts to shift the responsibility for coffee production to the dessa, or in practice to its headman, by leasing coffee plantations against a share of its income failed completely. The reform of the monetary system in the colony continued to gobble up large amounts of funds, and due to a fall in prices for coffee, sugar, and spices, income from compulsory deliveries dropped off steeply. Finally, the outbreak of war on Java in 1825, in which Dutch authority on the island was at stake, brought with it a sharp increase in expenditure. Therefore, Java, which Willem I (and his followers) primarily saw as a "gold mine," a source of money, from 1825 to 1829 regularly required significant injections of funds, which had to be borrowed in the Netherlands, increasing the burden on already seriously overstretched government finances.[72]

In this light it is understandable that proponents of a fundamentally different policy came forward. Two options were discussed between 1825 and 1829: encouragement of plantations financed and managed by Europeans (using only local wage labor), and a system in which the peasants themselves were obliged to grow cash crops, to replace land taxes. In a 1829 memorandum to the king, Van den Bosch analyzed what he considered the impracticality of the first option. In his opinion capital and entrepreneurial spirit were in short supply in the colony, and wages there were too high to sustain competitive business. According to him, under such circumstances profitability could be attained only if a system of forced cultivation of export crops, to be organized by the Indies government, was introduced. He was appointed governor-general of the East Indies to put this plan into effect.[73]

SECESSION AND RENEWAL OF THE COLONIAL NEXUS, 1830–40

Two events largely determined the course of politico-economic developments in the 1830s: the Belgian secession and the introduction of the Cultivation System on Java. The Belgian Revolt of August 1830 in fact effectively brought Willem I's economic experiment to an end. Elements of his policy that were focused on the southern Netherlands, such as the activities of the Fund for Industry, were severely curtailed, in part due to the financial problems incurred as a result of the loss of the south as a source of taxation. Increasing indirect taxation could partially solve these financial problems as southern pressure opposing any raise in this kind of tax disappeared as well. The share of indirect taxes in the estimated expenditure of households increased dramatically during the early 1830s (after a strong decline in the second half of the 1820s. This resulted in increases in the cost of living that depressed the domestic market, which had been the most important engine of industrial growth during the previous decade (see chapter 4).[74]

Of at least equal importance was the success of the system of forced labor that Van den Bosch introduced into the East Indies in the early 1830s. Local farmers were compelled to set aside part of their land for cultivating export crops such as coffee, sugar, and indigo and to supply these to the government in exchange for a certain planting wage, which was used to pay their land taxes. The headman of the dessa, who with the introduction of the land-tax system had become the point of contact with the local population, was made responsible for seeing that the system of coerced farming worked. The indigenous elite and Dutch civil servants were given a share in the profits of the system and therefore had a vested interest in ensuring that the local population met the responsibilities forced upon them. Finally, Chinese and later Dutch entrepreneurs were awarded contracts by the government for processing the produce (especially sugar); sugar contracts contained agreements on the supply of processed sugar from particular regions against certain conditions. Forced labor was also used in the transport and processing of goods for export. The NHM was given a monopoly over the purchasing and transportation, as well as their selling in the Netherlands, of these products. Although the colonial treasury was the recipient of the net profits from sales, the NHM was generously recompensed for the costs it incurred (including, for example, extra costs due to the higher freight charges of Dutch shipping companies).[75]

This system (of which only a rough sketch can be given here), due to its peculiar mix of forced labor and monetary incentives, was an instant success, as can be seen in the growth of exports from the East Indies: sugar exports rose from less than 7,000 metric tons in 1830 to nearly 62,000 metric tons in 1840; coffee exports rose in the same period from 18,000 to 70,000 metric tons; the export of indigo increased almost tenfold.[76] Concomitantly, there was a rapid growth in imports, pointing to an increase in purchasing power in the colony. Imports of cotton goods, something that was in demand by the local population in particular, grew spectacularly (see figure 4.3). Through payment of that portion of planting wages that was in excess of land taxes, the supply of money among the local population increased, part of which was used to buy textiles; perhaps, too, demand for labor had increased to an extent that there was less time available for spinning and weaving cotton. The surplus, the net income from the colonies that found its way into the Dutch government's coffers, grew enormously as a result. Official figures, which have to date always been used in the literature, and to a large extent still are, underestimate the true value of income flowing from the colony because they do not take into account the often hidden subsidies awarded to Dutch shipping, trade, and industry, as well as numerous other improper expenditures charged to the colony. In chapter 5 the results of extensive research will be presented that show that the true "colonial surplus" from the East Indies that the Dutch government appropriated in the thirties was nearly double that of the official figures, amounting to approximately fl 150 million in the 1830s (or 3 percent of the annual national income).

The success of the Cultivation System and the manner in which its profits generated demand and employment in large parts of the Dutch economy determined to a large degree developments in the economy after 1830. The colonial surplus was referred to as "the cork upon which the entire Netherlands floats," a statement that for 1830 through 1860 was hardly an exaggeration.[77] The textiles industry, shipbuilding and shipping, international trade, the sugar industry, the insurance sector, and all sorts of smaller activities and firms that were directly or indirectly dependent on these sectors were dominated by the booming trade with the Indonesian archipelago (see chapter 4). In all this, the role of the NHM was pivotal: to an important extent government policy was implemented through and by this body, which profited handsomely from the blossoming "colonial complex."

The obvious question that raises itself is of course related to the effectiveness of this policy, through which large sums in the form of subsidies were distributed to the textile industry, shipbuilding, shipping, the sugar industry, and the international trading sector. Traditionally in the literature this policy—particularly in relation to shipping and shipbuilding—is severely criticized because of its generosity and the fact that it held back modernization in those sectors.[78] The extremely high profits that could be made by building a ship and sailing for the NHM attracted large amounts of speculative capital and encouraged shipbuilding and shipping in towns where costs were much higher than elsewhere. An excellent study by Broeze on the rise in shipbuilding in Schiedam documents this: production costs in this industrial town were much higher than in, for example, Rotterdam or Amsterdam, but because of the overly generous NHM, it was still possible to profit from its policy of stimulating these sectors of industry (with the disappearance of subsidies, the shipping companies left Schiedam).[79]

One of NHM's goals was, certainly until 1840, to spread the advantages of its activities on different regions, groups of entrepreneurs, and laborers. This was one of the reasons for stimulating the migration of textile companies from Belgium to Twente, despite the poor economic prospects. For similar reasons the secretary of NHM's board, Willem De Clercq, to a certain extent the ideologist behind this aspect of NHM policy (although Willem I agreed with him), was in favor of spreading orders for calico among as many small manufacturers in Twente as possible, and at the same time financially supported efforts to introduce cotton weaving into other parts of the country, such as Zeeland. For

De Clercq, a proponent of the orthodox Protestant movement of the *Reveil,* the pursuit of "distributive justice" and to some extent the rejection of large-scale industry and capitalist entrepreneurship played an important role.[80] Be that as it may, De Clercq and the other members of NHM's board were also compelled to follow such strategies because in such matters the NHM was simply an instrument of the government, there to implement Willem I's policy of (with the help of the colonial treasury) stimulating regions and economic sectors in the Netherlands as much as possible. Nevertheless, the administrators of the NHM found themselves confronted with a paradox: in addition to being a "normal" profit-maximizing trading company, it was also expected to serve the common good, including combating the impoverishment of towns such as Schiedam, Middelburg, and Haarlem, and thus implement the policies of the king that were meant to revive the Dutch economy. The construction chosen for this was that of passing on the costs of financing the subsidies to the colonial treasury. In spreading the benefits of this policy widely among cities, towns, provinces, and social groups, Willem was at the same time actively attempting to strengthen his power base. The citizens of Schiedam could not be allowed to miss out on the fruits of the NHM system and for little extra cost to the treasury were thus able to share in the profits.[81] However, because "unemployment relief" was a prominent element of the company's policy, the system of protection introduced by the NHM was far from economically efficient.

Nevertheless, the NHM was no neutral intermediary between the government and commerce. Its board members and shareholders were drawn from the merchant elite of Holland, in growing numbers from Amsterdam, and therefore had a vested interest in seeing that the subsidies were allotted to enterprises in this part of the country. The difference in politics that was followed is conspicuous after the changes in 1840, when it became clear that budget cuts were necessary. Subsidies to the textile industry in Twente were phased out rapidly, and the system of tendering was liberalized.[82] Liberalization of trade and shipping policy was, however, much slower: freight charges were lowered slightly to reduce existing overcapacity, but a strongly protectionist measure, a waiting list system (*de beurtlijst*) for privileged ships and reders, was simultaneously introduced. In this way, protection for shipping companies already working for the NHM was continued, and reform and rationalization of the shipbuilding industry and the shipping fleet delayed.[83]

Policy changes with respect to the Twente textile industry in the forties eventually enabled this sector to adapt to changing conditions. Gradually, an increasing number of consignments passed through the hands of Amsterdam trading companies, indicating that costs were beginning to approach those of their international competitors. For the shipbuilding industry and the shipping fleet, however, the NHM's policy effectively postponed their exposure to international competition and prevented adaptation. As a result, by the 1850s the mercantile fleet was aging considerably and the shipbuilding industry had not

TABLE 3.4.
Subsidies to Industry, Trade, Fisheries, and Shipping, 1821–30 through 1861–70 (in million guilders).

	1821–30	1831–40	1841–50	1851–60	1861–70	Total
Industry						
Textiles	—	10.6	9.6	—	—	20.2
Shipping	1.7	—	—	—	—	1.7
Fund for Industry	18.6	10.1	—	—	—	28.7
Sugar	0.3	2.6	10.9	8.8	4.9	27.5
Other	—	3.2	0.5	—	—	3.7
Trade and shipping						
Freights NHM	4.4	18.5	35.6	28.6	16.1	103.2
Commission NHM	—	3.9	6.4	1.4	—	11.7
Others (insurances, etc.)	1.7	7.4	12.5	10.0	5.5	37.1
Herring fisheries	0.7	0.6	0.6	0.1	—	2.0
Total	27.4	56.9	76.1	48.9	26.5	235.8

Sources: textiles: Mansvelt, *Geschiedenis,* 2:210, 278–79; shipping: Mansvelt, *Geschiedenis,* 1:230; Fund for Industry: see note 54; sugar: Horlings, *Economic Development,* 367–68, Jansen, *Industriële ontwikkeling,* 340; other: ARA, Ministerie van Koloniën, verbaal 24-5-1866, no. 49; trade and shipping Mansvelt, *Geschiedenis,* 2:332–33, ARA, Archief NHM, no. 1886-1990, and Horlings, *Economic Development;* fisheries: Pons, *Bakens Verzet.*

introduced new production methods, so that the international depression that occurred after 1856 hit hard. Policies regarding marine insurance and the coffee and sugar trade were also characterized by similar inertia. Justly so, historians have been critical on these issues.[84] The very rough estimates of the subsidies given trade and industry summarized in table 3.4 bring these developments sharply into focus. In the twenties the subsidies extended by the Fund for Industry, with the intention of stimulating industry especially in the southern Netherlands, dominated. After 1830 subsidies connected with the "colonial complex" were prominent; subsidies to the textile industry were already being reduced considerably in the early forties, while the payment of excessive freight charges demanded by the shipping industry continued despite efforts to introduce reforms. Because such forms of protectionism were allowed to continue for far too long, the ability of numerous branches of industry to adjust to the new conditions that followed liberalization of international trade and cutbacks in subsidies was severely reduced.

The preceding pages have presented an outline of the economic and fiscal policies of Willem I, together with a description of the institutional context in which these emerged. The prime argument that we again want to underline here is that the institutions, especially the constitution of 1815, fixed the rules by which the newly defined game of Dutch post-Napoleonic politics was played. Accordingly, the activist and at times even autocratic policies of Willem I can be properly understood only against this background. The historiographical appreciation of these policies has varied considerably. In the nineteenth century especially, liberal economists and politicians passed a particularly negative judgment, notably with respect to the lack of political transparency, the suppressed role of Parliament, the extensive public deficits, and the resumed accumulation of the public debt. In the more recent literature, in which more attention is paid to industrial policy, colonial issues, and transport infrastructure, their positive sides have been emphasized. Of considerable importance in the emergence of this more positive image has been the fact that Willem was the one to take the initiative in the foundation of a number of more lasting institutions—notably the Dutch National Bank, the NHM, and the Brussels Société Générale—all of which were to make considerable contributions to the later economic development of both the northern and southern Netherlands. In this positive appreciation of William I's economic policies—there presently even exists a prize for entrepreneurship that bears his name—almost all attention is focused on the (presumed) beneficial effects of his activist economic policy, whereas its reverse side, the consequences for the nation's fiscal stance with which contemporaries were directly confronted, no longer appears to influence this particular judgment. In the next chapter, an effort will be made to reach a more balanced evaluation by means of a careful analysis of economic development in these years. The central question there is to what extent economic development during these years was influenced by these policies—whether positive or negative. One of the issues to be addressed in this respect is whether the accumulation of deficits caused a process of crowding out in domestic investment.

CHAPTER FOUR

Troubled Recovery

SECESSION, POLICY ADJUSTMENT, AND THE
COLONIAL NEXUS, 1813–1840

Postwar Instability into Sustained Growth

In economic terms, the demise of the Napoleonic Empire and the new independence in 1813 meant, first of all, the ending of the Continental System and the return of free access to the seas. In his famous proclamation of 17 November 1813, Gijsbert Karel van Hogendorp stated this in a nutshell: "The sea is open, trade revives, old times will return," but the latter part of this statement was mere wishful thinking. The long-term decline of the Netherlands as a commercial nation had accelerated during the years in which long-distance trade had virtually come to a standstill, as Dutch merchants would soon find out. Whereas in 1798 the Dutch share in world exports was still about 14 percent, it had declined to about half that in 1815.[1] Moreover, the United Kingdom, now the dominant economic power, increased its already strongly protectionistic stance during the years of the Congress of Vienna.[2] France was to follow soon, and introduced a very strict system to protect its industry in 1816, which created immense problems for the export industries of the southern Netherlands.[3]

Nonetheless, after the dramatic decline of economic activity during the final phase of the Napoleonic domination, a recovery set in during 1814–15, driven by pent-up demand for (imported) consumer goods. Value added in industry rose by almost a third between 1810–13 and 1816–17, and growth rates in transport and trade were even more impressive. The Baltic trade, for example, boomed as a result of extremely high prices (and harvest failures) in western Europe, and Rhine transport broke new records in 1816–17 (see chapter 2). The output of the Leiden textile industry, which had been halved between 1780 and 1813, recovered quickly to about 75 percent of the 1780 level.[4] It almost appeared if Van Hogendorp was right, and the old times would return.

The recovery did, however, not solve the problem of unemployment that had its roots in the long-term decline of (labor-intensive) industries during the eighteenth century and was intensified by the high prices of foodstuffs since the 1780s. Thanks to the intensified efforts of the state to collect statistics on poor relief and its causes, it is possible to show the extent of the problem (table 4.1).[5]

TABLE 4.1.
People Receiving Poor Relief as a Share of Total Population and Their Earning
Capacity in 1817.

	1807	1817	Earns More Than 50% of Income	Earns Less Than 50% of Income	Unable to Earn Any Income
Groningen	5.0	5.2	1.8	1.5	1.9
Friesland	9.0	8.5	2.5	3.4	2.6
Drenthe	—	4.7	1.6	1.7	1.4
Overijssel	4.5	5.6	2.9	1.8	0.9
Gelderland	8.0	7.1	3.2	2.4	1.5
Utrecht	12.0	9.2	3.9	2.7	2.6
North Holland	26.7	21.9	16.0	2.3	3.6
South Holland	12.5	11.2	4.2	2.0	1.0
Zeeland	6.3	8.1	2.8	2.9	2.4
North Brabant	—	10.1	5.5	3.0	1.6
Netherlands	—	11.0	5.8	2.6	2.6

Sources: Handelingen Staten Generaal (1817–18: 380); RA Overijssel, Sous Prefectuur Deventer, 4392; RA Gelderland, Gewestelijke besturen in de Bataafs-Franse Tijd in Gelderland 1795–1813, 722–24; RA Zeeland, Gewestelijke Besturen 1807–1810, 738; Noordegraaf, "Armoede"; RA Noord Holland, Gewestelijke Besturen 1807–10, 364.

The number of people dependent on poor relief fell hardly at all between 1807 and 1817. In Holland—not only the "depressed" north but also the southern part of the province—and Utrecht, 12 to 25 percent of the population received some kind of relief; the greater part of them were earning an income, which was, however, simply not large enough for their household. The strong seasonal pattern in the demand for labor was one of the main problems; many families received poor relief during the winter, when unemployment was extremely high. High prices and by implication low real wages—which increased hardly at all since the end of the seventeenth century—were the second cause of the enormous social problems that lay behind the statistics in table 4.1.

After the bust that followed the boom of 1816–1817, a rather sharp but short depression followed, which reached its nadir in 1819. After this typical postwar business cycle had ended, however, a process of almost continual growth began that was to last for two decades.[6] That remarkable growth, which stands in stark contrast to the stagnation during the 150 years prior to 1820, is the topic of this chapter: How to explain the appearance of this new dynamism around 1820; and why was it followed, after 1840, by a new period of relative stagnation? Finally, the changes in the direction of growth in about 1830—following the secession of Belgium—will be analyzed. In this, the important issue is what were the positive and negative effects of economic policy in this period, in particular Willem I's experiment?

For a long time the orthodox view of this period was that it was one of almost absolute stagnation, and that the attempts of Willem I to reform and reactivate the economy had failed because of the failure of private enterprise, which did not respond to the new challenges. Griffiths and De Meere have attacked this orthodoxy, showing that economic growth did occur and probably began in the late 1820s or (early) 1830s. The growth of agricultural exports and increased trade with Germany and the Indies have been analyzed to make this point, but no comprehensive account of the growth of GDP and its components was available to examine the process in detail. Moreover, because Griffiths and De Meere did not systematically analyze the consequences of the economic policies of Willem I, one may even draw the conclusion from their work that the revival of the Dutch economy after about 1830 was closely related to the beneficial effects of these policies. We disagree. We will show that growth predated the 1830s, and that during the 1820s it was, perhaps, based on a more solid foundation than after 1830. Furthermore, the change in the direction of economic growth after 1830 led, in our view, to the economic problems of the 1840s and 1850s. Our assessment of the effects of the economic policies of Willem I is, therefore, much more critical.

But let us first look at the estimates of the development of GDP (table 4.2). The expansion of 1816–30 was rather slow due to the negative influence of the 1818–19 depression. Moreover, it is striking that—perhaps as a result of the increase in real wages and standard of living in the 1820s—population growth in the period was significantly high. Just as striking, however, is the much more modest growth in population in the decades that followed, when food prices began to rise. The thirties witnessed a further acceleration of growth, to which agriculture, which between 1818 and 1825 had been afflicted by extremely low prices, was able to contribute. As mentioned earlier, after 1840 a noticeable slowing of growth occurred, particularly in industry, something that demands explanation. To analyze the growth of the economy in more detail, we will now turn to the individual sectors.

THE PRIMARY SECTOR: AGRICULTURE AND FISHERIES

Agriculture was, as has been described in chapter 2, one of the pillars of the Dutch economy at the beginning of the nineteenth century. Productivity was relatively high due to specialization of production; some grain for consumption

TABLE 4.2.
Estimates of the Growth of Real Value Added in the Most Important Branches of the Economy and
Their Contribution to Growth, 1816–50 (average annual growth rates and percentages).[a]

	Growth			Contribution to Growth[b]			Share in Value Added
	1816–30	1830–40	1840–50	1816–30	1830–40	1840–50	(1815/51)
Agriculture	0.60	2.25	0.89	14.0	37.3	28.5	26.5
Fisheries	−1.38	0.71	5.54	−0.7	0.2	2.9	0.2
Industry	2.67	2.42	0.54	33.8	24.9	10.6	30.8
Construction	1.39	0.64	-0.23	17.7	7.6	−11.0	11.2
Clothing	3.21	−0.85	0.31	12.2	−3.1	4.4	20.3
Leather	0.19	0.31	−2.85	0.7	1.0	−31.6	6.6
Mining	3.76	3.85	−0.54	6.8	8.9	−5.7	2.2
Metal	6.31	2.83	6.30	3.5	2.2	30.7	2.7
Shipbuilding	6.48	4.86	1.36	5.1	6.1	9.0	2.1
Textiles	4.98	6.17	−1.52	12.7	24.7	−29.3	16.3
Utilities	6.64	12.59	7.65	0.7	3.4	20.9	0.4
Foodstuffs	4.18	2.75	0.52	44.7	36.4	31.5	30.4
Services	2.08	1.95	1.54	52.7	37.7	58.0	42.5
International trade	0.11	5.87	1.28	6.2	28.1	18.8	17.8
Domestic trade	3.88	1.48	3.31	44.2	13.8	26.4	20.1
Shipping	4.50	9.79	2.32	6.1	17.9	2.9	5.9
River shipping	1.00	5.80	1.16	0.2	1.2	0.1	1.4
Internal shipping	0.56	2.51	0.92	3.9	12.0	0.9	18.4
Other transport	3.02	2.43	1.49	7.3	4.8	9.8	6.7
Banking	0.64	5.63	2.13	0.5	3.1	1.6	1.8
Insurance	1.87	5.85	5.11	0.5	1.4	2.0	0.8
Government	1.00	−0.76	1.11	12.4	−3.9	10.1	13.4
Housing	1.17	0.76	0.87	8.5	2.7	3.8	12.3
GDP	1.83	2.16	1.11	100.0	100.0	100.0	100.0
Population	1.16	0.93	0.70	—	—	—	—
GDP per capita	0.66	1.22	0.41	—	—	—	—

Source: Database national accounts.
[a] In this and in similar tables in chapters 6 and 8 we summarize the growth figures in the same way; each year
represents the average of three consecutive years: 1816 = 1815/17, 1830 = 1829/31, etc.; the first columns contain
the average annual growth rates; the next set of columns, the contribution of different branches to the growth of
the sector or of GDP in the period concerned; the final column, the average share of this branch in the sector or
in GDP during this period.
[b] Contributions do not add up to 100 percent because not all industries/services are included in table.

was imported, while other agricultural goods (in particular livestock products) were exported. Unfortunately, as a result of such specialization, the Dutch economy was vulnerable to barriers in the international trade of agricultural produce. On the one hand, the Continental System had hindered the import of grain from overseas; this led importers to search for alternative sources of supply to meet the great demand for this basic agricultural commodity, resulting in strong growth of trade along the Rhine.[7] On the other hand, export to England was forbidden, closing the door to one of the most important export markets. Due to the very high prices that all agricultural commodities could command during this period of scarcity, farmers experienced little inconvenience from the embargo; moreover, a large proportion of their former export to England was continued through the very lucrative practice of smuggling (the turning of a blind eye to the practice by Louis Napoleon being one reason for the growing rift between him and his brother, which eventually led to his dismissal in 1810).[8]

Reestablishment of international trade in 1813 had great consequences for Dutch agriculture. England had been denied imports from the Continent for so long that prices there rose to extreme levels. The return to normal trading relations meant that a large proportion of available supplies and considerable proportions of harvests were drawn immediately to the English markets, where they could command a high price. Coincidentally, in 1816–17 harvests all over Europe failed, fanning the flames of the boom in Amsterdam's grain markets even further. Its grain markets saw their turnover grow dramatically; traders made enormous profits by importing grain from the Baltic and reshipping it to England; it was as if Amsterdam was reliving the Golden Age.[9]

This boom was, however, short-lived. Prices in England fell rapidly, taking with them the very lucrative differences in prices with Continental sources of supply and eventually leading to the reintroduction of the Corn Laws, which closely regulated trade in agricultural produce. Great Britain was not the only country to do so: others, including France, retreated into the protectionism of the eighteenth century. The previous period of soaring grain prices had also led to the development of new sources of production. Southern Russia, with the port of Odessa as its point of export, evolved into an important exporter of grain, in direct competition with the Baltic region, which had been the most important exporter of wheat and rye since the sixteenth century. The steep rise in exports from Odessa considerably exacerbated the fall in prices, which after 1817 became inevitable.[10]

This combination of factors led to a sharp decrease in prices on the completely open Dutch grain markets. In Groningen, a trendsetter in the north, the price for wheat plummeted from fl 12.95 in 1817 to fl 3.95 in 1823, the lowest of the "postwar" depression; similarly, prices for rye fell by more than 70 percent.[11] Surrounding countries reacted to these developments by restricting the import of grain even further. In the early twenties landowners in the southern Netherlands and wealthy farmers in Groningen submitted petitions opposing the open-door policies of the new kingdom but with little result: after several years of maneuvering between northern free traders and southern protectionists, Willem I decided in 1821–22 to follow a liberal trade policy (see chapter 3). Nevertheless, in 1825 he introduced a modest increase in the import duty on grain (which in 1830, after Belgium's succession, was rescinded).[12]

The depression of the early twenties was felt severely in several regions. Especially in Groningen, where grain was almost the only crop cultivated, farmers were hardly or not at all able to cultivate alternative, more profitable crops. In other regions as well, to save on costs farmers dismissed workers or hired less labor. But only in exceptional cases was extensive farming the solution to the crisis. Prices for potato, madder, and particularly meat and dairy produce fell less sharply during this period, partly as a result of a renewed growth in exports to England. This stimulated farmers to intensify production of these products. Potato cultivation continued the trend already set in the eighteenth century, madder cultivation boomed (despite growing French competition), and areas specializing in animal husbandry, Friesland, Holland, and Utrecht, experienced possibly better times than they had before 1820. Because the prices of many industrial products declined even more than those of foodstuffs, the terms of trade for farmers improved, which induced them to increase market production.

Agriculture practiced on the sandy soils of the eastern and southern Netherlands underwent the most drastic change. The cultivation of arable crops—rye, buckwheat, oats—was fundamental to these areas, even though, especially in Brabant, a substantial proportion of income was derived from the sale of butter and livestock. Animals were kept mostly for their manure; an intensive application of manure, supplemented by cut turf and leaves from the scanty forests, was needed on the poor sandy soils. The sudden drop in grain prices and the far less pronounced decrease in prices for butter and livestock made it increasingly attractive for farmers to concentrate on animal husbandry. Expanding butter production was possible only by keeping more and better quality livestock. Because grain prices were extremely low, a large proportion of the grain harvests was fed to cattle; instead of selling rye, farmers sold the extra butter and calves they produced. Another approach to achieving the same effect was to improve the quality of meadow pasture, for example, by applying more manure and improving drainage. One obstacle met in the east of the country was that a large proportion of pasture was common property, managed by the marken. As a result of the changes in relative prices, however, the number of supporters for dividing up these commons grew. The combination of these forces and new government initiatives in this matter led to the actual division of the commons (see the next section). All in all, in the eastern and southern parts of the Netherlands the relative increase in the butter price was the cause of a reevaluation of the foundations of agriculture there, leading to a greater emphasis on animal husbandry, a process that continued to expand its influence in the second half of the nineteenth century.[13]

The depression of 1818–25 did slow down growth in agricultural production, however. Data for the first half of the nineteenth century are rather scarce. Nevertheless, careful analysis shows something of a recession in the twenties (see table 4.2). As the economic climate improved after 1825, production began to grow rapidly again, such that by the thirties the collapse of the early twenties had been completely nullified thanks to strong performance in the agricultural sector. The new Grain Act of 1835, which implied a greater degree of protection, was of symbolic importance in this respect. The act made the import duty on grain dependent on grain prices on the domestic market: as these increased, so duty decreased. The protective influence of the act was effective only for the first few years after its introduction; after 1837 grain prices on international markets rose to such an extent the import duty was extremely low (in 1845, during the most serious food shortages since 1816–17, the Grain Act of 1835 was repealed).[14]

Buoyed by the upturn in the economy, agriculture on the sandy soils of the eastern Netherlands enjoyed record harvests from 1835 onward. Farmers in the region profited handsomely from a combination of circumstances: growth in the textile industry in Twente and the Achterhoek region, and the expansion of peat digging greatly stimulated the region's economy. Besides, improvements in the region's transport infrastructure began to bear fruit; the construction of a network of sealed state highways, in particular, reduced transport costs and led to an increase in the intensity of traffic (a development, however, that only really set in after the introduction of railways in 1860; see chapter 6). The improvement of purchasing power in the countryside must have also benefited the agricultural sector. In the east, where at the turn of the nineteenth century yields at harvest were relatively low—for the most important grains no more that twelve hectoliters per hectare—production grew significantly; in the thirties and forties yields of fifteen to eighteen hectoliters per hectare were to become normal. The increase in production of livestock and their produce, under the influence of attractive butter prices, which led to an increase in livestock numbers so that more manure became available, played no small role in the increase in grain production. Increases in potato growing, which required intensive cultivation of the soil, may also have contributed to the economic growth. As a result of these changes, more and more labor was spent on arable cropping and animal husbandry, in turn leading to a growing demand for labor. This is apparent from the reduction in the seasonal migration of labor from the countryside of the eastern Netherlands to the towns of Holland in the 1830s and 1840s.[15]

Similar developments took place on the sandy soils in the south of the Netherlands: there, too, infrastructure was improved; industries grew in the countryside; and harvest yields increased. However, because agriculture there had always been labor-intensive, and animal husbandry had already been more important since the turn of the century, the potential profits to be made from agriculture as a result of the changes just described were smaller.[16]

As Batavian reformers such as Gogel and Goldberg had predicted, agriculture in the south and the east clearly profited from the new opportunities created by the establishment of a unified state; in the 1820s both relatively "backward" regions began an impressive process of economic change. Agriculture in the northern and the western parts of the country was much less successful; here, stagnation reigned. Market demand had diminished because international protectionism limited exports (most countries had, for example, banned the import of livestock) and because as a result of structural problems in the urban sector of the economy domestic demand had also ceased to grow. International comparative research has shown that growth in agricultural productivity is closely dependent on developments in the process of structural transformation of an economy: as, through the growth of towns, the demand for agricultural produce in other sectors of the economy increases and opportunities for specialization develop, it becomes possible to increase the productivity of labor in agriculture.[17] This explains why Dutch agriculture had already reached such a high level of productivity, which was a consequence of the early urbanization that took place in the Netherlands in the fifteenth, sixteenth, and seventeenth centuries. However, that urbanization stagnated between 1670 and 1860. The agricultural sector was unable to develop new markets for its produce, and the development potential of the sector collapsed as a result of stagnation in the rest of the economy. (This changed after 1840 through liberalization of international trade, allowing the sector to profit from growing demand in surrounding countries.)

Perhaps agriculture in the western provinces had run into a technological ceiling that, given the limitations of the preindustrial economy, could not be easily overcome. Harvests recorded in Zeeland at the beginning of the nineteenth century were hardly different from those known for the seventeenth century, perhaps an indication of the existence of such a technological ceiling.[18] Growth could be achieved only by cultivating more labor-intensive crops, such as potato, madder, and flax, which were profitable for farmers only as long as the increase in wages remained behind that of output prices. Population pressures, which continued to increase during the greater part of the nineteenth century, manifested themselves in a fall in real wages and a sharp increase in land prices and rents. Both were a great stimulus for increasing the intensity of agricultural land use. A case in point is the transformation in Groningen from mixed farming to the cultivation of only grains or cash crops, a transformation that was accompanied by plowing up pastures and increasing the area under arable crops; this clearly was a reaction to the scissor movement of falling real wages and rising land prices.[19] The "secret" of the success of agriculture in the east and south of the country was that it lagged behind and could therefore catch up as a result of gradual improvements in the transport net and the disappearance of all sorts of obstacles to the regional transport of goods.

CASE STUDY: THE DISSOLUTION OF THE COMMONS
IN THE EASTERN PROVINCES

During the eighteenth century the *markegenootschappen* (or *marken*) of the eastern Netherlands were the subject of criticism by "enlightened reformers" because, as managers of the commons, they were supposed to have prevented the reclamation of these wastelands. In theory this was correct. The communities attempted to maintain communal lands so that farmers could make use of them, but since for a small sum peasant farmers usually were able to reclaim and cultivate parcels of land, in practice it was not anywhere near so restrictive. Indeed, the marken received little attention from the Batavian revolutionaries; only a few reformers were quite vocal in their criticism of these institutions (the urban guilds, which were to some extent comparable to the rural marken, received much more coverage). The critics of the marken pointed out that in one of the most densely populated nations of Europe (second only to Belgium), enormous expanses of wastelands, particularly large areas of heath and peat bogs, were available, yet they contributed little to necessary production of food.[20]

The discussion that developed after 1798 on how the government should go about stimulating agriculture eventually led in 1809–10 to Louis Napoleon promulgating two decrees that were aimed at dissolving the marken. The conditions of the decree of 1810 were very strict. Each marke community was immediately required to appoint a committee to either draw up a plan for the division of their common lands or submit an explanation for why division was not possible at that time. In the latter case, the committee was obliged each year to hold a meeting until a majority voted for division of the lands.[21] At the same time, taxation of the wastelands increased sharply. In accord with the French system of taxation introduced in 1811, all land, even if uncultivated, was subject to land taxes. The marken were from then on liable to pay large amounts of tax each year.[22]

The regulations of 1810 met, however, with resistance from farmers almost everywhere. Sometimes committees were set up to meet the law, but thereafter nothing changed. Often the committee did not even bother to submit an explanation for why the land could not be divided up. In the few marken where a report was submitted, detailed explanations were given for why it would be impossible to continue farming without common land for grazing livestock and for cutting turf. The shifts in power that followed (in 1810 and 1813) and the fact that Willem I had to devote his time to more pressing matters created enough opportunity for these legal requirements to be ignored.[23]

All that notwithstanding, some years later, around 1820, a process began whereby gradually commons were either entirely or partially divided up, although it was not clear whether it was possible to fall back on the regulations of 1810. In 1820 the town council of Enschede, the most important center for textiles in the province of Overijssel, addressed itself in a letter to the leading politician of the day, G. K. van Hogendorp, requesting that he intervene to facilitate the division of commons. Only in this manner, in their view, could the foundations for a further expansion of the textile industry (i.e., the small-scale farm) be enlarged.[24] Despite this plea, clarification of the 1810 regulations was not given, so that the division of commons that took place between 1810 and 1837 had an irregular status. The *keuters* (i.e., those farmers who did not have a share in the marke and were therefore not allowed to make full use of the commons) were often inadequately compensated for the loss of use of these lands, which on occasions led to angry protest on their part. Pressure to continue with the division process usually came from large farmers, who needed more pasture to expand animal husbandry and the production of butter. The expansion of peat areas along the borders of Drente and Overijssel also played its part: land there that had originally been a worthless peat bog became very valuable as a result of the construction of the Dedemsvaart canal. Division of commons to profit from the situation immediately followed the canal.[25]

The division of commons gained momentum in the 1830s. Efforts to introduce cadastral surveying had been under way already since the turn of the century, culminating in the introduction of the land registry (*kadaster*) in 1832. This brought to an end many of the uncertainties surrounding landownership in the countryside: the precise boundaries of commons were registered now, something that made division a much simpler task than it had been previously. Prior to 1832 quite a few plans to divide the wastelands were considered impracticable because the exact boundaries were under dispute. The establishment of the kadaster also made it feasible to levy taxes on those lands, which encouraged moves to divide them up.

Nevertheless, a number of measures introduced by the government to force the dissolution of the marken were decisive in this respect. In 1837 Willem I decided that the regulations of 1809–10 were to be followed to the letter, and that provincial governors were to be held responsible for seeing that they were. From that moment on, governors began to push for the division of commons; simultaneously several proposals were made to ensure adequate recompensation of the interests of the farmers and the keuters. Plans to divide wastelands, which had to be approved by royal decree, had to make provision for the keuters by, according to principles of apportionment to be specified, allocating them a portion of the land. In addition, such plans for the dissolution of the marken had to be accompanied by plans for construction of roads to guarantee the accessibility of the new land parcels, and of ditches to improve drainage.[26]

The administrative offensive of 1837 met strong resistance in markegenootschappen containing a large proportion of keuters. At the same time as large landowners were pressing for a quick division of commons, the smallholders maintained that such measures represented a serious loss of their traditional use of communal land, even though each division made some provision for their compensation. Their resistance had little effect, however. Protest by keuters was seldom taken seriously; in any case, allowance was made for their situation by allotting each owner of a house and/or piece of land a small parcel of common land.[27] The resistance of the keuters to the division of common lands can be easily explained: through the loss of communal land they stood to lose their "social security," causing a further decline in their position. In exchange for common land they each received a piece of heath, but due to lack of means they were often unable to develop it.

Under government pressure, the commons of the eastern Netherlands were divided up in the decade following 1837. With the construction of roads and ditches and small canals, the land was immediately suitable for more intensive use. The better pastures, in particular, improved as a result of less overgrazing and investment in improved drainage. Simultaneously, reclamation of land increased from 1840 onward, in part a result of the dissolution of the marken.[28] Of course, other processes also played their role: the relative increase in butter prices, which led to dairy production becoming continually more attractive (and investing money in pastures becoming continually more profitable), the construction of sealed roads by the government, the expansion of the textile industry, and the exploitation of peat cutting after 1830. All these processes resulted in the rapid commercialization of the countryside in the eastern Netherlands, contributing to an increase in agricultural production and productivity in the region.

Two developments explain this expansion of private property at the cost of common lands. First, these lands became, through a combination of developments (of which the increasing importance of pastureland was probably the most important), more valuable, fueling interest in their "privatization." The cost of the division process, which on the one hand consisted of breaking the resistance of the keuters, and on the other hand the actual monetary costs, such as expenditures for the commission that was to supervise the division, and investments in roads and canals, was greatly reduced due to a number of institutional innovations. The most important of these was the legal framework of 1809–10, which was made law in 1837; the foundation of the land registry was also an important step in this respect. These fundamental changes in the relations between the potential returns of the division and its cost explain in large measure why this process could be by and large completed in the period 1837 to 1860.[29]

CASE STUDY: STAGNATION IN THE HERRING FISHERY

The herring fisheries and their problems are to a certain extent representative of the situation the entire Dutch economy faced during the first half of the nineteenth century.[30] This sector was characterized by close interrelationships between institutions, technology, and commerce that almost compulsively linked the economic boom of the sixteenth and seventeenth centuries with the subsequent decline of the eighteenth century and first half of the nineteenth century. Between 1500 and 1650 the sector blossomed as a result of several technological breakthroughs, such as the famous Dutch method of curing herring (*kaken*) that was taken over from the Flemish and the introduction of special designs of fishing boat, the herring buss (*buis*), which was highly suitable for fishing for long periods away from Dutch harbors (on Dogger Bank). The special "Dutch" method of processing the herring catch created a product that found a ready market throughout Europe. During this period the College van de Groote Visscherij (College of Deep-Sea Fisheries) was founded to protect the fishing fleet against piracy in times of war. The influence of the college, which as the representative of the interests of the sector and as an advisory body to the states of Holland had virtually acquired lawmaking powers, continued to expand, resulting in the detailed regulation of the entire herring production process. Its aim in this was, on the one hand, to ensure the quality of Holland herring—foreign traders had to have confidence in the quality of the product— and, on the other, to increase fiscal control because each ship had to share in the cost of collective protection. Ultimately the college was able to successfully protect the sector from external competition. For example, in 1752 fishers with *bomschepen,* small fishing boats working coastal waters, were explicitly forbidden to cure herring, to prevent their "inferior" product from competing with the "superior" herring of the established herring.[31]

During the second half of the seventeenth century, however, the herring fishery experienced a reversal of fortunes. International competition grew much stronger, particularly from Scotland, which was closer to the commercial herring grounds of the Dogger Bank. Moreover, protectionistic policies of the British government in that period led to supportive measures for Britain's growing fishing sector. Holland entrepreneurs responded to the competition by concentrating particularly on the upper segment of the international herring market, where the "superior" herring from the Netherlands was still preferred. Nevertheless, the Scottish (and later Norwegian and Danish) boats landed cheaper but relatively inferior herring on the quay, of which a continually growing proportion found its way to European markets that Holland had monopolized in the early seventeenth century. This made it necessary to extend the detailed regulation of the industry even further, to guarantee the quality of Dutch herring. Unintentionally it also

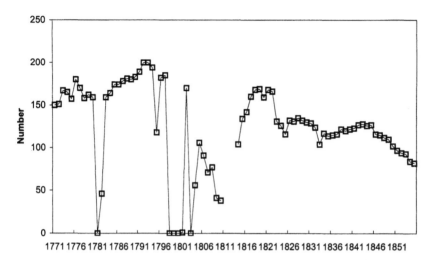

FIGURE 4.1. Number of herring boats putting to sea, 1771–1855. Data from D'Alphonse, *Aperçu*, 327; Pons, *Bakens verzet.*

led to the ossification of the industry. As the decline set in further, so the appeals for government support increased. In 1775 the organized fleet owners were successful in convincing the states of Holland to pay a subsidy of fl 500 per herring boat putting to sea, thus creating a rather unique position for the sector (only the sugar refining industry was awarded a similar subsidy, in 1776).

Neither the velvet revolution of 1795 nor the creation of the Kingdom of the Netherlands in 1813 put an end to this situation. In fact, just the reverse occurred: in 1801 an act was passed to regulate the herring industry by law; later, in 1814, Willem I took over this law in an adapted form. The government subsidy of fl 500 per herring boat was stopped in 1801 but reinstituted in 1814, and it was expanded in later years to include an export subsidy and exemption from salt taxes. In the period immediately following 1813, the fishing industry again boomed, under the influence of high prices generated by latent demand (little fishing had been undertaken between 1810 and 1813) (figure 4.1). After 1817, however, markets were saturated with cheap Scottish herring, and prices fell sharply (from fl 40 per metric ton in 1814 to fl 15 per metric ton in 1821) .

The continuing slump in the industry encouraged the ever-dynamic Willem I to organize an investigation into the situation. He wanted to know, for example, whether the subsidies offered by the Fund for Industry were effective.[32] The College van de Groote Visscherij defended the measures taken since 1775 and considered the decline only temporary. Perhaps in reaction to the king's initiatives, the Vereeniging der Zoutharingrederijen (Association of Salted-Herring Boat Owners) was founded in 1829 to create a cartel of the supply of herring and set prices. The association found favor in the higher levels of government; it was even decided that the subsidy of fl 500 per herring boat setting sail would be paid only to members of the association.[33] A central committee was made responsible for setting the market price of herring, a step that resulted in regular surpluses of unsold herring at the end of the fishing season. For this reason, the market prices probably stabilized, although all the while Dutch herring was losing export market share due to its high price.[34]

Despite these measures the decline in the herring fishing sector was not brought to a halt. Pons has demonstrated that after 1820 fishing became unprofitable for most boat owners; they continued only because they had invested most of their capital in their herring boats. Profits were made in years of exceptionally high catches or prices, but these paled in significance against the losses of the other years. Many owners were able to survive only by developing sidelines associated with herring fishing: selling nets, barrels, and rope to other boat owners; trading in herring; or fishing for cod during the winter season. Not all the boat owners were pleased with efforts of the Vereeniging der Zoutharingrederijen: because of its monopoly of the trade in herring, they lost the extra profits that could be made in exporting the herring abroad. In the 1830s the sector was able to achieve some stability and even growth, but the period from 1843 into the 1850s (when the industry was liberalized) was witness to a new decline in the number of herring boats putting to sea (figure 4.1).

The developments in the herring fishing sector provide a good example of how entrepreneurs went about protecting their direct economic interests (attracting subsidies, setting up cartels) within the institutional framework of the sector, without being able to solve the problems of the industry. The entanglement of interests in which the government, which followed the advice of the College van de Groote Visscherij, and the sector found themselves resulted in a continuation of the choices already made in the seventeenth century, ultimately resulting in protective measures and the establishment of a cartel, as well as the inability to find new, radical strategies to answer the sector's problems. To revitalize the sector, a transition to a completely different strategy was required: the struggle for control over the small and relatively shrinking market for high-quality herring had in the long run to be abandoned. The regulation of the sector, which led to the preservation of high cost levels, had to be dismantled and competition from outside—for example, from the bomschepen—admitted. The College van de Groote Visscherij, which represented the established interests of the sector, vigorously opposed such measures. In this it was able to make good use of the activist policies of Willem I, who was extremely sensitive to pleas for support and expected great results from it. In this case the policy clearly failed; only the complete liberalization of the herring fishing sector, in the mid-1850s, could bring the decline to a halt.

INDUSTRIAL DEVELOPMENT

Over the past decades, the late and slow industrialization of the Netherlands has been a topic of intense debate among economic historians. Essentially that debate dates back to a discussion during the 1840s over the causes of the failure of Willem I's economic policies. One of the best known contributions was published by E. J. Potgieter, a supporter of the reform politics of Willem I, who blamed the sluggish mentality of the Dutch for their failure, introducing the tragic character of Jan Salie in support of his claims.[35] Willem's liberal critics, on the other hand, pointed to the deleterious effects that protectionistic policies had had on trade and industry; but they, too, were tempted to describe the economic situation of the forties in somber terms.[36] This literature, the majority of which was written during the economic downturn of the 1840s, was a century later, in the 1950s and 1960s, a basis for debate among historians about the causes of the failure of the Dutch economy in the nineteenth century.[37] The literature cited in the debate was stripped of the political and economic context of the period in which it had arisen and was used to discuss *the* causes of the slow rate of industrialization in the Netherlands in this period. In this way Potgieter's negative judgment on the economic mentality of the day was used to prove that the supposed slow rate of industrialization was in particular caused by entrepreneurial failure.[38]

More recently, much attention has been paid to the economic factors that held back industrialization: for example, the high costs of basic inputs such as coal, and the high wages paid in the western provinces. Because the participants in the debate did not have solid statistical evidence on which to base their positions, the discussion was rather unfocused. One of the standard assumptions in this debate, until recently, was that industrialization in the first half of the nineteenth century had stagnated. It was only as late as the 1980s that several historians (e.g., R. Griffiths and J.M.M. de Meere) attempted to establish what had happened in the most important sectors of the economy between 1820 and 1850. Both arrived at the conclusion that this period had been always judged too negatively; they found that important changes had taken place across a broad cross section of Dutch industry.[39]

Our research has led to similar conclusions, at least as far as the period 1815–40 is concerned. Figure 4.2 illustrates growth in industrial production together with developments in real wages. Over the long term these series move in tandem (as has already been shown for Holland from 1764 to 1820): falling real wages and declining industrial production to approximately 1815; a modest improvement in the 1820s and 1830s; no clear trend between 1840 and 1860; and enormous increases in industrial production and real wages between 1860 and 1900. The relation between the two appears to be explained by the fact that developments in industrial production seem to be determined by domestic markets, which are in turn dependent on real wages.[40]

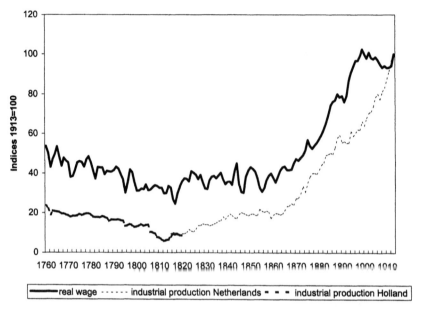

FIGURE 4.2. Industrial production in the province of Holland (1764–1820) linked to industrial production in the Netherlands (1807–1913) (lower line) and real wages in the western Netherlands (upper line) (indices: 1913 = 100). Data on industrial output in Holland before 1820, see figure 2.2; other data from database national accounts.

These data indicate a period of conspicuous economic industrial growth between 1815 and 1840. Upon closer analysis, two subperiods can be distinguished. The twenties were characterized by recovery from the deep depression in which industry found itself during the Batavian-French period. An increase in real wages after 1817 played an important role in that recovery. Characteristically, those sectors of the economy that were focused on the domestic market performed relatively well: the building industry and the clothing industry, for example, grew in this period but stagnated again from 1830 onward (see table 4.2). Growth in "mining" was dominated by an expansion of peat cutting, particularly in the eastern Netherlands, which was again driven by domestic demand. The food processing industry, which during the first half of the nineteenth century accounted for 60 percent of industrial production, enjoyed growth that could not be equaled in subsequent decades. The strong growth in the public utilities sector can be ascribed entirely to the founding of several of the first gas works in the 1820s.[41] In the textile industry, too, rapid expansion was based on domestic demand; this growth is remarkable considering that competition from the southern Netherlands and Britain was particularly fierce. However, the impression remains that this competition (and possibly the prosperity enjoyed by agriculture) was responsible for the rapid decline in home spinning in the countryside, an activity that had provided work for many (particularly women) during the French occupation. The Dutch textile industry was already to a large degree dependent on the import of thread, and this dependence increased further as a result of competition from British (and later Belgian) manufacturers.[42]

The importance of the development of a machine manufacturing industry in the 1820s for long-term industrial growth cannot be ignored. The metal sector had never blossomed in the Netherlands, in particular because one of the raw materials required, iron ore, was not directly available. A notable exception were several smelters in the Achterhoek (in the province of Gelderland), where iron was obtained from *oer,* a layer of soil containing iron oxide. Because of continually growing demand for articles made of iron, produced primarily for the domestic consumer and agricultural markets, several firms were able to grow into mechanized metalworking factories, which increasingly began to expand into machinery manufacturing. As a result they became more and more dependent on imported iron and steel, particularly as the supplies of oer became exhausted and the costs of transporting it from farther afield rose.[43]

This development of the iron-processing industry of the eastern Netherlands into a iron-working industry paralleled that of the engineering industry in Holland in the twenties and thirties. The most important factories there were by-products of the modernization of the shipbuilding industry that began in the 1820s. The Nederlandsche Stoomboot Maatschappij (Netherlands Steamship Company) was founded in Rotterdam in 1822, hiring G. M. Roentgen, a naval officer, as its technical expert. Since Cockerill, the entrepreneur who dominated the metal industry of the southern Netherlands, did not possess the know-how to build steamships, he drew up a contract with Roentgen in which the foundations for a cartel were laid for this new market. When it became clear, however, that Willem I intended to give Cockerill the monopoly in steamship building, many shipyard owners feared that they would lose their independence. Roentgen was approached to set up his own engineering works and shipyard, and he founded Fijenoord Company in 1825.[44]

These developments were being followed closely from Amsterdam. There, too, a group of businessmen had decided to found a steamship company, the Amsterdamsche Stoomboot Maatschappij (Amsterdam Steamship Company); and they too were afraid of becoming victims of a cartel, this time between Cockerill and Roentgen. Paul van Vlissingen, the driving force behind the Amsterdamsche Stoomboot Maatschappij, took the initiative and in 1827 set up his own metalworking firm and shipyard, initially to maintain steamships bought elsewhere, but he quickly started building ships himself.

Due to strong competition from the kingdom's southern provinces, both companies remained relatively small until 1830: Van Vlissengen's works employed eighty to one hundred people; Fijenoord probably had two to three times as many in its employ, given its total wage bill in 1830 was fl 75,000.[45]

Both firms had to import their iron, steel, copper, and coal from outside the country, which due to high transport costs and high import tariffs (to protect the Belgian iron industry) placed them at a great disadvantage. After 1830, however, this changed: several petitions by Roentgen and Van Vlissingen were sufficient to have the import tariffs adjusted to their advantage. Roentgen, moreover, who in addition to his business activities was an official adviser to the king on industrial matters, was able to obtain financial support from the government (as Cockerill had done before 1830).

From the very beginning, the machine works developed a broad range of products: steamships, and steam engines for just about any purpose, including, for example, steam-driven pumps for the Haarlemmermeer, sugar-processing machines for Java, products from cast iron, and machines for gas works.[46] The manufacture of steam engines is relatively easy to research because all steam engines had to be registered under the Hinderwet, and registration included details regarding the manufacturer. Table 4.3, which illustrates the development of this new industrial activity, was compiled from these registers. Up until 1830, nearly all the twenty-two machines installed had been made outside the Netherlands: eleven in Belgium, five in Great Britain, one in Germany, and four in countries unknown; only one had been manufactured in the Netherlands. This changed in the course of the 1830s: in the second half of the decade, the market share of Dutch manufacturers increased to more than 50 percent, where it remained. The Dutch manufacturers concentrated particularly on the market for smaller machines; measured in terms of the output (power) of the machines,

TABLE 4.3.
Steam Engines Installed in the Netherlands (made in the Netherlands or Elsewhere), 1816/25–1846/50.

	Dutch Machines			All Machines			Dutch Share	
	Number	Total Horse-power	Average Horse-power	Number	Total Horse-power	Average Horse-power	Machines	Horse-power
1816/25	0	0	0	6	38	6.3	0.0%	0.0%
1826/30	1	6	6.0	16	212	13.7	6.3%	2.8%
1831/35	8	89	11.1	29	403	15.0	27.6%	22.1%
1836/40	28	313	11.2	55	667	13.1	50.9%	46.9%
1841/45	34	420	12.4	69	1063	18.4	49.2%	39.5%
1846/50	63	533	8.5	120	1837	22.9	52.5%	29.0%

Source: Jansen, *Industriële ontwikkeling,* 303.

their market share was much less than 50 percent. The large machines came mostly from foreign manufacturers. In terms of the number of machines delivered, Belgium remained the most important foreign supplier, although the really large steam engines came from Great Britain.

The pattern of industrial growth changed dramatically in the thirties. The broad development characterized by expansion in almost all branches of the economy, based on the recovery and expansion of the domestic market, made way for growth in the industries associated with the growing trade with Java. Textiles, metal goods, and shipbuilding were the most dynamic, not counting the still quite small sector of public utilities (see table 4.2). The increase in real wages and the expansion of the domestic market came to a halt in the thirties, partly due to the reintroduction of and increase in various duties meant to help finance the enormous rise in military expenditure.[47]

The developments in cotton manufacturing, particularly in Twente, are perhaps the best-known example of the success of Willem I's experiment. A rather extensive textile industry already existed in this part of the country, although it provided almost exclusively for the domestic market. In the twenties, Flemish manufacturers had captured a significant portion of the markets in the East Indies, well supported in this by the NHM and several protectionist measures that made English imports more expensive. Subsidies from the Fund for Industry were also used to support them. It was in the interests of the NHM to promote the export of calico to the East Indies because such cargoes reduced the cost of sailing to the Indies—otherwise ships would have to sail carrying ballast—and calico was the most popular medium of exchange. To be able to capture an even greater market share on Java, it was essential to compete with British traders, who supplied cheap British cotton textiles.[48]

Belgian seccession in 1830 necessitated a sudden revision of these trade flows. Immediately following 1830, the British recaptured the Javanese market, weakening the NHM's position (figure 4.3). In August 1831, Johannes van den Bosch, the initiator of the Cultivation System, suggested that British and Belgian entrepreneurs be encouraged to set up businesses in the towns and cities of Holland, where a large proportion of the population was unemployed and stricken by poverty. Almost immediately several textile manufacturers, among them the confidential adviser of the NHM in the south, Thomas Wilson, announced their willingness to cooperate. At around the same time an Englishman, Thomas Ainsworth, after a visit to Twente, developed a plan to modernize the weaving industry of the region. Despite the NHM's preference for his plan, which appeared to be economically attractive, it could not ignore Wilson's advances in Holland, as he enjoyed the patronage of Willem I. Finally, it decided to carry out both plans: cotton textiles were to be woven in Twente, while dyeing and printing of cotton were to be done in Haarlem and Leiden. Three firms from the south, Wilson, De Heyer, and Prévinaire, relocated to Holland, and the bleaching works of De Maere relocated from the southern

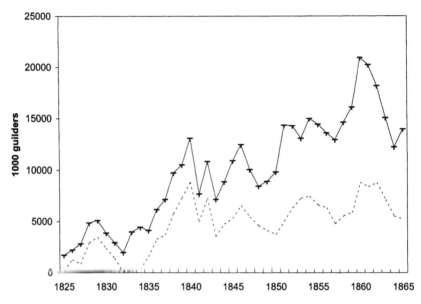

FIGURE 4.3. Imports of cotton goods on Java, total and from the Netherlands, 1825–65 (in thousands of guilders). Data from De Bruyn Kops, *Statistiek.*

Netherlands to Twente. Twente, which could already boast fairly important cotton textile and linen industries, was also chosen for political motives. Catholic North Brabant, with its extensive cottage industries, was politically not completely trusted in view of the escalating conflict with its southern neighbor, Belgium. In addition, there were fears that cotton goods would be smuggled into this province from neighboring Flanders.[49]

For a number of reasons, however, Twente was unable to compete with Gent: production techniques in Twente were obsolete, there was little experience in weaving calico for the Javanese market, and there was insufficient business acumen to make a successful start of things. By attracting Belgian and British businessmen and technicians, and by paying great attention to training on the spot—such as immediately setting up weaving schools—the NHM was able to solve these problems one by one. Entrepreneurs and laborers alike in Twente reacted enthusiastically to the new opportunities; newly introduced weaving techniques (particularly the flying shuttle) became common property, and businessmen rushed to invest large amounts of their capital in this new, extremely profitable activity, resulting in a rapid increase in production. In the early years costs in Twente were considerably higher than in Flanders, so that the NHM had to pay extra subsidies. However, costs declined rapidly, allowing subsidies to be reduced. Under the secret contracts concluded between the state and the NHM about this issue, the NHM was able to claim the subsidies to textiles back from the government, something that in view of tense trade relations with Great Britain had to be kept secret (there was already strong protest in England about the high degree of "open" protection enjoyed by Dutch exporters to Java).[50]

The success of these policies quickly led to the NHM being confronted with the opposite problem. With social considerations in mind, the executive of the NHM, which was in particular inspired by the ideas of its secretary, De Clercq, attempted to spread the advantages of this policy throughout the country, at the regional level, and to many small businesses. As a result, applications for orders from "philanthropic enterprises" (set up by local dignitaries of a town to combat poverty there) were usually met completely, as were those of small factories, whereas large entrepreneurs such as Blijdenstein, Salomonson, and Hofkes received only a modest portion of their application.[51] The least efficient entrepreneurs were rewarded, while the most efficient were kept small. De Clercq intended in this way to oppose the concentration of the textile industry in large factories; he feared the poverty and social injustice that he expected would be a direct result. However, the buoyant market for textiles produced a new draft of entrepreneurs, who learned how to reduce costs below those of the NHM's official tenders. The Salomonson brothers are a case in point. To ensure their expansion met the narrow limits laid down by the NHM, they subcontracted the work out to numerous small figurehead contractors, which because of their size were eligible for new contracts. The Salomonsons, moreover, developed plans to increase the spread of the weaving industry to other regions, in view of the shortage of weavers in Twente in the second half of the thirties. By recruiting laborers in other regions—such as the towns of Zeeland—they hoped to be awarded more work by the NHM. In this manner the weaving industry also expanded in regional terms in the 1830s; in 1842, for example, the NHM placed 29 percent of its orders in Zeeland and 12 percent in North Holland.[52]

Industries for the final processing of the product, such as the bleaching of calico and dyeing and printing of other cottons, became concentrated in Haarlem and Leiden. They boomed as a result of the generous orders of the NHM, supplemented by soft loans from the Fund for Industry. Attempts to mechanize the weaving industry in Haarlem and Leiden failed, however: the factories simply could not produce goods cheaper than cottage weavers in Twente, despite the most modern power-driven looms they had at their disposal.[53] Moreover, little employment was created in this more capital-intensive branch of the industry. Also, the Belgian owners took a part of their trained workforce with them; local laborers from Holland were considered suitable only for unskilled jobs.

Attempts by the NHM to establish spinning in the Netherlands were ultimately unsuccessful probably because of the lack of technical expertise. It was extremely difficult to match the quality of English yarns, and this branch of the cotton textile industry enjoyed little protection. This aspect of its industrial policy was abandoned by the NHM around 1840. In all, though, the company's textile policy was very successful: the market share of Dutch textiles on the Javanese market rose from 7.4 percent in 1834 to nearly 70 percent in 1839–40, and employment in the sector had, by the estimates of contemporaries, risen by fourteen thousand full-time jobs.[54]

The revival of the shipbuilding industry in the twenties and thirties was also in large part dependent on NHM policy. In 1823 the government introduced a subsidy into the industry that in effect amounted to 10 percent of the costs incurred in constructing a ship. According to Mansvelt, by the end of 1829 approximately fl 1.7 million in subsidies had been paid out.[55] In addition, NHM cargoes could only be carried by ships built in the Netherlands; in view of the expansion of the NHM's activities after 1830, this feature was by far the most important support for Dutch shipbuilders. Activities in the industry, which in the twenties had already received a boost, increased even further in the course of the following decade, reaching their absolute peak in 1840. Unfortunately, however, the support of the NHM did not stimulate increases in efficiency in the shipbuilding and shipping industries; as a result, modernization of the shipping sector, with few exceptions, such as steamship builders in Amsterdam and Rotterdam, did not take place.

A rapid modernization occurred in the sugar refineries, a sector that changed dramatically through the "industrialization policy" of Willem I and the NHM, and even more so due to the unexpected effect of duties introduced in 1819. Sugar refining was a traditional processing industry that was closely associated with international trade and had been the subject of government attention from the eighteenth century on. To combat growing international competition, transit tariffs were increased substantially (in 1771) and export subsidies introduced (in 1776). However, under the French regime the industry came almost to a standstill. After 1815 the industry had to face, once more, fierce international competition, including that from the southern provinces (Antwerp). Following pressure from the south a heavy duty was introduced in 1819 on imports of raw sugar to tax the use of this luxury good; a similar duty was introduced for coffee. Simultaneously, exporters of refined sugar received a rebate on the tax they had paid on the imported raw sugar that was related to the assumed technical efficiency of the refining process (e.g., how many kilos of refined sugar could be derived from a metric ton of raw sugar). The unintended effect of these changes was that entrepreneurs who were able to increase their efficiency could profit from the system: the rebate they received on exporting their product could be larger than the sums they paid when importing the raw sugar. As a result, opposition to this "southern" duty melted like snow on a summer's day; while duty on coffee was abolished in 1822, that on sugar remained because traders in Amsterdam had learned how to use it to their profit.[56]

Toward the end of the twenties, sugar refiners in Amsterdam again faced growing competition from Antwerp, where the NHM sold a large proportion of the sugar it imported from the East and West Indies. In 1828, the Amsterdam Chamber of Commerce approached the king with a request for an increase in the implicit "export subsidy" for refined sugar—to be paid by the Fund for Industry—with the argument that nearly all support for industry found its way to the southern provinces. The king granted this request in 1829, by which the duties of 1818 clearly acquired the character of an export subsidy.[57] It is likely that this favorable arrangement by Willem I played a role in stimulating the sugar refiner J. H. Rupe to completely modernize his factory. He introduced new, steam-powered techniques that produced important increases in refining yields from raw sugar—and thus a much higher rebate on exports. His example was followed quickly by other entrepreneurs (C. de Bruyn, Beuker, and Hulshoff), and by the midthirties the sector was dominated by several large steampowered refineries. The introduction of steam engines and the vacuum pan resulted in an enormous increase in production. The strong growth in the NHM's sugar imports, which arose from the Cultivation System in the East Indies, became dependent for its sales on a handful of businessmen who annually bought hundreds of thousands of guilders' worth of raw sugar—in a few cases more than a million guilders—on credit provided under customary terms of business. This was to lead to a further entanglement of interests between the NHM and the sugar refiners during the economic crisis of 1842.[58]

The large sugar refineries in Amsterdam, employing several hundred laborers, were in the first half of the nineteenth century among the first modern steam-powered enterprises, along with several machine manufacturers and shipbuilding yards (in particular those of Roentgen and Van Vlissingen), several textile manufacturers in Haarlem and Leiden (which were also to a large degree dependent on the NHM), a few spinning mills in Twente and Tilburg, and a small number of other factories spread throughout the country (Regout's potteries in Maastricht, for example).

The examples of textiles, shipbuilding, and sugar refining show that the second phase of industrial growth in the thirties was to an important extent dominated by the "colonial complex" that had developed as a result of NHM policies and the introduction of the Cultivation System on Java. This growth was not, however, generally accompanied by changes in the industrial structure and techniques of production used. The introduction of the shuttle in the weaving industry in Twente, one of the few exceptions, was responsible for a marked increase in the productivity of labor in the branch, although this occurred in a traditional cottage industry. Indeed, it was the express aim of the NHM to prevent the rise of large-scale industries: the company and others were afraid that this would proletarianize laborers and create social injustice—as it had in England. This conservative viewpoint was also reflected in the support given to the shipping and shipbuilding industries; specifically, all ship owners (not only the biggest and the most efficient) were meant to profit from the policy. The protection these businesses enjoyed also meant that there was less incentive to adapt new and better production techniques to combat international competition. The problems associated with this only became apparent after 1840.

The stagnation that held the economy in its grip after 1840 deserves some attention here, too—in anticipation of the discussion in chapter 6—because it clearly illustrates the limitations of the surge of growth experienced in the 1830s. The most important reason for the stagnation was to be found on Java: the extremely strong growth in exports of cash crops came to an abrupt end around 1840. The economic crisis on Java led to a shrinking demand for cotton goods. As a consequence of diminishing exports, demand for cargo space fell, leading to a great deal of overcapacity in shipping and, ultimately, shipbuilding.[59] The situation on Java after 1840 triggered a crisis in the "colonial complex." After 1840 the Dutch government gradually began to withdraw its protection from these sectors, so that increasingly they were confronted with international competition. Given the only modest modernization, partly due to NHM policy, that had been carried out in these sectors, this new course led to long-term stagnation in production in those branches of industry involved (particularly textiles and shipbuilding). The fundamental cause of the industrial stagnation that occurred after 1840 was, however, that industrial growth did not bring with it a commensurate expansion in consumer purchasing power; growth did not lead to a significant increase in the productivity of labor, which would have made wage increases possible and ultimately led to an increase in demand for industrial products. This "feedback" mechanism—to a certain extent the key of "modern economic growth" (see chapter 8)—did not begin to develop until the sixties. The expansion of the thirties did not, therefore, occur in sectors that served the domestic market but, as has been amply described, was concentrated in branches that focused on Java, so that the moment this market collapsed, the "natural limits" of this surge in growth were reached.

CASE STUDY: THE BLOCKED MODERNIZATION OF THE FOOD INDUSTRY

One of the most conspicuous characteristics of the slow pace of industrial modernization during Willem I's experiment was the retarded rate at which the steam engine was introduced.[60] The reasons for this are complex and will be discussed in detail in chapters to come: high coal prices; small-scale engineering that was still gaining experience in building steam engines (which as a result were expensive in the Netherlands); and the virtual lack of industrial sectors in which steam power was indispensable, such as coal mines and iron industry.[61] However, this economic view of the gradual introduction of the steam engine is only part of the story. To illustrate this, the spread of steam engines is described in an industry that measured in terms of value added was the largest in the Netherlands, that is, flour milling and bread making.

To be able to levy duty on flour, yet prevent any attempt at evading it and still leave international trade open, a system of checks and regulations had been created within the Republic that governed almost all activities within the sector. In Gogel's taxation system, duty on milled goods also played a central role, and the system of rules maintained in Holland was introduced throughout the country. The Excise Acts of 1821 (and 1833) continued this policy of taxation, despite fierce protests that arose from time to time in the south. According to this system, international trade in grain was completely exempt from duty—apart from minor import and export duties—but trade in flour and bread was strictly regulated and as a result made just about impossible. Flour millers were not permitted to trade in flour or grain: they were obliged to wait until clients approached them with an order, and they were not allowed to bake bread. Moreover, they had to process separately each grain lot offered—lot for lot—each with its accompanying duty documents, which continually held up milling. Requests to build a new mill required government approval, which was far from easy to get because each new mill made it potentially easier to evade paying duty. The millers' most important clients were, of course, bakers, who were also highly regulated in their activities. Local authorities set the price for rye and wheat bread, originally to protect the public, but in the course of the seventeenth century the system to regulate the price of bread evolved into an instrument for assuring bakers' income.[62]

In addition to national duties payable on flour, which but for a few short "interruptions" (1810–13, 1816–21, and 1829–33) were in force up to 1855, all cities introduced their own duties on flour, which were levied over and above the national duties. These local duties made it even more complicated to work in the sector: to prevent cheaper flour or bread from being brought in from the countryside, the local duties were levied at the city boundaries, and trade was strictly regulated. In effect, local bakers and millers operated in a virtually completely protected market in which prices were set by the local authorities.

In addition, both millers and bakers in various towns and cities had a long tradition of organization. Bakers' and millers' guilds could be found in nearly all large towns, and the system of duties and its regulations handed them the opportunity and means with which to control the market. Guild rules, which, for example, compelled the inhabitants of a particular area to mill their grain at a particular mill, had before 1795 limited competition even further.

As a consequence of this institutional structure, the production of flour and bread in the province of Holland was inefficient. The price of rye bread was considerably higher than elsewhere in the Netherlands and surrounding countries. The high duty levied on milling was partly to blame for this large price difference, but it was not the only cause: the costs incurred (and incomes earned) by bakers and millers were also much higher in Holland and Utrecht than elsewhere (table 4.4). For example, the cost of producing 100 kilograms of rye bread ranged from fl 1.48 in Kampen to fl 3.96 in Utrecht.

In view of the high cost levels of this sector, it is reasonable to assume that the profits to be made by not complying with its rigid structure were relatively great. However, as long as duties were levied directly at the mill, this was virtually impossible, and the complex regulations well nigh precluded any rationalization of the industry. Toward the end of the twenties, during a brief period

TABLE 4.4.
Regional Differences in Bakers' Wages, Milling Charges, and Local Taxes under the Assize Regulations (Dutch guilders per hectoliter of grain processed; average values of assize tables retrieved).

	Kampen 1826	Nijmegen 1831	Coevorden 1841	Helmond 1845	Leiden 1826	Utrecht 1822
Per hectoliter rye						
Milling wage	0.28	0.30	0.30	0.55	0.50	0.61
Fuel, oil	0.10	0.35	0.14	0.02	0.45	0.55
Bakers' wages	0.87	0.80	0.60	0.80	2.52	2.00
Salt, yeast	0.15	0.54	—	—	0.13	0.56
Production costs	1.40	1.99	1.04	1.37	3.60	3.72
Local excise	0.10	0.50	0.75	0.58	0.90	0.12
National excise	0.40	0.00	0.60	0.60	0.40	0.40
Conversion factor[a]	94.5	93.8	91.7	92.5	98.3	94.0
Per 100 kilo bread						
Production costs	1.48	2.12	1.13	1.48	3.66	3.96
Plus: local excise	1.59	2.66	1.95	2.11	4.58	4.09
Plus: national excise	2.01	2.66	2.61	2.76	4.99	4.51

Sources: Utrecht: GA Utrecht, Stadsarchief IV, 671, 673, 678; Groningen: GA Groningen, Nieuw Archief der Gemeente Groningen, 444 blauw; Leiden and Kampen: ARA, Archief Binnenlandse Zaken, Binnenlands Bestuur B, 1814–1831, 1366; Nijmegen: GA Nijmegen, Nieuw Archief, EA 738; Coevorden: RA Drenthe, Archief Burgelijk Bestuur Coevorden, 701 IV; Amsterdam: cited in GA Leiden, Nieuw Archief der Gemeente Leiden 1816–1851, 2105; Harkx, *Helmondse textielnijverheid,* 227.

[a] kilos of bread made out of one hectoliter of rye.

when the duty was abolished, a few attempts were made in Amsterdam to rationalize some aspects of the sector. To be able to understand the reasons for their failure, it is necessary to know more about the situation in Amsterdam at that time.

The millers' guild, which had been officially disbanded in 1805, was replaced by an agreement "between mill owners and millers in Amsterdam . . . for the purposes of preventing malpractice and to reduce competition among millers to fair proportions."[63] Under the "agreement," whose texts from 1817, 1833, and 1852 have been preserved, the milling wage was centrally fixed and a receiver was appointed to collect the fee and to prevent evasion of payment. A large proportion of the fee—in 1817, as much as 20.5 cents of the 70.5 cents charged per bag of wheat, and even more in 1833 and 1852—was not paid to the miller for his work but deposited in a central fund that was regularly distributed (per mill) among members. This practice implied a considerable evening out of income among millers. It is estimated that in 1843 (for which records are available) each miller received fl 1,448 from the central fund, so that the income of the miller who had milled the least was topped up from fl 431 (before distribution from the fund) to fl 1,713 (after distribution). Without the redistribution, the income of the richest miller would have been thirteenfold that of the poorest; after redistribution the difference was less than threefold.[64]

The redistribution of milling fees reduced to a large extent the incentive of millers to expand their businesses; the marginal profit remained, after all, relatively small. Moreover, it gave the millers' organization a powerful instrument—well-filled coffers—with which to pursue its interests. The cartel agreements were also imbued with elements taken from the old guild regulations. For example, articles were included that specified criteria apprentices had to meet, and which laid down details about the four commissioners that had to be chosen, who continued to meet in the guild building. If a mill was unworkable as a result of a fire or "common or uncommon repairs," owners of nearby mills were obliged "to mill for no recompense" for the unserviceable mill. In this way the income of millers was assured even in times of disaster.[65] In short, milling in Amsterdam was governed by a powerful cartel that in almost every aspect was nothing more than a continuation of the grain millers' guild that had been abolished in 1805. The cartel had various ways of ensuring the compliance of millers and was powerful enough to be able to redistribute incomes among members of the milling trade.

In 1828, at a time when national duties on milling were not levied (to placate the southern provinces), the first steam-powered mill was established. The protest was deafening. The millers of wind-powered mills submitted a petition predicting "only ruin" in the sector. Residents pointed out the dangers of the engine exploding, the inconvenience of clouds of steam, soot, unpleasant odors, and noise, and predicted an increase in rats and other vermin. The city authorities backed the residents in their opinions, and even the provincial authorities advised against it. King Willem I, however, allowed the mill to be built, although the site was not the one originally chosen by its founder, Lodewijk Cantillon. Cantillon came from Hasselt (Limburg), where he had already had experience with steam-powered grain mills.[66] He began his activities in Amsterdam by setting his milling fee considerably lower than that of the milling cartel. Nevertheless, millers in Amsterdam did not hesitate to follow his example, and they too lowered their milling fee accordingly.[67]

Thereafter Cantillon's mill faded into the background of daily events. Various sources report that in 1830 the milling fee was raised to levels that were common before 1828, which indicates that the cartel won the day.[68] In 1833, by no means a coincidence the year that milling duties were reintroduced, a new agreement was reached between mill owners that reinstated the situation as it was before 1828. Between 1838 and 1843, history more or less repeated itself in this respect: the establishment of a second steam-powered mill, by R. F. Hendriks and Company, was followed by the introduction of competitive milling fees, but by 1843 fees were back to levels similar to those of 1838.[69] Steam-powered mills had a hard time until 1855. Long, idle periods appear to have been normal; in 1841, for example, both mills were idle, and in 1843 only one of the three mills (only one more had been established since 1833) was working.[70] The upswing in international trade in grain and flour in Amsterdam in 1844 (partly due to the potato blight in this period) brought better times for several years, but the real breakthrough came only after 1855.

The fundamental problem for Cantillon and Hendriks was that they could produce flour cheaply only at rather high production volumes; only then was steam power cheaper than wind power.[71] But they were not successful in acquiring a sufficient market share, hence their idle mills. To win a sufficient share the steam-powered mill had to cut its fees below those of the cartel, but each time—in 1828 and in 1838—the cartel followed the steam mills' example. In fact, steam-powered mills had to contend with a "broken" demand curve common to oligopolies: price cuts did not lead to a significant increase in demand because competitors did the same. Theory predicts that entrepreneurs will not usually lower their prices because the resulting returns are too low. In such cases it is difficult for entrepreneurs to increase their market share.

Another factor contributing to this situation was the inelasticity of demand for flour. Local consumption of rye and wheat was almost entirely responsible for demand. The elasticity of demand for this staple was low, and in Amsterdam, as a result of falling standards of living, demand even stagnated. Milling fees made up a relatively small proportion of the total cost of bread—in 1826 as little as 4 percent of the price of wheat bread and 6 percent of that of rye bread—so that even halving milling fees would have had little effect on the price of bread, in the event that the reduction was passed on to consumers anyway.[72] Clearly, the opportunities for increasing market share by cutting milling fees were small.

As we have said, millers' most important customers were bakers. The price of bread was until 1854 fixed by the local government. An individual baker could, as a "free rider," profit from lower milling fees provided the lower fee was not meant for all bakers and therefore was not (in the long run) incorporated into the official price. Bakers did, therefore, try to avoid the cartel's prices by buying flour in the countryside.[73] For most bakers, however, the advantages of a general lowering of milling fees were limited because the official price would be adjusted accordingly, and the demand for bread was inelastic. Nor would they profit from a far-reaching restructuring of the branch by introducing the steam engine. This became clear in 1830, when attempts by the firm Riou, Barthe and Company—again an outsider (Belgian)—to establish a steam-powered bakery failed, once more with opposition from Amsterdam's bakers.[74] Without the support of the bakers, who generated almost the entire demand for flour, a steam-powered mill had little future, so that the market remained more or less closed but for the isolated activities of "free riders."

Finally, the law governing the levying of duties on milled produce forbade millers to trade in grain and flour and to bake bread, which reduced any motivation on their part to increase sales or to avoid the blockade of the Amsterdam bakers. For the same reasons, production for export, an option mentioned in various applications to establish steam-powered mills, was hindered. In summary, due to government regulations, steam-powered mills were severely restricted in their opportunities and opposed at every turn by other millers and bakers. It was virtually impossible for them to capture a reasonable market share; all they could actually do was hope for long periods of no wind or branch into an activity that did not have a cartel, such as husking rice.

Steam power made its breakthrough in flour milling and bread making after 1855, when—and all authors (e.g., J. A. de Jonge, H. Lintsen) agree that this was the most important reason—milling duties were abolished and all artificial limitations on trade in flour and bread were removed.[75] The Maatschappij der Meel- en Broodfabrieken (MBF), founded in 1855 by the philanthropist S. Saphati, was able to radically overturn the rigid market structure by introducing mechanized production of flour and bread and trading in grain and flour, thus undermining the position of the millers' and bakers' cartels. In 1856 the MBF sold wheat bread at 30 percent below the price set by the bakers.[76] The flour cartel suffered a similar fate: the agreement of 1852 appears to have been the last.

The MBF was an immediate success, perhaps not so much due to the radical cost reductions achieved with new techniques but especially because it broke the power of the local cartels, which had kept the price of bread artificially high. Success brought imitation: in less than ten years the number of flour and bread factories in Amsterdam increased to four. In the sixties, in most of the large towns of Holland, where bread prices had been the highest in the country, bread factories were established.[77] In addition to the premium on breaking the bakers' cartel, the large markets these town represented would have also played a role in their establishment. The number of independent bakers in Amsterdam, however, fell from 514 in 1859 to 400 in 1865. Millers met a similar fate: their numbers fell from 27 in 1843 to 5 in 1867.[78]

Why did the millers and bakers of Amsterdam themselves not modernize their firms by introducing steam engines? Perhaps it had something to do with the fact that in the 1830s, and again in 1856, it was outsiders who displayed initiative. Perhaps the millers and bakers lacked knowledge about the new technical possibilities, or, again, perhaps they did not have sufficient capital to invest in the technology. One could also see it as the outcome of a rational choice: so long as all bakers and millers refused to modernize (and kept outsiders at bay), their relative socioeconomic position would remain unaffected. Once a few of them modernized—and were forced as a result to try to increase their market share at the expense of the others—competition would increase, to the probable detriment of the majority of bakers and millers, as demonstrated after 1855, when many were forced out of business. Through the close organization of the cartel, deviant behavior was suppressed. As the millers' agreement stated, the aim was "to transform jealous behavior into fair competition." Before 1800 the guilds had attempted to enforce the same "traditional" form of competition on a much larger scale and across more sectors. The aim of these guilds, in view of the limited size of the market, was to create conditions that ensured a reasonable income for the trade, one commensurate with their social position. The redistribution of income of millers through their central fund is a clear example.

The specific form of taxation on milling (i.e., the levying of duty at the mill) and the closely knit organization of bakers and particularly millers in Holland prevented modernization of this sector for a long time. The price of bread, as a result, was considerably higher than elsewhere, contributing to the higher cost of living in the western Netherlands. Only after 1855, with the abolition of *broodzetting* and milling duties, was this rigid institutional structure broken down.

THE SERVICES SECTOR: DIFFERENTIATED DYNAMICS

The tertiary sector is to a certain extent a "rest" category, covering a multitude of diverse activities, ranging from prostitution to banking, from the lowliest clerk to the king. In fact they are all activities in which no material product is produced: to some extent a "service" vanishes the moment it is provided.

Although the sector was not prominent in terms of absolute numbers employed, in view of its strategic importance it is worthwhile to examine developments in international trade and transport first. In the eighteenth century, Amsterdam's role as the central European market for a wide selection of staples was gradually eroded due to increasing direct contacts between countries for which Amsterdam had previously been the go-between, and due to a shrinking of the Amsterdam traders' network (it is likely that trade with the Levant and parts of Africa and Asia even fell in absolute terms). Increasingly, Dutch merchants became primarily dependent on servicing imports and exports for the neighboring German hinterland and the import of a narrow range of tropical produce from the colonies (Surinam and the East Indies). Trade policies were traditionally based on these flows. The Republic had done its best to strengthen the position of Holland's ports by discouraging direct through transport—transit duties on this were higher than those for import and export—and by routing any trade with the colonies directly through the Netherlands (through monopolies such as the VOC and the WIC). The centuries-old blockade of the port of Antwerp was part of the *stapelmarktpolitiek* (e.g., the policies to protect the active trading of Amsterdam and Rotterdam). In this manner the Republic attempted to compensate for the protectionist forces at large in the world economy during the late seventeenth and eighteenth centuries. Continually, the close relationship between economic success—an increasing market share in international trade—and military power was affirmed. As the might of the Republic shrank, and it proved less able to react effectively to international threats to its position, the more the Dutch trading network was threatened. The continual decrease in trade after 1795, when the Netherlands lost almost all its overseas settlements to the British, must be seen against this background.

The military position of the Netherlands at the start of Willem I's reign was very weak: Willem had to depend on British support for reinstating the House of Orange and unification with the southern Netherlands. Most of the Dutch overseas possessions were returned, to strengthen the new kingdom, but in this, too, the new nation was dependent on the mercy of the British. The settlements in South Africa and Ceylon were not returned, for example. Under these new conditions, the blockade of Antwerp's port was, of course, a thing of the past, which meant that Amsterdam and Rotterdam acquired a new and formidable competitor.

When viewing the fierce struggle in trading policies of the early years of Willem I's reign, one should keep in mind the depression that followed the spectacular boom in the grain trade of 1816–17. In the period 1818–22, river transport on the Rhine, for example, fell by about 60 percent and shipping to European ports by nearly 40 percent, although this was compensated to some extent by growth in shipping to ports outside Europe, particularly Asia.[79] Just as was the case for industry, the twenties were in large part characterized by the recovery from this deep depression, with trade along the Rhine and with the East Indies expanding significantly. In both cases, trade policies played an important, if not decisive, role.

Among the important features of the stapelmarktpolitiek were measures aimed at preventing a completed liberalization of river trade along the Rhine.

The Treaty of Vienna in 1815 stipulated that shipping along the Rhine should be completely open *jusque à la mer*, but the Netherlands did not want to relinquish its old powers in this respect. It interpreted the stipulation to mean "as far as the sea" (and not "into the sea"), which meant to the Dutch as far as the spot along the river where the influence of ebb and flood could be first noticed.[80] Moreover, Willem I had been able to negotiate having this provision not apply to the Waal, on the formal grounds that it was a tributary of the Maas and not part of the Rhine. Based on this position, the Dutch maintained that they were entitled to regulate trade and impose levies—transit trade was explicitly forbidden until 1826[81]—and moreover to protect barge transport, which was controlled by Dutch skippers. This rather peculiar interpretation of the Treaty of Vienna led to thirty-five years of trade conflict with the Prussians, the country's eastern neighbors. In determining their position, the Dutch failed to appreciate sufficiently that the international balance of power had changed; the political and economic emancipation of the German hinterland that was taking place in this period made it impossible to maintain the traditional position of power of Dutch ports in this manner.

The first breakthrough occurred around 1830, when Belgian independence launched a new round of competition between ports in Holland and Antwerp. Already in 1831, Willem I had been forced to sign the Treaty of Mainz, which abolished protection for Dutch bargemen and led to a considerable reduction in duties and tolls; otherwise, the issue of *jusque à la mer* remained unsolved. Further, the Netherlands continued to thwart Antwerpen trading via the Rhine, and in general the tensions in trade relations with its neighbors increased rather than decreased.[82]

Dutch trade policies concerning their German neighbors and Rhine shipping continued under Willem I's rule to promote the time-honored stapelmarkt as a noneconomic means of extracting trading advantages for Amsterdam and Rotterdam. Despite this "conservative" policy, the volume of shipping along the Rhine grew explosively: more than 50 percent in the twenties and easily 100 percent in the thirties, when Amsterdam was able to recapture its strong position in the international distribution of sugar, coffee, and other colonial products. In downstream trade, imports of coal and grain, in particular, increased. The loss of their privileges in the Rhine shipping worked to the distinct disadvantage of Dutch skippers, who after 1831 saw their market share fall from what had been approximately 70 percent to around 55 percent in 1840, and further to 40 percent in 1850.[83]

The boom in Rhine shipping was in part due to the blossoming of trade with Java, to a large degree due (likewise) to the protectionist policies of Willem I. Despite dependence on Great Britain, measures were already being introduced in the twenties to ensure that trade on Java would flow through Dutch markets. The introduction of the Cultivation System after 1831 and the de facto award of a trading monopoly to the NHM created a virtually complete "guided economy" that was protected to an important degree from international competition.

The NHM, over which Willem I had great influence, was the linchpin in this network. As a national institution, which up until 1830 also had large interests in Antwerp, one of its aims was to introduce some measure of reform and uniformity into the trade practices of the ports of Holland. An extremely complex system of terms of business had evolved during the seventeenth century that Mansvelt has characterized as follows:

> The conditions of sale in our country were extremely diverse in the various towns and for a wide variety of goods. Tare weights were calculated here in such a manner and there in another manner, in general, always too much, as part of a discount or hidden profit. . . . Pickup times and conditions of payment also varied greatly. Discount for payment in cash was 1.5%. The list of broker's fees was no less attractive. . . . Nor were their fees for the same goods the same in different places. One should view the origins of these conditions as special favors among intermediaries . . . now these intermediaries view these conditions as their "trade secret." For them these were a means of mystifying the true cost price; an attempt by the importer to create higher prices. The source of the higher prices of the towns of Holland, over which there were many complaints, can be explained to some extent by this costly system of distribution. And as for foreigners on the market, they had no choice, or they had to be frightened off by the existing terms of sale, as no uninitiated person knew what the value was of the charge made for services and how much disappeared into the pockets of intermediaries. . . . They (the intermediaries) fought tooth and nail to defend the existing conditions. . . . They were so committed to the old conditions that in Middelburg, for example, merchants no longer sold tea because of attempts there in 1818 to change the conditions.[84]

In his detailed recollections of trade in the city, the Amsterdam trader Van der Hoop cites "the high city taxes, the high rents on houses and warehouses, the high broker's commissions, the high wages, the high trading costs, ... weighing house porters, packers, lighters, bargemen, all of whom charge dearly for their services" as the reason for the decline.[85] He calculated that, for example, warehousing of a shipment of sugar in Amsterdam cost nearly four times as much as in Antwerp.

Certain groups in Amsterdam, however, strongly resisted any attempts to change the situation. Shipping agents, to whom we will limit this discussion, tried to limit access to the commodities trade in Amsterdam; only those who were very experienced in the practices of the exchange were able to survive. Only in 1837 did an anonymous trader publish a comprehensive book describing all the sizes, weights, and customary practices of Amsterdam, comparing them with those of Hamburg (which had already been published): "Continually, some traders attempt systematically to keep their practices a secret . . . In Hamburg these same practices are generally known because of their publication; in many towns and countries these are simple pieces of information; but here, despite so many efforts to simplify things, little has changed. Moreover, it is far from seldom that these practices are implemented at whim, and that broker and buyer are inclined to conspire to cheat the trusting seller, or conversely broker and seller conspire to cheat the buyer."[86]

However, these trading practices were staunchly defended by the brokers' guild, which had survived the abolition of the guilds in 1806 and continued to exist as a broker's office that was run indirectly by the city of Amsterdam. The number of brokers was limited to a certain maximum, and new agents could be appointed only by the municipal executive. Brokers were bound to charge fixed fees, which were laid down in a city bylaw.

In short, trading in Amsterdam was extremely costly, and the community of merchants were able to keep outsiders in order to stick to the old—still relatively profitable—routines. But because of the high costs of trading in Amsterdam, the city's international position was declining. Following the introduction of the metric system in 1820, the Chamber of Commerce attempted to rationalize the system of customary practices in Amsterdam. A group of seventy-five traders, who had experienced firsthand the disadvantages of the complex practices of brokers, brought pressure to bear on the chamber, and in 1823 the latter drew up a proposal for a greatly simplified system of conditions of sale.[87] This proposal met strong opposition not only from the brokers but also from other groups—sugar refiners, shopkeepers, and wholesalers—who believed they would be disadvantaged under the new system.[88] Willem I was, however, of the opinion that by adjusting its tariffs Amsterdam could again become competitive; he wanted these reforms to be carried out as part of NHM policy, which in 1827 took the offensive against these notorious customs and practices.[89] New ceilings were set for the different sales conditions in order to bring those in Amsterdam and Rotterdam to levels that were used in Antwerp. Instead of authorized agents, the NHM used "moonlighters," who were willing to accept lower commissions.[90] This of course led to protest from the brokers' office, which took action to improve the legal status of authorized agents (which resulted in some degree of protection being included in the Commercial Code of 1838). The continual friction between the trading elite of Amsterdam and the NHM came to an end in 1830, coincidentally at the same time as the NHM moved its registered office to the capital, and led to the discontinuation of the offensive against the brokers: "As the efforts of the management to reform terms of business did not result in changes in practice and had only harmed the NHM by creating opposition to its auctions, its board of directors, in anticipation of approval by the king, decided to stop its campaign and return to the messy maze of the traditional terms of sale."[91]

The winds of liberalization that swept the forties were to bring the monopoly of the brokers to an end. In 1843 the city of Rotterdam issued new regulations that led to a significant reduction in the brokerage to be paid on coffee.[92] In 1845 Amsterdam followed suit with its own new regulations for the broking profession in which fees were lowered by as much as one-third. Strong opposition by brokers against these and other measures were to no avail. Moreover, in the long run the Municipalities Act of 1851 brought an end to the privileged position of this group, as was confirmed in 1853 by the Municipal Council of Amsterdam.[93] The specialized brokerage firm, with the exception of real estate agents, was to gradually disappear.

The shipping sector profited as no other from the NHM's policies. Several initiatives had been taken in the 1820s to modernize this industry through the introduction of steamships and the establishment of regular shipping services. The latter comprised to some extent the modernized continuation of barge shipping, which had since the seventeenth century maintained connections with a large number of domestic and foreign destinations. Roentgen's Nederlandsche Stoomboot Maatschappij (NSM) and Paul van Vlissingen's Amsterdamsche Stoomboot Maatschappij (ASM) turned out to be hardly profitable undertakings. Only the regular service with Hamburg was a stable source of income for ASM. The NSM was especially active in steam shipping along the Rhine; the introduction of steam-powered towboats was an almost immediate success. Willem I strongly supported these plans, from which Roentgen in particular profited. Willem I also advocated that the NHM set up a regular packet service with Java, employing either sailing ships or steamships.[94] However, the shareholders' meeting unanimously rejected this plan, effectively bringing to an end NHM support for steam shipping. In Amsterdam in the 1830s there was, with the experiences of ASM in mind, also little enthusiasm to be found for Willem I's grand plans to open up a steamship line for "several prominent European seaports" because steam shipping was not profitable and Amsterdam's harbor was not well situated for steamships, which had to make a large detour over the Zuiderzee to approach it.[95]

The surge in modernization triggered by the introduction of steam power in the twenties waned not just as a result of NHM policy, which from 1824 onward was completely committed to supporting sail-based shipping. The profits of the two steamship companies were extremely modest because steamships were still more expensive than sailing ships, even on relatively short routes. Only for routes on which passengers and high-quality mixed cargoes ("urgent manufactures, small packages and property, and the like," according to a brochure from the Amsterdam Chamber of Commerce) were transported were steamships able to compete with sailing ships.[96] Moreover, because of NHM policies, in the 1830s many more profitable opportunities developed for sail-based shipping as trade with the East Indies grew. The freight charges set by the NHM for shipping bound for Java were so high that the cost of building a ship that was to carry only cargoes for the NHM could be earned back within several years. Initially the high charges had been set to stimulate the availability of domestic ships, but when it became clear the extent of the profits to be earned, even by outsiders, the supply of shipping increased drastically. Even places such as Schiedam, which had no traditional ties with shipping or the shipbuilding industry, was through its political contacts successful in acquiring a share in the excessive profits. Large shipping owners such as B. Kooy and A. van Hoboken, both of whom had a great deal of influence over the management of the NHM, were also able to share in the profits of the latter's policy. As the fleet grew, so freight charges gradually dropped, following a general fall in freight charges on international markets, so that the degree of protection was more or less maintained at its original level. The overcapacity that occurred at the end of the boom, around 1840, did not bring about a drastic fall in freight charges; instead, a waiting list was introduced. This "rationing" of freight over shipping companies only further increased lethargy in the industry: all a ship owner had to do to ensure a healthy profit was to have his ships placed on the waiting list to carry freight.[97]

Marine insurance, in this period by far the most important branch of the insurance industry, also profited handsomely from NHM policies. In this, too, the premiums were very advantageous. In the 1820s these had been generous to encourage new supply. Once this was achieved, however, the premiums were insufficiently adjusted downward, so that marine insurance became a very lucrative business, particularly because the merchant fleet consisted mostly of newly built ships, so that there were relatively few cases of damage and shipwreck. Here, too, the situation led to the introduction of quotas.[98] Without doubt Amsterdam profited most from these new developments. By relocating the NHM's registered office to Amsterdam, Willem I attempted to bridge the differences between it and the principal city of the country, and to seal an alliance between its citizens and the colonial complex.

The two pillars of the revitalization of the international services sector—Rhine shipping and trade and shipping with Java—were responsible for a considerable proportion of the growth of this sector in the 1820s and 1830s. The expansion was not, however, limited to these activities. Improvements in infrastructure resulted in a significant growth in the flow of goods. Transport over inland waterways gained momentum (once the depression of the early twenties had been overcome) in part due to the construction of new waterways. To an important extent, however, they were built primarily to strengthen the position of the central ports: the best example is the Noordhollandsch Kanaal, built to stimulate Amsterdam's trade.[99] The rapid growth of peat transport from the northern and eastern Netherlands to Holland also played a significant role in the renewed growth of transport by inland waterways.

In a similar manner, the construction of a national network of sealed roads encouraged growth in road traffic, although in quantitative terms it was less important than water transport. In several regions where good waterways were lacking (e.g., Twente and the Achterhoek), state roads, which were supplemented by a network of provincial and local roads, played an important role in the continuing expansion of activities on a regional scale.

The third and in the long term most dramatic change in infrastructure was the construction of railways. Directly in the thirties, in part under the management and inspiration of Willem I, a serious beginning was made to introduce railways into the country. In the decades that followed, until the early 1860s, the pace of construction slowed down, however (see the next section).

In contrast with these dynamic branches, the contribution of large parts of the services sector to economic growth was only modest. A large proportion of retail businesses enjoyed only limited turnover, and their profits were very low; comparisons with the "informal" economies of current developing countries come to mind. The domestic distribution system was partly dependent on protection of local markets and trade barriers created by provincial and local taxes. Numerous shops and small businesses in towns were often run for extra income, for example, by married women or widows. Large groups of hawkers and peddlers that are mentioned in taxation documents could barely scrape together an existence from their activities. The turnover of this informal economy was probably in step with the rhythm of the purchasing power of the local population; an increase in real wages due to low food prices in the twenties without a doubt resulted in an increase in this element of the services sector. This is comparable to the modest growth in employment for servants between 1815 and 1830, another sign of increasing purchasing power, this time among the middle and upper classes (between 1799 and 1815 the numbers of servants employed had dropped significantly).[100] Typical of such changes in growth processes is that in the forties growth slowed considerably (domestic trade) or even declined (servants' employment). Therefore, in the services sector, too, there was a shift in the pattern of economic expansion: in the 1820s growth occurred across more or less the entire economy, stimulated by expansion of the domestic market; in the 1830s it shrunk to those sectors most closely associated with the "colonial complex" (see table 4.2).

CASE STUDY: THE CAPITAL MARKET AS A BOTTLENECK?

In much of the literature on the slow pace of industrialization of the Netherlands in the first half of the nineteenth century, a great deal of blame is laid at the feet of the capital market. In this line of thinking, new industries were unable to profit sufficiently from the enormous wealth accumulated by the inhabitants of Holland because they preferred to invest passively, that is, in low-risk bonds issued by the Dutch and foreign governments. In reaching these conclusions historians rely on statements made by citizens of that time, ranging, for example, from the words of the writer Nicolaas Beets to those of economists such as Portielje and Koenen, in whose opinion citizens preferred to earn low interest from government securities rather than investing their wealth in industry. The slow pace in construction of railways, for example, has been attributed to the lack of venture capital.[101]

There are other questions related to the Dutch capital market of the time: What influence did the continual increase in the public debt in the twenties and thirties have on the capital market, and what effect did declining confidence in public finances have on the willingness of investors to put their money actively to work? Did government borrowing "crowd out" investment in private ventures? Or did the growing distrust of public financing under Willem I drive investors to avoid investing in government bonds?

Jonker, in a recent study of the financing of industry in Amsterdam during this period, concluded that there appeared to be no bottlenecks in the supply of capital for industry. Most businessmen were able either through family networks or through a more or less informal capital market to borrow sufficient funds.[102] Of course they had to have a certain level of "credit" to do so: their creditworthiness had to have been established in the past or be apparent from the standing of their family. Moreover, plans for the borrowed funds had to be realistic. Those who did not possess this "credit" found it difficult to borrow money, even though a relatively large number of "outsiders" did succeed in doing so, sometimes due to support from the Fund for Industry. Of course, Amsterdam was not representative of the country as a whole, but comparative research on the capital markets in the countryside of Twente has indicated a similar degree of activity and mobility. To a certain extent the citizens of Twente had an excess of capital and were looking for ways to invest it, from which, for example, farmers in this area profited considerably. By taking out mortgaged loans, they were able to buy large tracts of agricultural land in the region.[103]

This image of a fairly efficient and dynamic capital market with few bottlenecks needs some adjustment, however. To begin with, there are indications that interest rates in the 1820s and 1830s were relatively high, even significantly higher than in the second half of the eighteenth century, something that probably should be seen in connection with strong government demand for capital. The general development of interest rates on mortgages during the period 1760–1869 is known for three regions: Groningen, Twente, and de Beijerlanden (an island in the southern rim of Holland) (table 4.5).

During the second half the eighteenth century, interest rates gradually increased, in particular due to rising inflation in the period (after correction for

TABLE 4.5.
Interest Rates on Mortgages in Three Regions, 1760/69–1860/69.

	Nominal			Real[a]		
	Groningen	Twente	Beijerlanden	Groningen	Twente	Beijerlanden
1760/69	—	3.10	3.63	—	2.89	3.41
1770/79	3.94	3.20	3.57	3.32	2.58	2.95
1780/89	3.84	3.29	3.69	3.08	2.53	2.93
1790/99	3.95	3.49	4.17	3.25	2.79	3.47
1800/1809	4.31	4.00	5.20	3.09	2.78	3.98
1810/19	4.65	4.19	5.12	3.53	3.07	4.00
1820/29	4.68	4.22	4.96	5.71	5.25	5.99
1830/39	4.66	—	4.90	5.84	—	6.08
1840/49	4.47	—	4.88	3.90	—	4.31
1850/59	4.30	—	4.85	3.44	—	3.99
1860/69	—	—	4.86	—	—	4.35

[a] We have corrected the nominal interest rate by subtracting the average rate of inflation in the preceding twenty years following Fisher, *Theory.*

inflation, the increases between 1760 and 1810 are negligible). Deflation after 1817 did not, however, bring with it a fall in interest rates; these remained until the end of the 1830s at levels that were notably higher (by more than 1 percent) than before 1780. Once again, after correction for long-term developments in prices, real interest rates in the 1820s and 1830s were more than 2 percent higher than levels normal for the eighteenth century. This is striking because one would, as a result of institutional and legal developments, expect just the opposite: the introduction of the Napoleonic Code and the detailed description of mortgages and landownership in the land registry was an important improvement, reducing the risk to capital of underwriting mortgages. Nevertheless, this did not result in lower interest rates—indeed, just the opposite.

The cause of continuing high rates of interest on the private capital market should be sought especially in problems associated with rising public debt. In the eighteenth century, when the province of Holland was able to behave as the monopsonist on the capital market, the phased reduction of interest rates for public debt induced a general fall in the level of interest. Because of general confidence in the government, the rate of interest for government notes formed a bottom for the capital market; lowering the bottom rate, only feasible because of the surplus of capital within the Republic, was partly responsible for a fall in interest rates on the market for private capital. In the twenties and thirties this mechanism had the reverse effect: interest rates on government notes were higher than for the private capital market because confidence in Willem I's financial policies was lacking, thus effectively raising interest rates on the private capital markets.[104]

The effect on the private capital market of this increase in interest rates was probably limited; by international standards interest rates in the Netherlands were quite low (4 to 5 percent), so that it is not likely that the competitiveness of businesses in the Netherlands was adversely affected (although they did lose the advantage of their traditionally low interest rates after 1800, which had been of strategic importance in the opinion of Adam Smith). More important, perhaps, was that the marked increase in public debt led in the long run to the reduction of government investment. In the twenties both investment and public debt increased without check; the Kanalen-koning was responsible for a significant boom in investment in waterways. In the thirties and forties investments by the central government fell sharply, however: at first due to the expenditures needed for the war with Belgium, and later because the necessity to reorganize government finances and to implement cuts in spending had priority. It appears likely that for these reasons especially the construction of railways fell behind. Willem I's proposals that the state should participate in the construction of railways was rejected by Parliament in 1838 (although he still proceeded without parliamentary consent). After Willem I's abdication, the distressed condition of the state's finances made it unthinkable that the government would undertake any initiatives in this area.[105] Only after completion of the reorganization of the government's finances and after large surpluses from the Cultivation System solved the financial problems did such plans have enough support to be noted on the political agenda. There is, therefore, every reason to assume that the financial crisis of the state was a contributing factor to the meager levels of government investment between 1830 and 1860.

Initial plans to construct a railway met other sorts of problems, too. The two military engineers who drew up the plans, W. A. Blake and W. C. Brade, based them especially around improving the infrastructure of Amsterdam, in particular by building a railway to Cologne. They were supported in this by Amsterdam's merchants and bankers; those in Rotterdam firmly opposed these plans because in their opinion this would compete with transit shipping and so adversely affect their city's trade. Despite the support of some of the country's wealthiest citizens, the first emission of shares (in the Rhine railway) failed, and the second emission generated only fl 1 million of the fl 4 million required.[106] In her investigations of both failures Fritschy concluded that legal problems were especially to blame for the situation. A public limited company could be founded only by royal decree, which effectively implied that the definitive versions of the statutes and concessionary conditions were decided by Willem I after the emission. This brought about uncertainty. In 1834 and 1835 Van Hall, a representative of Amsterdam's business community, strongly opposed this practice, through which "the independence of business in establishing public limited companies" was threatened. This debate resulted during Willem I's reign in various adjustments that were finally incorporated in the Commercial Code of 1838 to guarantee the "independence of business."[107]

The reason for the Amsterdam business community to distrust Willem I can be traced back to the intrigue associated with the foundation of the NHM in 1824. The first royal decree, by which the foundation was announced, spoke of an independent trading company, which was not to have "any relationship with the state other than that similar public companies enjoyed by law," with working capital of fl 12 million and certain privileges for trading with the colonies.[108] Moreover, the king had given the impression—according to Amsterdam businessmen—that the NHM would establish its head office in Amsterdam. The subscription was extremely successful, reaching a total of fl 69.6 million, probably because Willem I had personally guaranteed a dividend of 4.5 percent on the shares. Subsequently the king decided, in contradiction to the original prospectus, to limit the total subscription to fl 37 million (only his subscription was honored for the full 100 percent). In the definitive royal decree in which the company was formally founded, a form of shareholder representation was included that was disadvantageous to Amsterdam: the city was allotted only eleven of the forty representatives' seats although in the original decree proportional representation was proposed, which in effect would have given half the seats to Amsterdam. Moreover, The Hague was chosen as the site for the company's registered offices, much to the disappointment of Amsterdam's businessmen. The reason given for this choice was that of the close ties the NHM was to maintain with the government, a statement that seemed to contradict earlier concessions concerning the independence of the trading organization.[109] Amsterdam's opposition to the affair was to no avail, in part because other cities supported the sovereign. Later Amsterdam got its way, and the NHM moved to Amsterdam in 1831. During the 1830s the NHM became so entangled in the financial problems of the state (because it could not escape the influence of Willem I) that bankruptcy loomed in 1839–40, and it was only through the abdication of Willem and the subsequent reorganization of the state's finances that this could be averted.

The foundation of the NHM, including the approval of its statutes, was carefully orchestrated by Willem I. Because a royal decree was stipulated, at crucial moments Willem I was able to control the entire process. This experience probably played an important role during discussions in the 1830s on the independence of the public limited company as a legal form of organization. The two initiatives to build railways, which were supported by Willem I, could therefore expect to meet distrust from Amsterdam's business community, despite the great advantages improved transport connections with the German hinterland represented for them. It is quite likely that other plans of Willem I's—for example, the creation of the General Society for the Support of National Industry in Brussels—were also torpedoed because of this distrust.[110] It is not clear whether other limited companies were stillborn due to similar circumstances or whether firms avoided the transition to this legal form so as not to offer the king the opportunity of meddling in their business. It is clear, however, that this problem—this lack of clarity concerning definition of proprietary rights, to use the words of Douglass North—did interfere with the workings of the capital market during Willem I's reign.

The modernization of the financial system was seriously delayed due to the lack of trust between the financial world (primarily in Amsterdam) and the government. The Nederlandsche Bank (DNB), Willem I's first significant creation, suffered for a long time from lack of confidence in financial circles. DNB was founded in 1814 as a public limited company that was permitted to play a role in all banking affairs and was to become the central bank for the government, as well as being given the monopoly over issuing banknotes. Of course it was of great importance that this institution should acquire the confidence of the general public, which, for example, had to accept the notes issued by the bank as legal tender. The dominance of Willem I over the bank—he appointed its president, and until 1847 the government had a large share in its capital—meant, however, that Amsterdam's merchants were not inclined to accept this new institution. Up until 1830 there was only a gradual increase in the issue of banknotes; fluctuations of confidence in the government's finances were reflected in fluctuations in the value of the bank's shares.[111] Also, Amsterdam's pride was wounded by the definite liquidation of the Exchange Bank in 1818, a process in which Willem I took the initiative because he had lost confidence in the future of the institution.[112] Finally, many of Amsterdam's bankers saw in the DNB a formidable competitor that could only do harm in their sector.[113]

Up until the 1830s the DNB developed slowly, and its activities remained limited to the Amsterdam money market. Initiatives to expand its sphere of activity to, for example, Rotterdam, the second financial center in the country, met with opposition from Rotterdam banks, which feared competition from the DNB, nor were such moves supported by the bank's managers. In their view, the establishment of agencies and branches would only complicate the bank's organization and even threaten its internal solidarity.[114]

Distrust of the DNB by business circles in Amsterdam was not entirely without foundation. During the thirties, when Willem I's need for money rose sharply as a result of the quasi war with Belgium, he brought great pressure to bear on the bank to extend credit to the state. Initially the bank's executive was successful in resisting this plan, but it finally succumbed in 1834. Because of the desire for secrecy—rightly, they feared that publicity about the loan would affect confidence in the DNB—the credit was registered to a "straw puppet." This loan, which at no time had any adverse effects on the bank's solvency, grew to a total of fl 6.6 million in 1843 before being subsequently gradually reduced.[115]

The sluggish development of the DNB and especially the slow acceptance of the banknote as legal tender were considered by contemporaries as signs of the conservatism of the Dutch public in such matters.[116] In the foregoing, however, we have shown that the lack of public confidence in banknotes was indeed based on reality. Without doubt the example of the Exchange Bank's demise after it extended credit to the city of Amsterdam and to the VOC was fresh in their minds, as was the dramatic fall in the value of the French assignat due to unlimited and unsecured issue. The rumors of the well-nigh unlimited credit NHM was forced to extend to the government based on shipments of tropical goods from Java—credit that grew to such an extent during the thirties that the company faced bankruptcy—were common knowledge. A central bank that until the 1830s was unable to escape the influence of Willem I and was forced to lend the government money was rightly viewed with some suspicion. Only after the business world's lack of confidence in the government was removed in the forties, by the political reforms of 1840–41 (and 1848) and the financial reforms of 1843–45, did DNB banknotes begin to play a growing role in the economy.[117]

ECONOMIC DEVELOPMENT AND THE AUTOCRATIC EXPERIMENT

To what extent did the economic growth of 1820–40 actually bring an end to the "stationary state" of the eighteenth century? Can one speak of structural changes, of qualitative improvements in production techniques, and of improvements in institutional structures, or was the pattern of development established in the eighteenth century continued? There are several arguments for evaluating this spurt of growth positively. Certainly in the twenties, when growth in agriculture slowed and industry shot ahead, when migration to the towns and cities again increased after the reverse migration—back to the countryside—of previous decades, there was to some extent a relatively modern pattern of economic development supported by an increase in purchasing power (due to low prices of agricultural produce) of the population. This was, however, short-lived: after 1830 this impulse faded again (due to increases in taxation), and a new phase in the process of growth began in which the trend was to a large degree set by several sectors "traditionally" connected with the stapelmarkt—shipbuilding, textiles (no longer from Leiden, but now Twente), shipping, international trade, and marine insurance. Nevertheless, modernization did occur: the steam engine was slowly put to use, and the engineering industry gradually expanded.

There was in other respects, too, a break in the trend that had been taking place before 1780. One of the characteristics of the "stationary state" was the continual expansion of the financial sector, but as a result of the demise of the Exchange Bank, loss of a great deal of the capital holdings of Holland, and London's supremacy on the international capital markets after 1815, this was now out of the question.[118] Agriculture, the other "strong" sector of the "stationary state," was, however, after a temporary slump after 1820 able to fulfill this role once again; in the long term the net export of agricultural produce increased considerably. Parallel to this, the import of industrial products only gradually increased, despite a fairly rapid increase in production. The trend of comparative advantage that had already appeared in the eighteenth century, one in which the agricultural sector became an increasingly important exporter and more and more industrial products were imported to satisfy demand, continued in this period. The large net export of services (shipping and international trade) continued to support this trend of specialization. In this respect the process of ongoing specialization in the agricultural and services sectors that had begun in the late seventeenth and eighteenth centuries continued after 1814, notwithstanding Willem I's policy of industrialization.

Of course the great difference was that during the "stationary state" of the eighteenth century no increase in per capita income had been achieved, whereas this changed after 1820, as stagnation and decline were transformed into cautious growth. Many contemporaries were decidedly positive about economic development during the first fifteen years of Willem I's experiment. Based on detailed statistical research, Drieling in 1829, for example, found many signs of the "prosperous state" of the Kingdom of the Netherlands: "Everywhere in our fatherland new houses are being built, existing houses renovated and embellished; factories built. . . . Add to this the low interest rates and the eagerness with which every opportunity is taken to transform circulating capital into productive or fixed capital."[119] Writing in 1830, A.J.L. van de Bogaerde, of Brugge, in the south of the Netherlands, also discerned an almost unbelievable increase in industry, trade, and shipping, which he accredited in particular to "the active and strong influence of our institutions and government on the development of the public welfare."[120] No less positive is the opinion of A. H. van der Boon Mesch on the twenties, during which time not only did industry in the south develop but "the northern provinces also did not remain behind, where many manufacturers reorganized and improved their old factories or even established new ones . . . of which the number of steam- and other-powered machines introduced in this period is convincing proof."[121] These judgments contrast sharply with the picture historians have traditionally painted of this period.

Of course one can only speculate about what would have happened if the events of the early thirties—the seccession of Belgium and the introduction of the Cultivation System—had not taken place. If the growth of the twenties had continued, it may have been transformed into increasing industrialization and structural reform. Although growth during the thirties was a little faster than in the previous decade, it was in large part based on protectionism, the result of a tedious coalition between the elite of Amsterdam and Willem I. To a certain degree the economic problems that arose after 1840 were inherent in this structure—the artificial nature of the colonial complex. The offensive against obsolete institutions, which began in the twenties, stagnated at the same time, so that sources of endogenous growth were insufficiently utilized.

This brings us to the most important limitation of this spurt in growth: reform of the incumbent institutional framework of economic life, an inheritance of the seventeenth and eighteenth centuries, was insufficiently realized. Since the peeling away of the first layer of the framework during the French-Batavian period, when the decentralized infrastructure of the Republic had to make way for the centralized nation-state, reform had stagnated. In all layers of the economy small groups of entrepreneurs—herring fishers, flour millers, and brokers—continued to oppose strongly the policies of reform introduced by the state, policies that after 1814 threatened to grind to a halt. Due to a combination of factors, such as the necessity to levy taxes (milling duties) and the desirability of establishing common ground with the elite of Amsterdam, Willem I was only to a limited extent able to overcome these attitudes. Sometimes his activist policies met agreement among the organized interest groups, as was the case with owners of herring boats.

Coincidentally, Willem I's policies in these years were strongly oriented toward the traditions of the *stapelmarkt;* the protection of the privileged position of the ports of Holland was still (or, after the failed attempt to form a coalition with the special interest groups of the southern Netherlands after 1816, again) a key element in his trade policies, which led to great problems especially with the Prussian state and the Zollverein. New waterways particularly served the interests of the very same ports. Attempts at reforming the inefficient and expensive trade system had to be abandoned after 1830, when his source of power in the north needed strengthening. The sectors of shipping and international trade profited far above all others from the striking innovations launched around 1830, and from the Cultivation System and the role of the NHM in it. These conservative approaches did not reflect the personal preferences of the sovereign but rather the political-economic forces to which he was exposed. He was forced after 1830 to seek renewed support from the citizens of Holland because of the sudden loss of support from the south. In effect he became a prisoner of the dilemmas of the "stationary state" and thereby lost the opportunity to overcome the ossified institutional structures of the economy.

The second phase of Willem's "industrialization policy" faced limitations. Of course, there were sound economic reasons for maintaining a degree of economic protection for new "infant industries": industrialization could increase economic growth in the long term. However, this protection was provided at the cost of the domestic market, in which taxes and duties were raised and purchasing power smothered, and resulted in inefficiencies in the industries concerned, for which there was less incentive to modernize. The social goals of the "industrialization policy" also constrained policy making: the creation of employment and its distribution over as many entrepreneurs, workers, and regions as possible was in conflict with efforts to improve efficiency and strengthen the country's international competitiveness. Industries that enjoyed far-reaching protection in the 1830s were confronted with great problems when faced with an increase in international competition in the following decade.

Without a doubt, Willem I was the most forceful and powerful sovereign the Netherlands has ever known; his reign was characterized by an unprecedented highly centralized political decision-making process, which he was able to dominate, certainly in economic and financial matters (but also, for example, in matters of education, language politics, and religious politics). Moreover, he was an extremely competent ruler: his working capacity was impressive; his knowledge of his kingdom's economy was huge; he had an eye for detail and involved himself in all sorts of decisions; and although he sometimes lost sight of his main goals, his approach was usually sound and consistent. He combined his extensive expertise in financial and economic matters with the ability to continually develop new plans in which he often made use of the ideas and understanding of others (although those others often found that they could barely recognize their original ideas and intentions in the version Willem I finally presented). In certain aspects he was a financial genius, who with astonishing ingenuity was able to find new sources of income for his many plans. Moreover, he was able to combine this rare collection of qualities with, as provided in the constitution of 1815, a very strong power base. Nevertheless, his reign came to a dramatic end, and many contemporaries—in particular the liberals, who held political control in subsequent decades—judged him and his great experiment extremely negatively. To be able to understand this paradox—why an experiment in managing the economy could in certain respects go so wrong—one first must realize that his power base was not that strong after all: from 1815 onward he was forced to expend much effort in legitimizing his regime, particularly in the southern provinces (he was not "chosen" as sovereign by the Belgians themselves but rather selected by Great Britain and the other participants in the Congress of Vienna). His source of power in the south was very weak, something made more complex by the clear conflict of interests between the southern and northern provinces. Unfortunately, his first instinct, to oblige his southern citizens, whose loyalty still had to be won, failed him. The financial crisis of 1818–19 demonstrated that the taxation system drawn up in 1816 was defective, which forced him to give priority to the wishes of the northern provinces. There were two moments, during the reform of the national debt in 1813 and during the drafting of the Beginselenwet of

1821, when he clearly chose to win over the citizens of the northern provinces to his regime, although in the latter case he did attempt to conciliate his southern citizens by offering subsidies through the Fund for Industry. The "conservative" leanings of his policies can be explained by this fact: from 1821 onward he was forced to link his fate to the interests of the elite of Holland, and his policy reflected in important measure the force and point of view of this pressure group. After 1830, when the counterbalance of the southern provinces no longer existed, this tendency grew stronger. His vulnerable position as the constant negotiator between numerous interest groups in the Netherlands demanded that he develop plans for each new group that joined the throng of plaintiffs, thereby requiring new funds to be found, while levying higher taxes on certain groups was already all but impossible. Because power was so centralized, because the threshold to power was so low, because Willem I felt responsible for all social groups in his kingdom, and because of his unbridled activism, there was an almost continual shortage of means for the financing of these new plans. This dilemma was sometimes so intense that he often used his own private means to avoid it: he participated with his own capital in nearly all his large plans, or he strengthened the guarantees on the interest based on his own wealth. The drama of Willem I, his great successes, and his inevitable fall are all attributable to this combination of factors. The actual economic development of the Netherlands in the decades following 1815, and especially in the thirties and even forties, must be found in this same combination of circumstances. Ultimately it was the deficiencies in the political system—of the constitution of 1815—that are the root cause of Willem I's failure. The countervailing power that could ensure more careful management of government finances was missing: Parliament had little power, ministers were no more than implementers of Willem I's ideas, and public opinion had no weight. Only when the true nature of the financial problems became known in 1839 was public opinion aroused and could reforms be set in motion to put an end to Willem's autocratic rule. At that point the way was cleared for the painful transition to a political system in which responsibilities were more evenly distributed and less power was vested in the sovereign.

CHAPTER FIVE

The Liberal Offensive, 1840–1870

UPBEAT: THE FINANCIAL CRISIS OF 1839–40

In the thirty years after the abdication of Willem I, Dutch society saw the evolution and execution of a liberal reform program that is universally seen as having shaped its current parliamentary system, redefined electoral influence, and cast executive government into a three-tiered structure of municipal, provincial, and central rule with subsidiary responsibilities and coordinated funding. Yet notwithstanding these dominant features of its historiographical perception, the thrust of the liberal offensive did not originate in philosophical criticism of the 1815 constitution per se. Through its normative accounts of the personal events surrounding the crucial 1848 constitutional reform, political history has typically downplayed the fact that the liberal movement of the 1840s had come together on an agenda aimed at the joint reorganization of political institutions and public finance—issues that, as we have seen, were joined at the hip under the 1815 constitution. It was in relation to this agenda that changes in the structure of taxation, in trade policy, and in the regulation of factor and commodity markets were made possible. It was under the influence of liberal reforms in the institutions of government that municipal fiscal and executive autonomy were finally curtailed to lift numerous coordination problems in taxation and infrastructure. And it was the control achieved over public finance that created the possibility for enhanced government investment in this infrastructure, in means of transport, and in urban overhead, even though the cloud of public debt would continue to hang over Dutch politics until the last decades of the century. As such, the economic implications of the "liberal offensive," through a reform of public finance and the institutional effects of coordinated executive rule, are seen here to have been essential in changing the structure of Dutch nineteenth-century development. To be sure, none of this discounts the influence on the pace and pattern of Dutch industrialisation of more traditional arguments on comparative factor costs and natural resource endowments. In fact, by arguing that distributional interests—related to region as much as factor incomes—cemented product markets, factor mobility, and public finance by political means, it apportions a large part of these effects to institutional restraints.

The liberal program, of which Johan Rudolf Thorbecke (1798–1872) was the most prominent spokesman and political leader, owed much of its consistency to the failure of the experiment of Willem I and the criticism it engendered. A descendant of a Zwolle family of tobacco traders and a professor of diplomatic history and constitutional law at the universities of Ghent and then Leiden, Thorbecke had first joined the States General in August 1840 as an associate delegate for the province of Holland to partake in the deliberations on the proposed constitutional amendment. It was in the years between the abdication of the first hereditary king of the Netherlands and the subordination of the political rights of the royal office to ministerial responsibility in 1848 that Thorbecke was able to assume leadership over the building liberal offensive. Although by no means in a position to exert executive power for even most of the time in between, it would be only one year before his death in 1872 that the third and last cabinet under his leadership would be forced to hand in its resignation.

With respect to the period before 1840, a wide range of politicians may be argued to have promoted a variety of liberal ideas. For example, both Van Hogendorp and Gogel—opponents at the extreme end of the political spectrum, according to contemporary opinion—have been credited with the fatherhood of Dutch liberalism.[1] Traditionally, the Dutch bourgeoisie strongly preferred free trade, albeit in the most pragmatic of ways, that is, if and for as long as this converged with the interests of the Amsterdam staple market. Moreover, the resistance against too prominent a role for the sovereign in politics undoubtedly had its roots in the traditional aim of urban regents to restrict the power of the stadtholder. But the fact that over the course of the 1840s these diffuse political and economic ideas converged into a consistent program in a relatively short term should probably be attributed to the fact that Willem I had personified the antithesis of these traditions: he increasingly demonstrated his lack of concern about the interests of the urban middle-class taxpayer, he opted for interventionist policies, and he mismanaged government finances to such an extent that bankruptcy of the state seemed imminent. As we have shown using newly reconstructed figures on the public budget, sources of income (such as the Batig Slot, the net income from the Indies), and the true size of outlays, the various elements of his experiment were interconnected and based on the legislative and executive powers provided by the 1815 constitution. A reform of economic and fiscal policy could therefore not be seen in isolation from fundamental changes in the constitution. This inherent necessity constituted the core of the liberal criticism coherently voiced by increasingly prominent spokesmen such as Donker Curtius and Thorbecke in the 1840s. To be sure, none of them could claim to be the first proponent of modern liberalism, which was also able to gain in strength because it was increasingly able to mirror itself to foreign movements with similar political aims. Early liberal criticism of this kind on Willem I's financial policies—and the 1815 constitution that had allowed it to take root—had already flared up in relation to the second ten-year budget in 1829–30, as well as having been voiced in still more traditional terms by Van Hogendorp between 1816 and 1820.[2] Especially in the southern Netherlands criticism of this kind had been forceful and as such had played a significant role in the secession of 1830. Yet in the northern part of the realm, too, oppositional opinion gained currency. Moreover, the necessity to adapt the constitution also sprang from the acceptance of Belgian independence, causing the 1815 text to become partly obsolete. Following the ratification of the Treaty of London in 1839, which finally settled the independence of Belgium, the pressure for constitutional change increased. The budget for 1840 as presented to Parliament the previous autumn for the first time since 1829 contained a survey of the state of public finance, as well as a proposal for a new public loan "chargeable to the East-Indies." Based on the growth of the East Indian exports after 1830, investors had retained a certain amount of confidence in this economy, which had been abused by securing loans redeemable from the remittances gained by the auction of the products of the colonial economy, but in fact used to cover the burgeoning deficits of the domestic budget.[3]

The background to this financial crisis, which ended the experiment of Willem I, was provided by the fact that the state, through the Department of Colonial Affairs, had received large sums of credit from the NHM in anticipation of remittances flowing from the auction of colonial produce. By locally—that is, in Batavia—recording the proceedings of the textiles imported into the East Indies against the produce in consignment, a theoretically consistent system of accounting had been set up. However, the financial need of the Dutch government after the 1830 secession and the associated creed for the postponement of financial obligations disrupted the balance. Consecutive ministers of colonial affairs (Clifford, Brocx, Van den Bosch, and Baud), working from the assumption of stable or increasing revenues, continued to raise the sum of future remissions, with the result that in 1837 the advances received from the NHM totaled of fl 22 million. However, when prices, especially for coffee, started to fall, the advances assumed the character of a blank check. In 1837 revenues remained fl 6 million and in 1838 even fl 8 million (some 6.3 and 8.5 percent of total government expenditure, respectively) below expectations. When the government urged additional advances to cover domestic deficits, the situation came to a head. In 1839, on the eve of the presentation of the budget in Parliament, the debt with the NHM had reached no less than fl 39 million, and the company's directors refused further cooperation without prior redemption. With its back against the wall, the government sought for a last way out. In the autumn of 1839 the king advanced considerable sums from his own means, and clandestine money-changing operations in the amount of fl 6 million were carried out.[4] Yet all this was highly insufficient, and little else remained but to expose the situation to light and add a proposal for a new public loan of no less than fl 56 million to the budget—a sum of which, as Van de Bosch informed a closed session of Parliament, 40 million would be spent to redeem the advances with the NHM, fl 10 million would be used for the redemption of sums used by the Department of War, and fl 4 million would be spent on the financial legacy of the Amortisatiesyndicaat—all this against the background of a total annual amount of government expenditure of some fl 97 million.

As had been the case on the two previous occasions, the debate on the ten-year budget drew the attention of the national press and accordingly served as a political catalyst for the opposition. The rejection of the loan proposals was broadly carried by the liberal, and as such repeatedly summoned, *Arnhemsche Courant*, which instantly referred to the events as a "moral revolution."[5] Shortly afterwards the implacable rejection of the budget itself followed; this time repeated submission was to no avail. The lack of confidence in the government had even assumed such proportions that the final vote consisted of fifty rejections and only one approval: that of the minister himself. Following this defeat, the minister of finance, Beelaerts van Blokland, resigned at his own initiative. In response to the earlier rejection of the loan proposal, largely earmarked to cover the colonial debt, the minister of colonial affairs Van den Bosch—inventor of the Cultivation System—had already gone before.[6] Following these events Willem I abdicated. The official motive was a personal one: dissent among the Protestant community had emerged over his plan to marry a member of the Belgian, Catholic aristocracy.

THE REORGANIZATION OF GOVERNMENT FINANCE

These first experiments in ministerial responsibility (never before had a minister resigned after a conflict with the States General) signified the possibilities for institutional change. Yet the constitutional amendment of 1840, partly under pressure by Willem I, had remained limited: a restricted form of ministerial responsibility had been introduced, and the ten-year budgets were replaced by biennial ones. The most important change introduced in 1840, however, was that all information about government finance was to be made public, ending the period of hidden and semilegal operations by the state in the previous years and opening up the possibility for effective parliamentary control. The appointment of Rochussen as interim minister of finance (like Six before him and Van Hall after him an Amsterdam banker), provided with the special instruction to chart all financial liabilities of the state, resulted in his "survey of the probable state of the public treasury on 1 January 1841," which, having been leaked to the *Arnhemsche Courant*, provoked a public debate. As a result, as of 1840 considerable pressure existed to cut back on spending and reduce the public deficit. The extent to which successive ministers of finance were successful in this respect highly determined their political fate. Starting with the 1841 budget, numerous retrenchment programs followed in which no item of expenditure was exempt from reevaluation. At the same time, various proposals were launched to reorganize the public debt. In 1841 the remaining bulk of Willem I's "deferred debt" was paid off against its prevailing—very low—market price. More extensive proposals to reorganize the public debt stranded in the States General, however, forcing both Rochussen and his successor, Van der Heim van Duivendijke, to resign.[7]

In 1842 and 1843 the financial crisis was deepened by the further decline in the Batig Slot due to the depression in East Indian trade. A breakthrough was forced only in late 1843, when the confidant of the Amsterdam banking community, Floris van Hall, was appointed the new minister of finance. His proposal for the reorganization of state finance essentially consisted of a "voluntary loan" of fl 127 million, yielding a low 3 percent rate of interest and earmarked to pay off (at fixed rates) the much higher-yielding government paper of the 1830s. Hedging the scheme was the threat that, should the loan fail, an incidental tax to the same effective amount would be levied on income and wealth (a threat not without a postwar precedent, since such a tax had in fact already been imposed in 1831). Additionally, the loan would be used to redeem a large part of the debt owed to the NHM, as well as to provide funding for the public deficits of 1843 and 1844. Given the fact that the average yield on current government paper hovered around 4 percent, there was an implicit element of force within these proposals. Only as a result of personal pressure on the Amsterdam banking community on the part of Van Hall, setting forth the eventual financial dangers of individual free riding on the time inconsistency of fiscal policy, the loan in the end succeeded. As a token of his support and so as to set an example, in 1844 the new king Willem II contributed nearly fl 2 million to Van Hall's voluntary loan. Moreover, the "East Indian" debts, on which a 5 percent rate of interest rested, were converted into 4 percent bonds. As a result of these measures and the simultaneous solution of the dispute with Belgium over outstanding debt transfers, interest payments could be reduced by nearly fl 4 million, whereas the nominal debt remained essentially unchanged.[8]

The success of these measures was substantial: the confidence of the financial markets in the management of government finance increased strongly, which expressed itself in a rise in the quotations for NWS (see figure 3.1). With the coming of Van Hall, Amsterdam finance had in effect regained control over the management of the treasury—albeit at a price and only after the forced solution of coordination failure and underlying free riding, generating holdup problems in fiscal stabilization.[9] With hindsight, the 1840 constitutional amendment and the preceding abdication of Willem I would appear to have provided sufficient preconditions for the reorganization of public finance. During his short yet pivotal period of rule between his accession in October 1840 and his death in March 1849 (only four months after Thorbecke's constitutional amendment had been carried), Willem II turned out to be a much less dominant head of state who lacked interest in financial issues, even though his views on the competence of Parliament (at least until early 1848) were hardly more liberal than those held by his father. Of further importance was the fact that the pressure of public opinion and the States General for spending cuts persisted, whereas in 1820 and 1830 the system of ten-year budgets and the political evaluation of fiscal change versus a constitutional standoff had caused this pressure to subside. As previously emphasized by Bornewasser, these circumstances have caused the importance of the 1840 constitutional amendment—in the light of the events of 1848—to have been underestimated. [10]

The upbeat to the 1848 apogee of Dutch post-Napoleonic constitutional change was provided by the fact that the economic situation continued to worsen during the 1840s. The downturn of the business cycle in the early 1840s—following in the wake of the crisis in the Cultivation System—was followed in 1845 by the first systematic outbreak of the potato blight. The fungal disease largely ruined the crop and in the longer term resulted in a sharp decline in yields. Potato prices soared, to be followed by the prices of other foodstuffs, not only as a result of cross-elasticities of demand but also due to the failure of the harvest of the staple cereals in 1846—rye in particular. Given still relevant subsistence relations and the lessened dampening effect of grain imports since the late eighteenth century (cf. chapter 2), the mechanism of the "premodern business cycle" also resulted in a shrinking demand for nonagricultural products on domestic markets, causing especially inland industry and services to contract. This Ancien Régime type of economic crisis, ignited by harvest failure, led to growing popular unrest. In neighboring countries—France, Austria, and Germany—this social turmoil resulted in strong oppositionary and nationalistic movements.[11] Introduction of a constitution or, wherever this already existed, adaptation to allow for a democratization of the polity and an enhanced influence for the broadening urban middle class invariably featured prominently among the goals of this revolutionary striving. In combination with the liberal pursuit of accountability, the separation of executive and legislative powers, and the subjection of fiscal policy to electoral consent, these formed the platform for the famous revolutions of 1848. The Dutch political elite—first and foremost Willem II himself—feared similar movements. In the all but distant past, foreign revolutions had exerted strong destabilizing effects upon the polity of the Netherlands, most recently in 1830. Moreover, in the 1840s a coherent liberal opposition—a faction of still largely independent provincial delegates, of which Thorbecke was the undisputed leader—had gestated on an agenda of closely defined institutional change.[12] Having dismissed all of the 1840 proposals as insufficient, he had already put forward a coherent plan for constitutional change with nine other members in 1844 (henceforth known as the "nine-man proposal"), which specified ministerial responsibility and direct elections under a restrictive census. In May 1845, with twenty-one votes in favor and thirty-four against, the chamber decided not to take the proposal into consideration. It would be just over three years before the tide of events would sweep all these conservative objections aside.

As elsewhere, periods of political instability in Dutch history had been used by different factions of the contemporary political elite to strengthen or regain their position. On previous occasions—events during the "disaster year"1672 and those of the second, 1747, Orangist Restoration first spring to mind—*stadtholders* had both stirred and used popular support in order to reclaim their executive positions and curtail the influence of the regents. Whenever *stadtholders* did hold office, however, a similar moment of political instability could turn against them, as the broad impact of the Patriot movement between 1781 and 1787 showed. In certain respects the political changes of 1848 fitted this tradition: riding the wave of popular unrest and international instability, the liberal opposition was able to fully exploit the moment. Willem II, before 1848 a staunch defender of his privileges, "turned liberal within twenty-four hours" and now suddenly supported their infringement, as a result of which the liberals were able to introduce their new constitution. This first of all meant that the initially strengthened power of the post-Napoleonic monarchs was to be curtailed, forging an end to the bifurcated nature of Dutch politics, which since the final quarter of the sixteenth century had been based on a tension between the regents and their lieutenant army commanders from the House of Orange. After a period in which an institutionally strengthened representative of the latter—Willem I—had dominated at the political and financial expense of the other, the Dutch bourgeoisie now managed to eliminate the monarchy from the competition for formal executive and legislative power. Through the 1848 constitution, the urban elite finally gained control over the unitary state that had been created in 1798.

Yet the doctrinaire liberal opposition of the 1840s had not merely put its sights on the monarchy. It also set out to break the coalition that had emerged between the king and those interest groups that were closely linked to the experiment of Willem I: shipowners, merchants, shipbuilders, industrialists, and Amsterdam bankers who profited from the Cultivation System and the NHM-led system of rent-seeking. Their views found political shelter from Protestant conservatives, fearing not only the moral decadence of liberalism in general but also the impact of reform on account of the free trade agenda upon government finance. After 1840 Amsterdam became the center of this preacher-merchant alliance, whereas support for the new liberalism came from outside Holland, that is to say, from inland provinces such as Overijssel, Gelderland, and Limburg. It was therefore no coincidence that Thorbecke was born in one of the outer provinces (as were other leaders of the liberal opposition). The tension between conservative Amsterdam and the liberal inland provinces would become an important factor in political life up to the 1860s and as such would play a large role in dictating the pace and character of economic reform—especially so in colonial policy.[13]

At the same time, the constitution of 1848 can be seen as the conclusion of the process of institutional change that had begun with the liquidation of the

Republic in 1795. The relations between king, Parliament, and ministers were regulated with precision and care; direct election of the Second Chamber was introduced (replacing indirect election, which had been open to manipulation of the constitution of 1815); an annual budget, to be approved by Parliament, was introduced, which became the cornerstone of parliamentary power. After the strongly centralized constitutions of 1798 and 1815, a new equilibrium between the central government, the provinces, and the municipalities was found, which gave distinct but limited powers to the lower layers of the state. This ended the old autonomy of the cities but also meant that for large areas of public policy (e.g., industrial policy, health care, social issues, and environmental matters) the new municipalities became the primary units of policy making. There is no doubt that this new constitution, written to a large extent by Thorbecke, was well ahead of its time. Some resistance against it existed, and this resurfaced during moments of political conflict, in 1853 (when Catholics were allowed to reestablish the organization of their church) and again in 1866, but it was never seriously under discussion.

This does not mean that the period after 1848 was dominated by the liberals. Modern political parties as we know them now did not exist then. In fact, many liberals maintained that such parties would constrain the actions of their members and that they were inconsistent with the duty of members of Parliament to act according to their conscience. Broad political groups—liberals and conservatives—did exist in Parliament, but their fidelities were fluid, and MPs changed their affiliation and voting behavior easily. The unpredictability of Parliament meant that cabinets found it difficult to implement a clear program and were often forced to resign as they could not reach agreement with the parliamentary majority.

On financial policy the consensus was, however, that more cuts were necessary to balance the budget. The first Thorbecke cabinet (1849–53) adopted an even more staunchly conservative fiscal policy stance than its predecessors. An important factor that made large reductions in spending possible was that the Netherlands had finally come to terms with the fact that it was a second-rank power, one that no longer had an important role to play in international politics and one that in case of war would always be dependent on its allies (in the 1820s Willem I still had the duty to forge the United Kingdom into a strong state to control the northern border of France). The share of the budget going to defense, therefore, fell sharply. A similarly disproportionate decrease in expenditures also befell the monarchy: from fl 1.25 million in 1848 to fl 0.8 million in 1849 (in the 1820s this had been fl 2.6 million), a highly symbolic decline.[14] For the first and last time in the history of the Kingdom of the Netherlands, in 1849 total expenditure fell below fl 70 million. The decline of government spending as a share of national income was also without precedent: dropping from about 12 to 14 percent in the early 1840s to 8 to 9 percent

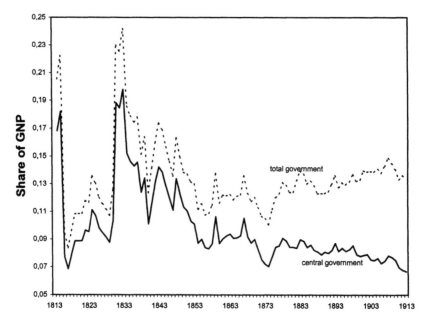

FIGURE 5.1. Expenditure by the central government and total government as percentage of GDP, 1813–1913. Data from database national accounts.

in the late 1850s, and to less than 8 percent in the 1870s (figure 5.1). The relative decline of government spending was made possible by a significant fall in the share of interest payments in the budget. In the 1840s the ratio between interest payments and total expenditure had been as high as 60 to 65 percent; this dropped to slightly more than 50 percent in 1860 and further to about 40 percent in 1880.

As a result of these changes and the recovery of income from the Cultivation System (see later discussion), the financial crisis was finally overcome, and confidence in government finance returned. From the early 1850s onward, the liberals could realize other parts of their program. A crucial element in this was the reform of the taxation system, of which indirect taxes, in particular, were considered burdensome and inefficient. As was shown in the case study of duties on milling (chapter 4), these taxes restricted internal trade, limited competition, and drove up the cost of living. Moreover, some excises were evaded on a large scale; Gogel and Van Hogendorp had already pointed out that such duties stimulated "unethical" behavior and should, therefore, also be condemned on moral grounds.[15]

In the early 1850s, when the financial crisis seemed to be a thing of the past, the liberals began to institute a long series of tax reforms, the most important of which were the abolition of excises on pork and lamb (1852), on milling

(1855), and on peat and coal (1863), and the special stamp duty on newspapers (1871). In 1865 the extremely inefficient system of local excises was abolished. To finance these changes, the excise on sugar was rationalized, which meant that the "export premium" on refined sugar was revoked (which increased the state's income from this source) and excises on consumption of jenever were strongly increased, with the additional motive of discouraging consumption.[16]

The importance of these measures can hardly be overstated. Case studies of excises on milling and on coal and peat will show the effects of their abolition in some detail (chapter 6). The abolition of the local excises also freed internal trade from many cumbersome restrictions. Before 1865 the import and export of many goods was controlled and taxed at the city gates, which increased transport costs and contributed to the fragmentation of internal markets. The law of 1865 therefore also brought to an end the protection of the domestic markets of cities.[17]

Another important element of the liberal program, which was realized after the first reforms in the tax system had been implemented, was the increase of investment in infrastructure. The favorable development of government finances, which was also made possible by the continuous flow of colonial surpluses into the treasury coffers, also made this possible. We have already argued that the sorry state of government finances that developed during the reign of Willem I made it difficult to take effective initiatives for the construction of a network of railways, although some initiatives had already been supported in the 1830s. This changed during the 1860s (see chapter 6). Similarly, a private, English-based company was the first to begin construction of a canal connecting Amsterdam to the North Sea, but when this initiative failed halfway, the government took over the project and completed the canal. In order not to favor Amsterdam exclusively, a similar canal was constructed to improve Rotterdam's link with the sea: the Nieuwe Waterweg. Growing prosperity during the 1860s also made it possible to begin to implement another part of the liberal program, to improve the quality of the educational system, and to increase participation in it. Again, this was made possible by allocating more funds to it.

Possibly the apogee of the liberal policy doctrine was the abolition of the Patent Act in 1869. For its time, the Republic had used a relatively modern system for patenting inventions. Nevertheless, in 1817 a new patent law for the new kingdom had been introduced, which according to its liberal critics did not function well. On the one hand, it did not require that the applicant submit a detailed specification or drawing of the new product or technology, which meant that what exactly was being patented was not always clear. On the other hand, the law specified that a patent would be nullified if the patentee obtained a patent for the same invention abroad, which strongly reduced the attractiveness of patenting at home. The number of patents of original inventions remained, therefore, very low. But the liberals did not seriously consider amending the law or replacing it with a better one. The proponents of total abolition of patents, who considered the law a remnant of "mercantilistic" practices that had to give way to a free exchange of ideas and technologies, had the upper hand in the debate of 1869. For a small open economy, which in those years made a negligible contribution to technological innovation, this made sense, as long as the international community allowed the Netherlands to "free ride" in this way.

COLONIAL POLICY AND THE BATIG SLOT

The crisis in public finance around 1840 was exacerbated by a sudden fall in the colonial surplus, referred to as the Batig Slot, which in 1837 had still amounted to fl 20 million but by 1840 had fallen to a mere fl 311,000. Two principal factors were responsible for this dramatic decline: the eventual unwillingness of the NHM to extend credit to the state; and a fall in the price of coffee and sugar on the Amsterdam market that resulted in a prolonged recession in the international trade of these products—a situation that was to continue until the end of the 1840s. The reaction of the administration in Java was to reduce local expenditure in order to keep the colonial surplus, but this only worsened the economic situation. The Javanese population was unable to maintain its level of expenditure on textiles, for example, which led to a dramatic fall in sales by the NHM (from 600,000 pieces in 1840 to 132,000 in 1843).[18] Money (once again) became very scarce in the Javanese countryside, which may have contributed to the severity of famines that occurred between 1844 and 1847 and again in 1849–50.

This dual crisis showed just how strong the connections between Java and the Netherlands had become. In Java it led to the first reforms of the Cultivation System: the unprofitable and burdensome cultivation of indigo was abolished, but the culture of sugar—equally burdensome but more profitable—was stimulated even more. At the same time the government attempted to limit the degree to which forced labor was used, and the contracts with sugar manufacturers were streamlined to skim off some of the huge profits that were being made by these entrepreneurs.[19]

It was only after the constitutional changes of 1848 that opposition to the Cultivation System was voiced in the Parliament (Van Hoëvell, a well-known critic, was elected in that year). But the liberal opposition of the system could not ignore the fact that the colonial surplus was vital for Dutch public finances, and that for some time to come these resources would be necessary for the implementation of the liberal program. The inherent contradiction in this position gave rise to the saying "a liberal in the Netherlands, a conservative in the colonies." The streamlining of the system of colonial exploitation, in order to end the most severe excesses and to increase the colonial system, was the main policy goal after 1848. The latter meant that the—often covert—subsidies to shipowners, merchants (the NHM in particular), insurance companies, and the manufacturers of sugar and textiles were gradually abolished.[20]

Obviously the NHM had to play a large role in the implementation of these reforms, but it was also going to be one of their major "victims." It had built up an impressive position in colonial trade and was very influential both within and outside government. Indeed, it could count on the support of large sections of the financial elite of Amsterdam, who as shipowners, merchants, and insurers had substantial interests in the colonial sector and were therefore directly dependent on the NHM. This made it almost impossible to make drastic changes in colonial policy. In 1849, for example, Parliament did not dare to amend the contract with the NHM in such a way that its privileged position could be changed in the immediate future.[21] At the end of the debate the conservative Groen van Prinsterer therefore concluded that it would be better to acknowledge the role of the NHM in colonial trade and in the financing of the state through the colonial surplus.[22]

But in spite of resistance from "Amsterdam," certain changes in the system aimed at reducing the hidden subsidies to the private sector were gradually introduced.[23] The immediate effect of this was that the colonial surplus grew even larger, the more so as the prices of coffee and sugar on world markets started to increase strongly in the 1850s. Official figures on the magnitude of the colonial surplus are not very reliable. During the 1830s (and to a much lesser extent after 1840), numerous ad hoc payments by the state had been financed from the colonial treasury. The "legal" basis for this was that the constitution of 1815 gave the king sole responsibility in colonial affairs, which under Willem I meant that he alone was in charge of colonial finances. The constitution of 1848 changed this, too, ending the separate status of the colonies, which meant that their administration became an integral part of government policy and therefore had to be controlled by Parliament. These payments were unrelated to the administration of the colonies and therefore should have been included in the colonial surplus. The same applies, of course, to hidden subsidies that were allocated to the NHM and other parts of the private sector. The official figures on the colonial surplus were literally a "surplus," that is, the gross income from the sale of Javanese export crops minus all these costs and subsidies. However, the costs resulting from the decision to subsidize textile manufacturers in Twente, for example, were not included in the colonial budget but in the overall budget of the government.

New calculations shown in table 5.1 give an impression of the size of the colonial surplus according to the official figures and our estimates.[24] The difference between the official and the reconstructed surplus was largest in the 1830s and amounted to almost 50 percent (i.e., the reconstructed surplus was almost twice as large as the official one). This means that public finances were even more dependent on the colonial exploitation than they had ever thought to be. The direct contribution of the surplus to GDP was between 2.8 and 3.8 percent,

TABLE 5.1.
Estimates of the Size and Composition of the Batig Slot, 1831/40–1861/70 (in million guilders).

	1831/40	1841/50	1851/60	1861/70
Gross proceeds of sales, NHM	227.0	473.9	652.7	641.8
Costs of NHM				
Freights	55.4	106.7	85.9	63.4
Insurance	6.9	8.1	11.1	6.0
Commission	9.8	16.5	14.4	12.8
Other costs	15.9	34.1	27.3	32.5
Total costs	88.0	165.4	138.7	114.7
(as a percentage of sales)	(39)	(35)	(21)	(18)
1. Net proceeds	139.0	308.5	514.0	527.1
Expenditure paid for by the colonial treasury				
West Indies	3.4	7.4	7.0	3.6
NHM (interest and debt)	20.9	18.7	3.7	1.1
Amortisatiesyndicaat	11.0	—	—	—
Other subsidies	5.7	1.8	—	—
Total "extralegal" expenditure	41.0	27.9	10.6	4.6
Expenditure for East Indies	18.2	147.2	264.7	272.0
(as a percentage of gross proceeds)	(8)	(31)	(41)	(42)
2. Total expenditure	59.2	175.1	275.3	276.6
3. Batig Slot according to *official statistics (1 − 2):*	79.9	133.2	238.7	250.5
4. Corrected Batig Slot I[a]	120.8	161.1	249.4	255.1
5. Corrected Batig Slot II[b]	150.6	215.6	289.4	276.7
5. As % of GDP (annual average)	2.8	3.6	3.8	2.9
5. As % of tax income state	31.9	38.6	52.6	44.5

Sources: Mansvelt, *Geschiedenis,* appendices; ARA, Archief NHM no. 1886–1889, 1905; De Waal, *Aanteekeningen,* II, VII, 145 e.v.; ARA, Ministerie van Koloniën, no. 1757 en verbaal 24-5-1866, no. 49; *Bijblad De Economist* 1856/57, 461.
  [a] Batig Slot plus "extralegal" expenditure.
  [b] Batig Slot (4) plus hidden subsidies of NHM to shipping, insurance companies, and itself.

which is a quite substantial net addition to income. When compared with total internal taxation in the Netherlands, the colonial surplus was huge indeed, ranging from more than 30 percent in the 1830s to more than 50 percent in the 1850s.

The reforms instituted during the 1840s meant that hidden subsidies declined and unofficial payments disappeared. The streamlining of the system of colonial exploitation is evident from the gradual decline in the hidden subsidies, which implies that the margins between the official figures and our estimates become increasingly smaller. Up until the mid-1860s liberal colonial policy meant that to an increasing extent the private sector was being rewarded with world market prices for its activities. Expressed as a share of total sales, the costs that the NHM was allowed to charge to the state declined from 39 percent in the 1830s to 18 percent in the 1860s. An important part of this decline was the gradual convergence of the freight rates charged to world market levels.

During the 1860s the direction of colonial policy changed: the focus became the abolition of the Cultivation System and its replacement by a system in which private enterprise would play a pivotal role in the exploitation of the colony. The liberal ministers of colonial affairs, Fransen van der Putte (1863–66) and De Waal (1870–71), achieved the complete liberalization of trade with the colony (and abolition of the NHM's monopoly), the termination of forced cultivation of sugar for the colonial government, and the opening up of the colony to private enterprise.[25] The Agrarian Law of 1870, perhaps the most important step in this process, made it possible to lease "unused" land for a period up to ninety-nine years to entrepreneurs who wished to start a plantation of export crops (tea, coffee, tobacco). These changes resulted in a sharp decline of the colonial surplus, which was replaced by net subsidies to the colonial treasury in the second half of the 1870s. The question arises, of course, of why the government set out to abolish a system that brought such huge returns to the treasury.

Three explanations for the abolition of the Cultivation System have been suggested in the literature. The first stresses ideological reasons: a system of forced cultivation (based on the coercion of Javanese peasants for labor) and the monopolization of colonial trade by the NHM was inconsistent with the liberalism that had become dominant after 1848. The criticism of the system by the left, which reached its apogee with the publication in 1860 of "Max Havelaar" by Eduard Douwes Dekker (a former civil servant turned writer after a sharp conflict with the colonial administration), could not be ignored indefinitely by the Dutch bourgeoisie. A different interpretation has been put forward by Fasseur, who stressed the gradual reforms in the system that had already been introduced there in the 1840s and 1850s, laying preparations for the more radical changes in its operation in the next decade.[26] A third view stresses the economic interests behind the changes in the 1860s. A side effect of the growth of exports from Java after 1830 was the rise of a group of merchants who were involved with—for example—the processing of the crude cane into sugar, or the trade in tobacco and coffee. They became increasingly confident that they could organize the export agriculture in a more efficient way themselves, that "free" wage labor could often be used much more efficiently than the forced labor on which the Cultivation System was based. They began to argue, therefore, in favor of the ending of the system.[27]

These different views are to a large extent complementary. The growth of "free" export agriculture in the 1850s and 1860s was an important factor in the gradual erosion of the system and resulted in a fast growth of trade in export commodities beyond those monopolized by the NHM. But in the 1850s resistance to the abolition of the Cultivation System was still very strong, and—apart from a few critics on the left—nobody really seriously suggested bringing it to an end.

The crucial changes to the system were brought about in Amsterdam. As Theo van Tijn has shown, although Amsterdam in the 1850s was the center of resistance to any proposed changes—for obvious economic reasons—its position shifted in the early 1860s. One important reason for this switch was that thanks to the gradual streamlining of the Cultivation System the profits that could be earned within the NHM system were rapidly declining, whereas free trade on Java, organized by private companies, was expanding. Textile entrepreneurs from Twente, for example, increasingly made use of private companies to sell their products overseas, and the imports of "free" Javanese commodities also expanded strongly. A symbol of this changing orientation was the establishment of two colonial companies, the Nederlandsch-Indische Handelsbank and the Nederlandsch-Indische Spoorweg-Maatschappij, both focused on investing large amounts of funds in the Indies. Politically this reorientation of the elite of the city had already taken place in 1859, when after an exciting campaign (perhaps the first real campaign in the political history of the city) a liberal candidate was elected to represent Amsterdam in Parliament, bringing to an end the easy conservative domination of previous elections. In 1861 the same group of liberals also gained control over the city's chamber of commerce, the institution that officially represented the merchant elite and was often consulted by government on economic issues. These changes prepared the way for a new stage in the implementation of the liberal program: the abolition of the Cultivation System and further liberalization of international trade (see later discussion).

Of course, the liberals hoped to have their cake and eat it as well. Some expected that they could abolish forced labor and liberalize the Javanese economy, and continue to reap a sizable colonial surplus to support public finances. Not all forced cultures were abolished, however: for example, in parts of Java the growing of coffee remained based on coerced labor, and its sale continued to be an important source of income. The hopes of the liberals were in vain: the colonial surplus disappeared, and from the 1870s onward private enterprise was the main benefactor of riches in the colonies.

THE LIBERALIZATION OF TRADE POLICY

The shift toward economic liberalism in taxation, the organization of domestic markets, and external trade that occurred in the Netherlands as of the 1840s can on no account be interpreted as an isolated phenomenon. On the contrary, foreign examples—such as that provided by the new Belgian constitution—played a prominent role in Dutch debate, and the liberal reforms in the United Kingdom that began with the 1842 Peelite reform and the 1845 abolition of the Corn Laws were a significant factor behind comparable changes in Dutch politics.[28] In chapter 3 we have shown that trade policy after 1815 had been exposed to the divergent interests of the different parts of the kingdom, that is to say, the call from Holland's merchants for low tariffs and claims from the southern provinces for the adequate protection of new industries. The new Tariff Act of 1821 implied that northern interests had gained the upper hand in this issue (whereas southern industrialists were placated by the establishment of the Fund for Industry). Judged by international standards, the degree of protectionism had already been relatively low, and so it remained during the 1820s and 1830s. Ironically, independent Belgium now also accepted a relatively liberal regime. Other western European countries—France and the United Kingdom, for example—protected their markets much more heavily (table 5.2).

It would be incorrect to characterize Dutch commercial policy before 1840 as an early manifestation of laissez-faire. Low tariffs clearly were a pragmatic means, with the restoration of the international trade of Holland as its primary goal. Colonial policies resulting in the establishment of the decidedly unliberal Cultivation System are a case in point. Another area where liberal attitudes did not predominate was constituted by shipping and trade along the Rhine, a vital link between the major harbors and the German hinterland which the government eagerly sought to control. Traditionally this meant that a rather diffuse system of differentiated import and export levies was applied, geared to channeling trade from the hinterland to the staple markets of Rotterdam and Amsterdam. Tariffs on transit trade, for example, were extremely high, so as to discourage trade that would bypass either Rotterdam or Amsterdam and protect the interests of the skippers' guilds within these cities as well as those in Dordrecht, the third center of river trade. Moreover, a large number of tolls—some based on feudal privileges dating from the Middle Ages—were levied on river trade, again restricting the free movement of goods. During the Napoleonic period, the French attempted to liberate Rhine trade as much as possible from these constraints. Implementing reforms that would eventually also be accepted by the Congress of Vienna, the Rhine was formally declared an open river. The Netherlands continued to resist, however, since it feared that the reforms would harm the privileged position of its ports. In 1829 international pressure led to the formal acceptance of free transport on the Rhine.[29]

TABLE 5.2.
Yield of Tariffs on Imports and Exports as a Percentage of the Value of Imports, the Netherlands, Belgium, United Kingdom, and France, 1816/20–1911/13.

	Netherlands	Belgium	United Kingdom	France
1816/20	3.2	—	—	—
1821/25	3.7	—	53.1	20.3
1826/30	3.9	—	47.2	22.6
1831/35	2.9	—	40.5	21.5
1836/40	2.5	4.8	30.9	18.0
1841/45	2.4	5.1	32.2	17.9
1846/50	2.2	5.2	25.3	17.2
1851/55	2.2	4.4	19.5	13.2
1856/60	1.5	3.2	15.0	10.0
1861/65	1.1	2.5	11.5	5.9
1866/70	1.1	2.3	8.9	3.8
1871/75	1.0	1.7	6.7	5.3
1876/80	1.1	1.5	6.1	6.6
1881/85	1.2	1.8	5.9	7.5
1886/90	1.2	2.0	6.1	8.3
1891/95	1.3	2.1	5.5	10.6
1896/1900	1.7	2.4	5.3	10.2
1901/05	1.7	2.0	7.0	8.8
1906/10	1.6	1.6	5.9	8.0
1911/13	1.5	1.5	5.4	8.8

Source: Horlings, *Economic Development*, 136.

However, Dutch resistance against the liberalization of Rhine traffic did not end with the ratification of the Treaty of Mainz (1831) intended to settle the issue. The government continued to obstruct implementation of the treaty, justifying its stance by a very narrow interpretation of the its clauses, which stated that the river would be free *jusque à la mer*—the question being, of course, on which side of this borderline the Dutch ports should be reckoned, and hence would they fall under the terms of the treaty or under the normal jurisdiction of national trade policy? For another twenty-odd years, relations between the Netherlands, Prussia, and the Zollverein would continue to be tense, especially on the subject of Dutch commercial policy. Under Willem I, economic policy had been aimed at strengthening the position of the large seaports, at the implicit expense of the Dutch and German hinterland. By obstructing transit trade and manipulating import and export tariffs, a distinctly protectionist attempt was made to retain as much of German trade flows in Dutch hands as in the past. Under the terms of this policy, which formed a continuation of eighteenth-century staple market politics, the Dutch government underestimated the growing economic and political importance of its eastern neighbor, acting as if the Netherlands was still able to dictate the terms by which the Rhine trade was to be pursued. In response, Prussia began to develop a close relationship with Belgium, undermining the position of the Dutch ports. The construction of the "Iron Rhine," a railway connection between Antwerp and Cologne, in 1843 was a decisive move that provided the latter with a strong competitive position in transit trade.[30]

The "Iron Rhine" and the withdrawal of Willem I—a staunch defender of Dutch privileges in this matter—from the political arena in due course resulted in a policy change. Given the more complaisant Dutch stance, new negotiations—although delayed by political instability in both Prussia and the Netherlands—resulted in a treaty that granted equal rights to Dutch and German ships and skippers in 1851.[31] In the meantime, however, the diplomatic frictions with Prussia had also resulted in a substantial delay of railway construction connecting the Dutch network with that of the Zollverein; it would take until 1856 before the line linking Arnhem to Oberhausen would be opened and Amsterdam and Rotterdam also became directly connected to Cologne—thirteen years after Antwerp.[32] Other important steps toward the liberalization of international trade in the 1840s were also closely linked to the changing relationship with Prussia. The Tariff Act drafted by Van Hall in 1845 and Van den Bosse's 1850 Shipping Act, which ended discrimination in transit trade and against foreign ships, cannot be seen in isolation from the change in the Dutch policy position with respect to the economically unfolding German hinterland. At the same time, the increased Belgian competition forced the Dutch government to step up its efforts to improve the infrastructure of both major ports, Amsterdam and Rotterdam, leading to the construction of the Noordzeekanaal—the first direct shipping route between Amsterdam and the North Sea, cutting through the western dunes—and the Nieuwe Waterweg, which improved access to Rotterdam for a larger number of seagoing vessels with an increasing draft.[33]

The effects of the liberalization of Rhine traffic were sweeping: the volume transported increased spectacularly, also due to the strong economic expansion of the Zollverein. Yet the market share of Dutch reders decreased perceptibly as a result of the loss of protection. Up until the 1830s this share had hovered between 65 and 70 percent. Already by the end of the 1840s it had fallen to around 40 percent.[34] Simultaneously, the regular services of skippers' guilds, with their turn-based allotment of cargoes, were increasingly replaced by the efforts of independent reders. Finally, transit trade swiftly gained in significance, at the expense of staple trade in both Amsterdam and Rotterdam; transshipment rather than staple trade became the dominant international function of both harbors. As a result of these changes, especially the position of Amsterdam in these trade flows declined. Even so, on balance the effects of liberalization were highly beneficial: in the decades after 1830, Rhine shipping became one of the most dynamic sectors of the Dutch economy.

Apart from the doubtlessly important reform of Rhine trade, the period between 1815 and 1842 in international respects was marked by reinvigorated protectionism. Seen from this perspective, Dutch foreign economic policy was by no means exceptional. The establishment of a new, post-Napoleonic regime in France in 1816 was almost immediately followed by the introduction of a high degree of protection of its industries. In the United Kingdom the fall of grain prices on international markets initiated a return to the Corn Laws in 1815, whereas the highly discriminatory Navigation Acts, dating from the days of civil war were still in force. Likewise, whereas to its constituents the German Zollverein may have meant the creation of a large free-trade area, to outside nations such as the Netherlands it resulted in high and rising protectionism along its eastern border (see table 5.2). The unhappy effects of Dutch diplomacy and the British resentment of the overt protection in the Indies had done little to reduce trade conflicts with neighboring countries.[35] For a small open economy such as that of the Netherlands, this kind of protectionist tit for tat—a continuation of eighteenth-century practice—constituted a serious restriction of economic possibilities. Especially trade, shipping, and, as we shall see, agriculture would in due course be able to profit strongly from the international move toward free trade and open seas.

The 1840s brought a radical turn of events. Even in 1839 the Zollverein had lowered its barriers to the import of livestock products. In Britain the Peel cabinet, under pressure from the Anti–Corn Law League, in 1842 abolished numerous trade restrictions and lowered some of the existing tariffs. This, for example, made it possible to export live animals to Britain—a crucial effect, since it removed the comparative disadvantage of having to pay the excise on slaughtered animals.[36] The repeal of the actual Corn Laws followed in 1845, carrying the almost complete liberalization of agricultural imports in its wake. In 1848 the much-resented Navigation Acts were also abolished. Acting under British as well as German pressure, Van Hall now followed suit by introducing elaborate reforms in trade legislation and lowering both import and transit tariffs. The positive discrimination of Dutch ships was dispensed with in 1850; only the trade with the East Indies continued to be under tight regulation, which did—for reasons already described—not bend until the late 1860s.

Under the emerging type of British leadership in commercial and monetary affairs—a role that Maynard Keynes would later famously coin as that of "directing the international orchestra"—a radical liberalization of international trade gathered momentum. The definitive breakthrough of the movement was achieved by the Cobden-Chevalier Treaty of 1860 between Britain and France, which brought about a second round of abolished trade restrictions and introduced the "most-favored country" clause to the abstract language of international trade negotiations. The strongly diminished revenues from import and export tariffs in both Britain and France (see table 5.2) serve to indicate the success of this movement. The Dutch government followed suit and, after having first suspended the Graanwet (a system of a sliding scale Corn Laws) in 1845, in 1862 introduced a system of tariffs that even by international standards specified very low ad valorem values. Halfway through the nineteenth century, an era of about two centuries of international mercantilism, which had formed a persistent barrier to the expansion of the open Dutch economy, thus drew to an end. Oliver Cromwell's first Act of Navigation (1651) and the protectionism of Colbert and Louis XIV (1667) had served the explicit purpose of undermining the economic supremacy of Holland, a goal that eventually had been reached. Nearly every politician or economist who has been engaged in this issue viewed international protectionism as a principal cause for the relative decline of the Dutch economy—even Adam Smith, as the archfather of advocated liberalism in foreign trade, had acknowledged the advantages of the subsequent Lord Protector's economic policy initiative to the British economy. After 1840, however, this long-term cause of relative stagnation was removed at a moment when surrounding nations had caught up with or surpassed the Dutch income level. In what follows we will start by focusing on the way in which this radical change in the international trading environment affected the Dutch economy.

CHAPTER SIX

Market Integration and Restructuring, 1840–1870

THE MIDCENTURY PRODUCTIVITY SLOWDOWN

The first few decades after the restoration of independence in 1813 were a period of relatively fast growth. In particular, between 1820 and 1840 the rate of economic expansion was impressive, something that did not escape the notice of contemporaries. Growth in the northern Netherlands may have been as fast as in the southern Netherlands—perhaps even faster. In the 1840s this first spurt of growth came to a halt, and the industrial sector entered a period of stagnation that would continue until the early 1060s. Agriculture, on the other hand, profited considerably during this period from the liberalization of international trade, which resulted in growing exports and rising prices. For the development of the services sector things were more complex: those branches that were linked to the Cultivation System also went through a period of stagnation, but other parts of the services sector expanded very rapidly, as we will show. The implementation of the liberal program resulted in an acceleration of processes of integration that resulted from the rapid growth of trade and trans-

TABLE 6.1.
Growth of Value Added in the Most Important Sectors of the Economy (average annual growth rates) and Their Contribution to GDP Growth (in percent), 1840–70.

	Growth of Value Added			Contribution to Growth		
	1840–50	*1850–60*	*1860–70*	*1840–50*	*1850–60*	*1860–70*
Agriculture	0.89	−0.06	1.80	28.5	−3.4	24.5
Fisheries	5.54	0.88	0.32	2.9	1.1	0.1
Industry	0.54	−0.28	3.40	10.6	−9.9	29.8
Services	1.54	1.45	2.28	58.0	112.2	45.5
GDP	1.11	0.59	2.38	100.0	100.0	100.0
Population	0.70	0.66	0.84	—	—	—
GDP per capita	0.41	−0.08	1.54	—	—	—

Source: J. P. H. Smits, Horlings, and Van Zanden, *Dutch GNP.*

port. The net result of all these influences was a deceleration of growth: growth of GDP fell from an average of 2.3 percent annually in the 1830s to 0.6 percent in the 1850s, when GDP growth was marginally below population growth (table 6.1). After 1860, however, and in particular after 1865, things improved dramatically, especially in industry, and a new phase of rapid growth began.

An analysis of this phase of retardation is important for understanding the economic development of the Netherlands in the nineteenth century. The debate over the "late" or "slow" industrialization of the Netherlands, which has been the focus of much economic–historical research from the 1950s onward, is basically about what happened (and perhaps what should have happened) in this period. As we will show in the chapters that follow, after 1870 (in fact 1865), the modernization of the Dutch economy accelerated, and economic development was by all standards comparable to trends in neighboring countries. This was most certainly not the case in the period 1840–65, and this "failure" has therefore received much attention from contemporary writers and economic historians. New data now make it possible to shed additional light on this matter.

Our approach in analyzing the performance of the economy is to compare the pattern and pace of economic development in the Netherlands with that in Belgium, a classic example of a mid-nineteenth-century "success-story."[1] Belgium industrialized rapidly in this period, as a result of which its GDP per capita, which had been below Dutch GDP before the 1840s, definitely left the Netherlands behind after 1865. In 1870, when its growth spurt ended, Belgium's lead was about 10 percent (figure 6.1). Between 1840 and 1870, economic

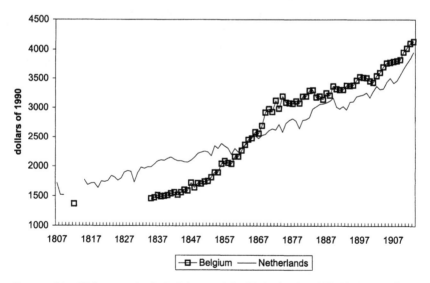

FIGURE 6.1. GDP per capita in Belgium and the Netherlands, 1807–1913. Data from Smits, Horlings, and Van Zanden, *Dutch GNP;* Horlings and Smits, "Comparison."

retardation in the Netherlands resulted in the relative decline of its GDP per capita, creating the relative "backwardness" that became a feature of the economy during the rest of the century.

The literature suggests two possible interpretations of the lag in growth during the mid-1800s. The traditional view, which is prevalent in much of the contemporary literature, is to see it as a history of missed opportunities, of the failure of entrepreneurship to respond to the challenges of the times, for example. A more recent view stresses that since the mid-1820s the Dutch economy had been characterized by a process of "balanced growth," which in particular resulted in the expansion of agriculture and the services sector.[2] Perhaps this second interpretation does not fully take into account the problem of the slow growth of industry in the 1840s and 1850s—a problem that is the center of attention of much of the older literature on this subject. A number of developments, for example, liberalization of international trade and a fall in transport costs, resulted in a relative increase in prices of agricultural products and stimulated "unbalanced" growth of this sector. Moreover, until the mid-1850s (when the excise on grain milling was abolished), the high prices of foodstuffs depressed real wages and the domestic market for industrial goods, contributing to the retardation of industry. "Balanced growth" does not, therefore, seem to be the right description of what happened in this period.

The liberal reforms of the mid-1800s are an obvious starting point for our analysis. These reforms and a number of technological developments (the establishment of railways, building of steamships, introduction of the telegraph) that resulted in a steep decline in transport costs brought about a rapid integration of national and international markets. The Dutch economy responded differently to those changes than did that of Belgium. There a strong industrial basis had been built: steel mills, engineering works, mining and woollen manufacturing flourished in the southern part of the country, while Flanders was an important center for the cotton industry. Belgium obviously had a comparative advantage in those industrial products, and the coming of free trade led to a sharp rise in industrial exports. Belgian entrepreneurship, supported by a number of big banks, played a role in the construction of railways abroad, for which Belgian industry supplied the rails and locomotives. The growth of industry and the construction of a dense network of railways by a state that was not burdened by a huge public debt led to a strong increase of investment at home. In short, the liberalization of trade led to a classical "industrial revolution" because already in 1840 Belgium had a strong comparative advantage in industry.[3]

The Dutch starting point was fundamentally different. The comparative advantage of the economy was in agriculture, not in industry. The primary sector's productivity was very high, and it specialized in products with a relatively high income elasticity of demand (butter, cheese, meat, vegetables, horticultural products).[4] Agriculture therefore profited most from the changes in the international environment, although certain parts of the services sector also

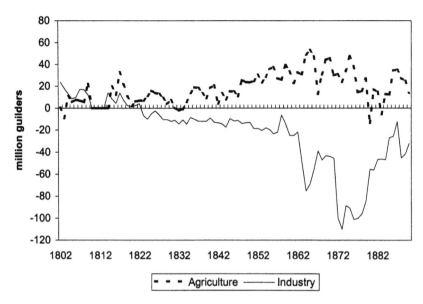

FIGURE 6.2. Net exports of agricultural and industrial products, 1802–90 (in million guilders). Data from database national accounts.

did quite well (e.g., the transit trade to Germany boomed during these years). Between 1842 and the mid-1860s, agricultural exports increased significantly; net imports of industrial products grew even more rapidly, however, a clear sign of the relatively weak competitiveness of the industrial sector (figure 6.2).

The strong expansion of the demand for agricultural products resulted in an increase in output and productivity, but the primary sector was not able to play the role of "engine" for economic growth (as industry did in Belgium). In fact, during the 1850s the growth of agricultural output also slowed (see table 6.1). Moreover, the increase in relative prices of foodstuffs resulted in stagnation in real earnings; harvest failures in the mid-1840s and again in the mid-1850s also depressed the domestic market for industrial products. The per capita consumption of agricultural commodities also fell in the 1840s, returning to 1830s levels only following the 1860s (see figure 6.4). The combination of a stagnating domestic market, increased competition from abroad, and the abolition of the protectionist policies of Willem I resulted in the decline of industrial growth.

In addition, the difficult financial situation meant that until the 1860s state investments were kept to a minimum. Railway construction lagged, and investment in new canals was delegated to private enterprise—until it became clear that this delayed the construction of vital new infrastructure. These attitudes changed in the early 1860s, when the decision was made to construct a national network of railways, the building of which was financed by the state: its exploitation was delegated to a private company. Similarly, the decision to

TABLE 6.2.
Structure of Employment in the Netherlands and Belgium, 1807–1910 (in percent).

| | *Netherlands* | | | | *Belgium* | | |
	Agriculture	*Industry*	*Services*		*Agriculture*	*Industry*	*Services*
1807	43	26	31				
1849	40	31	29	1846	46	36	18
1870	39	31	30	1866	40	39	20
1889	37	32	32	1890	27	43	30
1909	30	34	35	1910	23	47	31

Source: Horlings and Smits, "Comparison," 92.

finance the digging of canals between the two port cities of Amsterdam and Rotterdam was made in 1863 (after the insolvency of the British company that had begun to construct the canal between Amsterdam and the North Sea had become evident). Those undertakings resulted in a major surge in total investment during the 1860s, bringing with it strong growth-enhancing effects in the long run.

TABLE 6.3.
Structure of GDP in Belgium and the Netherlands, 1808/12–1910 (in current prices).

	1808/12	*1836*	*1850*	*1870*	*1890*	*1910*
Belgium						
Agriculture	30	20	21	14	11	10
Industry	29	37	38	49	43	40
Services	41	42	41	37	45	50
Total	100	100	100	100	100	100
Netherlands						
Agriculture	25	22	26	30	21	19
Industry	30	32	26	24	32	31
Services	45	46	48	46	47	50
Total	100	100	100	100	100	100

Source: Horlings and Smits, "Comparison," 87

The fundamental difference between the growth paths of Belgium and the Netherlands can be seen in the contrasts in their comparative advantage. The expansion of agriculture in the Netherlands did not result in a process of structural transformation. On the contrary, the structure of the labor force remained almost the same in the period 1849–70 (table 6.2). In Belgium, on the other hand, the share of agriculture in the labor force began to fall significantly during these years. Changes in the share of these sectors in GDP were even more pronounced: in the Netherlands the share of agriculture grew between 1836 and 1870, whereas the share of industry declined sharply, a pattern that is also caused by diverging trends in relative prices (table 6.3). In Belgium the "industrial revolution" can be seen in the significant increase in the share of industry in total income, along with a parallel decline in the share of agriculture. The atypical pattern of the Netherlands—usually economic development leads to a decline of the share of agriculture and an increase of industry's share—can also be seen in the estimates of the development of the labor productivity in the two sectors (figure 6.3). Because the estimates are in current prices, they are affected by the—at times—violent changes in them. Figure 6.3 shows that the "normal" pattern, that is, a positive productivity gap between industry and agriculture, prevails in the 1820s and 1830s, and again after 1870. But before 1818 (high prices in agriculture) and again during the 1850s and 1860s, the gap disappears, and value added per worker in both sectors is rather similar.

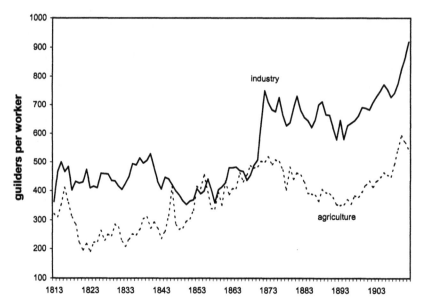

FIGURE 6.3. Labor productivity in agriculture and in industry (current prices), 1814–1913. Data from database national accounts.

This means that at the macro-level no clear incentive seemed to exist to transfer labor from agriculture to industry, which explains the lack of structural transformation during this period. In Belgium, by contrast, labor productivity in agriculture was only a fraction—30 to 45 percent—of that in industry, which stimulated structural transformation and meant that the transfer of workers to industry was an important source of growth.[5]

The results of liberalization of international trade for the two economies were therefore very different: it ignited an industrial revolution in Belgium but led to a slowing down of growth in the Netherlands. Part of the explanation for the difference seems to be the growth-stimulating effects of the process of structural transformation and related processes of urbanization.[6] In Belgium both processes contributed to a rise in investment and an acceleration of growth. The expanding demand for agricultural commodities from the growing cities also led to a widening of the domestic market for agriculture there, whereas high prices and slow urbanization had the opposite effects on the evolution of the demand for foodstuffs in the Netherlands (see later discussion). The growth of export demand was therefore to a large extent nullified by the stagnation of the domestic market. The paradoxical result of these developments was that labor productivity in agriculture in Belgium increased more than that in the Netherlands, despite Dutch agriculture profiting so much from the growth of exports.[7] Labor productivity in Dutch agriculture, which at the beginning of the nineteenth century was probably as high as in Great Britain, and much higher than in most Continental countries, began to decline relatively— between 1810 and 1870 the lead over Belgian agriculture declined from 50 percent to 23 percent.[8] The specialization in agricultural products was, therefore, in the long run, a dead end because it was not possible to increase labor productivity in this sector substantially without a parallel process of structural transformation of the economy.

These disparities in the growth of labor productivity were even more striking in the industrial sector. Stagnation in Dutch industrial growth resulted in a comparable retardation of productivity growth, whereas in Belgium the "industrial revolution" led to rapid growth in labor productivity. Economies of scale and learning effects were much stronger in the technologically dynamic new industries that dominated Belgium's growth performance than in the booming—but technologically not very innovative—agricultural sector of the Netherlands, or in its stagnating industrial sector. Again, we can use the estimates produced by Horlings and Smits to make the point: labor productivity in Belgian industry grew by 4.1 percent annually between 1850 and 1870, whereas its northern neighbor experienced an increase of only 0.9 percent in the same period.[9] In short, Belgium concentrated on new activities in which large advances in productivity could be made, whereas the Netherlands found itself locked into a highly prosperous agricultural sector that was, however, unable to increase productivity in a similar way.

The contrasts in the development of capital formation are a final point to be made here. Belgian industrialization and the construction of railways resulted in a boom in investment, which probably grew from less than 10 percent of GDP in the second half of the 1840s to more than 20 percent by about 1870. In the Netherlands this share stagnated at about 7 to 8 percent of GDP before 1870.[10] An added difference is that because of the absence of a developed capital goods sector, much of the expenditure on railways, steamships, and steam engines went abroad, whereas in Belgium the rise in the investment ratio directly stimulated the domestic market.[11]

The net effect of these different paths was that, in terms of GDP per capita, Belgium overtook the Netherlands in the 1860s and remained the more developed economy throughout the rest of the nineteenth century (see figure 6.1). The only advantage of the path of growth followed by the Dutch economy was that it allowed specialization on products the price of which increased rapidly between 1840 and 1870, resulting in a marked improvement of its terms of trade. Between the mid-1820s, when the prices of agricultural commodities reached rock bottom, and the 1860s, the terms of trade improved by about 80 percent (they would be more or less stable during the rest of the century). Income per capita, therefore, developed more favorably than GDP per capita. The Belgian terms of trade, by contrast, fell because of specialization on industrial products, the international prices of which declined (a result of growth in productivity in those new sectors, of course).

This comparative analysis leads to a different interpretation of the retardation of the Dutch economy during the mid-1800s. The explanation that is put forward is that it was the result of the comparative advantage of agriculture and the relatively poor international competitiveness of industry. However, this cannot be seen in isolation from other forces—institutional and political—that have been analyzed in preceding chapters. The crisis in public finance was identified in the analysis as a major factor in low levels of investment and the delayed construction of new infrastructure. The poor competitiveness of modern industry was, as will be shown, linked to the fragmentation of the markets for coal, machines, and other inputs, while the stagnation of the domestic market was connected to the system of excises on national and city levels. Finally, the technological stagnation of industry was related to its overregulation and the fragmentation and stagnation of the domestic market. Liberal reforms to remedy these defects in the institutional structure were, in the long term, quite successful in this respect. Although the details of this story are explained in the rest of this chapter, the "bottom line" is that an accelerated integration of the domestic market created the basis for a new period of industrial expansion that began in the middle of the 1860s. Integration resulted in an increase in competition on the domestic market, which enhanced specialization and made it possible to profit from economies of scale. It also resulted in the lowering of the prices of coal and steam engines, which made the transition to steam more attractive. Moreover, as a result of the relative stagnation of the Dutch economy from 1840 to the mid-1860s, nominal wages increased much less than abroad, which also contributed to the competitiveness of industry.[12]

At the same time, the strong expansion of agricultural exports came to an end. In the 1840s the Netherlands was by far the largest exporter of livestock products to the British market. Slowly it lost its predominant position to new competitors: Denmark at first, followed by British colonies (e.g., Australia and New Zealand). The quality of the Dutch export product had in the meantime deteriorated—perhaps its strong position on the British market had led to complacency—which contributed to the fall in market share. Finally, the domestic market picked up again in the 1860s. These changes resulted in a leveling off of the export boom in the second half of the 1860s.

The change during the 1860s is, again, apparent from the development of net exports of agricultural and industrial products (see figure 6.2). Net exports of agricultural products decline from the mid-1860s onward; after 1871 a similar break in the series of net imports of industrial products is apparent. Therefore, during the mid-1860s, a fundamental reorientation of Dutch economic development took place. The growth path based on comparative advantage in agriculture, which had resulted in increased specialization in this sector, was abandoned, and industry became, again, the most dynamic part of the economy. The current chapter explains this change in detail by going into the underlying institutional and economic developments that made this transition possible.

AGRICULTURE: FROM POTATO FAMINE TO EXPORT BOOM

The liberalization of international trade in the 1840s initiated a new period of expansion for the agricultural sector. But at the same time the potato blight and the harvest failures of the mid-1840s showed the vulnerability of this sector and the economy in general to such exogenous shocks. The first of these was the rapid spread throughout large parts of Europe of the fungus *Phytophtera infestans*, which almost destroyed the potato crop. The effects varied from region to region, but in those places where potato was cultivated on a substantial scale it brought massive poverty and unemployment. In the river clay area of Gelderland, for example, small farmers had concentrated almost completely on the cultivation of this crop, which was highly labor-intensive (the labor input was three to five times as high as that for rye or wheat) but could produce higher yields and incomes.[13] For farmers with small holdings, the possibility of consuming part of the yield themselves—unlike most other crops, the potato did not need industrial processing—and selling the rest to meet taxes, rents, and other expenditures made the crop a highly attractive option. These farmers were very hard hit by the failure of the crop in 1845 and the following years.

The gradual increase in cultivation of the potato that occurred between 1770 and 1840 had been made possible by parallel changes in patterns of consumption. During the final decades of the eighteenth century, when grain prices were increasing rapidly, the poor classes of the population had gradually accepted the potato as a new staple food, which was relatively cheap thanks to the very high yield and the absence of excises on its consumption. After 1820, when grain prices were falling rapidly, the consumption of the potato continued to spread—it not only replaced bread in the diet of the poor but also replaced the relatively large consumption of peas and beans in the diet of the middle classes and the rich.[14] From a nutritional point of view, however, this was a mixed blessing. The potato supplied more calories per guilder, and the fact that it contained vitamin C also counted in its favor, but its rise resulted in a rather unbalanced diet that was especially poor in protein.[15] This was partly compensated for by growth in the supply of pork, which became cheaper because potatoes were also increasingly used as fodder.

The potato blight of 1845 brought the rather fragile structure of those regions that were highly dependent on this crop to light. In the river clay area of Gelderland, in the Bommelerwaard in particular, and in parts of Friesland and Zeeland, the harvest failure resulted in a sharp increase in poverty and malnutrition. At one stroke the rural population lost its main source of income and food. Throughout 1845 most people coped with the situation by slaughtering their livestock, by not paying rents and taxes, and through poor relief. Unfortunately, in 1846 the rye harvest also failed—and the potato blight returned—which together resulted in skyrocketing food prices. This time the traditional mechanisms failed to absorb the double shock: poor relief collapsed because the institutions no longer received any income (rents were not being paid, nor were taxes for poor relief as the middle classes had also lost their sources of income).[16] In the most depressed areas a wave of emigration to the United States of America began that was to continue for several decades. The increase in malnutrition is also evident from data on the height of military conscripts, which shows a sudden fall in these years (and again during the harvest failures of the mid-1850s).[17] The per capita consumption of foodstuffs, which had been more or less stable during the first four decades of the century, now started to decline and only slowly recovered from the level attained before the 1840s (figure 6.4).

Mortality increased markedly in these years, and for the first and last time during the nineteenth century, the death rate—in 1847—was higher than the birthrate, resulting in a net decline of the population. The demographer Hofstee estimated that "surplus" mortality due to these causes was equivalent to about 2 percent of the population, but these estimates are highly tentative because the country was also struck by the cholera in 1847–49 (although the severity of this epidemic was of course not unrelated to the malnutrition and poverty in those years).[18] Marriages were postponed on a massive scale, which

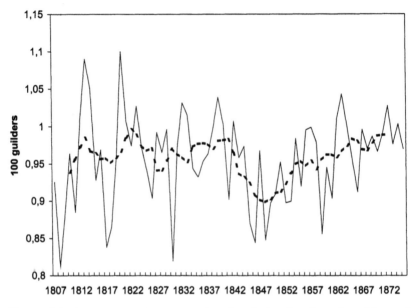

FIGURE 6.4. Average per capita consumption of agricultural products (in guilders and prices of 1913), 1807–75. Data from database national accounts.

resulted in a rise in the average age of first marriage, reducing the birthrate even more. The potato famine of the mid-1840s has all the features of a classic "subsistence crisis," to which the population reacted in a similarly classic way.

Yet not all regions went through a similar crisis. Its severity depended on the degree to which the rural economy was dependent on the potato; in "monocultures" such as the Bommelerwaard, the decline in yields was much stronger than in regions practicing a more diversified agriculture. Because the price of potatoes went up sharply, it even became profitable to cultivate the crop in regions that did not have good access to the main centers of demand in the west of the country. On the sandy soils of the eastern Netherlands, cultivation of potato in fact increased during the 1840s because the decline in crop yields was much smaller there, and because of the higher prices potatoes could command. Therefore, this region continued to prosper in the 1840s.

Rapid recovery set in after 1847, following abundant harvests and decline in the severity of the potato blight (but yields never returned to levels that were normal before 1845). In the mid-1850s the specter of hunger returned, however: in 1853–55 the Crimean War disrupted the import of grains from the Baltic, coinciding with poor harvests. Extremely high prices of rye and wheat brought about a return of malnutrition, now concentrated in the cities (as the countryside had already profited from the export boom that began in the 1840s).[19] This crisis is also evident from the decline in consumption of agricultural products to be seen in figure 6.4; the internal market for agricultural products remained weak until the 1860s. The stagnation of consumption was also related to the changes in relative prices: the prices of livestock products rose sharply due to the export boom, and consumption of meat and butter especially decreased in those years (contributing to imbalance in the diet). The average height of conscripts fell to an all-time low; Hans de Beer has shown that the height of Dutch inhabitants had probably been declining since the Middle Ages, and the drop of the mid-1850s was the end point of this long-term trend.[20]

The strong growth of exports of agricultural products in the decades after 1840 had important consequences for the structure of the sector. The share of exports in total gross output, which fluctuated between 10 percent and 15 percent in the 1820s and 1830s, increased considerably during the next few decades until it reached a new plateau of about 30 percent in the 1860s (figure 6.5). About 75 percent of these exports were livestock products: butter and cheese alone accounted for about 50 percent, and the rest consisted of meat and live cattle, sheep, and pigs. Madder was the most important product from arable

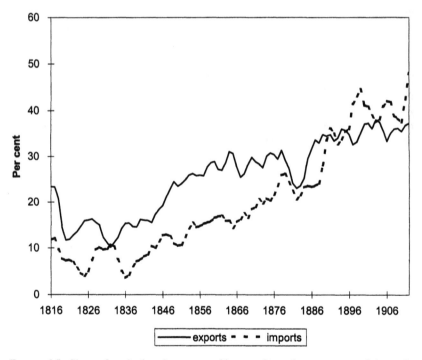

FIGURE 6.5. Share of agricultural exports and imports in total gross output of the agricultural sector, 1816–1913 (in percent). Data from database national accounts.

agriculture: together with oats and processed potatoes, it accounted for the remaining 25 percent.

As figure 6.5 shows, the strong expansion of exports did not result in an equivalent growth in output. An increase in production was to some extent restricted by the decline in potato yields. Other causes were the introduction of new, more resistant varieties and changes in cultivation practices; the *Phytophtera* fungus had, for example, badly affected potatoes that were harvested late in the season, but harvesting earlier did result in lower yields. The average yield declined from 170 to 200 hectoliters per hectare before 1840 to about 120 hectoliters per hectare in the 1850s, a fall of about one-third. Because the potato had become by far the most important crop, accounting for 12 percent of total output, this decrease meant a serious loss in total output. The decline in potato yields therefore helps to explain why the agricultural sector did not respond more favorably to the rising prices of this period (table 6.4). Livestock farming responded much more favorably to the changing situation, as might be expected: its growth was relatively strong, but not strong enough to completely compensate for the stagnation in the arable sector.

An important and lasting change that resulted from the expansion of exports was the improvement of the relative price of livestock products. Grain prices did not show a clear trend in the mid-1800s, in spite of some extremely strong fluctuations, but prices of butter, cheese, and meat went up by 100 percent or more. This induced large numbers of farmers to switch to livestock farming, in particular in those regions where arable yields were relatively low and the prospects for improving livestock farming were relatively great. In the river clay area this process accelerated in this period, and large parts of the region turned to specialized cattle farming in the second half of the nineteenth century. Similar changes occurred in sandy-soil regions—the eastern and southern parts of the country. Livestock had been kept there mainly for the production of manure, to fertilize the relatively poor soils, although some pockets of more

TABLE 6.4.
Growth of Value Added in Agriculture, 1840–70 (average annual growth rates).

	1840–50	*1850–60*	*1860–70*
Agriculture	0.89	−0.06	1.80
Arable farming	0.50	−0.21	1.58
Animal husbandry	1.34	0.03	2.19
GDP	1.11	0.59	2.38

Source: J.P.A. Smits, Horlings, and Van Zanden, *Dutch GNP.*

specialized butter production did exist (in Noord-Brabant, for example). This began to change fundamentally in this period: the rising prices of butter induced farmers to feed an increasingly large part of their grains (mainly rye and oats) to their cattle, and sell larger amounts of butter on the market. At the same time, the buying of (imported) feedstuffs began to spread, and attempts were made to import new fertilizers (such as guano) to solve the problem of the low productivity of the sandy soils. The production of pigs for the international market also began to spread rapidly, and the potato harvest was increasingly used as fodder.[21]

This switch to the production of butter and pork, whereby the harvest of rye and oats, instead of being sold directly to the market (as was the case before the 1840s), was now being used as feed for growing livestock, was part of an ongoing process of intensification of agriculture in these still relatively "backward" regions (see chapter 2). On the small family farms in this region, with their relatively elastic supply of labor, the addition of another labor-intensive stage to the production process—the transformation of rye into butter, and potatoes into pork—made economic sense, and the region became strongly focused on this mode of (mixed) livestock farming. In the areas of specialized livestock in the coastal provinces—in large parts of Holland, Utrecht, and Friesland—the expansion of production was made possible by increasing livestock densities, through the buying of more (imported) feedstuffs, and the increase of the yield of the hay harvest. Investment in the quality of the land, such as the construction of steam pumps to drain the land more effectively, also played a role.[22]

The period preceding the "great depression" of the 1880s and 1890s has often had a rather bad press. The standard literature on the agricultural history of this period emphasizes that farmers had become rich in those years of high prices rather than improving their institutions and techniques in those times of prosperity, and that they had not anticipated that this prosperity would come to an end. The catchy expression used to characterize this was that farmers had become "rich while sleeping."[23] More recent literature has tended to de-emphasize these failures and instead stress the many changes that were introduced in the 1850s and 1860s. New farm implements, such as new types of plows (imported from the United States and rapidly copied in the Netherlands), and new types of fertilizer (guano, Chile saltpeter) were introduced, all of which contributed to productivity growth.[24] On the other hand, there is no doubt that farmers profited enormously from the rise in produce prices, which was not matched by a comparable increase in wages and rents. Consequently, the profit income of farmers increased dramatically. Whereas before 1840 costs and revenues were about equal, and the profit income of farmers was close to zero, this increased to about 25 percent of value added in the 1860s and 1870s (see figure 8.6). The large profits made by the farmers—especially by large farmers in the coastal provinces—resulted in a huge growth of luxury consumption in the countryside: urban silversmiths and goldsmiths profited greatly from the growing demand for their products (which, characteristically, collapsed after the beginning of the great depression).[25] The growth of capital exports, of investment in U.S. railways and Russian public debt, also had its roots on the countryside. Many farmers invested part of their profits in this way.[26]

Yet there appears to be some truth in the criticism of the reformers of agricultural institutions of the 1890s and early 1900s that this generation of farmers had become rich while sleeping. The Dutch share in exports to the most important export market, Great Britain, showed a strongly declining trend, in particular after 1860. The share of cheese, for example, fell from 63.5 percent in 1860 to 40.6 percent in 1870; butter's share fell from 39 percent to 35 percent in the same years (reaching 24 percent in 1875).[27] Exports of live cattle collapsed after the rinderpest epidemic of 1865–66. British authorities began to restrict the imports of live animals after that year, but the Netherlands was relatively slow in switching to the export of meat. The fall in market share of butter was linked to growing complaints about the declining quality of the Dutch product, which also depressed prices for "Frisian" butter on the London market. The success of Brabant's margarine industry, which manufactured a product that competed effectively with lower-quality butters and was intended to taste and look like butter, contributed to the confusion about the quality of Dutch export butter. The growing strength of competitors—Denmark, France, and to some extent Germany, on the butter market, and the United States, on the market for cheese—was therefore also related to the failure of the Netherlands to defend its position.[28]

The agricultural sector lacked the right institutions to respond adequately to these challenges. It was almost unthinkable that the government would intervene in the market for butter and cheese, to suppress the fraud with butter (cheap and inferior butter was, for example, imported from Germany and repacked in Friesland to be sold as "superior" Frisian butter), or to regulate the trade in meat and promote the necessary restructuring of the export trade in the product. Farmers, too, were unable to act effectively. The Danish method of butter production, which resulted in a product of higher quality, was, for example, propagated by the Frisian Society of Agriculture, but to no avail. It required a much larger scale, and farmers were unable to find ways to adapt the method to the conditions that prevailed in Friesland. A real breakthrough did not occur until the late 1870s, with the introduction of cooperative butter processing (see chapter 8). Only after 1890, when the more dogmatic version of laissez-faire politics of the mid-1800s had disappeared, did the government begin to take a more constructive stance toward the agricultural sector.

The story of the agricultural sector from 1840 to 1870 is a rather complex one: on the one hand, growing exports, and rising prices and profits made growth in production and employment opportunities possible; on the other hand, the stagnation of the domestic market (until about 1860), the decline of per capita consumption (during the 1840s), and potato blight and harvest failures all point to the economic weaknesses of this period. The profits of export growth were distributed unequally: farmers' incomes boomed, in particular in those regions that already specialized in livestock farming or that had succeeded in switching to it, but real incomes of laborers were depressed, especially in the cities, as a result of the rising prices of basic foodstuffs. In spite of the fact that it profited most from the liberalization of international trade, agriculture was unable to become the "leading" sector of the economy, which might have pushed the economy onto another growth path. The growth of production and productivity was rather limited (as explained, due to a stagnating internal market and negative output shocks), and already in the 1860s the limits to the growth of this sector became apparent. In any event, the services sector was to take on this role in the mid-1800s.

SERVICES AS LEADING SECTOR

The services sector was by any standard the most dynamic sector of the Dutch economy during the period of deceleration of growth in the mid-1800s: it demonstrated the fastest increase of production and productivity (table 6.5). Two developments contributed to the strong performance of the sector: the liberalization of national and international markets and trade; and the spread of a number of fundamental innovations, such as the telegraph, railways, and the steamship. Liberalization stimulated strong growth in trade, which in itself—in view of the learning effects and economies of scale involved—would have resulted in productivity growth. The new technologies created new modes of transport that competed with each other and with older systems—railways and transport via waterways, or sailing ships and steamships—which resulted in a decline in transport costs. In combination these developments led to a very sharp fall of transport costs and transaction costs, which in turn stimulated output growth. The new systems—the telegraph and railways—showed by far the highest rates of growth (see table 6.5), although the "old" modes, which were forced to rationalize quickly, also profited from the rapid growth of exchange.

The negative effects of the gradual liberalization of trade with the Indies— which were not felt much before the crisis of 1856—were therefore more than compensated for by the growth-enhancing effects of these developments. A fundamental breakthrough was the construction of a network of railways, which had been delayed in the 1840s and 1850s by financial problems of the state. In the late 1830s and 1840s, the most interesting lines—from a commercial point of view—had been constructed: a short circuit connecting the major cities of Holland and Utrecht, and a line between Amsterdam and Rotterdam in

TABLE 6.5.
Growth of Value Added in Services, 1840–70 (average annual growth rates and percent).[a]

	Growth			Contribution to Growth[b]			Share in Value Add(
	1840–50	1850–60	1860–70	1840–50	1850–60	1860–70	1840–70
All services	1.54	1.46	2.28	100.0	100.0	100.0	100.0
International trade	1.28	−1.58	0.74	18.8	−20.7	5.0	18.9
Domestic trade	3.31	5.21	5.52	26.4	57.9	56.0	17.2
Shipping	2.32	1.88	−1.12	2.9	2.6	−0.9	4.9
River shipping	1.16	4.02	3.26	0.1	0.4	0.2	0.9
Railways	23.56	9.60	12.21	1.7	2.7	5.5	0.6
Inland transport	0.92	1.81	0.86	0.9	1.9	0.6	9.7
Other transport	1.49	1.82	1.00	9.8	12.8	4.3	5.1
Communications	1.72	11.29	9.12	0.1	1.1	1.3	0.4
Banking and insurance	3.25	2.89	2.83	3.7	4.0	2.8	2.1
Government	1.11	1.72	0.55	10.1	16.3	3.1	7.1
Housing	0.87	2.68	4.05	3.8	12.5	14.2	9.3
Domestic services	1.05	1.46	0.75	10.3	14.6	4.4	6.6
GDP	1.11	0.59	2.38	—	—	—	—

Source: J.P.A. Smits, Horlings, and Van Zanden, Dutch GNP.
[a] See the method of table 4.2.
[b] Contributions do not add up to 100 percent because not all services are included in table (domestic servi(

the west and Arnhem in the east competed with the transport via the Rhine that was to be linked to the German network in 1856). Other initiatives to construct a more encompassing network failed, mainly because it was unclear whether those new lines would be profitable in themselves.[29] Toward the close of the 1850s, it became apparent that private enterprise was unable to do the job, and after some plans by different groups of MPs had been aborted, in 1860 minister Van Hall submitted an integral plan for such a railway network. The basic idea was that its construction would be financed by the state, although later, in 1863, it was decided that a private company would be set up to manage the network.[30]

In certain respects it was advantageous that the national network was created in such a way, and not by the uncoordinated plans of private enterprise. In the

United States and in Britain, where private enterprise played a leading role, the lack of cooperation between privately owned railway companies meant that transit trade (which used the tracks of more than one company) was often discouraged if it was thought that a competitor might profit to any great extent from it. Some connections—between London and the Midlands, for example—were covered by multiple lines of competing companies; during the planning of an individual track, the effects it had on the network and the ways in which it might contribute to a better functioning of the network as a whole were not sufficiently taken into account.[31] Some of these problems would emerge in the Netherlands, too, as the newly created *staatsspoorwegen* (state railways) operated only that part of the network that was constructed after 1860; it had to compete with the two older companies, which managed the lines with Germany and the circuit within Holland. But the failure of the market to supply railways to the rest of the country meant that a balanced plan for a comprehensive network could be made. Political debate between 1858 and 1860 also centered on the efficiency of the different networks proposed. Which city, for example, had to become the central hub of the system, Arnhem or Utrecht?[32] Regional interests played a big role in this debate. Van Hall succeeded in breaking the stalemate by promising the delegates of the different cities that construction would begin in almost all regions at the same time, which allayed MPs' fears that their city or region would not profit from the coming of the railways. The accelerated construction of the railways, made necessary by this decision, resulted in a significant increase in investment, which contributed to the economic boom in the 1860s.[33]

Another sector that did exceptionally well was Rhine river shipping, which profited from the strong expansion of the German economy (which underwent an industrial revolution between 1840 and 1870) and the liberalization of this mode of transport in this period. The effects of this liberalization were drastic: the share of Dutch skippers in Rhine shipping declined from 65 to 70 percent in the 1830s (when they were still protected) to about 40 percent by the end of the 1840s. The regulated services of the skipper, who was a member of the guilds, gave way to tramp shipping. Transit trade grew much more rapidly than the active trade of Rotterdam and Amsterdam, and the position of the latter city, in particular, in the Rhine river trade came under serious pressure as a result. But the huge growth in volume of transport and trade compensated for these negative effects of liberalization, and real incomes increased rapidly in this industry.

Several other industries in the services sector also felt the negative impact of the liberalization of the domestic and international markets. Smits has shown that the strong growth of competition on the domestic market led to a reduction in margins of retail trading, especially in the province of Holland.[34] The value added in this branch, therefore, shrank considerably, and the sluggish growth of the domestic market did not compensate for this difference (see table 6.5). In the international arena similar changes occurred. The gradual streamlining of the Cultivation System meant that trading margins for export crops from Java were reduced. Some merchant houses successfully developed new activities and profited from the gradual liberalization of the system. For example, privately financed exports of textiles boomed. Other houses went down with the liberalization, protesting against the monopoly of the NHM, which seemed to suffocate trade with the Indies.[35] The gradual lowering of freight rates for the Indies also depressed the incomes of reders, and the shipping industry would remain in the doldrums until the 1870s (see table 6.5).

These "victims" of the abolition of protectionism did not loom large in the services sector as a whole. The sector also pioneered the development of new organizational structures: big railway companies, set up in this period, became (together with the NHM) the largest firms in the country, employing many hundreds, if not thousands, of people (although they were still relatively small when compared with the VOC in its days of glory). Despite—in the 1820s—a number of aborted attempts to run a profitable steamship line, new shipping companies were established, copies of their foreign brothers and sisters. In 1856, the Amsterdam elite set up the Koninklijke Nederlandsche Stoomboot Maatschappij, with the aim of running regular services between Amsterdam and other major European ports. At the same time the Stoomvaart Reederij De Maas, a Rotterdam initiative, was established, later to be taken over by its competitor from Amsterdam.[36] The poor connections of both cities with the North Sea were among the reasons that steamships did not have a great impact on Dutch shipping in this period.

To evaluate the important role played by the services sector in more detail, and to show how markets changed during this period of rapid integration, we are going to analyze in detail the development of three markets fundamental to the Dutch economy in this period, those of energy (coal), capital, and communication. This discussion will illustrate how this process of accelerated integration occurred and what its effects were.

CASE STUDY: THE INTEGRATION OF THE COAL MARKET

One of the features of the British Industrial Revolution was the application of a macro-innovation, the steam engine, to production processes in many branches of the British economy.[37] This resulted in large increases in productivity. Because the new processes that arose offered important economies of scale, they also favored the concentration of large numbers of workers in factories, which had enormous consequences for the social and economic development of Britain. The slow development of Dutch industry in this period is also often related to the delayed introduction of the steam engine as a source of energy.

The question of why this happened has been the subject of much new research. The new consensus that has arisen is that the high price of coal played an important part in delaying the introduction of steam power to the Netherlands. A limitation of this new research is that the price of coal is seen as exogenous; most research has focused on the way this affected entrepreneurial behavior.[38] Sometimes it has been noted that high coal prices were the result of the Netherlands having to import almost all its coal; mining was restricted to the deep south of Limburg, where most output was exported to neighboring Germany.

The explanation for the high price of coal is not that straightforward, however. Political-economic forces also played their role. After 1816 the import of coal into the new kingdom had been taxed at an almost prohibitive rate of fl 7.17 per metric ton because Willem I wanted to protect the Belgian mines and to forge stronger links between the south and the north. Traditionally the already large imports of coal for the breweries and gin distilleries of Holland came from the north of England (Newcastle) or Scotland, but this trade was cut off by the new tariff, which resulted in an increase in coal prices in the western part of the country. Coal imports from Germany also ceased.[39]

The secession of Belgium in 1830 caused a sudden crisis in the supply of coal, which resulted in the abolition of the tariff. It was replaced by an excise on the consumption of peat and coal, which also resulted in a strong increase in the relative price of the imported products. The new excise was about 100 percent of the price at the pithead. The peat excise was much lower: 10 to 30 percent of the production price. The way in which the excise was levied also differed: the excise on peat was imposed at the source, which meant that trade in the product and its consumption were not hindered by it, whereas the excise on coal was paid for by the consumer, which resulted in the coal trade being strictly regulated. The new excise law did allow the most important industries using coal a refund of 90 to 95 percent of the excise, but this did not limit the administrative burden of the coal merchants and consumers, who had to cope with it.[40]

The new law effectively meant that peat maintained the quasi monopoly it had on the energy market for domestic consumption. The sector profited greatly from this protection: in the northeast of the country, new production areas were developed through the digging of new canals, which resulted in a marked increase in peat consumption (from about 14 million barrels in 1810 to 40 million barrels around 1860).[41]

The peat market was well developed and highly integrated. Large amounts were shipped from the northeastern part of the country via the Zuiderzee to Holland and Utrecht; the transport of this "black gold" over canals and the Zuiderzee was also one of the pillars of the large domestic transport sector. Compared with peat, the market for coal was highly fragmented. A number of port-related industries already imported sizable quantities of coal in the seventeenth and eighteenth centuries, but farther inland this trade was almost nonexistent. When in 1825 Pieter van Dooren established the first steam engine in the Brabant town of Tilburg, he personally had to buy the coal in Liège, arrange its transport to the city of Den Bosch, rent a warehouse there, and finally organize transport to Tilburg by road. Moreover, a dispute arose between him and the city of Den Bosch about payment of an urban excise on the import of the coal; it took seven years to reach an agreement.[42] Because of the underdevelopment of this market, the costs of importing coal into Tilburg were enormous.

The growing volume of coal imports slowly lowered these transaction costs. But because peat remained predominant, the coal market developed rather slowly, and coal prices were kept at a high level. In this way the early modernization of the Dutch economy—its focus on peat, which persisted due to the protection peat received—retarded a rapid transition to a new, coal-based economy. Data on coal prices in different parts of the country clearly show the fragmented nature of this market (table 6.6). During the French period, when import of coal from Great Britain was blocked, the price of coal in Middelburg or Leiden was more than six to eight times that at the pithead in Limburg. Between 1015 and 1830 the difference fell somewhat, but the introduction of the excise in 1833 resulted in a new divergence of coal prices.

The rapid integration of coal markets began in the 1850s. The first significant event in this development was the connection with the German railways of

TABLE 6.6.
Prices of Coal in Different Cities and at the Pithead in Zuid-Limburg, 1804/13–1904/13 (in guilders per metric ton).

	Pithead	Den Bosch	Nijmegen	Utrecht	Middelburg	Leiden
1804–13	4.31	—	—	—	38.22	39.85
1814–23	3.90	27.96	11.60	—	24.25	29.17
1824–33	3.73	12.40	9.90	—	21.03	25.71
1834–43	3.89	15.13	12.10	19.46	22.39	31.02
1844–53	3.70	14.43	11.20	—	23.20	27.65
1854–63	4.72	15.40	12.49	9.72	19.71	28.22
1864–73	5.27	9.31	7.14	10.01	14.51	12.05
1874–83	5.33	8.65	6.72	8.48	9.35	9.02
1884–93	4.72	9.41	5.78	9.24	10.61	10.56
1894–1903	4.62	10.88	7.38	11.71	12.77	11.93
1904–13	5.88	—	8.82	13.36	15.25	13.36

Source: Database national accounts.

1856, which made it possible to import coal directly without transshipment. The delay in establishing this railway link, the result of the tense relationship with Prussia during the 1830s and 1840s, may have been an important cause of high coal prices before 1856.[43] At the same time, new German mines were opened, which were situated relatively close to the Dutch market and began to export large quantities of coal. The creation of a national network of railways in the 1860s further stimulated the growing integration of the coal market.

The abolition of the excise on coal and peat in 1863 inaugurated the final stage in the process. Imports of coal jumped, and the demand for peat fell sharply, as a result of which the share of peat in total energy consumption suddenly declined from 50 percent in 1863 to 38 percent in 1865. Table 6.6 shows how radical the consequences for coal prices were: the difference between Limburg and any other city in the Netherlands decreased markedly after 1863 (Leiden is perhaps the most spectacular example: the spread fell from more than fl 23 in 1854–63 to about fl 7 in 1864–73 and to less than fl 4 in 1874–83).

These changes brought about a dramatic change in the relative price of coal, which induced many consumers to switch to coal for heating and made investment in a steam engine attractive for many entrepreneurs. Figure 6.6 presents estimates of the relative price of coal (including the excise) and the related

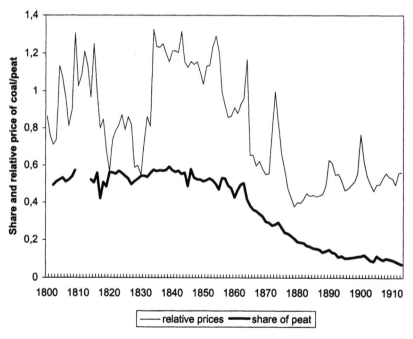

FIGURE 6.6. Relative price of coal versus peat (peat = 1) and the share of peat in total energy consumption, 1800–1913. Data from database national accounts.

changes in the share of peat in total energy consumption. The prices of peat and coal are made comparable by expressing them in the estimated amounts of energy they produce. These figures show that between 1833 and 1855 peat was, as a result of its protection, probably cheaper than coal, but that after 1855 the price ratio changed significantly because of the fall of average coal prices. As a result, at the end of the 1870s the price of coal had fallen to almost one-third that of peat. The structure of consumption closely followed those developments in relative prices: before the mid-1850s peat dominated the energy economy and accounted for about 50 percent of total consumption. During the late 1850s this began to change, and the share of peat started to fall, a process that accelerated after 1863. By the end of the nineteenth century the share of peat had dwindled to close to 5 percent. The quick integration of the market for coal in the 1850s and 1860s was one of the most important causes of the rapid spread of the steam engine during these decades. Lintsen has shown that after the sluggish diffusion of this vital innovation in the period before 1850, a change set in after the middle of the century, one that in his view is clearly linked to the development of the price of coal.[44] Before 1863, high coal prices, the result of policies to protect the peat industry (and the Belgian coal mines) and of the underdeveloped nature of the coal market, therefore played an important role in the slow spread of the steam engine.

CASE STUDY: CURRENCY REFORM AND THE
INTEGRATION OF THE CAPITAL MARKET

The organization of its currency had perhaps been one of the weaker elements of the Dutch economy in the seventeenth and eighteenth centuries. Many different currencies circulated, both foreign and domestic. The domestic currency was supplied by twelve mints—each province and some cities had maintained this privilege—which to some extent competed with each other, and sometimes produced coins of a lesser quality to maximize output and profits. The mint of Zeeland in particular struck such low-quality coins, which tended to drive out the high-quality coins of the other mints.[45] The mintmasters-general attempted to ban such practices, but jealously guarded provincial autonomy made it impossible to centralize the issuing of currency completely. The centralization of the state in 1798 did not bring about a solution to this issue either. Although it succeeded in closing down the provincial mints and unifying the currency, the state lacked the means to reform money supply, which meant that old coins remained in circulation.[46]

Currency reform was one of the desiderata of Willem I, his main purpose being to integrate the monetary standards of the two parts of the new kingdom. In the southern provinces of the Low Countries the French franc was in use and had to be replaced by new coins; talks on the new currency began in 1815.[47]

The representatives of the southern provinces resisted these changes, however: they wanted to stick to the franc because France was by far their most important trading partner. The ensuing negotiations resulted in a fixing of the relative value of the franc at a rate that was somewhat above its intrinsic value, a concession designed to win the support of the southern delegates.

Unfortunately, the new standard, which was introduced in 1816, impeded the circulation of money in two ways. In an attempt to introduce the new standard, new money was issued in large quantities in the northern Netherlands. This circulated along with the old coins, which had lost part of their intrinsic value due to wear and tear and clipping. The premium of the new money was at least 5 percent in 1820.[48] This dual standard did not really resolve the problem of the confused state of the money supply. Furthermore, in the southern provinces it became attractive—in view of this premium and the relatively high value of the franc—to melt the new coins and remint the silver in France into new francs. The new coins therefore disappeared from circulation, and the old situation— separate currencies in the northern and south provinces of the Low Countries— persisted.

Only abolishing the franc as a legal means of exchange and forcing the south to exchange its coins for new guilders could end this situation. This measure, introduced in 1825, met with stiff resistance and was in reality boycotted in the south, contributing greatly to growing tensions between the two parts of the kingdom in these years.[49] After 1830 the problem of the sorry state of the currency continued to drag on. The enormous cost of totally reforming the currency—replacing all old coins with new ones—postponed any plans until the mid-1840s, when the financial reorganization by Van Hall created some room to maneuver. The operation, which was carried out after 1845, cost about fl 10 million.[50] Between 1845 and 1849 all coins dated earlier than 1816 had to be handed in; a total of fl 86 million in old currency (of which fl 29 million consisted of *rijksdaalders* from Zeeland) was exchanged for new guilders.[51] Between 1849 and 1851 the coins that had been issued between 1816 and 1839 were withdrawn (but of the total coinage of 16 million three-guilder pieces, only 1 million were handed in again).[52]

This currency reform ended a long period of relative chaos in the money supply. During the eighteenth century the drawbacks of this situation were mitigated by the existence of the bankgulden, the currency that was deposited at the Amsterdam Wisselbank, which was used to conduct a large part of national and international payments. The value of the bankgulden was stabilized by the Wisselbank and the Amsterdam municipal authorities.[53] The decline of the Wisselbank meant that Amsterdam lost its important function in the international systems of payments.

During the first decades of its existence, the newly established Nederlandsche Bank (DNB) restricted its operations almost exclusively to Amsterdam.

Its board did not want to comply with a section of the Bankwet of 1814 (which had established the DNB), in which the setting up of branches in other parts of the country was announced. The slowly growing trust in the DNB, which is clear from the relatively moderate growth in demand for its banknotes, also limited its sphere of influence. In addition, outside Amsterdam its banknotes were valued at (slightly) less than par, which did not help speed up their circulation (see chapter 4).[54]

The 1840s brought important changes in the role of the DNB. Trust in the bank increased, in part because the danger of being manipulated by the king disappeared. The currency reform of 1845–49 also enhanced confidence in its activities. The issue of temporary paper money during the currency reform—to bridge the gap between the handing in of old coins and the issue of the new ones—contributed to the growth in supply of banknotes.

The new Bankwet of 1838 once again ruled that another branch of the DNB had to be opened in Rotterdam. The new board began to make plans to implement the decision; for example, it printed new banknotes in a different color from the "Amsterdam" notes, which had to be issued in Rotterdam (which also indicated the limited spread of the Amsterdam money). The Rotterdam cashiers, who were making a living from conducting the payments in the city, resisted the coming of a branch of the DNB for fear of competition from this "monopolist." This gave the DNB a reason to postpone setting up the branch.[55] In 1847, when the DNB board again tried to comply with the stipulation laid down in the Bankwet, the play was simply repeated. Only in 1852, after long consultation between the Rotterdam Chamber of Commerce, the DNB, and the Rotterdam cashiers, was it decided that four Rotterdam cashiers would become official agents of the DNB, and that they would provide their services at rates comparable with those of the DNB. The Rotterdam cashiers, who were de facto a cartel trying to defend its market against outside competition, had to lower their rates substantially as a result.[56]

The idea of 1838, to issue separate banknotes at the Rotterdam branch of the DNB, had not been taken up again in later plans. "Amsterdam" banknotes began to circulate in Rotterdam (and elsewhere) during the 1840s, and the notes issued by cashiers (against the deposit of money) now rapidly lost ground to the DNB banknotes. A further step in the integration of the system of exchange was taken after 1863, when the next Bankwet (which again renewed the monopoly of the central bank) stipulated that the new board set up a network of agencies, not only in Rotterdam but also throughout the rest of the country. The DNB's board acted immediately, and in 1865 an office was opened in Rotterdam, twelve agencies were set up in other major cities, and fifty-six corresponding agents were integrated into the system.[57] In a very short period a new network of banking services was set up, which integrated the system of exchange. This led not only to a strong increase in activities by the DNB (in 1868 already 50 percent of activities originated from outside Amsterdam) but also to a leveling of tariffs on payments and short-term credit.

Parallel to the expansion of the DNB into the provinces, a national market for short-term investment and credit, the on-call market, came into existence. This *prolongatie-markt* was based on the supply of credit against stocks for a period of three months, which might revolve automatically (as a result of which this short-term credit could often satisfy demand for much longer periods). Separate on-call markets probably existed before the 1850s—their history still has to be written—but the changes during the 1840s and 1850s caused a convergence of credit supply and demand on the Amsterdam market, which became the central hub of the national on-call market.[58] A precondition for the creation of a national market was rapid communication of interest rates and security prices between the different parts of the country, a condition that was now being met through the introduction of the telegraph in all parts of the country. It is clear, for example, that the decision of the Rotterdam cashiers to become agents for the DNB led to the integration of both markets and reinforced the dominant position Amsterdam already occupied.[59]

This on-call market had many advantages. Thanks to efficient mediation by brokers and cashiers, almost everyone with surplus money or a (temporary) shortage could participate on this market. Moreover, investment in stocks became more attractive because they could always be used as collateral for on-call credit; therefore, securities were almost as liquid as coins and banknotes. The rise of the on-call market went together with a strong expansion of investments in securities. Because domestic supply of securities was extremely limited—the state was concurrently liquidating part of its debt, and private enterprise did not need much capital for expansion—surplus savings, which to a large extent came from the countryside, were invested abroad.

The huge outflow of capital that began in the 1850s and probably reached its peak in the 1870s was, therefore, closely related to changes in the domestic capital market, which facilitated and even encouraged it. Russian public debt and American railways were the most favored stocks. Veenendaal has documented the growth of investment in American railways.[60] It was a highly speculative market, in which the great distance to the location where the capital was invested resulted in major information asymmetries. The Dutch investor was unable to evaluate properly the risk involved in projects or the quality of their management. The best projects were often financed in the United States itself, whereas external funds were necessary for the more risky ones. The Dutch investor knew the reputation of the bank issuing the stock; this intermediary was therefore crucial for the success of the emission, but it was expected that the bank would also play a role in monitoring the railway company in which the funds were invested. To that purpose, a unique Dutch institution was created: the *administratiekantoor*. Bankers involved in a syndicate that launched a certain railway company placed the original shares in an administratiekantoor and sold certificates to their clients. Payment of dividends or interest on bonds was automatically channeled to the owners of the certificates, but the right to monitor the activities of the company could now be executed by the bankers, who controlled the administratiekantoor (if the original shares had been sold to many thousands of investors, almost nobody would have been able to collect the necessary information for monitoring the company, let alone travel to the United States in case of major difficulties). In this way bankers tried to uphold their reputation and influence, if necessary, the activities of the railway companies.[61]

The administratiekantoor was an attempt to deal with some of the problems of information asymmetry and adverse selection that arose from capital exports to the United States. The rise of the financial press had a similar background: the number of periodicals on financial issues increased rapidly, and their focus was, of course, on the reputation and prospects of the many different funds in which Dutch investors had put their money. These solutions were not very satisfactory, however, as the many bankruptcies of companies in which the Dutch invested after 1870 would show (see also chapter 8).

The integration of the national capital market and the growth of international capital movements went hand in hand in the mid-1800s. The development of the on-call market also had a disadvantage. Because of its efficiency in bringing together the demand for and supply of credit, specialized banks had difficulties in developing their own niche of the capital market. Bankers, merchant houses (which traditionally provided financial services as well), and cashiers profited from the on-call market, which made their securities more liquid and was a source of income as well. But because of its efficiency, the margins for financial intermediaries were very small indeed—it was limited to a small brokerage fee—which meant that no bank could survive from attracting money on this market and lending it out again. Because the on-call market used stocks as securities, the risks were also very small indeed, which also limited the potential role of banks (which specialize in spreading risks and monitoring their clients in such a way that risks are reduced).[62]

The booming on-call market therefore stood in the way of a more rapid development of the banking system. Banks did not succeed in attracting sufficient deposits to enlarge their credits; deposits were not very attractive because interest rates on the on-call market were higher (until 1861, when the Twentsche Bank introduced interest on deposits, one did not get any interest on money deposited with cashiers).

It is against this background that the final stage of the changes in the financial system of the Netherlands must be understood. Between 1863 and 1873 a number of joint-stock banks, based on the model of the Crédit Mobilier, were set up.[63] The idea that big banks could play a decisive role in the industrialization of a country was based on German and French examples. The first successful example of this was the Algemeene Nederlandsche Maatschappij ter begunstiging van de Volksvlijt, established in 1822 and better known as the Société Générale. This had been designed by Willem I as a new central bank for the southern provinces, and as such was expected to invest its large resources in economic development. In the long term this experiment proved to be very successful, and in the 1850s and 1860s many plans were made to transplant this new type of bank into the Netherlands. The first initiatives were suppressed by the DNB—in its view the new banks were based on speculation only—but in the 1860s the tide could be held back no longer. One of the most important arguments in favor of these new initiatives was a change in colonial policy: it was clear that the development of private enterprise in the Netherlands Indies was handicapped by capital shortage, and a number of the new banks set out to remedy this.

At first most new banks were not very successful. The Rotterdamsche Bank, for example, soon found that it was unable to get access to the market in the Indies; instead it became, much to its chagrin, a tough competitor of the cashiers who had financed the establishment of the bank in 1863.[64] The Algemeene Maatschappij voor Handel en Nijverheid, the comparable Amsterdam initiative of the same year, went bankrupt as a result of financial mismanagement, although it did create two longer-lasting companies (Staatsspoorwegen and the Nederlandsch-Indische Handelsbank) before it went down.[65] The Amsterdamsche Bank of 1871, a mainly German initiative, also failed to find the large projects to render a profit from its substantial resources, and it had to be trimmed back after a few years.[66] The most successful newcomer was the Twentsche Bank, established in 1861, which built on a well-established clientele of textile entrepreneurs from the eastern part of the country, to whom its predecessor, the company of B. W. Blijdenstein, had already supplied financial services.[67] Therefore, this generation of joint-stock banks did not yet inaugurate a new phase in the financial history of the country.

CASE STUDY: INTEGRATION AND COMMUNICATIONS

In the course of the early modern period, a decentralized system of postal services developed that played a large role in the exchange of information between markets and cities. City governments were mainly in charge of the system, although in Holland in 1752 a more centralized postal system was introduced to supplement the services supplied by cities. The Batavian revolutionaries had placed the reform of postal services prominently on their agenda; the Postwet of 1807, the result of their plans, made postal services a state monopoly and brought about centralization of their management. However, the monopoly created was used later to make postal services a major source of income, which did not encourage the intended use of this means of exchange.[68]

The new Postwet of 1850 brought about a major breakthrough, as the aim to use the postal service as a source of income was replaced by that of providing a cheap and efficient means of information transfer. Rates were cut by 50 percent or more, and the number of postal agencies increased significantly because the new law stipulated that all communities should have at least one.[69] Further reductions followed in 1855 and 1871, bringing the costs down to about a quarter of the pre-1850 level, and the number of letters being sent increased enormously (from 4.3 million items sent before 1850, to 10.5 in 1853, and up to 15 million in 1860).[70] After 1860 the coming of the railways sped up the delivery of mail.

It was the introduction of the telegraph, however, that brought on the real revolution of the communications sector. The necessity to send messages quickly—especially in times of war—had already in the eighteenth century resulted in systems of interconnected signposts to rapidly transmit information, but these new methods had clear limitations (when operating during periods of darkness, fog, or cloudy skies, for example). The development of the electric telegraph, which became ready for practical use in the 1840s, had been followed closely in the Netherlands. In early 1845 the first requests were made to the minister for the interior to construct a railway telegraph alongside the lines of the two railway companies; the first line was already working in June 1845.[71] The network of the Hollandsche IJzeren Spoorweg Maatschappij (HIJSM), the company that managed the railway network throughout Holland, was opened for public use in 1847, and became an immediate success. But as a result of the lack of integral planning by private enterprise—in 1854, four different but partial networks, which were not interconnected, were in use—the possibilities of the new technology were not fully used.[72] A commission appointed by Thorbecke to study whether the state had to intervene clearly exposed the failure of private enterprise. It advised exploitation by the state, mainly because the interests of the state itself were at stake—the telegraph would be crucial in future defense—and because an efficient and extensive network could not be constructed and operated by private enterprise (which would, for example, not be willing to operate lines that did not show a profit).[73] The Telegraafwet that was submitted by Thorbecke in 1851 adopted these proposals, calling for the construction of a national network of telegraph lines and linkage to international networks. Exploitation was to be focused on providing a service at cost price; within a few years the state also took over any private lines that still existed.[74]

The next step was the construction of links with foreign networks. The connection with the Indies was, of course, at the top of the agenda, but it took until 1871 before a direct line was finished.[75] This link was perhaps even more important than the national network because communications with the colony had always been very time-consuming. In the seventeenth and eighteenth centuries it took about two years for the VOC to receive an answer to letters sent to Batavia. After 1780 the use of special mail boats reduced this time to about a year, but this experiment proved too costly to continue. A number of innovations, such as overland mail via Suez (instead of the trip around the Cape) and the use of steamships to speed up the mail, had reduced this even more, but in 1850 it still took almost two months for a letter from London to arrive in Batavia. This changed suddenly in 1871, when the opening of the telegraph connection with Batavia (which was, however, largely in British hands) made it possible to exchange information within one or two days.

Not much research has been done so far on the consequences of the introduction of the telegraph for the economy. It was an important factor behind the rise of the national on-call market centered in Amsterdam. Cashiers, bankers, and investors in the provinces could, thanks to the telegraph, use the financial services of Amsterdam at minimum cost and have access to almost the same information as did their counterparts in the city. This greatly enhanced the city's position as the indisputable financial center of the country.[76]

We know a little more about the effects of the construction of a telegraph connection with Batavia, which was finished at a moment when almost all parameters of trade with the Indies had changed decidedly. The opening of the Suez Canal in 1869, which suddenly made steam a profitable option on this very long trip, also changed the pattern of trade radically. The abolition of the Cultivation System and the protection to Dutch shipping and trade this implied had a significant impact as well. The net result of all these changes was that trade flows to and from the Indies were redirected in a major way. Before 1870 a Dutch company that owned a coffee, tea, or sugar plantation in the Indies would ship the goods to the Netherlands and try to sell them there as profitably as possible. The local administrators of the plantation did not take commercial initiatives. After 1870 new options opened up: to sell the goods locally or in Singapore, or on their way to the Netherlands (and inform the captain by telegraph where to land the goods—in London, Marseilles, or Rotterdam). The local administrator in the Indies had a new commercial role to play. He could consult headquarters via telegraph and by telegraph could be informed about the prices in different markets and any other information relevant for local decision making. In a similar way the role of merchant houses that specialized in the import of goods into the Indies changed: manufacturers in Twente could quickly be informed about the qualities that were desired by the market and their prices, so the supply of goods could be adapted much more quickly to changes in demand.

The flows of goods to and from the colony became much more flexible and responsive to changing markets. In practice this also implied that a much larger part of exports from the Indies were no longer going to the Netherlands but to other Asiatic ports, or to England or the United States.[77] In this way the Indies became much more directly involved in international exchange.

The communications sector is a good—but somewhat exceptional—example of the large increases in productivity that were created by the development of the services sector, from which other sectors could and did profit as well. The process of (national and international) integration that occurred in this period strongly enhanced the competitiveness of Dutch entrepreneurs; the "revolution" of the transport, communications, and capital markets lowered the costs that entrepreneurs had to make to compete on international markets. A good example is, again, the relative price of coal. Figure 6.7 compares average Dutch, English, German, and Belgian coal prices, measured in terms of the deviation of Dutch prices from those in the other countries. Clearly, until about 1860 the disadvantage of Dutch entrepreneurs was huge.[78] The price fluctuated between fl 12 and fl 18 per metric ton (whereas average pithead prices were less than fl 6); the spread began to decrease in the second half of the 1850s, and continued to do so until the turn of the century. The cost penalty Dutch manufacturers had had in comparison with their foreign competitors almost disappeared. Another way to interpret these figures is that between 1831 and 1855

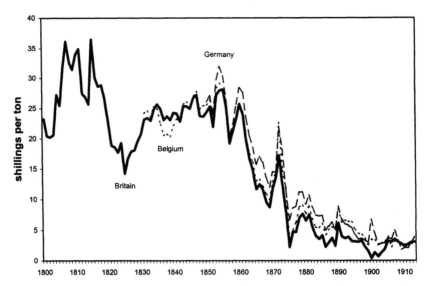

FIGURE 6.7. Differences between average prices of coal in the Netherlands and in Britain, Germany, and Belgium (in shillings per metric ton), 1800–1913. Data from Deane and Mitchell, *Abstract*, 482–83; Kuznets, *Secular Movements*, 447–49; Jacobs and Richter, "Grobhandelspreise," 62–63; exchange rates: Posthumus, *Nederlandsche Prijsgeschiedenis*, 613–38.

about 75 percent of the price of Dutch coal consisted of transaction costs (in the broadest sense, including excises, for example), a share that declined to 25 percent by 1875 and 18 percent by 1913 (the rest, going up from 25 percent between 1831 and 1855 to 82 percent in 1913, was the price at the mine). The strong decline in transactions costs was not restricted to coal, as Griffiths has shown, but also affected other inputs (cotton, iron, copper, etc.) being imported and important finished products such as calicoes, which had to find their way to the world market. At first Dutch industrialists were confronted with a sharpening of international competition, but in the long run they profited from these changes and managed to improve their competitiveness as a result.

We have stressed that parallel to this process of international integration, national markets also became much more closely linked. Regions with traditionally low prices of agricultural products saw the prices of foodstuffs rise relative to regions in which the cost of living had traditionally been high (see chapter 2 for a detailed examination of these regional costs of living in the early nineteenth century). An example is the price of butter, of which the regional variation declined between the mid-1840s and about 1870; the coefficient of variation went down from greater than 12 percent to less than 8 percent.[79] These changes ended the relatively fragmented structure of the Dutch economy, which was one of its features during the seventeenth and eighteenth centuries. Technological changes accomplished part of the job, as we have shown, but institutional reforms were perhaps as important in bringing this about.

SLOWDOWN INTO ACCELERATION: INDUSTRIAL PERFORMANCE

The development of industry was in many respects the mirror image of that of agriculture. Industry was increasingly confronted with the greater competition that resulted from the liberalization of international trade and the gradual abolition of the system of colonial protectionism. The stagnation of the domestic market until the mid-1850s, the result of high prices of foodstuffs, also had a clearly negative impact on demand for industrial commodities. In the 1860s the trends changed radically, however, and an accelerated modernization of the industrial sector began that was to continue into the years beyond 1870. This development, the transition from stagnation to rapid expansion, is the subject of this section.

Before doing that, however, we need to look at the retardation of growth after 1840. The weak spots in the system of colonial protectionism were already mentioned in chapter 4. The policies of the NHM had been geared to the creation of employment and had not resulted in a rapid modernization of the industries that profited from it. The realization of economies of scale and rationalization of production processes had in fact been held back by the NHM because of the predominance of its social motives and a dislike of large-scale production methods. Moreover, the colonial sector had not anticipated the economic downturn of

1840–41, which resulted in huge surplus capacity and large unsold stocks of calicoes. Slow communications with Java and the limited knowledge of the market that the NHM possessed made matters worse.[80] During the liberal reforms of the 1840s the ongoing protection of shipbuilding, textiles, and shipping was strongly criticized. The desire to be transparent in public finance was inconsistent with the continuation of hidden subsidies for the export of textiles to the Indies, subsidies that were in defiance of the 1824 Treaty of London. As a result, the textile industry was the first to be confronted with the abolition of protectionism. Already in 1843 the Raad van Commissarisen (Supervisory Board) of the NHM urged the abandonment of the export trade in calicoes in view of the huge losses of the previous years. The fact that the company still had large stocks of textiles in its warehouses in Batavia, however, made it impossible to implement this advice immediately. Moreover, the government did not want the NHM to stop ordering calicoes right away because large parts of the country were very much dependent on them, and most entrepreneurs themselves were still not able to organize the export of textiles. During the famine of the mid-1840s the government even induced the NHM to step up production again, which was also made possible by the recovery of the Javanese market, but this new phase ended with another crisis in 1848–49.[81]

One of the changes that were introduced was a more profit-oriented system for placing orders, from which the big entrepreneurs who produced at the lowest cost profited the most. They began to develop new channels for distribution, too, following the example of the Salomonsons, who had started this move toward independence in the 1830s. A few Rotterdam and Amsterdam merchant houses were prepared to send goods to Java on commission. This meant, however, that the entrepreneurs themselves had to finance the initiative and accept much of the risk; it took eighteen months to four years to actually get the proceeds of the transaction. Previously the risk had been taken by the NHM, and the entrepreneurs had received their money after delivering their goods to its warehouse in Twente. But the big advantage was "direct" contact with the market: the NHM had monopolized knowledge regarding what products were in demand in which regions, and it had not always been able to transmit this information to the entrepreneurs.[82] The merchant houses that gradually took over its role were specialized in these activities. Out of necessity the NHM had concentrated on the cheap segments of the market and had left the more interesting parts to British competitors. New options for upgrading the export products opened up as a result of these changes.

At first, however, these changes led to a strong decline of market share in Java. In the 1830s this share had risen to almost 70 percent; declining after 1840 to reach 38 percent in 1850, and fluctuating between 35 and 50 percent during the next decade. At the same time export volumes stagnated, which caused total output of the textile industry to fall during the 1840s and to remain more or less constant in the 1850s (table 6.7). The peak in exports around 1840 was not surpassed again until the early 1860s (see figure 4.3). The rationalization of the industry that occurred in the intervening years resulted in the disappearance of many small entrepreneurs and the concentration of the industry in Twente (and the neighboring Achterhoek).[83]

Slowly the textile industry adapted to the abolition of protectionism in the 1840s and 1850s. After a strong reduction of output, employment, and market share and important changes in its organization (see the case study on the rise of the factory), in the 1860s, when a new phase of growth began, it was able to meet international standards. In shipbuilding this reorganization took much longer, in part because protection for shipbuilding and shipping was abolished much more slowly: for example, in 1849 the NHM introduced a system of shipping services to the Indies that created new opportunities for building ships

TABLE 6.7.
The Growth of Value Added in Industry, 1840–70 (average annual growth rates and percent).

	Growth			Share in Growth[a]			Share in Value Added[b]
	1840–50	1850–60	1860–70	1840–50	1850–60	1860–70	(1840–70)
All industry	0.54	−0.28	3.40	100.0	100.0	100.0	100.0
Construction	−0.23	0.01	2.24	−11.0	−0.9	15.5	11.3
Clothing	0.31	1.72	3.60	4.4	−49.8	9.7	14.5
Leather	−2.85	−0.63	1.88	−31.6	11.0	2.5	4.6
Mining	−0.54	2.31	−0.29	−5.7	−50.1	−0.5	2.8
Metal	6.30	0.27	2.01	30.7	−3.3	2.0	4.0
Shipbuilding	1.36	−0.63	0.92	9.0	8.2	0.9	5.4
Textiles	−1.52	0.46	4.72	−29.4	−15.7	15.0	16.2
Utility	7.65	4.95	3.36	20.9	−47.1	3.4	1.4
Foodstuffs	0.52	−0.40	2.57	31.5	46.1	23.2	31.9
Paper	−2.17	2.18	5.47	−0.9	−1.8	0.5	0.5
Chemicals	0.29	4.95	2.72	0.3	−12.8	0.7	1.5
GDP	1.11	0.59	2.38	—	—	—	—

Source: Smits, Horlings, and Van Zanden, Dutch GNP.
[a] Shares do not add up to 100 because not all industries are included in table (ceramics, wood, print, diamond).
[b] See the method of table 4.2.

for this protected market. This resulted in a brief boom (until 1856) in the building of relatively small and inefficient ships.[84] The official freight rates of the ships that were chartered by the NHM were lowered substantially during these years, but they remained at a level well above the world market. Indeed, the building boom after 1849 shows that these freight rates were still much too high.

Shipbuilding therefore did relatively well in the 1840s; shipping and shipbuilding also profited from the harvest failures of the mid-1840s and mid-1850s because the strong demand for grains led to a sudden revival of the Amsterdam grain market and the shipping industry related to it. The time of the Crimean War, when imports from the Baltic suddenly regained the importance they had had during the seventeenth and eighteenth centuries, represented the final "golden years" of the wooden ship. The downturn of 1856 ended this last boom, and shipbuilding went into a long depression that lasted until the 1880s (see table 6.7).[85] The new shipping and tariff laws of 1850 and 1862 meant shipbuilders were now completely exposed to international competition. Because of their focus on constructing (small) wooden ships, the traditional shipbuilders were unable to switch to making (large) iron ships. The large factories of Paul van Vlissingen in Amsterdam and Roentgen in Rotterdam, which had built a number of steamships, had not been able to develop sufficient capabilities to become competitive internationally. They concentrated on other activities in which they had developed more expertise, such as the building of machines for the sugar industry (Van Vlissingen) or of Rhine ships (Roentgen).[86] The new companies that were set up in the 1860s and 1870s to operate steam lines bought their ships abroad, mainly in Great Britain.

Shipbuilding and textiles are two examples of industries that profited from protection and had to face its abolition later. It took almost forty years before shipbuilding adapted to international competition; the textile industry managed to do this in a much shorter period. In 1840 the German economist Friedrich List published an economic interpretation of protectionism that was based on what is now called the "infant industry" argument. The central idea is that industrialization is a learning process, which means that in due course, given the right incentives, the growth of industrial production will result in an accumulation of skills that will make it possible to lower production costs and become competitive internationally. A country that does not have an industrial basis can try to create one by protecting key branches and inducing entrepreneurs to establish new industries or reorganize old ones. To be successful in the long run, the degree of protectionism has to be lowered beyond a certain point, in line with the lowering of production costs that result from the collective learning process.

The development of the textile industry was almost by accident more or less in line with this scenario, in spite of the fact that the initial policies of the NHM were not focused on the enhancement of efficiency and the lowering of production costs. A few entrepreneurs, the brothers Salomonson, for example, already in the 1830s went beyond these changes by developing their own export channels (the lower returns per calico they received were compensated for by the economies of scale achieved in this way).[87] A transition to an industry that worked for a largely unprotected export market was in this way prepared from within the branch itself, which made the change easier (the small entrepreneurs who had to close down their activities in the 1840s and 1850s were also part of this process of adjustment).

The development of shipbuilding shows the penalties of the same policies of protectionism: in this branch the technology of production became frozen—because the NHM chartered only wooden ships—which meant that protection did not bring important learning effects or economies of scale. In addition, before 1870 steamships were not competitive in the transport to Java because of the long distance of the trip, which meant that a ship had to carry too much coal in relation to its other cargo. The opening of the Suez Canal and the introduction of the compound machine, which made much more efficient use of coal, changed all this after 1870.[88] The NHM could therefore not have stimulated the use of steamships, but it might have opened up its shipping activities for larger and more efficient sailing boats and brought freight rates down to world market levels. The most important reason it failed to do so before the 1860s was that the directors of the company, and others closely linked to it (the members of the supervisory board, for example), had strong interests in the shipping industry itself and in related activities in trade and insurance. The textile entrepreneurs from Twente were, on the other hand, outsiders to the financial elite of Amsterdam who ran the NHM; their objections to the abolition of the hidden subsidies clearly did not carry the same weight as the reasons the directors of the NHM had not to harm their own (albeit short-term) interests.

The retardation of industrial growth was not only caused by the decline of branches linked to the Cultivation System. The liberalization of trade and the growth of exports of livestock products also led to an increase in the prices of foodstuffs, whereas nominal wages did not go up much at all. Previous chapters have discussed the link between the development of real wages and domestic demand for industrial products (see figure 4.2). The same link caused a stagnation of domestic demand, which in turn caused in stagnation (1840s) and even decline (1850s) in the production of foodstuffs. Annual meat consumption per capita declined from 31 kilograms in 1834–38 to 27 kilograms in 1849–52.[89] The consumption of rye bread (with a relatively low value added) expanded at the expense of wheat bread. Beer consumption declined until the 1850s. Sugar processing, too, went through a crisis, although this was related to the lowering of the export premium (part of the streamlining of the Cultivation System) and growing competition from beet sugar in Western Europe. Other industries that were dependent on the domestic market did not fare any better. The building trades also stagnated, mainly as a result of the low level of investment in the economy (see also chapter 8). Stagnation of real wages, low investment, and the abolition of protectionism together explain the slow development of industry in the years prior to 1860.

The flourish experienced by agriculture did create some new options for industrial growth, however. In the regions that were almost completely dependent on export agriculture—in the agricultural "zone" encircling the Randstad Holland—new agricultural industries were set up that brought some more balance to their economies. The processing of madder, a red dyestuff cultivated by farmers on the clay soils of the southwest, is the first example of industrial regeneration in this zone. This branch of industry had existed in parts of Zeeland and the southern islands of Holland since the seventeenth century, and its history shows similarities to that of the herring fisheries analyzed in chapter 4. In order to ensure an export product of a constant high quality, the industry was closely regulated by the provincial government (in cooperation with the traders in the product from Rotterdam). The strict rules made it almost impossible to introduce new production methods, but since the madder from Zeeland had a near monopoly on the British market, it appeared rational to try to protect this position as much as possible. After 1815 a French production center developed that specialized in producing large quantities of dyestuff of constant quality; the disadvantage of the Zeeland methods was that there were many qualities of the dyestuff, which were all graded differently according to a complex set of standards. French competition resulted in a deep crisis in madder processing after 1837.[90] This induced the provincial government to abolish the regulation of the industry in 1845. Within a few years the whole industry was transformed: with the aid of outside capital, new, centralized factories were set up for the production of garancine, a dyestuff of a much higher quality produced from the same raw material. This brought about a recovery of its share on the British market and initiated a final phase of expansion in madder cultivation and processing (until the invention of chemical dyestuffs based on coal in the early 1870s).[91]

In the northeast of the country, two new agricultural industries arose that were dependent on the processing of potatoes and straw. The distilling of potatoes (a new industry dating back to the 1820s) collapsed after the blight of 1845. Its successor was the processing of potatoes into potato flour, an industry that took off in the 1860s (after a slow start between 1842 and 1860).[92] Almost all its products were exported to England, where the starch was used in the textile industry. The processing of straw into cardboard began later, after 1867, and was also completed geared to the English market.[93]

The opening up of international markets therefore created opportunities for the growth of new industries based on the processing of agricultural raw materials. The rise of the margarine industry in Brabant is a similar story; in this case the export trade of butter from the Netherlands (and increasingly Germany) to Britain was the main stimulus (see chapter 8). A final example of a processing industry that arose in this period is that of sugar refining. Leading entrepreneurs from the Amsterdam sugar refineries played an important role here: they feared that the supply of raw sugar from Java would end after the termination of the Cultivation System. Moreover, the competition from beet sugar from Germany and France was becoming increasingly intense on the European markets, and the new industries that arose in these countries managed to protect themselves against imports of cheap sugar from the colonies.[94] The Dutch government had, however, discouraged the growth of beet sugar because of its huge interests in sugar imports from Java. This changed in 1852 when the introduction of a new law regulating the excise on sugar created opportunities for the government to indicate that the introduction of this culture would be tolerated.[95] In 1857 the first factory was opened, soon followed by others, located primarily in the northwestern part of Brabant, near the centers where the cultivation of the sugar beet had spread fastest.[96]

The sudden revival of industry in the second half of the 1860s can to some extent be attributed to coincidence. A number of important industries benefited from spurts of growth between 1865 and 1875, often caused by exogenous factors. An important event was, for example, the abolition in 1871 of a stamp tax on newspapers, which resulted in a sudden reduction in their price and a marked increase in demand.[97] The paper industry, which had lost its traditional protection with the tariff law of 1862, reacted to these challenges by changing its production methods in order to supply the rapidly growing market of (news)paper.[98] Another exogenous event was the discovery of diamonds in South Africa, which brought about a strong flow of raw diamonds to the Amsterdam industry in the early 1870s. During this Kaapse Tijd real incomes of diamond workers soared, and large slices of these incomes were reinvested in the Amsterdam economy.[99] The American Civil War (1864–66) caused cotton supplies for the Twente textile industry to dry up, but entrepreneurs used the time that left on their hands to build steam factories that changed the structure of the branch fundamentally. Besides these "external" events, two factors were behind the rather sudden change of course of industrial development. We have already discussed the role played by the liberalization of domestic and international trade, the lowering of transaction costs, and the rapid integration of markets. This led to the creation of new patterns of specialization, of which the agricultural industries that arose in these years are fine examples. At the same time, wages of Dutch laborers lagged behind those of workers in neighboring countries,[100] and the costs of inputs—such as coal—declined as well.

Good examples of industrial activities that took off as a result of the liberal reforms of this period are to be found in bread baking and flour milling. The abolition of the excise on milling in 1855 ended the fossilized structure of the branch and created opportunities for large gains in efficiency. The new factories—the first was set up in 1856, in Amsterdam—brought about a significant and lasting decline in the price of bread because total production costs (i.e., the margin between the price of bread and that of the grain used) fell by more than 70 percent, much more than could be expected on the basis of the abolition of the excise alone (figure 6.8). The impact of these advances in productivity (which were largely passed on to consumers) were very large indeed: real incomes of workers, whose budget was dominated by bread, were affected strongly by these changes. Another activity that profited much from changes in the tax system was brewing; until the mid-1850s it was one of the few industries that saw its output decline, but during the 1860s—when the excise was reformed in such a way that new production methods could be introduced—it slowly began to modernize again and to sell new types of beer (in particular Bavarian beer) that had previously been imported from Germany.

The development of shoemaking illustrates new patterns of specialization. This branch became increasingly concentrated in the northwest of Brabant (in the Langstraat), where employment and output doubled in the 1860s and 1870s. Urban protection of this industry, which had been advocated by the guilds, was now a thing of the past, and shoemaking in the large cities declined as a result.[101]

A key sector in economic development, metalworking and engineering industries, remained relatively weak links in the structure of the Dutch economy. It did profit from the increased demand for steam engines that manifested itself especially after 1860, in response to the sharp decline in coal prices. The

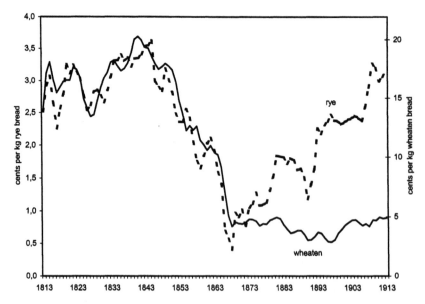

FIGURE 6.8. Margins between the average price of rye bread and wheaten bread and the costs of the rye and wheat, 1813–1913. Data from database national accounts.

share of Dutch industry in the market for newly installed steam engines, which in the 1840s had gone up to about 50 percent, remained more or less constant (it was 54 percent in 1876).[102] A significant part of the metalworking industry was linked to shipbuilding, a sector that sank into deep depression after 1856. The construction of a railway network in the 1860s created new stimuli for the sector, but this also remained restricted as a large proportion of the locomotives and the coaches required were bought elsewhere.[103] The orthodox-liberal policies of the period meant that when large orders were placed, the only selection criterion was price, and Dutch companies sometimes did not get the job even if they were only marginally more expensive than their foreign competitor. The Nederlandsche Vereeniging van en voor Industriëlen (the Dutch Association of and for Industrialists) was set up in 1861 by a group of entrepreneurs in the metalworking trades to protest these practices and to oppose proposals for tariff reform that would harm the metalworking industry even more.[104] They had no impact on public opinion.

CASE STUDY: THE RISE OF THE FACTORY

One of the most radical changes in the institutional structure of the Dutch economy during the nineteenth century was the rise of the factory. The British industrial revolution was to a large extent characterized by this development, which meant that the organization of the labor force changed fundamentally. According to the classic picture that has been drawn by Friedrich Engels in *Die Lage der arbeitenden Klasse*, the laborer exchanged the harmonious existence in the countryside, where he as a small farmer or craftsman could organize his work himself, for the "slave labor" of the factory, in which the pace was dictated by machines, and he did not enjoy his work anymore. Working in the factory meant being disciplined by bosses and capitalists, who put penalties on all kinds of violations of their rules, meant becoming dependent on the rhythm of the clock and the steam engine, and meant the exploitation of women and children on an unlimited scale. Engels ended his description of the situation of English workers with the words: "Such is the condition of the English industrial proletariat. Everywhere we find permanent and temporary suffering, sickness and demoralisation all springing either from the nature of the work or from circumstances under which they are forced to live. Everywhere the workers are being destroyed."[105]

This negative image of the British industrial revolution has no parallel in the Dutch literature on this subject. On the contrary, the retardation of the Industrial Revolution in the Netherlands is often seen as the most important cause of the country's relative "backwardness" in the nineteenth century. J. A. de Jonge, in his classic study of industrialization in the Netherlands, concluded that the rise of the factory system did not occur before the 1890s.[106] The data collected

TABLE 6.8.
Estimates of the Average Number of Laborers per Company in Industry, 1819–1909

	1819	1859	1889	1909
Total	14	15–16	20	40
Textiles	53	65	63	82
Metal/shipbuilding	3	14	34	60
Foodstuffs	4	18–19	28	47
Other	8	6–7	10	28

Sources: 1819: *Statistieken* and Horlings, *Economic Development,* 333; 1859–1909: De Jonge, *Industrialisatie,* 228–32; De Jonge, "Role," 220.

in table 6.8 confirm this picture: before 1889 the industrial enterprise was relatively small, and only a minor part of the labor force worked in factories of more than ten workers. A significant change began after 1889, however, and in 1909 the number of relatively large enterprises had doubled compared with 1889. The exception to this rule seems to be the textile sector, where already in 1819 more than half the labor force was employed by enterprises comprising more than ten workers; many of these were cottage workers, who spun or wove for a manufacturer but did not work in a factory. The transition to mechanized production within a factory occurred between 1860 and 1880 and is not properly reflected in these data.

This case study concentrates on two branches in which the mechanization of production processes began in the period before 1870 and tries to analyze the dynamics and some of the consequences of this change. Why did entrepreneurs opt for this radical reorganization of the manufacturing process (and with it the input of labor), and why did workers start to work in those factories (keeping in mind the dark interpretation of its consequences by Engels)? Usually this process is linked to technological change: the introduction of the steam engine, in particular, made it possible to mechanize large parts of the production process in certain industries. One of the consequences of using the steam engine was the creation of large economies of scale. A doubling of the power of the engine only necessitated, for example, an increase in invested capital of about 50 percent.[107] Similar economies of scale existed in the operation of the engine. In the early years it was often necessary to hire English stokers or engineers to maintain and operate the machine, which, again, was a fixed cost. In short, the larger the engine, the lower its cost per horsepower. The introduction of steam in a particular branch was, therefore, often profitable only if production was above a certain threshold (see also chapter 4 on the introduction of steam into the milling industry). Moreover, production had to be concentrated at one place, and in view of the large economies of scale of the new technology, there were strong incentives to increase the scale of production.

The slow rise of the factory system was therefore closely related to the sluggish introduction of steam power. An international comparison of data on the horsepower or industrial steam engine and the consumption of coal per capita clearly illustrates Dutch "backwardness" in this respect (table 6.9). After 1850 the gap with the United Kingdom and Belgium slowly narrows—at least in relative terms—and at the end of the century the installed capacity of steam engines was almost on par with that of neighboring countries. Coal consumption remained smaller than elsewhere (with the exception of France), however.

The current consensus is that the delayed introduction of steam power and the factory was driven by changes in relative prices. Bos and Griffiths interpreted the cause of this process to be the very high level—by international standards—of the price of coal and other inputs (steam engines included) and

TABLE 6.9.
Estimates of the Capacity of Steam Engines (in horsepower per 1,000 inhabitants) and the Consumption of Coal (in metric tons per capita) in European Countries.

| | Steam Engines Capacity | | | | |
	1840	1850	1870	1880	1896
United Kingdom	23.2	46.9	128.7	219.5	346.0
France	2.6	10.4	48.1	82.0	153.6
Germany	1.3	7.8	63.2	113.5	153.2
Belgium	9.8	15.8	69.2	111.0	183.2
Netherlands	0.?	3.3	36.0	61.8	122.6

| | Coal Consumption | | | | |
	1830	1850	1870	1890	1913
United Kingdom	1.25	2.16	3.30	4.16	4.28
France	0.06	0.12	0.49	0.96	1.62
Germany	0.06	0.19	0.83	1.84	3.88
Belgium	0.61	1.31	2.01	2.69	3.71
Netherlands	0.08	0.16	0.50	0.82	1.54

Sources: Jansen, *Industriële ontwikkeling*, appendices; De Jonge, *Industrialisatie*, 104, 495–96; Landes, *Unbound Prometheus*, 194–212; Mitchell, *International Historical Statistics*, 416–19, 466–69, 490–97; 655–59; Maddison, *Dynamic Forces*, 226–31.

the relatively low level, compared with Britain, of wages, which together did not induce entrepreneurs to mechanize rapidly.[108] When after about 1860 relative coal prices came down and wages began to rise, mechanization accelerated, and the closing of the gap with the neighboring countries began.

This interpretation explains the delayed industrialization rather well, but, as has been argued already, it does not address the question of why coal prices remained so high, or how to explain the development of nominal wages. Wages could have been "sticky" because of the institutional structure of the labor market, and coal prices were high—and the market for coal remained fragmented—because of the protection given to peat (or to coal from Belgian mines). Therefore, the relative prices, which to some extent governed the pace of industrialization, cannot be taken for granted but were related to the institutional structure of the economy. Another notable point is that the actual transition to steam power in any branch of industry was often affected by many institutional factors, which can be studied only at the branch level. To analyze the determinants of this transition process in more detail, we will examine two specific industries, the textile industry in Twente and the diamond-cutting industry in Amsterdam.

The textile industry in Twente is arguably the most intensely studied branch of the nineteenth-century Dutch economy. A number of studies have shown that important improvements in the infrastructure between 1850 and 1860 resulted in a lowering of coal prices and the cost of (imported) textile machinery, setting in motion a transition to the factory system in the 1860s and 1870s.[109] Yet it is still not completely clear why the factory system was that much more profitable after 1860. Two sets of calculations of the cost structure of production in a steam-powered factory show that the cost of weaving one piece of calico was about 80 cents (table 6.10). At the same time, the wage for a handloom weaver was about 50 cents per piece of calico. The first inescapable impression is that a switch to mechanized weaving could hardly be a good idea. However the Salomonsons, who set up the first steam-powered weavery in 1853, supplied some more details about the cost of the new technology. The piece wage of their workers was 22.5 cents per calico,[110] but because their labor productivity was about twice that of a handloom weaver working at home, the daily wage of both workers was about equal. To make the factory profitable the Salomonsons had to finance their other expenses out of the "remaining" 27.5 cents (the 50 cents a handloom weaver would get minus the wage per piece of the worker in the steam factory). Interest and depreciation of machines and buildings were about fl 75 per loom (15 percent on a total investment of fl 500 per loom).[111] To make a steam-powered factory profitable, it was necessary to use the looms as intensively as possible: if each loom produces 300 calicoes per year, these fixed costs would be 25 cents per calicoes, leaving almost no profit for the entrepre-

TABLE 6.10.
Two Estimates of the Costs of a Weavery Using Steam in Twente, 1850 and 1860
(in guilders).

	Total Costs (1850)	Per Calico (1850)	Total Costs (1860)	Per Calico (1860)
Depreciation	5.000	0.14	6.200	0.11
Interest	2.500	0.07	3.100	0.05
Coal	6.125	0.16	6.538	0.11
Wages	11.143	0.32	22.752	0.39
Other costs	—	—	8.439	0.14
Total	24.768	0.82	47.029	0.80
Number of looms	100	—	128	—

Sources: Fischer, *Fabriqueurs,* 272; Ter Meer, "Patroonvarianten," 34.

neur. If the Salomonsons succeeded in increasing output to 500 calicoes per loom per year, fixed costs would fall to 15 cents, and a substantial profit margin of 12.5 cents per calico would be achieved.

The large fixed costs of the factory explain, therefore, to some extent the changes in the organization of labor that occurred. To make a profit the number of hours that the machines were being used had to be extended, and the labor force that was working at the machines had to be disciplined not to waste "machine time." Strict rules were implemented to suppress Saints Monday and other practices that could harm the tempo of production (drinking alcohol at work, for example). To increase the speed of the machines, children were hired to perform all kinds of odd jobs that in the past had interrupted the rhythm of work of the adult laborers. Understandably, laborers did not like these changes. The new steam-powered factories had great difficulty in getting workers. The Salomonsons had to recruit workers from almost all parts of the Netherlands, since the textile workers in Twente preferred to stick to their handlooms (and the Salomonsons did not pay a higher wage than that to be earned in cottage industry).[112]

The problem of recruitment of laborers for the new factories was not restricted to this first steam weavery. Because of the strict discipline of work within them, and a natural preference of laborers to regulate their work themselves, mechanized factories had to pay much higher wages than were usual in cottage industry or in "manufactories," that is, enterprises in which handlooms (and hand-spinning machines) were concentrated in one building, and where workers still dictated the pace of work themselves; in 1841 one of these "manufactories" stated, for example, that the workers take "free hours at their own choice." Two censuses of working conditions and wages in the Twente textile industry make it possible to compare wages in these different segments (table 6.11). The big gap in earnings between the steam-powered factories and the "manufactories" is clear from these data; in part, the gap is probably due to the premium an entrepreneur had to pay for a more disciplined workforce. Furthermore, the average daily wage of workers in cottage textile industry was about forty cents in both years, well below the average wage in industry. Differences in working hours can partly explain such wage gaps: in steam-powered textile factories the average working day in 1841 was about thirteen hours, compared with eleven hours in the "manufactors."[113] One-third of the wage gap of about 50 percent can therefore be explained by longer working hours. By 1860 the wage gap had declined noticeably (but the gap with the cottage workers had in fact increased): the premium for work discipline was by then down to about 20 percent.

The entrepreneur who set up a steam-powered factory therefore had to pay relatively high wages to attract laborers, which only adds to the puzzle as to how these factories were profitable at all. One more factor that should be taken into account is the high cost involved in the organization of the cottage textile industry. Again the history of the company of the brothers Salomonson is illuminating. To manage the enormous growth of this company in the 1830s, when they employed thousands of cottage workers, they set up an elaborate network

TABLE 6.11.
Wages in Textiles in Overijssel: Firms with and without Steam, 1841 and 1860 (in guilders per day).

	1841			1860		
	Steam	No Steam	Difference (%)	Steam	No Steam	Difference (%)
Men	0.92	0.52	76	0.81	0.66	23
Women	0.50	0.31	63	0.59	0.53	12
Boys	0.44	0.35	25	0.54	0.44	22
Girls	0.44	0.29	53	0.50	0.39	27
Children	0.24	0.23	6	0.29	0.23	24
Average	0.54	0.35	48	0.63	0.51	24

Source: Gorter and De Vries, "Gegevens."

of middlemen to provide the workers with yarn and to collect the calicoes produced.[114] The cost of maintaining this network were huge: a middleman could claim between five and twenty cents per calico, costs that came on top of the piece wage of the weaver.[115] Moreover, the supply of calicoes was characterized by strong seasonal fluctuations: during the harvest period, for most crops in autumn, not much was produced, whereas during spring (at the end of a winter), when there was not much to do in agriculture, deliveries to the company's warehouses were at their peak. Because neither the entrepreneur nor the middleman could manage the labor input of the cottage worker, the scheduling of production was almost impossible. Only in the long term, through the handing out of yarn, could some scheduling be arranged, but the entrepreneur could never be certain of when the produced goods would be handed in. The development of the industry was therefore characterized by short, marked cycles in which periods of scarcity of weavers alternated with times of overproduction that could not be cut back by the entrepreneurs. One of the most important reasons for building a steam-powered factory was the possibility to plan ahead, because the Salomonsons were at times unable to honor their contracts with the NHM because of the inherent problems associated with decentralized production by cottage workers.[116]

The advantages of the factory were therefore that the expensive network of middlemen could be abolished and that the possibilities for directly scheduling and managing the production process increased considerably. As we have already argued, this required the disciplining of the workers, because the large investments in fixed capital required could only be made profitable through intensive use of the new machines. An added, very important advantage was the possibility to diversify the output. Cotton goods of a much higher quality could be made only by powered looms (the cottage workers were trained only to produce cheap calicoes), which made it possible to conquer more profitable segments of the Javanese market that had been dominated by British goods up to the 1860s. This also required another type of organization of the export trade and more direct contact with markets, markets in which the NHM was becoming less and less important (see the previous case study on the communications sector).

British practices played an important role in this transition to the factory system. In the 1830s and 1840s, Twente textile families began to send their sons to England to gain an intimate knowledge of the organization of industry and trade in Lancashire and London, places where they learned to appreciate new technology.[117] This younger generation considered the introduction of steam power the logical next step in the development of the industry, which would be taken once the infrastructure was ready for it. The railway links with Germany (for coal) and with the Dutch port cities (for the transport of yarn and finished products) that were constructed in the 1860s were therefore fundamentally important for the rise of the factory system. The switch from cottage industry to the factory took place in a relatively brief period: the number of handloom weavers declined from an estimated 8,500 in the 1850s to 4,050 in 1866 and to 2,100 by 1876. During the same period the number of power looms increased from 500 in 1856 to 7,100 in 1866, surging to 9,800 in 1876 (and 13,000 in 1886).[118] Twente became the primary center of new industry in the country, and the large size of its factories was exceptional by Dutch standards.

The mechanization of an urban-based industry that was based on highly skilled labor—diamond cutters in Amsterdam—followed a different path. In the seventeenth century immigrants from Antwerp and the Iberian Peninsula established this industry in the city. It was closely related to the world trade in diamonds, which also came to Amsterdam. At the end of the eighteenth century this trade moved on to London, however, but the skilled craftsmen—mainly Jews—had stayed in Amsterdam. Diamond cutting still was a typical cottage industry, in which the men did the actual polishing of the diamonds on a rotating mill, while the women and children drove the mill and did all sorts of other jobs associated with cutting.[119] The cutter was in fact a small entrepreneur, who was hired for a specific job by merchants in unpolished diamonds, that is, jewelers. Wages were relatively high but fluctuated greatly: the industry was heavily dependent on the supply of diamonds from overseas, meaning that periods of high incomes alternated with periods of unemployment. Many diamond workers therefore had activities on the side, for example, in the retail trade, to earn a living in bad years.

By the 1820s there was already a limited concentration of work. Between 1822 and 1830, four "manufactories" were set up in which workers could rent mills that were driven by horsepower. In 1840 the plan was launched to replace the horses by a steam engine, and in fact five jewelers received a patent for this innovation.[120] In 1845 the big jewelers decided to set up a society (i.e., partnership) for the exploitation of these factories, the Diamantslijperij Maatschappij, which bought the old "manufactories" and established a large steam-powered factory. It soon turned out that steam was much cheaper than horsepower, due in part to the high grain prices (i.e., horse feed) of the mid-1840s.[121] But in the new steam-powered factory, too, the diamond cutter remained an independent worker who relied on getting an order from a jeweler and was paid per piece of work. The income of the Diamantslijperij Maatschappij consisted of the rent it received from the diamond cutters for the mills they used.

The switch to steam had other potential advantages. One of the sources of conflict had been (and continued to be) the optimal use of the horsepower in the "old manufactories": the cutters wanted to use the production capacity as fully as possible, which meant that they worked simultaneously with two or more tongs, into which the diamonds were fixed during polishing, whereas the "manufactory" managers feared that this would wear down the horses, reason for them to introduce the rule that no more than two tongs could be used at the same time.[122] The cutters protested against this restriction because it resulted in an underexploitation of their own labor; they wanted to work with three or four tongs and so be able to earn more. In spite of the ongoing conflict over the issue, the new steam-powered factory had, however, also adopted the rule of using only two tongs, in this case because it would save on coal. It took twenty-five years before the rule, which did result in inefficient use of labor (and capital), was abolished.[123]

This institutional lethargy was connected to the specific organization of labor in the diamond industry. If the diamond cutters had been wage laborers employed by the factory, it would have been in the interest of employers to use their labor as efficiently as possible. In that case they would have been forced to use more than two tongs at once to maximize output and minimize costs (just as the weavers were urged to operate more than one loom—for the same reasons). The independent position of the diamond cutters meant that a conflict of interest existed between the owners of the factory and the workers about the precise conditions of renting the mills by the workers.

A further element in the delicate balance between the jewelers, who were also the owners of the Diamantslijperij Maatschappij, which owned the factories, and the diamond cutters was a fund that was introduced in 1845 to bind the cutters to the Diamantslijperij Maatschappij. Part of the rents paid by workers went into this fund, from which allowances in case of sickness, invalidity, or old age would be paid to the cutters, or to their widows and orphans. But any cutter who rented a mill with another company would lose these benefits immediately. At the same time, the jewelers who founded the company agreed that all their work would be done in their mills. These conditions created a strong, quasi monopoly for the owners of the Diamantslijperij Maatschappij. Only a few marginal "Christian" diamond cutters, who specialized in certain low-quality products, remained outside its control.

The first few years after the establishment of the new society were highly profitable. New diamonds from Bahia flooded the market, and demand for cutting and polishing boomed. This resulted in a number of enlargements to the first factory; the rental price of the mills was, however, kept at its old level, which meant that all reductions in costs were paid out in the form of dividends to the shareholders (who in 1853 received the equivalent of their invested capital as a return).[124] The next twelve years were much less profitable, however, as the Bahia sources dried up, and the most important export market, the United States, became involved in a civil war. Moreover, attempts by the managers of the Diamantslijperij Maatschappij to extend the discipline required of cutters resulted in a number of conflicts, culminating in a one-day strike in 1865 (confirming their independent position in this respect). The next year, in 1866, they established a society of diamond cutters (Vereniging van Diamantslijpers), which demanded, during its first strike in 1867, lower rents for the mills.[125] During the same years two new, independent factories were set up, which ended the monopoly of the Diamantslijperij Maatschappij; obviously this also strengthened the bargaining power of the diamond cutters.

These two case studies show that the introduction of steam power had important consequences for the way in which industry was organized. In both cases the economies of scale of the new technology led to a concentration of production in large factories and resulted in the decline of cottage industry. But this is only part of the story, as the case study of textiles in Twente shows. Other factors, for example, the possibility of scheduling and controlling production and monitoring quality, also played a role. This went together with a disciplining of the labor force, the introduction of a system of strict hierarchy, and, in some cases, the increased use of women and children for labor. The case of the diamond-cutting industry shows that these results were not inevitable, however. In spite of the near monopoly that was established by the Diamantslijperij Maatschappij, the diamond cutters maintained their relatively independent position as small entrepreneurs who worked for local jewelers. During the 1860s, when the company lost its monopoly, they were able to reestablish their relatively strong bargaining position. Yet diamond cutters were in an exceptional position; other factory workers were being subjected to much stricter regimes, and perhaps they felt they had become the slave laborers from the writings of Engels (and Marx). This process of "proletarianization" would receive increased attention after 1870, when the "social question" became a central issue in politics.

THE LABOR MARKET: FROM URBAN CRISIS TO STRUCTURAL CHANGE

The changes in the position of the laborers described here bring us to the subject of the labor market, which underwent important changes in this period. Schumpeter saw the process of economic development as one of "creative destruction," under which, to realize more efficient modes of production, old practices and labor relations will inevitably be demolished.[126] The labor process in a particular trade, which is based on the accumulated expertise of generations of craftsmen, may become redundant due to the development of a new technology or be replaced by a new machine that can be run by an unskilled laborer. Economic development means that new patterns of specialization are being created and that old jobs disappear. At the same time, new incentive systems will develop, and new ways to discipline labor will be invented. In short, economic development will always hurt those who suffer from these changes, but it will also result in rising expectations among those who profit from it. Social conflicts, about the distribution of the gains in productivity that can be made and about the reorganization of labor relations, are directly linked to the process of economic growth.

It is striking that these kinds of social conflict were almost absent from the Netherlands between the middle of the seventeenth century and the middle of the nineteenth century. Labor relations in large parts of the economy were almost completely rigid. The craftsmen knew this themselves: when in 1869 the shipwrights of Amsterdam organized the first "modern" strike for the improvement of their working conditions, they argued that their wages had not changed since 1664! This has been confirmed by recent research: the wages of craftsmen in Holland remained frozen from about 1650 onward, a rigidity that continued into the second half of the nineteenth century.[127]

This ossification of labor relations was a feature of a special (but important) segment of the labor market. On the basis of a case study of the Amsterdam construction industry, Ad Knotter has shown that there were in fact two segments. The first segment, focused mainly on maintenance and renovation, was characterized by a steady supply of work and was organized by individual craftsmen who employed "their" workers on a more or less regular basis. Workers received a fixed daily wage (which varied only with the season and the length of the working day), while the income of the master was based on a small surcharge on top of the wage of the employee (often the master himself also worked as a carpenter or mason). The cost of this work—the sum of wages and other expenses—was paid for by the client. The master's risk was negligible, but so, too, was his income and profit.[128]

In large projects—the building of new warehouses, for example—the labor supply was organized differently. Building contractors who had agreed to do the job for a certain amount of money hired laborers on a short-term basis—for the duration of the project. They could make a handsome profit if their costs remained below the contracted sum. Often piece wages were paid here, or (teams of) workers subcontracted out a part of the work. The pace of work was often faster in this sector, and earnings could also be more lucrative, but the demand for labor was much less stable and was concentrated in the summer months.[129] This segment of the labor market was therefore dominated by seasonal migrants from different parts of the (eastern and southern) Netherlands and Germany. By contrast, the first, stable segment of the construction trade, that is, maintenance and renovation, was dominated by inhabitants of Amsterdam. The migrant workers were a kind of buffer for the Amsterdam labor market: when the demand for labor was high, they came in large numbers, which kept the market more or less in equilibrium.[130]

The Amsterdam construction industry is probably a typical example of the labor market in large parts of the country, in particular for the cities of Holland. Labor relations in the first segment were characterized by relatively stable relationships between craftsmen—between masters and their workers—in which, until the end of the eighteenth century (and in some cases until the

1850s), guilds played an important role as regulators and mediators. From the 1850s onward, slow changes began to occur in this segment that were also related to the second, flexible segment of the labor market.

The rapid integration of markets during the mid–nineteenth century was one of the causes of change. Urban markets had previously been protected by high transport costs or the side effects of urban excises (competing products from the countryside were often banned from the cities because no town excises had been levied on them); this kind of protection disappeared in this period, and urban producers had to face increased competition from "foreign" producers. The shoemakers of Brabant, who had established a strong position on the domestic market in this period, are a case in point. The introduction of steam power in a number of industries also changed the rules of the game: in the new factories, labor relations were reorganized in a fundamental way, as we have seen.

At the same time, the flexible supply of labor from the "periphery" of Holland began to decline. Even for the 1840s it is clear that seasonal migration from the eastern Netherlands was all but disappearing because of the relatively fast growth in the demand for labor in this region. The rapid economic development of Germany's Ruhr region, which attracted large numbers of workers from other parts of Germany, had similar consequences. Political developments, such as Bismarck's wars, which drew many young men from the labor market after 1865, accelerated the process.[131]

The consequences of these changes were complex. In the Amsterdam building industry they led to a radical restructuring of traditional labor relations, in which profit-making motives became much more important. The contracting out of projects was also introduced into the maintenance and renovation sector, which meant that traditionally operating masters who did not adapt to the new circumstances became unemployed, and relations between employer and employee became more businesslike. During the 1870s, growing demand for housing led to the rise of a new group of entrepreneurs, who began to undertake the construction of houses at their own risk and for their own profit, and who were very keen to reduce (labor) costs. They hired laborers for the duration of a project and introduced new production methods (such as the production of parts of the house—windows, doors, etc.—in standard series) and incentive systems to cut costs. The labor productivity in construction increased markedly as a result. At the same time, the drying up of the flexible supply of seasonal laborers from outside the city meant that the rigidity of the wage system also disappeared, and nominal wages increased significantly, beginning in the 1860s. The activities of a number of trade unions, set up after 1870, probably contributed to the wage increases of the early 1870s.[132]

These qualitative changes in labor relations were not restricted to the building industry of Amsterdam.[133] In the printing industry of the city, another well-documented case, the growth of competition, the introduction of steam power (which simplified certain tasks), and the increasing employment of low-paid juvenile workers during the 1860s had similar consequences for labor relations. The highly skilled craftsmen in this branch resisted these changes, which in their view led to a deterioration of their position. This resulted in the setting up of a trade union in 1866 to defend their interests.[134] Similar changes occurred elsewhere. In Groningen, for example, the spread of piece wages in agriculture accelerated between 1850 and 1870, and the system of labor relations seems to have been reorganized, too.[135]

The rationalization of wage systems that occurred during this period, and in particular the rapid spread of systems of payment of piece wages in large parts of the economy, meant that, increasingly, not the *subject* (i.e., labor with its particular needs) but the *object* (i.e., the amount of labor that was performed) was being remunerated. Since the rise of wage laborers in the Middle Ages, fixed wages had been replaced by wages that were differentiated according to the season (i.e., the number of hours worked), and piece wages had been introduced in different parts of the economy, but in the second half of the nineteenth century this process clearly accelerated. In the eyes of Marx and his followers, it signified the "commodification" of labor, which became a "commodity" like all others.[136]

There is no doubt, on the other hand, that the qualitative changes in labor relations were an important source of economic expansion in this period. The doubling of the productivity of laborers in the construction industry—to give one of the most spectacular examples—was made possible by these changes.[137] The reform of labor relations that occurred between 1850 and 1870 created great opportunities for enhancing productivity and growth. This reform can be interpreted as the final phase of the dismantling of the "stationary state" and the ossified institutional structures of the eighteenth-century Republic. After the introduction of the unitary state and the slow decline of the special interest groups in the half century that followed 1795, the institutional changes penetrated to what is probably the "core" of the economy—the way in which the labor process is organized, which now began to change in a fundamental way.

The ending of the long period of wage rigidity was one of the immediate results. The growing demand for labor in agriculture and for infrastructural projects (drainage of the Haarlemmermeer, for example) in combination with the dwindling supply of laborers from the "periphery" created shortages in the lower segments of the labor market during the 1850s and 1860s. Wages of unskilled workers went up much more than those of skilled workers in this period.[138] This was one of the reasons that skilled laborers, such as printers in Amsterdam, felt deprived: they complained that their wages had now fallen below those of an unskilled worker. Wage increases accelerated in the years after 1865, when also the higher segments of the labor market profited from growing shortages.[139]

The result was that average wages began to rise rapidly during the 1860s, an increase that outstripped inflation by a substantial margin. Real wages almost doubled between 1853–55 and 1880, an increase that was supported by a decline in food prices after the mid-1870s (see figure 4.2). This was indeed a radical break with the past: after centuries of—at best—stagnant real wages, during which the standard of living was maintained by more hours worked on a per capita basis and increased participation of women and children in the labor market, a substantial increase in the real wage was realized, making possible a considerable improvement in the standard of living. Other evidence points in the same direction: food consumption recovered strongly after its midcentury nadir, and the height of military recruits began to increase during the 1860s, again after a decline in the previous decade.[140]

CONCLUSION

The changes sketched in the previous section signify the third and final stage in the gradual relaxation of the institutional structures that were inherited from the Dutch Republic. The rapid integration of national and international markets, which was closely related to the implementation of the liberal program during these years, also played a large role in this third stage. These reforms put an end to the influence some special-interest groups had on taxation and redistribution (as the case studies of the integration of the coal market and the aborted introduction of steam power into the milling industry have shown). Liberal reformers such as Thorbecke knew that they were finishing the reforms that had been begun after 1795. It is ironic that they could be so successful thanks to the legacy of the colonial policies of Willem I: the enormous colonial surplus made possible the reform of the public debt, the abolition of many excises, and finally the construction of a system of railways (and two canals, one connecting Amsterdam and the other connecting Rotterdam with the North Sea).

During the first half of the period 1840–70, liberalization of international trade and the growth of exports did not result in a comparable acceleration of growth. On the contrary, economic growth slowed. By comparing the Dutch and the Belgian reactions to these changes, we have argued that this was related to the fact that the Dutch economy had a comparative advantage in agriculture, but that this sector was not able to drive the process of growth as was the case in Belgium, where industry was the principal benefactor of the liberalization of international trade. Moreover, the abolition of protection for those industries that had profited the most from the system of colonial protection of the 1830s, and growing international competition for certain key industries (i.e., the metalworking industries) also contributed to the initial stagnation.

In the medium-long term, the rapid integration of markets brought substantial advantages for Dutch industry. In the slipstream of the expansion of agriculture, new processing industries arose in this period. More important still, it resulted in a lowering of relative input prices, which enhanced industry's international competitiveness and stimulated processes of specialization that also contributed to growing efficiency. This resulted, for example, in the introduction of steam power in a growing number of industries, often revolutionizing labor relations and market structures. A broadly based process of economic growth, beginning in the 1860s, resulted from these changes, as is characterized by a strong expansion of the domestic market, important qualitative changes in labor relations, new patterns of specialization, and—finally—the rise of the factory, which was the end result of these developments. This new dynamism went together, however, with the introduction of regimes of discipline imposed on laborers in the new factories, with changes in earning systems, and, more generally, with a "commodification" of labor. Reactions to these processes of change were at the center of political debate following 1870.

CHAPTER SEVEN

Emancipation, Pluralism, and Compromise

TOWARD THE POLITICS OF ACCOMMODATION, 1870–1913

The "Social Question," Pillarization, and Civilization

Between early 1870 and the end of the First World War, Dutch politics was dominated by three main issues: the relationship between state and church for the organization and financing of education; the extension of franchise; and social reform to improve the position of laborers. These concerns were not entirely new—in particular the discussion on the "neutral" character of the educational system had already been on the agenda before 1870—but they became more urgent as the second decade of the twentieth century was drawing to a close. At the same time, the way in which politics was conducted changed fundamentally: modern political parties were established, and new forms of collective actions were introduced. Large-scale protests, ranging from the *volkspetition-nement* (the people's petition) organized by the orthodox Protestant leader Abraham Kuyper against liberal reforms in the educational system in 1878 through to the general strike of 1903, became part of the political repertoire.

These changes resulted, in the long run, in the formation of a number of more or less independent networks of organizations tied together by ideology or religion: three highly regulated "pillars"[1]—the Catholics, the orthodox Protestants, and the socialists—and one more loose network of the liberal, nonorthodox Protestant "rest." This segmentation of society into homogeneous groups, which was characteristic for Dutch society between the First World War and the 1960s, was related not only to political organization but covered almost all aspects of daily life.[2] Trade unions, farmers' organizations, schools and universities, the press (including new media), the health care system, sports clubs and other leisure activities, and even agricultural banks and insurance companies were all segmented along these lines.

A crucial aspect of this process of pillarization that began in the 1870s was that it constructed links between organized interest groups—workers, farmers, teachers, employers—and the state. The dismantling of interest groups that had been the result of the reforms carried out between 1795 and 1850 was undone by the rise of new interest groups after about 1870. Each pillar, which was dominated by its political party (which participated in the political decision-making process), created strong links with farmers' or workers' organizations that were part of the pillar. The dynamic development of the process of pillarization was to an important extent related to the creation of a neocorporatist structure: "new" social groups got access to power via their pillar, which created strong incentives to organize. But the political parties also had to show that they were able to "deliver": the rise of pillarization was accompanied by growing pressure for social reforms, for the expansion of the educational system, and for policies in the interests of farmers. In this way, pillarization was a crucial element in the change from the liberalism of the mid–nineteenth century to the neocorporatism of the twentieth century.

It is impossible within the constraints of this book to analyze in detail the complex processes that were behind these changes. Sociologists, political scientists, and historians have attempted to understand the causes underlying the rather unique transition that took place in Dutch society in this period, but this has not resulted in a consensus about its roots. Within the context of this book we will concentrate on a few changes that were in our view of fundamental importance, knowing full well that the rise of pillarization is an even more complex story.

An important cause of the change after 1870 was that the liberal program was all but finished. It was concluded with the colonial reforms, the abolition of the death penalty, and the abolition of stamp duty on newspapers in 1870–71 and was marked, symbolically, by the third and final cabinet of the great liberal leader Thorbecke (1871–72), who died in 1872. Only a few elements of the program remained unfinished, the most important being reform of the tax system (which would be effected by Pierson in the mid-1890s). The liberals simply had done their historic job.

Moreover, from 1870 onward the state was confronted with two new issues, the result of changes that had been set in motion during the previous decades. These issues, the extension of the franchise and the effects of economic modernization on workers, were closely interrelated and created, in combination, much of the new political dynamic of the postliberal period.

Thorbecke had already in 1844 concluded that universal (male) suffrage was the logical end result of the process of democratization that had set in with the French Revolution of 1789.[3] The time was not yet ripe for it, he thought, and the constitution of 1848 did not extend the franchise but had significantly increased the direct influence of those who voted, as it had removed the layers in the voting process that had restricted voters' power before 1848. From the early 1870s onward a number of left-wing liberals, of whom Sam van Houten was the best known, put extension of the franchise on the political agenda again. The debate centered not so much on whether this should happen but on the pace of an extension, and on the character of the new sociopolitical system that it would bring with it. Abraham Kuyper, for example, who in these years was at the beginning of his career, wanted as the spokesman of the orthodox Protestant minority to introduce a system in which only the male head of the household would have the right to vote.

The underlying issue fueling the debate was what the extension of the franchise would mean for the relationship between the state and society. When, in the future, the *census*—the threshold in terms of wealth for voting rights—would be lowered so as to include "new" social groups in the political community, the balance of power was bound to be affected. The fundamental issue was how the "old" elites that had been in charge of the state for so long (since the days of the Dutch Revolt of 1572, in fact) would manage this process and integrate "new" social groups—farmers, craftsmen, laborers—into the political system. At the same time, these changes induced political "entrepreneurs" to stand up as the representatives of those new social groups, to formulate programs that served their interests in an attempt to gain access to power on their behalf, and to hasten the process of democratization. The emancipation of those social groups, which is at the core of much of the historical literature on this period, consisted in the first place of the desire to obtain the right to vote, which would inevitably change the balance within the political system.[4] The socialists, who in the 1870s presented themselves as the representative of the working class, had developed an ideology that formulated the "objective" interests of workers. To be able to carry out their program, they insisted on universal suffrage, which would "automatically" bring them to power. Perhaps the best example of such a political entrepreneur is Abraham Kuyper, who spoke on behalf of the Protestant men of small means (*kleine luyden*) from the lower middle classes (shopkeepers, farmers, and craftsmen), who were excluded from the political process. A brilliant organizer, he not only managed to reformulate their "ideology" (resulting in a split of the Reformed Church in 1886, when the orthodox Protestants followed Kuyper and formed their own congregation) but also set up a political party (the first, in 1879), with its own newspaper (1872), schools, and university (1880). Only in the 1890s did the Catholics follow this example and form their own political party, trade unions, and affiliated organizations.

Pillarization was, therefore, to some extent a by-product of the process of democratization that began after 1870. The process created its own dynamics, too: the constitutional changes of 1887, which resulted in a major increase in the proportion of the population that was allowed to vote, strengthened those parties that could profit from further extension of the franchise—the socialists, the orthodox Protestants, and the Catholics.[5] More extensions followed in the 1890s, but universal suffrage was only introduced in 1917 for men and in 1919 for women. The gradual nature of this process of enlargement of the political community is clear from table 7.1. Whereas elsewhere the introduction of universal suffrage often came suddenly, as the consequence of a dramatic conflict—such as in Belgium in 1893—in the Netherlands this was brought about by a slow and "controlled" lowering of the *census*.

TABLE 7.1.
Share of Male Adults Allowed to Vote, 1870–1913 (percent).

	1870	1880	1890	1900	1910	1913
Netherlands	11.3	12.3	26.8	45.8	59.1	67.0
United Kingdom	32.2	35.8	62.4	61.5	62.2	62.4
Germany	80.8	91.3	92.3	94.2	94.0	86.8
Austria-Hungary	24.7	24.8	30.5	34.3	94.5	94.5
France	87.0	86.4	86.6	90.0	91.5	90.5
Italy	8.9	9.0	32.0	26.5	32.2	89.8
Belgium	8.5	8.2	8.1	90.7	91.6	91.6
Denmark	72.9	78.3	84.2	85.4	87.9	87.8
Norway	21.0	20.7	32.2	89.7	95.0	95.0
Sweden	21.5	23.5	22.9	27.5	77.5	76.5

Sources: Jaarcijfers 1913, 7, 301; Joh. de Vries, "Censuskiesrecht"; Flora, et al., *State,* 89ff.

The fact that new social groups had to be integrated into the political system became manifest in the years around 1870, when the Dutch bourgeoisie was suddenly confronted with a new phenomenon: large-scale labor conflicts. There had been a small number of strikes already during the 1860s, but the first "modern" strike was organized by Amsterdam shipwrights in April 1869 and aimed at increasing wage levels. A trade union was set up to organize the strike. Moreover, in May it became a member of the international organization of socialists (the Internationale). Over the next few years a wave of strikes rippled across the country.[6] Many new unions were established. Some of them became members of the Internationale; others joined the liberal Algemene Nederlandsche Werklieden Verbond (ANWV), which had been set up as a counterweight against the influence of the socialists.

This brief period of social unrest had a major impact on liberal thinkers and politicians. It induced "enlightened" liberals to question the future of orthodox liberalism and to formulate a new program to meet this challenge. This resulted in the establishment of a Comité ter bespreking van de Sociale Questie (Committee for the Discussion of the Social Question), in which politicians, employers, and workers participated: the "social question" was born.[7]

This "social question" was the result of the acceleration of economic development in the previous period, leading to the rationalization of labor relations (see chapter 6). At the same time, the urban economy grew rapidly, and large numbers of laborers, pushed by the poverty in the countryside during the agricultural depression, came to the cities in search of jobs and a better life (see chapter 8).[8] Social mobility—both horizontal and vertical—was, in general, on the rise. Some workers improved their position, but many also felt that they did not profit much from these changes because rationalization of labor relations also led to proletarianization.

This "relative deprivation" is only part of the story, however. The standard of living of large parts of the population—of farmers in particular, but also of laborers and members of the lower middle classes—was clearly improving. In the 1860s more children went to school than ever before, and illiteracy was decreasing rapidly.[9] From the early 1860s onward, real wages rose to unprecedented levels. The claim for participation in the political process of those "new" social groups was related to a revolution of rising expectations. This trend was suddenly disrupted in the mid-1880s, however, when a cyclical downturn of the urban economy coincided with the worst period of the agricultural depression, and unemployment hit on a huge scale. This resulted in a new wave of social unrest, which in turn pressed the controlling elite of the state to accelerate the implementation of a number of reforms (the most important of which were the constitutional changes of 1887).

The focus on the "social question" in a period of gradual improvement in the population's standard of living suggests that the poverty of the working classes was not itself the primary concern of the liberal elite. The social conflicts around 1870 (and, again, around 1886), the growing influence of socialism and anarchism that became evident during those conflicts, were the real reasons behind the changing views of the ruling elite. The "social question" was not so much an issue of poverty and proletarianization of the working classes but one driven by the fact that the elite knew, given the ongoing process of democratization, that those laborers would get their say in politics, and that ways had to be found to integrate this group into the existing political system.

In this way the "social question" exposed some of the contradictions of the liberal program that had been enacted after 1840. On the one hand, laborers were supposed to become, in the long run, full members of the political community. On the other hand, the rationalization of labor relations tended to degrade workers, to make them "commodities" whose price was set by blind market forces. In politics laborers were deemed to be responsible persons who could help to shape the future of the country, whereas in economy, the workplace, they were highly disciplined by their boss and subjected to the pace of the steam engine. The social philosopher Thorbecke had already in 1844 foreseen that universal suffrage was the inevitable consequence of the principles of liberalism, but the economist Thorbecke had in 1830 already pointed out that modern industrialization meant that workers had to subject themselves to the logic of the machine and the power of the industrialist.[10] The "social question" therefore consisted of the fundamental tension between the political emancipation of the laborers and the "commodification" of labor, both direct consequences of the liberal program.

We end this broad-brush sketch of the dynamics and some of the main causes of the sociopolitical changes of the years following 1870 with a brief outline of the structures that evolved from them. The famous pacification hypothesis of Arend Lijphart states that the pillars that came into existence as a result of these sociopolitical changes might have endangered the stability of the political system because of the strong ideological tensions between them.[11] However, the political elites who dominated the top of the pillars learned to communicate with each other and to develop stable patterns of cooperation, in particular between the orthodox Protestants, the Catholics, and the liberals. Because no group could hope for a majority in Parliament—even the socialists had to abandon this idea after the extension of the franchise in 1896 did not bring the landslide victory they had taken for granted—coalitions of parties were necessary to run the country. These were based on the need to "accommodate" the existing contradictions. According to the new rules of the game, as they developed in the decades after 1878, policy making was based on bargaining between the elites of the various minority groups (i.e., the pillars), who in their turn represented different interest groups (e.g., the Catholic pillar promoted the interests of the farmers in certain parts of the country, of Catholic employers, trade unions, etc.).[12] Compromises were the logical product of this structure. In fact, it became well established with the historical compromise of 1917, in which universal suffrage (demanded by the Left) was traded off against the complete financing of "special" (i.e., religious) education (desired by the religious Right). Another mechanism that kept the system working was delegation of authority to corporate bodies—trade unions, employers' organizations, farmers' organizations, and so forth—that were to implement government policies or develop policies themselves.

The final product of these developments was a neocorporatist state in which the pillars (or segments thereof), dependent on their political weight and skills, brought about important changes in the distribution of income. Rent-seeking behavior kept the system going to a large extent: the rise of social legislation, the granting of equal (financial) rights for "special" education, and many other measures were directed at pacification of the contradictions between the pillars. The full implications of such neocorporatism only came to light after 1914 (and, in some respects, even only after 1945). The period between 1870 and 1914 was one in which the new structure slowly came into existence, and in which new and old elites developed the rules that were to govern politics in the century to come.

Another reaction by the liberal elite to the challenge of the "social question" was a systematic attempt to educate and civilize the working classes. Much like the process of pillarization, this project of civilization was the result of largely spontaneous and to some extent uncoordinated actions by individual members of the bourgeoisie, who wanted to change the "hearts and minds" of the poor. They wanted to convince them that through self-discipline, industriousness, thrift, and devotion to duty, they—the poor—could become full members of society. The diagnosis of the "social question" that was behind this response was that it was mainly an individual, moral issue, and that by changing the behavior of the poor, they could be raised from their sorry state.

The efforts to raise up the poor predated the 1870s, and in fact predated the nineteenth century. During the second half of the eighteenth century a similar movement began, which, for example, resulted in the founding of the Maatschappij tot Nut van 't Algemeen (Society for the General Good), one of the activities of which was to stimulate education of the lower classes.[13] Since 1818 the society had taken initiatives to set up local savings banks, where servants, craftsmen, and laborers could "further their own welfare through saving."[14] Because these savings banks invested their money in the public debt, the financial difficulties of the state in 1830 and again in 1848 resulted in a number of bankruptcies, which did the reputation of these banks no good. After 1848 the movement gained more momentum, but it remained restricted to the slightly more prosperous segments of the working class. In 1881 the state-owned postal bank was set up, which, through its possession of a dense network of post offices and because the state guaranteed the savings, was able to attract large groups of new customers who had even less money to save than the clients of the savings banks. Spurred by this competition, the activities of the savings banks also increased rapidly.[15]

Savings banks are just one example of an institution that was organized by the elite to educate the poor. Poor relief was increasingly used for the same purpose. In 1871 a new society for poor relief was set up in Amsterdam, *liefdadigheid naar vermogen,* which pioneered a much more direct form of help. Families who received assistance had to be educated in thrift and hygiene, the finding of employment, and the raising of their children. Direct visits of this society's volunteers to families in need were part of the new program.[16] Poverty was no longer seen as inevitable but as the result of failure on the part of the members of the family concerned. Work and education could help the poor to improve their lot, and the volunteers of this organization would teach them how to realize that.[17] Gradually this new view on the old theme of poor relief became generally accepted.

The educational system was another instrument for the civilization of the working class. After 1870, left-wing liberals began to argue in favor of a radical improvement of primary education, which finally resulted in a new law (in 1878) that practically doubled expenditures.[18] Before the 1870s, spending on education had been relatively stagnant and below that of neighboring countries (it was just 0.8 percent of GDP in 1870). The explosion in spending after 1878 reversed this situation and brought it, by international standards, to a high level of 2.0 percent of GDP in 1884.[19] Budget cuts in the 1880s and conflict with the orthodox Protestants, who were unable to finance their "special" schools in a comparable way without government subsidies, resulted in a moderation of the growth. But, increasingly, Protestants and Catholics also wanted expenditure on education to increase if their special schools were to profit as much from the new measures as the public schools did. The first compromise on this issue was forged by the first confessional (nonliberal) cabinet that came into office in 1889; from now on liberals and the confessional parties would continually outdo each other in spending on education (and its share in the economy went up to 2.5 percent in 1900).[20]

The project of the liberal bourgeoisie to civilize the "poor" was also adopted by the new, confessional elites who came to the fore. The new religious and political leaders had equally strong interests in educating their "pupils" and often possessed far more effective means to influence their hearts and minds. The intricate network of pillarized organizations that was to dominate almost all aspects of social life in the twentieth century also proved an effective channel to civilize their supporters. The socialists played their role as well: they also needed disciplined members for the party and trade unions. As the socialist and anarchist Domela Nieuwenhuijs used to say, "A labourer who drinks does not think, and a labourer who thinks does not drink."

This process of civilization was highly effective. For example, efforts to improve the hygiene and health care of the working class brought a drastic decline in mortality. Drinking habits, one of the primary concerns of all segments of the new elite, changed dramatically, as is evident from the huge decline in the consumption of alcohol consumption (especially jenever).[21] Other indicators of "improper" behavior—such as the number of extramarital children—also fell rapidly. As a result, the Netherlands became a very decent, "suburban" society.[22]

Collective Action and the Gestation of a New Corporatism

Between 1795 and 1870 the state had been the main instrument of "top-down" movements to reform the institutional structure of the economy. The Batavian revolutionaries, Willem I, and the liberal reformers of the 1840s and 1850s had all used the power of the state to introduce new rules for the organization of the economy, and all had clashed with defenders of the various interests favored under the old rules. The process of institutional development that began after about 1870 had a different character: the new institutions that arose were to a large extent the result of new forms of collective action by "new" social groups that were trying to improve their economic and sociopolitical situation and get access to the power of the state. It was a process of "bottom-up" change, initiated by new leaders of trade unions and farmers' organizations—skilled laborers, teachers, preachers (and ex-preachers)—who had not been part of the ruling elite and who found new ways to organize the groups they represented.[23]

The explosion of institutional experiments in the period after 1870 was a very special phenomenon. In almost every field of social, economic, and political life, new institutions and organizations were set up, which, as we have shown already, resulted in the neocorporatism of the twentieth century. Demolishing the old corporatism of the eighteenth century had been one of the main aims of the reform movements of the 1790s and the 1840s, but once this aim was realized, a powerful countermovement began to rebuild strong networks of interest groups: trade unions, employers' organizations, farmers' organizations, and other interest groups became parts of the "pillars," which controlled access to the state in the twentieth century.

The rather sudden appearance of these organizations of "new" interest groups demands an explanation. Why were farmers and laborers "suddenly" able to organize themselves effectively? These new organizations were able to arise because large groups of people changed their behavior: workers joined trade unions and established cooperative shops, which often meant challenging their employer; farmers set up cooperative dairies, purchasing societies, and banks (and ran into conflicts with the middlemen who had purchased their butter in the past) and formed their own organizations. These new forms of collective action were risky: it was not certain that the experiments would work, that it would be worthwhile changing old modes of behavior and challenging the vested interests of the day. Many of the pioneers of the trade union movement, for example, lost their jobs and incomes and paid a high price for the role they played.

In retrospect, the advantages of the new modes of behavior are evident, but these advantages were dependent on the fact that large groups of laborers and farmers decided *collectively* to adopt the new rules. On a theoretical level Mancur Olson analyzed this problem of collective action in the following way.[24] The results of collective action are often public goods: when, for example, a trade union wins a pay raise, all workers will profit from it, not just the workers who are members of the trade union. The question is, therefore, why should workers join a trade union when for each individual worker the costs of membership will be higher than the very marginal contribution one extra member can make to the success of the union (i.e., the direct benefit that a worker can expect from membership)? According to Olson, the "free rider," who profits from the existence of the union but does not pay the related costs of collective action, exhibits strictly rational behavior. But if all are free riders, the union will never come to be.

One of the ways to overcome this problem of collective action is to offer "selective stimuli" to members.[25] Trade unions tried to attract members by organizing insurance against illness, old age, or unemployment, thus providing inducements for workers to become a member of the organization. Of course, the question arises as to why unions were able to offer those services more efficiently than others (i.e., private enterprise). Marco van Leeuwen has argued that trade unions had access to information that made them more efficient in this role. A relatively small group of laborers in a specific branch—for example, printers in Breda—knew the reputation of all their members and could monitor their behavior at almost no cost. This informal source of information was of vital importance in organizing insurances: the problems of adverse selection and moral hazard could be solved in this way. Private entrepreneurs who did not have access to this information could not, in this respect, compete with the trade unions. From the start, trade unions therefore concentrated much time and energy on developing these "selective stimuli," and they were often quite successful at doing so.[26]

In some European countries there existed a direct link between the guilds from the ancien régime and the oldest trade unions, but in the Netherlands such a link was absent. The guilds had been abolished between 1798 and 1820 as part of the "top-down" reforms of the Batavian revolutionaries, and as it turned out their abolition had important consequences for the system of social insurances. In the eighteenth century about 30 percent of the labor force in the cities had been members of a guild, which had organized social insurances for these craftsmen. The guilds enjoyed the same advantage as the early trade unions, that is, they had access to information that made it possible to regulate (access to) these insurances efficiently.[27] The dissolution of the guilds also meant that the *knechtsbossen,* the social funds set up by the workers (not the masters) in a certain guild, lost their function. Abolition of the guilds therefore created, according to Van Genabeek, "a completely open market for social insurance."[28] New suppliers entered the market: mutual insurances grew significantly, savings banks were being set up by the members of the Maatschappij tot Nut van 't Algemeen, and, slowly, commercial insurance companies and factory funds set up by entrepreneurs became more important. The development of trade unionism was, however, hindered by a stipulation in the Code Pénal (introduced in the Netherlands in 1811) that prohibited all trade unions (and employers' organizations) and ordered that all societies with more than twenty members had to be approved by the government. It was only in 1872 that the ban on trade unions was officially lifted.[29]

The first wave of trade unionism arose between 1865 and 1875 and consisted of local organizations of skilled workers in the same trade (and a few more general workers' organizations). Highly skilled laborers that already had a long tradition of conviviality—printers, diamond cutters, shipwrights, and blacksmiths—dominated the movement.[30] Many saw their relative position decline in these years, and they feared the consequences of a further rationalization of labor relations; at the same time, they had the human capital and the networks to organize themselves relatively quickly. Insurance activities played an important role in their efforts. They aimed to improve working conditions (a goal that was facilitated by the strong performance of the economy in these years) and to "decommodify" their labor by setting up production cooperatives. The first wave of the labor movement was to some extent, according to Theo van Tijn, a "defensive reflex" of the upper layers of the laboring class, an attempt to reaffirm their social position.[31]

The strategy of setting up production cooperatives was unrealistic: workers had neither the capital nor the know-how to run them. The cooperatives that were being set up did not function well and were often handicapped by frequent conflicts between the participants (and the absence of a means to resolve these conflicts).[32] This experiment in "bottom-up" institutional change did not bring its members the advantages they had envisaged, and the movement collapsed in the 1880s.

In the 1890s a new generation of trade unions sprang up—again, first in Amsterdam. These tried to be less dogmatic and more focused on immediate gains for their members, on wage increases and on the shortening of the working day.[33] The most successful example of this new approach was the Algemeene Nederlandsche Diamantbewerkers Bond (ANDB; General Dutch Unions of Diamond Cutters), set up in 1894. Van Tijn has analyzed in detail the, to some extent unique, success of this truly first "cartel of labor." These highly skilled laborers were confronted with a very fragmented group of jewelers who commissioned their work but who were rather weak in comparison with the cartels in the unpolished diamond trade (the De Beers syndicate) and the buyers of polished diamonds on the export market. As a result, the margins between import and export prices had declined substantially, which had reduced the profits of the jewelers and put downward pressure on wages in the diamond industry. By forming a strong cartel of labor in Amsterdam, the laborers created a counterweight against those pressures, which was also welcomed by the jewelers (who acquired a stronger bargaining position on their margin as a result). The independent position of the diamond workers, who did not have to fear repercussions from an employer (see chapter 6), also helped to set up a strong union.[34]

The defining feature of the new unionism of the 1890s was that while the changes that had occurred on the labor market were acknowledged, the union aimed to regulate and control the "new" labor market as much as possible.[35] In that respect the new strategy was fundamentally different from that of the 1870s, when the undoing of these changes had been at the top of the agenda. By creating a cartel of labor, workers hoped to increase their bargaining power and restrict the room for maneuver of the employer. Their first aim was to convince employers that labor conditions had to be regulated in collective contracts, the result of the bargaining between trade unions and employers (or employers' organizations), to replace bargaining between individual workers and the entrepreneur.[36] This, of course, threatened the bargaining position of the employer, and the unions often had to fight long and hard before their position in the bargaining process was recognized. The situation in the diamond industry, where it was to the advantage of jewelers that the union was recognized and that one set of labor conditions was introduced, was rather exceptional. Although it did occur in some other industries, too, the unions were a welcome instrument to regulate competition within the industry. At the same time unions were keen to develop their other activities—such as social insurance—and from 1906 on, municipal governments subsidized these efforts.[37]

A final transformation in the structure of unionism occurred after 1905, when national federations of trade unions were set up. The logic of this development was that by pooling resources and centralizing wage negotiations the position of the unions could be greatly strengthened. This implied, however, that local unions lost some of their influence, as they were not allowed, for example, to decide for themselves if and when to strike (at least if they wanted to have access to the strike funds of the national federation). Despite trade unionism's rather late start in the Netherlands, the shift to these national structures was very rapid. Part of the explanation for this swift change was the experience of the failure of the national strikes of 1903. The sharp divisions within the trade union movement became apparent during this conflict. The anarchistic unions (which expected the national strike would herald the radical overturning of society), the socialist "new" unions (which were forced into the strike and only hoped to improve the position of their members), and the Protestant and Catholic unions (which opposed the strike) were clearly disunited. The conflict reached a bitter climax when the government—headed by Abraham Kuyper—imposed a number of draconian measures to suppress a railway strike, measures that proved successful as the strike ended in a clear victory for the government. The conflict meant that each segment of the labor movement began to follow a different route. The Catholic and Protestant unions grew rapidly, profiting from the fact that they had not participated in the strike, while the socialist unions finally seperated from the anarchistic ones and formed a strong, central federation in 1905 (which would make it impossible for them ever again to be drawn into such an "anarchistic" experiment against their will).[38] The anarchistic unions, however, lost much of their vitality after 1903. The example of the "new unionism" of the ANDB played an important role in these changes: Henri Polak, the founding father of the ANDB, also played a central role in the formation and growth of the Nederlandsch Vak Verband (NVV), the socialist federation of trade unions.[39] Under his guidance the NVV developed into a strongly centralized but rather effective organization of trade unions, which began to participate in all aspects of social and political life and became perhaps the strongest organization in the emerging socialist pillar. The example of the NVV was soon copied by Protestant and Catholic trade unions, also setting up their own national federations.

The rise of trade unionism was only one aspect of the process of "bottom-up" institutional change that began during the final decades of the nineteenth century. In chapter 8 more attention will be paid to comparable developments in the agricultural sector, which resulted in a strong cooperative movement and related organizations of farmers, another building block of the neocorporatism of the twentieth century.

THE GOLD STANDARD AND PUBLIC FINANCE

In 1875 the Netherlands adopted de facto the gold standard, but only after some public discussion, since it involved the abandonment of the silver standard that had been in force prior to that.[40] The immediate reason for doing so was the adoption of the gold standard by the newly formed German Reich in 1873, a step made possible by the imposition of a large war indemnity on France after the German-French war of 1870–71 and a major transfer of gold to the new Reich in 1871–73.[41] The German announcement meant that in the immediate future one could expect a demonetization of a comparable amount of (German) silver into gold, which would have a strong impact on their relative prices.[42] As a result, a number of European countries, in fear of a relative decline in the price of silver, which would lead to inflation in any currencies that remained tied to that metal, switched to gold. The Dutch authorities followed their example in 1875.

Before 1871 the debate on the currency standard had focused on the issue of, on the one hand, greater stability in the exchange rate vis-à-vis the dominant trading partner, Great Britain (which had already moved to the gold standard), which was to be expected if the gold standard were to be introduced, versus, on the other hand, the disadvantages of dropping the silver standard when all neighboring countries were still sticking to it.[43] Moreover, French monetary policy had guaranteed a stable relationship between silver and gold, in spite of the radical changes in the supply of both metals, in particular after large discoveries of gold in California and Australia. The developments in the early 1870s changed the outcome of this balance fundamentally, and the cabinet De Vries–Geertsema appointed a commission already in 1872 to formulate proposals to change monetary policy.[44] After an initial rejection of their proposals by Parliament in 1874, because it feared a loosening of the monetary union with the East Indies, a redrafting of them in 1875—the new proposal boiled down to the introduction of a gold coin of ten guilders besides the silver guilders that would remain in circulation—was successful. In combination with changes in the policies of the Central Bank, which were to focus on the sale and purchase of gold, this meant a transition to the gold standard that would be the central concern of monetary policies until September 1936.[45]

The de facto introduction of the gold standard had important consequences for financial and monetary policies. First of all, it led to a strong growth in demand for gold, which, in combination with a highly inelastic supply, resulted in more than two decades of almost continuous deflation in all countries that had adopted the gold standard. This happened in the Netherlands, too, albeit that deflation began relatively late (in about 1878 instead of directly after 1873) (figure 7.1). On world markets, the prices of agricultural commodities became severely depressed during the 1880s and 1890s—although the agricultural depression of this period had other causes as well (see chapter 8)—and the general level of prices continued to decline until the mid-1890s.

Another unintended consequence of the gold standard was that as a result of deflation, the burden of public debt grew once more during these years. The ratio of public debt to GDP had fallen dramatically during the 1850s and 1860s (when its decline began to level off as a result of huge investments in infrastructure and in the abolition of slavery in Surinam) but was still about 80 percent. Deflation and some net borrowing brought it back to 100 percent in the late 1880s, when a new decline set in that returned it to the 80 percent level by about 1900. Interest payments on the public debt continued to be about 40 percent of total public expenditure during the final decades of the century, limiting the possibility of new expenditures (e.g., to respond to the "social question").

The advantages of the gold standard were mainly associated with a lowering of transaction costs, in particular those related to capital movements.[46] If a country stuck to its rules, the risk of changes in the exchange rate was minimal, and interest rates could fall to the low levels of the international (British)

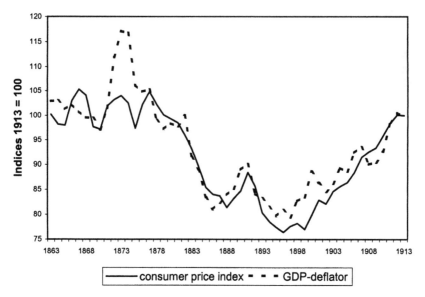

FIGURE 7.1. Two indices of the development of prices in the Netherlands, 1863–1913 (1913 = 100). Data from database national accounts.

market.[47] This indeed occurred in the Netherlands between 1870 and 1913: the difference between the interest rate on NWS and British consols that had leaped to 40 percent during the years of political and monetary instability in the early 1870s, fell to 10 percent around 1895 (figure 7.2). This not only had consequences for public finance, which profited from this decline, but was of some importance for the economy as a whole, as it stimulated investment (see chapter 8).

Among the rules of the game that had to be obeyed, one was that monetary policy had to be able to manipulate gold reserves in such a way that they could be kept above a certain threshold (40 percent of the money supply). At the end of the 1870s, when the economy was still booming and, as a consequence, deflation on world markets had been much more severe than on domestic ones, deficits in the trade balance in combination with high levels of investment abroad resulted in a significant decline of gold reserves, which necessitated a number of increases in the base rate in 1880–81.[48] The economic crisis that set in after 1882, and the sharp decline of domestic price levels that followed, restored the balance, which resulted in a strong increase in gold reserves. A similar external crisis did not occur again before the First World War, but then DNB was able to manipulate gold flows rather easily.

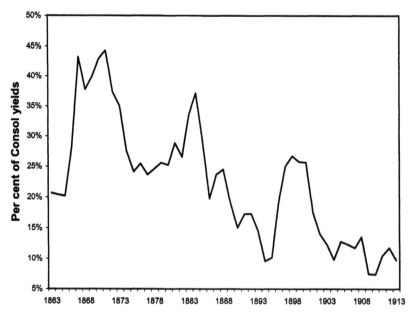

FIGURE 7.2. Spread between NWS 2.5 percent bonds and British 3 percent consols, 1863–1913 (in percent of the interest on consols). Data on NWS from Jonker, *Merchants;* Homer and Sylla, *History;* Klovland, "Pitfalls."

The gold standard also dictated the margins of financial policy. Large deficits and a sharply growing public debt would undermine confidence in the guilder and would show that the Dutch were not able to manage their economy properly. Because of the small margins of financial policy, and the fact that after 1875 the colonial surplus turned into net subsidies to the colonial empire, the state did not really respond during the 1880s and 1890s to the challenge posed by the "social question." Pressure to do so increased after the constitutional changes of 1887, however.

The rather conservative management of public finance is evident from the fact that the share in the GDP of public expenditure by the central government fell slightly during the period between 1870 and 1913, although this was to some extent compensated for by the growing importance of municipalities (see figure 5.1).[49] After the sharp decline in public spending between 1850 and 1870, on balance the role of the state in the economy stabilized, but the structure of expenditure did change. The share of public finance (i.e., the debt) fell in the long run, which created some room for education (rising from 1 percent to 12 percent of expenditure), infrastructure (peaking at 29 percent of expenditure in the mid-1860s), and "economic affairs," including agriculture (table 7.2). Spending on poor relief and health care also rose in the long run, but the municipalities funded most of this. On the income side of the budget, the introduction of income taxation by Pierson in 1893 was the most important change.[50] The importance of excises on staple foods slowly decreased, with the exception of those on alcohol and sugar.

Other evidence points into the same direction: "laissez-faire" remained the dominant ideology during these years, in spite of growing pressures for more interventionist policies. The estimates of the level of protectionism presented in chapter 5 also point to the fact that free trade remained the dominant ideology in the Netherlands, in spite of the fact that in neighboring countries (Germany, France) the tide was changing from the mid-1870s onward. Estimates presented by Peter Lindert on the scale of income transfers (to the poor) in western Europe show that the Netherlands was lagging behind in this respect, too: between 1850 and 1875 income transfers may even have declined from 0.50 percent of GDP in 1850 to 0.45 percent in 1875, followed by a very moderate increase (again to 0.50 percent) until 1890.[51] The most important factor Lindert singles out to explain these patterns is the process of democratization. The data on the extension of the franchise (see table 7.1) seem, indeed, to confirm this connection. In short, the Netherlands remained one of the most liberal countries in Europe, in which the state continued to lean strongly toward laissez-faire.

The role of the central government in the economy therefore changed only very slowly in the decades following 1870, in spite of increasing demands from voters for the state to do more. Some of the pressure for more active policies to

TABLE 7.2.
Structure of Income and Expenditure of the Central Government, 1850–1913 (in percent and million guilders).

	1850	1860	1870	1880	1890	1900	1913
Structure of income (%)[a]							
Income tax	0.0	0.0	0.0	0.0	0.0	11.3	14.6
Other direct taxes	35.3	36.4	30.8	26.3	27.4	18.2	16.7
Excises on sugar and drink	10.5	14.1	27.6	30.5	31.4	34.6	32.9
Other excises	27.2	18.4	12.5	11.5	11.5	7.2	6.4
Other indirect taxes							
(including tariffs)	27.0	31.1	29.1	31.8	29.7	28.6	29.4
Total income	100.0	100.0	100.0	100.0	100.0	100.0	100.0
Total tax income (10^6 fl)	54.0	55.6	69.7	94.1	102.5	121.5	169.6
Total income (10^6 fl)	59.2	61.9	79.7	109.5	123.1	146.7	225.2
Structure of expenditure (%)							
Core tasks[b]	10.7	15.4	25.3	11.7	12.0	14.9	22.1
Debt and finance	58.9	51.3	45.0	39.1	37.2	39.8	31.0
Defense	19.5	22.2	25.5	27.6	24.5	25.8	22.2
Other	10.9	11.1	4.2	21.5	26.2	19.5	24.8
Total expenditure	100.0	100.0	100.0	100.0	100.0	100.0	100.0
Of which, infrastructure	4.2	4.3	16.9	16.8	10.9	9.2	6.6
Education	0.7	0.7	1.8	4.4	5.5	7.2	12.2
Total expenditure (10^6 fl)	69.3	74.4	88.5	106.8	111.2	127.4	194.2
Budget surplus (10^6 fl)[a]	−10.1	−7.4	−8.8	2.8	11.9	19.3	31.0
Expenditure/GDP (%)	12.2	10.5	9.4	9.7	8.9	8.8	8.0
Budget surplus/GDP (%)	−1.8	−1.0	−0.9	0.3	1.0	1.3	1.3

Sources: Van der Voort, *Overheidsbeleid,* 208–76; GDP: database national accounts.
[a] Exclusive colonial surplus.
[b] King, justice, and internal affairs; all figures are three-year averages.

serve the interests of large parts of the population resulted in changes in policy at the local level. Relations between the central government and municipalities had been clearly regulated in the new Gemeentewet of 1851, a direct consequence of the new constitution of 1848. The central issue was that, on the one hand, the (former) autonomy of the cities, in particular in the matter of taxation, was severely curtailed, while, on the other hand, certain responsibilities and tasks were allocated to this lowest layer of the state. The authority to levy excises, for example, was restricted, in return for which the municipalities received a share of central taxation. However, responsibility for health care, for example, and public utilities was delegated to the municipalities, which were expected to play a large role in the implementation of policy in the field of education and of economic affairs. A certain balance between municipalities and the central state developed, in which, naturally, the central state was the source of legislation in these fields, but major tasks were delegated to the local level.

The growing pressure to change the role of the state resulted, therefore, in the first place in changes at this level. Whereas the limitations of public finance made it almost impossible to introduce new taxes at the national level before the 1890s, local direct taxes increased sharply after about 1870, both to replace the old excises and to cater to the growing needs at this level. In particular, direct taxes on income proved to be a highly elastic source of tax income, greatly facilitating the expansion of spending that local politicians thought was necessary.[52]

A major concern of the "new" politics at the local level was health care. Since the seventeenth century, the cities of Holland and Zeeland were infamous for their unhealthy environment and resulting high death rates. In other cities of Europe, for example, in rapidly expanding London, public investment in the improvement of the system of health care and related infrastructure (such as water supply and sewage disposal) had resulted in lower death rates. But in the "grave of Europe," as Malthus called Amsterdam, no comparable investments had taken place, and the renewed growth of the cities threatened to make the situation worse.

A group of young medics, who became known as the *hygiënisten,* started a publicity campaign after 1848 to attract attention to the problem and induce local governments to act. With modern statistical methods they tried to analyze the cause of the problems and raise support for their proposals for public investment in new infrastructure and better housing. Their ideas gradually gained acceptance. When after the cholera epidemic of 1866 it turned out that the number of deaths in Amsterdam was much lower than in other cities— because, according to the hygiënisten, the city had a system that brought clean drinking water from the dunes—other cities were induced to construct similar systems (the Amsterdam company supplying drinking water was, strikingly, the result of a British initiative).[53] The problem of sewage disposal was dealt with in a similar way. Cities gradually began to invest in systems to clean up the environment (and sell the collected manure to farms in the surrounding countryside).[54]

After 1870 these changes, in combination with the process of "civilization," in which the need for greater personal hygiene was greatly stressed, began to have an impact on the public heath. Death rates began to decline slowly after about 1870, in particular among infants. These changes originated in the cities of the western part of the country, where death rates had been relatively high before 1870. In the years prior to the First World War, cities became more healthy places to live than the surrounding countryside, which was a reversal of a centuries-old pattern.[55]

In the late 1880s city politics were greatly affected by the constitutional changes of 1887, which broadened the electorate at the local level. Left-wing liberals (known as radicals), for example, dominated city politics in Amsterdam for quite some time, urging more dynamic city politics. The nationalization of public utilities was at the top of their agenda, as were new initiatives in the field of public housing and the first attempts to regulate the labor market.[56] To recapitulate, whereas the central state "stagnated" relatively in this period, local governments began to experiment with a new, more active role in society, in response to the "social question" that was of course particularly urgent at the local level. No city government could, for example, continue to ignore massive unemployment in times of economic depression, and the 1880s saw experiments with the first systematic plans for unemployment relief.[57] These experiments were important and were often interlinked with the development of unions or other interest groups (local schemes to subsidize the unemployment insurances of the trade unions are a good example). But in the end, progress at the local level was constrained by the legal and budgetary framework that was defined by the central state. Increasingly, therefore, attention was again focused on this level.

But at the central level, progress in the field of social policy was slow. After initiation of the law against child labor in 1874, it took another fifteen years before new initiatives materialized. The Inquiry into the Situation at Factories and Workplaces that was induced by growing complaints about the exploitation of women and child labor during the 1880s resulted in a new law in 1889, which established more detailed rules, and an organization, the Inspection of Labour, that was to monitor its implementation.

The next stage in the development of social legislation consisted of plans to introduce legislation to insure workers for loss of income due to an accident in the workplace. It is typical for the situation before the rise of neocorporatism that neither employers nor laborers (nor their organizations) were involved with the preparation of the new law, which was submitted to Parliament by Lely in 1898.[58] There was a consensus that something should be done about the issue, and that all employers had to be covered by the new law. But the centralist approach of the proposed Ongevallenwet (Industrial Accidents Act), meaning, for example, that one central fund for its administration would be created, was strongly criticized.[59] Kuyper argued in favor of a decentralized administration in which the employers in each branch of industry would manage the implementation of the law. This approach was supported by the Vereniging van Nederlandsche Werkgevers (Association of Dutch Employers), an organization set up in 1899 to argue the employers' case for a more privatized and decentralized administration of the law (it was to become the foremost organization of employers during the twentieth century). They could argue, too, that in important industries "social entrepreneurs" had already developed comparable, often more generous, schemes for their workers, and that the new law would interfere with those—more efficient—experiments at the local level. In this discussion the question of who would control the new organization—the "neutral" state or the employers themselves—was closely linked to the issue of its efficiency: the (left-wing) liberals expected a centralized bureaucracy to be more efficient, whereas their critics praised the advantages of decentralized management and control. The initial proposal was approved by the Second Chamber of Parliament, but that did not convince a majority of the (often more conservative) First Chamber, and afterward the proposal was rewritten to meet their criticisms.[60] The final result, which passed Parliament in 1901, created a few possibilities for private management of the implementation of insurance against accidents.

This debate was more or less representative of the discussion on social policies in the years before the First World War. There was consensus that something had to be done, and that laws had to be introduced to improve the lot of the workers, who were dependent on an unstable source of income, that is, wage labor. Reducing the uncertainties that resulted from the "commodification" of labor was seen as an important goal. The way forward was to "force" them (and/or their employers) to insure themselves against accidents, unemployment, illness, and old age. The social security that people had in mind consisted of a "postponed" wage, paid for by premiums on the wage income of the laborers (which could be considered a part of this wage income). An alternative approach, advocated by only a small minority, consisted of schemes of national social insurances for everyone (i.e., also farmers, shopkeepers, etc.) that was to be paid for by the government.[61] This approach was considered to be *étatiste* and to ignore the responsibilities of those involved (as well as being too costly, for that matter).

In view of the fact that there was consensus—among the (left) liberals, the Christian parties, and the socialists—that an extension of social legislation was necessary, it is striking that so little progress was made before 1913. As in the debate on the Ongevallenwet of 1901, disagreement focused on the precise role of the state and how much should be delegated to the trade unions and employers and their organizations. The left-wing liberal and the Christian parties were unable to reach a compromise on this issue, which meant that both boycotted the proposals of the other, and the legislation stagnated as a result. The political elites of both groups were not yet able to work together closely: they were still involved in a learning process, in developing the rules of the "politics of pacification" (Lijphart) of the interwar period. The pressure from "below" to make more progress in this field, from organized labor and from employers' organizations, was also still relatively weak (compared with the post-1914 period). Therefore, in this respect as well the 1870–1914 period saw only the initial development of the new rules of the game that were to regulate sociopolitical and economic matters during the twentieth century.[62]

CHAPTER EIGHT

Modern Economic Growth and Structural Change, 1870–1913

THE TRANSITION TO ANOTHER PATTERN OF ECONOMIC GROWTH

The 1860s were an important watershed in economic development, since they ushered in the beginning of "modern economic growth" as defined by Simon Kuznets.[1] In his pioneering international comparative research Kuznets stressed the relationships between the growth of output and income, on the one hand, and structural changes of the economy, on the other. This is immediately evident from his definition of "modern economic growth": "a sustained increase in per capita or per worker product, most often accompanied by an increase in population and usually by sweeping structural changes."[2] He stressed the same patterns of changes that were already identified by Colin Clark:[3] growth goes together with a decline in the share of agriculture in the economy, whereas industry and, in a more limited way, services will increase as a share of employment and income. Parallel to this, capital intensity will rise, an increasing proportion of the population will be concentrated in cities, the mobility of labor and capital will increase, and the size and structure of companies will change.[4] These structural changes, in their turn, were an important cause of continued growth: moving laborers from (low-productive) agriculture to (high-productive) industry, for example, will in itself contribute to increased productivity and income.

In previous chapters we have seen that in the Netherlands the relationship between growth and structural change was not that straightforward. A sustained growth of income and output per capita had already begun around 1820—although it decelerated markedly in the 1840s and 1850s—which means that we would have to date the beginning of "modern economic growth" to that time. Simultaneously, however, the economy's structural transformation stagnated until the 1860s: the share of industry in income was lower at about 1860 than at the beginning of the century (due to a decline in the previous two decades), whereas the share of agriculture had been growing strongly during the 1840s and 1850s (see table 6.3). Moreover, the relative performance of this economy had been rather weak; whereas at the beginning of the century GDP per capita was probably on a par with that of the United Kingdom, its relative position had declined to about 80 percent of that level in 1870. The other western European countries, too, had done much better than the Netherlands (table 8.1). The

TABLE 8.1.
Nineteenth-Century European Growth in Output and per Capita Value Added, Selected Intervals
1820–1913 (in 1990 international dollars, indices of U.K. domestic per capita product and
annual growth rates).

	1820	1850	1870	1913	1820–50	1850–70	1870–90	1890–1913
	Per capita GDP, levels (1990 $)				*GDP, growth rates*			
Netherlands	1,784	2,306	2,660	3,970	1.79	1.45	2.05	2.32
Germany	1,112	1,476	1,913	3,833	1.82	2.25	2.36	3.13
Belgium	1,291	1,808	2,640	4,130	1.99	2.57	2.10	1.90
France	1,218	1,669	1,946	3,452	1.65	0.87	1.23	1.81
Denmark	1,225	1,700	1,927	3,764	1.96	1.78	2.13	3.05
United Kingdom	1,756	2,362	3,263	5,032	1.84	2.29	2.03	1.75
Euro sample[a]	1,338	1,670	2,074	3,570	1.34	1.00	1.80	2.23
	Capita GDP, indices (UK = 100)				*GDP per capita, growth rates*			
Netherlands	101.6	97.6	81.5	78.9	0.85	0.71	0.88	0.98
Germany	63.3	62.5	58.6	76.2	0.94	1.30	1.42	1.79
Belgium	73.5	76.5	80.9	82.1	1.12	1.89	1.20	0.90
France	69.4	70.7	56.9	68.6	1.05	0.75	0.98	1.66
Denmark	69.8	72.0	59.1	74.8	1.09	0.63	1.15	1.91
United Kingdom	100.0	100.0	100.0	100.0	0.99	1.62	1.14	0.89
Euro-sample[a]	76.2	70.7	63.6	70.9	0.74	1.07	1.12	1.40

Source: Maddison, *Dynamic Forces;* database national accounts.

[a] The Euro-sample is the aggregate of eleven nations (Austria, Belgium, Denmark, Finland, France, Germany, Italy, Netherlands, Norway, Sweden, United Kingdom), all adjusted for boundary changes.

slow changes in the structure of the labor force suggest a similar "abnormal," relatively slow pace of development. In chapter 6 we analyzed the divergent development of the Dutch economy by focusing on a comparison with Belgium, which brought out these contrasting experiences quite well; for the Netherlands slow growth without structural change was characteristic for the period before about 1860.

The particular features of the pattern of growth can be analyzed in a more rigorous way. The literature on the process of modern economic growth has examined correlations between per capita GDP and a broad range of economic

TABLE 8.2.
Comparative Development Characteristics: The Netherlands Compared with the
Stylized European Norm at Dutch per Capita Income Levels, 1810–1910.

| | | | | | Netherlands | | | |
		European Norm			1810	1850	1870	1910
Income level (1990 $)	1,515	2,306	2,660	3,726	1,515	2,306	2,660	3,726
Urbanization ≥20,000	8.4	22.8	26.3	36.4	19.0	21.0	24.1	40.4
Urbanization ≥2,500	21.9	34.3	38.4	48.0	36.2	36.6	38.4	54.8
School enrollment[b]	18.4	20.6	44.5	54.8	n.a.	41.4	44.2	49.1
Labor allocation (employment shares)								
Primary	63.7	50.5	46.1	35.2	43.1	40.6	39.0	29.6
Secondary	18.4	28.5	32.0	40.3	26.2	31.0	31.4	34.7
Tertiary	17.9	21.0	21.9	24.4	30.8	28.4	29.6	35.7
Resource allocation (GNP shares)								
Primary	46.1	34.5	30.8	21.9	26.3	25.7	29.9	18.9
Secondary	21.5	26.3	27.8	31.5	24.3	26.1	24.0	31.2
Tertiary	32.4	39.2	41.4	46.6	49.5	48.2	46.0	49.9
Exports	11.6	14.9	16.3	20.7	18.9	16.8	37.3	29.6
Private consumption	81.4	78.6	77.7	75.5	65.4	68.7	79.2	76.7
Gross private investment	12.3	15.0	15.9	17.9	7.8	7.0	8.7	12.8
Government spending	7.5	6.9	6.7	6.1	15.4	14.2	11.3	9.4

Source: Burger, "Dutch Pattern," and authors' own calculations on the basis of the database national accounts.

indicators, such as the sectoral structure of the economy, levels of urbanization, and school enrolment ratios (table 8.2). For nineteenth-century Europe, these patterns have been modeled by both Crafts and Burger; the results of this type of analysis are stylized patterns of economic change, linking GDP growth to economic and sociopolitical indicators.[5] By analyzing the differences between these stylized European patterns and the actual development of the Netherlands, we can gain insights into specific features of the latter's development. Table 8.2, which presents the results of this experiment, shows that levels of urbanization in the Netherlands were much higher than was "normal" in Europe at similar levels of GDP per capita; the same also applies to school enrollment. The structure of the economy was also rather atypical in that the share of agriculture in GDP was much lower than might be expected on the basis of the European "norm," whereas the share of industry and, in particular, services was consistently much higher. In other words, the relatively modern structure of the labor force and GDP, which were already present in the Netherlands at the beginning of the nineteenth century, did not result in a comparably high level of GDP. Interestingly, in his study of structural transformation in Great Britain, Crafts found similar deviations from the European norm (e.g., the share of agriculture in Britain was also consistently lower than "normal").[6] Between 1800 and 1870 the Netherlands slowly converged upon the European norm; Great Britain, on the other hand, continued on its special growth path throughout the nineteenth century. That around 1800 both Great Britain and the Netherlands diverged from the European norm—that is, the structure of their labor forces and GDPs did not "match" the European norm—is significant. Both countries were pioneers of early modern economic growth, characterized by their precocious specialization in international services and related industrial activities. If these estimates are correct, this early growth did not bring the advances in productivity and growth in GDP consistent with the nineteenth century's (post–industrial revolution) "norm." Great Britain sustained its growth path well into the twentieth century, as is evident from Crafts's analysis. For the Netherlands the process of convergence with the European norm was more or less completed by 1870, which is clearly apparent from the changes in the sectoral structure of its GDP (see table 8.2). Another way, therefore, to interpret the "deviant" development of the Dutch economy between, say, 1780 and 1870 is that it was in this period that the "traverse" from its "preindustrial" economic structure to its "industrial" structure was completed. From about 1870 onward, the Dutch economy more or less followed the European norm, and GDP growth and structural change went hand in hand.

In the second half of the 1860s this began to change, and the process of economic growth began to fit the patterns analyzed by Clark and Kuznets: taking, for example, the ratio between the share of industry and that of agriculture as a measure, the change can be dated to 1865: after that year a sustained increase in the GDP began, which was to last for about a century (figure 8.1). Growth accelerated strongly during the 1860s and remained relatively high for the rest of the century (see table 8.1). Between the mid-1860s and mid-1870s the growth of value added in industry also exceeded that in services, resulting in a marked shift toward the former sector (see figure 8.1).

The beginning of "modern economic growth" was therefore characterized by a decisive acceleration of industrial growth during the 1860s and 1870s; industry contributed more than 50 percent to total growth in the latter decade (it was already one-third during the 1860s) (table 8.3). After 1880 growth was

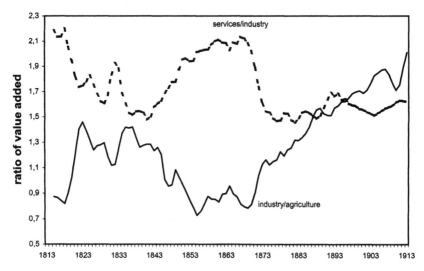

FIGURE 8.1. Ratio between the value added of industry and agriculture and of services and agriculture, 1813–1913 (three-year moving averages). Data from database national accounts.

less dominated by one particular sector, and services and industry were more in equilibrium.

Economic historians have been debating the issue of the start of the "industrial revolution" in the Netherlands for quite some time, major contributions being those of I. J. Brugmans (who dated its beginning in the 1850s) and J. A. de Jonge (who put forward evidence in favor of the 1890s).[7] The debate was based on rather fragmentary information—related to the growth of particular branches of the economy or sources of income—which made it difficult to make robust statements about the timing of industrialization. De Jonge, who published the classic study on this issue in 1968, gave great emphasis to changes in the structure of industry: he basically saw the rise of large-scale industry in engineering, shipbuilding, and metalworking in the 1890s as evidence for the "takeoff" that occurred.[8] But more recent research has shown that the rapid spread of the steam engine began after 1850, and that this had already changed the structure of many industries (see chapter 6). Moreover, the rapid acceleration of growth that De Jonge and Griffiths found in the 1890s is not corroborated by the research presented here: it was restricted to a few industries (mining, metalworking) and was by all measures not as rapid as the growth spurt of the 1860s and 1870s (see also figure 4.2).

During the 1860s and 1870s the transition from the "stationary state" of the eighteenth century toward the process of "modern economic growth" was completed. In chapter 1 we have tried to analyze more in detail how this "stationary

TABLE 8.3.
Growth of Value Added of the Different Sectors of the Economy, 1860–1913 (annual average growth rate).

	Growth (of Value Added)				Contribution to GDP Growth			Share in GDP
	1860–70	1870–80	1880–95	1895–1913	1870–80	1880–95	1895–1913	
Agriculture	1.80	-0.64	0.83	0.82	-10.5	9.0	5.7	21.2
Fisheries	0.32	-0.20	-0.19	6.85	-0.1	-0.0	1.5	0.5
Construction	2.24	4.16	0.73	2.63	13.4	2.0	5.3	4.3
Mining[a]	-0.29	-1.42	-1.85	4.42	-0.7	-0.5	0.9	0.4
Manufacturing	4.08	5.12	2.92	2.84	57.2	33.3	29.3	25.0
Government	0.55	0.96	0.74	1.58	3.0	1.6	2.4	3.6
Domestic services	0.75	0.38	1.01	0.89	1.3	2.3	1.3	3.4
Other services	2.87	1.74	2.88	3.16	36.4	52.4	53.6	41.5
GDP	2.38	1.70	2.09	2.52	100.0	100.0	100.0	100.0
GDP per capita	1.54	0.57	0.92	1.12	—	—	—	—
Population	0.84	1.13	1.17	1.39	—	—	—	—

Source: Smits, Horlings, and Van Zanden, Dutch GNP.
[a] Including peat.

state" can be interpreted; here we intend to focus on how growth and structural change interacted and caused a cumulative process of economic development that is still going on. We will therefore, as we did in chapter 1, focus on the equilibrium between investments and savings, between supply and demand on the labor market, and between exports and imports.

Another important argument in favor of the 1890s as the takeoff period was some evidence De Jonge presented on the development of *investment*. He estimated that the share of investment in GDP increased from 5 percent in the 1880s to more than 10 percent before the First World War.[9] Seen in the very long term, this increase in the share of investment would signify the end of an extended period of low capital formation that began with the sharp decline of investment during the final quarter of the seventeenth century that inaugurated the "stationary state." The new evidence that has been assembled to estimate the level and development of capital formation during the nineteenth century does not confirm the interpretation of De Jonge, however. At the beginning of the nineteenth century the share of investment in GDP was already about 8 percent; it rose to between 9 and 10 percent during the boom in canal construction in the 1820s. In the next few decades the investment ratio remained at a relatively low level of between 7 and 8 percent—the trough bottoming out at "only" 6.5 percent (figure 8.2) around 1860. This was followed by a very strong increase in investment, in particular during the 1870s (when it peaked at 13 percent of GDP), a recession during the 1880s (approximately 10 percent) and

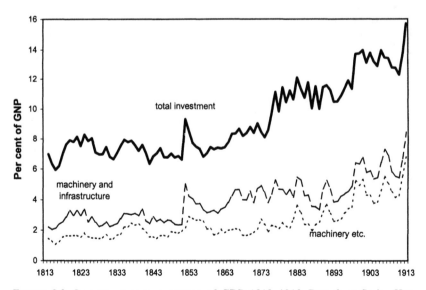

FIGURE 8.2. Investment as a percentage of GDP, 1813–1913. Data from Smits, Horlings, and Van Zanden, *Dutch GNP.*

another surge during the second half of the 1890s. In short, between the mid-1860s and about 1900 the investment ratio showed a strong upward trend—from 6.5 percent to 14 percent—after which stabilisation followed. The "decisive" upsurge in investment therefore began much earlier than De Jonge assumed.

It is possible to analyze the increase in the share of investment in GDP in more detail. Two factors turn out to be important in attempts to estimate the investment function of these years: the relative prices of labor versus capital goods, and the interest rate.[10] The first factor predominates: wages rose strongly in this period, whereas the costs of purchasing and maintaining capital goods fell sharply. Figure 8.3 shows two estimates of the ratio between these relative prices: during the first half of the century the incentive to mechanize does not increase strongly, but this changes during the 1850s, when the cost of coal and of (imported) machines begins to decline significantly, whereas at the same time nominal wages begin to increase. Between 1855 and 1870 the price ratio halved; this is repeated in the following twenty years.

The second factor, the relative decline of the interest rate (in comparison with the "world market"), was the bonus the international capital market awarded for the reorganization of government finances and the stability of the financial

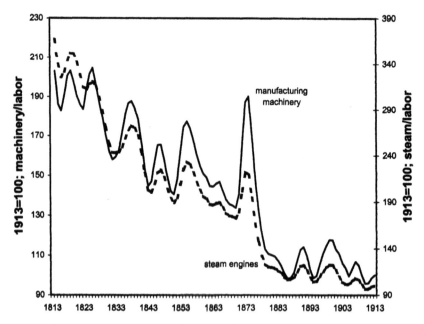

FIGURE 8.3. Estimates of the development of the relative price of machinery (all machinery in manufacturing and steam engines) versus labor (indices 1913 = 100). Data from database national accounts; Albers, *Machinery Investment.*

and monetary system. The declining difference between the interest rate on NWS and on British consols has already been analyzed in chapter 7. Together these factors explain the increase in the investment ratio; the effect of other variables was marginal.

Another way to approach the increase in investment is to distinguish between different kinds of investment goods: infrastructure, buildings, machines, and transport equipment. In his detailed study of investment in infrastructure, Peter Groote showed that the first group was dominated by the transport sector. Before 1865 this type of investment was relatively small, except for a brief boom in the 1820s and another temporary surge during the reclamation of the Haarlemmermeer in the mid-1850s. Things changed during the 1860s, when the combination of investments in the railways, in large canals, and a national system of telegraphs resulted in a long boom that lasted until 1888.[11] This was followed by fourteen years of more limited investment activity in infrastructure—the main reason for the decline after 1888 was that the national network of railways had been completed in that year. New investments in tramways and in public utilities (electricity, gas) brought about another boom in investment after 1902, but in these years investment in infrastructure was much less important than in the previous boom between 1866 and 1888 (see figure 8.2).[12] Econometric research has also indicated that after 1853 there existed a strong connection between investment in infrastructure and the rate of economic growth (it is striking that such a link could not be established for the first boom of investment in canal building and road construction during the 1820s).[13]

There is no comparable study of the causes and consequences of investment in buildings, which means that we cannot identify the reasons for its growth in a similar way. This kind of investment was dominated by residential dwellings, which are by nature the result of a complex interaction between demographic and economic variables, resulting in the famous "building cycles" of about twenty years that were identified by Kuznets and others. The demographic changes that began in the 1860s, resulting in a renewed growth of the cities (see later discussion), led to a long period of expansion in the construction industry, which lasted between 1866 and 1883. The building boom became in itself a major force behind the revival of the cities, as it created a strong demand for relatively unskilled laborers from the countryside (the flexible supply of seasonal migrants from the eastern Netherlands and Germany had dried up; see chapter 6). The depression of the 1880s was very severe, however, and recovery during the early 1890s rather slow; the next upward phase of the building cycle ended in 1907.[14] Again the enlargement of the major cities of Holland—and the growth of new industrial towns in Twente and Brabant—was the most dynamic element of the boom.

The third type of investment, in machines and transport equipment, consisted of investments in rolling stock (linked to the extension of the railway system), in shipping, and in machines. The growth of the latter and most important group

TABLE 8.4.
Savings and Investments in the Netherlands, 1814–1913 (annual averages).

	(1) Gross Capital Formation $(10^6 fl)$	(2) Increase Public Debt $(10^6 fl)$	(3) Balance Current Account $(10^6 fl)$	(1–3) Domestic Savings $(10^6 fl)$	International Transfers $(10^6 fl)$	I/Y^a (%)	S/Y^b (%)
1814–23	38.1	5.6	−7.7	36.0	14.8	8.3	7.7
1824–33	40.4	20.5	−16.0	45.0	22.1	8.6	9.6
1834–43	44.5	5.7	0.5	50.7	32.7	8.0	9.1
1844–53	48.3	−0.1	12.5	60.7	30.2	8.2	10.3
1854–63	61.0	12.4	55.5	128.9	42.5	8.2	17.4
1864–73	86.5	12.9	82.1	181.5	22.0	9.1	19.1
1874–83	136.9	1.1	34.9	172.9	2.8	12.1	15.3
1884–93	144.5	−8.2	160.3	296.6	0.0	12.2	25.1
1893–03	202.5	−16.8	39.8	225.5	0.0	14.6	16.3
1904–13	294.4	−25.8	−55.5	213.1	0.0	15.0	10.9

Source: Smits, Horlings, and Van Zanden, *Dutch GNP.*
[a] Investment as a share of GDP.
[b] Savings as a share of GDP.

was linked to the spread of the steam engine and, after 1890, the even more dramatic rise of electricity and electric power; its underlying causes—the changes in relative prices of labor and capital—have already been discussed.[15]

To sum up, the increase in the investment ratio during the first period (1866–83) was the result of investment in infrastructure (railways, canals), in dwellings, and in steam engines (and related technologies and buildings); during the second period (1894–1913), mechanization was again important, as were dwellings and, to a lesser extent, tramways and railways. Moreover, the increase in investment had a strong effect on the economy: expenditure was concentrated in the construction and metalworking industries, two parts of the industrial sector that expanded rapidly during the 1870s and again after 1895 (see table 8.10). Construction had strong backward lineages with brickyards and woodworking. The engineering industry succeeded in capturing a growing share of the national market (after the decline in market share during the 1850s and 1860s).

The growth of investment was made possible by the constant high level of domestic *savings* (table 8.4). During the greater part of the nineteenth century, net savings were much higher than domestic investment, which created ample space for large investments abroad. The interest rate, the best indicator of the degree of "tension" on the capital market, continued to decline until about 1895. Afterward interest rates went up slowly, following price trends, but real interest rates remained remarkably low (between 2 and 3 percent), and Dutch interest rates were among the lowest in the world.[16] The export of capital, which began again after 1850, did not slow down during periods of high investment activity at home. The value of the capital invested abroad continued to rise, but because much of this was the result of the reinvestment of profits made elsewhere (in the Indies, in particular), it is unclear how much money actually left the country. Given the low interest rates and the ongoing exports of capital, there are no signs that at any point the supply of capital was a bottleneck.[17]

The changes in the *labor market* that occurred during the early stages of "modern economic growth" have already been sketched in chapter 6. These changes meant that new employment was created in expanding branches of industry and in places where labor was sometimes in short supply, and that employment disappeared in other trades and places. Table 8.5 shows that in the long run

TABLE 8.5.
Development of the Structure of the Labor Force, 1807–1909 (in percent).

	1807	1849	1859	1889	1899	1909
Agriculture, fisheries	43.1	40.3	40.4	36.5	34.1	30.4
Construction	6.7	6.6	6.9	7.1	7.0	7.0
Mining	0.2	0.2	0.2	0.9	0.8	1.0
Industry	19.3	24.2	24.3	23.6	24.8	26.2
Trade	7.1	6.9	7.0	8.0	9.2	9.7
Transport	4.5	6.2	6.3	6.0	6.0	6.8
Government	3.8	3.4	3.5	3.5	3.0	3.1
Domestic services	11.7	9.1	8.6	9.7	9.9	9.3
Other services	3.6	3.2	3.0	4.7	5.1	6.4
Total	100	100	100	100	100	100
Turbulence (%)	—	0.15	0.07	0.16	0.30	0.43
Turbulence (absolute number)	—	1,680	947	2,515	5,675	9,376

Source: Smits, Horlings, and Van Zanden, *Dutch GNP.*

agriculture was in relative terms the declining sector, and that the growth of employment was concentrated in industry, trade, and other services. A rough measure of the degree to which people have to switch occupation (or children will have to choose another job than that of their parents) is the turbulence index, calculated in the bottom rows of the table. It shows that not much changed before 1859, but that after that date "turbulence" accelerated slowly but consistently.

The relative decline of agriculture had the severest consequences for the predominantly agrarian rim of Holland, that is, the regions of specialized agriculture in Zeeland, Friesland, and the "peripheral" parts of Holland.[18] Population growth accelerated in the cities of Holland and Utrecht, also caused by the migration of large numbers of agricultural laborers, shopkeepers, and craftsmen from agrarian zones.[19] After two centuries of stagnation, Amsterdam in the 1860s was home to 240,000 inhabitants, the population it already had in the late seventeenth century.[20] Rotterdam, Den Haag, and Utrecht underwent a similar growth spurt, which even accelerated during the 1880s and 1890s, when large numbers of agricultural laborers were pushed out of the primary sector (table 8.6).

TABLE 8.6.
Growth of the Cities of Holland (in thousands and in percent).

	1814	1829	1849	1879	1899	1909
Amsterdam	180.2	202.4	224.0	317.0	510.9	566.1
Rotterdam	58.6	72.3	90.1	148.1	318.5	418.0
Nederland	634.2	778.6	897.5	1,274.9	2,040.9	2,427.2
Holland	406.6	483.3	560.1	815.0	1,373.0	1,646.4
Rates of growth						
Amsterdam	—	0.77	0.51	1.16	2.39	1.03
Rotterdam	—	1.41	1.10	1.66	3.83	2.72
Nederland	—	1.37	0.71	1.17	2.35	1.73
Holland	—	1.15	0.74	1.25	2.61	1.82
Urbanization ratio						
Nederland	28.6	29.6	29.0	31.6	39.7	41.0
Holland	52.7	53.9	53.5	54.9	65.0	65.9

Sources: Horlings, *Economic Development*, 323; *Jaarcijfers*, various issues.

After 1900 the countryside recovered from the agricultural depression, and the urbanization ratio more or less stabilized. Migration to Holland continued, however, and the north (Groningen and Friesland) and Zeeland lost about half their "natural increase" (the difference between births and deaths) to migration. Emigration to North America or other destinations remained limited, however; the East Indies attracted increased numbers of—mostly temporary—migrants, and small numbers went to other destinations overseas. In sum, the beginnings of "modern economic growth" had important consequences for the spatial distribution of the population.

The decline of agriculture led to a sharp fall in employment in this sector. The demand for labor in other parts of the economy, however, grew much more rapidly. It can be inferred from poor relief statistics that the rate of unemployment fell significantly in the 1860s and 1870s, went up during the next decade (when the depression in agriculture and in construction coincided), but started to fall again after the mid-1890s (figure 8.4). The growing tensions in the (urban) labor market resulted in a strong increase in nominal and real wages after 1860, which even accelerated after 1880, when food prices came tumbling

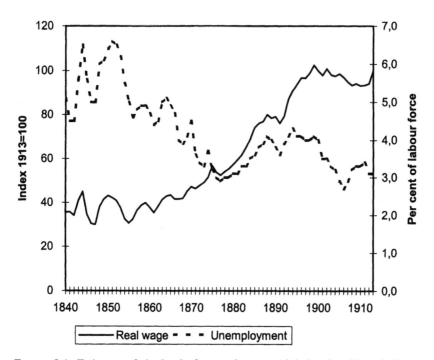

FIGURE 8.4. Estimates of the level of unemployment (right-hand scale) and of the development of real wages (1913 = 100, left-hand scale), 1840–1913. Data from database national accounts.

down. Between 1860 and 1900 real wages increased by more than 150 percent, after which they stabilized.

This great increase in the standard of living of the laborers had important consequences for the structure of consumer expenditures. In the 1860s and 1870s the increase in real wages resulted in growing consumption of livestock products such as meat, butter, and cheese (and fish), and of stimulants such as coffee, tea, tobacco, and gin. As a result, the share of bread and potatoes in the household budget declined sharply (from 32 percent to 20 percent), but the total share of foodstuffs remained at about 56 percent (table 8.7).

TABLE 8.7.
Budgets of Laborers' Households, 1852/63–1910/11 (expenditure as a share of total).

	1852–63	1870–72	1880–82	1886–97 Holland	1886–97 Other Cities	1910–11 Holland	1910–11 Other Cities
Bread	20.4	18.4	12.0	11.6	17.1	11.6	12.6
Potatoes	11.3	13.2	8.6	5.9	6.5	4.0	3.9
Total bread and potatoes	31.7	31.6	20.6	17.5	23.6	15.6	16.5
Dairy products	5.7	6.3	11.0	7.9	10.7	10.9	10.5
Meat, fish	5.4	4.4	8.2	7.0	9.3	8.7	10.2
Sugar, coffee, tea	3.4	3.0	5.6	5.7	7.4	5.2	5.7
Vegetables, rice, flour	11.5	10.5	11.3	5.5	7.5	8.3	9.3
Total foodstuffs	57.6	55.6	56.7	43.6	58.5	48.5	52.2
Clothing, apparel	15.0	8.4	12.2	15.6	13.9	11.9	11.0
Housing	10.8	14.9	15.8	23.3	10.2	15.1	13.3
Energy	8.5	7.5	9.1	7.5	7.6	5.9	6.3
Soap, etc.	3.3	4.4	2.8	1.0	0.9	2.1	1.9
Drink, tobacco	0.9	1.7	3.4	2.7	1.8	1.7	1.1
Other	2.9	3.9	n.a.	6.3	7.1	14.9	14.3
Total expenditure	442.23	358.84	587.36	632.94	548.94	965.68	795.56
N =	15	10	16	16	22	38	32

Source: Database national accounts.

After 1880 this share began to fall, in particular in the cities. In the countryside the standard of living did not improve much during the "agricultural depression," which is also evident from the budgets presented in table 8.7. In the cities, income growth was spent on clothing, shoes, education, and housing.[21] This shift away from foodstuffs and toward products of industry and services in its turn accelerated the process of structural change. Higher wages, on the one hand, stimulated industrialists to invest in machines and, on the other hand, induced households to spend more on the products made by the same industrialists. This interaction between demand and supply was one of the mechanisms that ensured the sustained character of industrial growth.

Changes in the external equilibrium have played only a modest role in these initial phases of modern economic growth. It is remarkable that the shares of imports and of exports in GDP, which are often used as an index of the degree of openness of an economy, did not change much during the period of rapid growth after 1865, whereas both shares had gone up very rapidly in the previous twenty years (figure 8.5). The liberalization of international markets had resulted in a greater than proportional growth of international flows of goods and services, but after 1865 GDP, on the one hand, and exports and imports, on the other, grew at almost the same rate. Growth after 1865 was therefore not "export-led," although for some industries exports were the most important, if not only, source of demand (margarine is a case in point).[22] Agricultural growth between 1840 and 1865 had clearly been "export-led," but this, too, changed after 1865, and the share of exports in total demand did not grow much anymore (see figure 6.5).

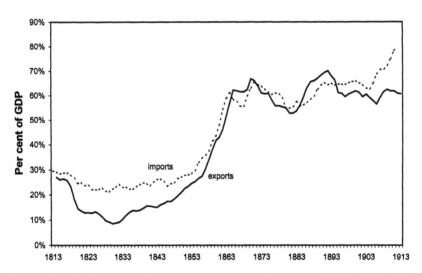

FIGURE 8.5. Ratio between the value of exports and imports and GDP, 1813–1913. Data from Smits, Horlings, and Van Zanden, *Dutch GNP*.

Chapter 6 has already been pointed out that the large surpluses on the agricultural trade balance that were a feature of the 1840–70 period disappeared afterward; imports and exports of agricultural products were more or less in equilibrium during the decades that followed (see figure 6.5). Industrial exports became more important after 1870, but the changes were not very large, and the imports of industrial products rose almost as rapidly as exports (table 8.8).

The rise of industrial exports did not crowd out agricultural exports, but it did have that effect on mainly tropical (colonial) products because the liberalization of the East Indies trade meant that a declining share of its exports could be channeled to the markets of Holland. The same factor explains the strong decline in the net export of services after about 1870 (see table 8.8).

The net result of a declining surplus on the balance of services, a deficit in industrial products (except for brief periods between 1864–73 and 1874–83, imports continued to exceed exports), and a declining surplus on the agricultural trade balance was that the trade balance showed large deficits, which were covered by large income transfers from abroad (table 8.9). Between 1815 and 1830 these consisted of the net taxation the north received from the south; between 1830 and 1870 the colonial surplus filled the gap; and after 1870

TABLE 8.8.
Structure of Exports and Imports, 1815–1913 (in million guilders, three-year averages).

	1814/16	1829/31	1845/7	1872/4	1894/6	1912/4
Exports						
Arable agriculture	23.5	24.6	12.9	8.5	16.4	12.9
Dairy products	9.9	20.9	17.2	8.4	10.7	15.6
Tropical products	31.4	23.7	44.3	45.6	30.3	25.7
Raw materials, semifinished goods	2.4	2.9	3.0	12.0	5.1	7.2
Industrial products	32.8	27.9	22.6	25.5	37.5	38.6
Imports						
Arable agriculture	16.7	19.5	17.1	6.9	18.3	14.6
Dairy products	3.8	1.3	1.1	1.2	1.5	1.0
Tropical products	55.5	41.8	50.7	40.2	31.7	26.2
Raw materials, semifinished products	3.4	9.4	9.0	24.3	20.4	23.1
Industrial products	20.6	28.1	22.2	27.4	28.0	35.1

Source: Database national accounts.

income from foreign investment (which had boomed since the 1850s) played the same role. On balance the current account mostly showed a surplus, used for capital exports (the large size of the surplus between 1854 and 1873 correlated with large investments abroad in these years).[23] At the end of the period the slow growth of exports and the more rapid expansion of imports (following growth of GDP) resulted in a deficit on the trade balance that exceeded the estimated flow of income to the Netherlands, but there are no indications that this led to an outflow of gold or the tightening of the capital market in this period.[24]

The sketch of these developments in the external sector shows that the process of structural transformation—the relative growth of industry and services—was not in the first place caused by exogenous factors but highly dependent on changes in the structure of the domestic market. It was changes in the composition of domestic demand, such as the rise of the investment ratio and the changing pattern of consumer expenditure, that drove the process of structural change. We have also seen that this process of "modern economic growth" tended to reinforce itself. Productivity growth led to wage increases, which induced entrepreneurs to substitute capital for labor (which further contributed to the growth of labor productivity), and stimulated households to switch to

TABLE 8.9.
Items of the Balance of Payments, 1814–1913 (in million guilders and as a percentage of GDP).

	Trade Balance (10^6)	Net Transfers from Abroad (10^6)	Service Balance (10^6)	Trade Balance (% GDP)	Net Transfers from Abroad (% GDP)	Current Account (% GDP)
1814–23	−32.92	29.78	−4.57	−7.2	−6.5	−1.7
1824–33	−56.10	39.26	0.86	−12.0	8.4	−3.4
1834–43	−51.34	48.71	3.17	−9.3	8.8	0.1
1844–53	−38.80	43.95	7.39	−6.6	7.5	2.1
1854–63	−16.40	64.29	7.65	−2.2	8.7	7.5
1864–73	18.23	59.08	4.73	1.9	6.2	8.6
1874–83	−35.82	70.93	−0.17	−3.2	6.3	3.1
1884–93	66.13	88.46	5.66	5.6	7.5	13.6
1893–03	−58.33	96.45	1.69	−4.2	7.0	2.9
1904–1913	−212.90	154.19	3.19	−10.9	7.9	−2.8

Source: Smits, Horlings, and Van Zanden, Dutch GNP.

other industrial items of consumption. The growth of cities, in response to the decline of employment opportunities in the countryside and their expansion in industry and services, had a comparable function: it enhanced productivity (which was relatively low in agriculture) and created stimuli for (among others) the construction industry in the cities, which also increased the level of investment. These and comparable mechanisms set in motion a cumulative process of economic growth that resulted in a significant increase in real income and an ongoing structural transformation of the structure of the economy.

The sustained character of growth after 1870 was remarkable because agriculture almost disappeared as a source of growth between 1880 and 1900. Between 1830 and 1880 there had been a rather strong correlation between the growth of agriculture and the development of GDP: quick expansion in the primary sector correlated with rapid growth for the total economy, and vice versa. During the "agricultural depression" of 1882–96 the link was broken: the economy grew, strongly, whereas agriculture struggled to overcome the crisis.

This agricultural depression was the consequence of the large-scale imports of American grain, leading to a marked decline in the prices of agricultural products. It was a watershed in economic development on both sides of the Atlantic.[25] Before 1870 two worlds existed next to each other: in the Old World real wages were relatively low, and population pressure caused land to be relatively expensive, which drove up food prices. Capital was, certainly in the Netherlands, amply available. In the New World land was abundant, and labor scarce, which resulted in contrasting relative prices (i.e., high real wages, low food prices, and low rents). To develop the huge continent, capital was constantly in high demand, which drove up interest rates. During the second half of the nineteenth century both continents became increasingly integrated economically, due to the sharp fall of transport costs (both overseas and on land), the arrival of the telegraph, and other reductions in transaction costs. This resulted in increased exports of capital to the United States—to profit from the high interest rates there—and a modest stream of migrants (emigration from the Netherlands remained relatively small by international standards).

The process of integration that began in the second half of the nineteenth century was made possible by a significant decline in the costs of transporting goods both overseas and within the United States, from the areas that produced the agricultural surpluses in the Midwest to the port cities. The steamship and the railways played an important role in the process. The decline of transport costs made it possible to export American commodities at competitive prices to European markets, which resulted in a fall of prices there. The low prices of foodstuffs sustained the movement toward higher real wages that had begun in the 1850s and 1860s but of course depressed the incomes of farmers. This also resulted in a (relative) decline in land prices and rents. The net effect was a leveling of income disparities as laborers profited from the redistribution of income that occurred, at the expense of landowners and farmers. The redistribution of income also sped up the process of structural change, as many agricultural laborers were forced to look for employment outside the sector. Between 1840 and 1860 the high level of agricultural prices and the growing employment opportunities in this sector had retarded structural transformation; after 1880 the ongoing integration of transatlantic markets had the opposite effect.

The process of "modern economic growth" was in many respects the opposite of the "stationary state" that was analyzed in chapter 1. In the eighteenth century, industry declined as a result of a shrinking domestic market, due to falling real wages. After 1860 the increase of real wages stimulated the growth of industrial output and induced an acceleration of productivity growth. The role of agriculture was the mirror image of this: it expanded during the eighteenth century and began to decline radically again in relative terms in the final decades of the nineteenth century. Shrinking investment opportunities led to growing levels of investment in the public debt and investment abroad; rising investments after 1865 did not "crowd out" the export of capital (which continued during this period, albeit at perhaps a slightly lower rate than in the 1850s and 1860s), but the public debt certainly became a much less important destination of savings for the private sector. Behind these changes was a fundamental transformation of the role of industry in the economy: during the eighteenth century it had been a relatively weak sector that was unable to compete internationally; during the second half of the nineteenth century it became the most dynamic part of the economy, attracting a large part of the workers who left the agricultural sector. The constant factor in a certain sense was the services sector. During the eighteenth century the sector was very significant and remained so without interruption in the nineteenth century. It profited, as it were, from every change in direction of economic life.

AGRICULTURE: NEW INSTITUTIONS AND STRUCTURAL CHANGE

In the decades after 1840, the agricultural sector was the most important "beneficiary" of the liberalization of world trade. Due to the growing market potential in England and Germany, prices had increased enormously, and farmers and landowners were enjoying high incomes. During the 1870s this great prosperity came to an end, a result of the emergence of new competitors. In the years that followed, agriculture would become perhaps the most important victim of "globalization." Due to the emergence of steamships and steam locomotives (which opened up the expansive Midwest of the North American continent), American grain could be brought to the European market more and more cheaply. This resulted in falling grain prices, and in their wake the prices of virtually all agricultural products began to decrease sharply. In large areas of western Europe this decline of agricultural prices began as early as 1873. It is characteristic of the strength of the Dutch economy in the 1870s and the dynamism of the domestic market (because the market share abroad declined greatly) that agricultural prices remained at a fairly high level and began to decline rapidly only after 1882, following the next crisis in the business cycle.[26]

This "agricultural depression" continued until around 1896. Grain prices fell significantly more than prices in livestock farming or horticulture. In Groningen—the most important domestic grain market—the wheat price fell by about 40 percent between 1875–79 and 1895–99, while during the same years, the butter price fell by about one-third. This sudden decrease in prices led to a sharp reduction in farm income, which was partly reflected (with some delay) in lower rents. During the 1890s the rents in the clay soil region, which was more dependent than other regions on arable crops, fell to about 15 percent below the level of 1881–85; in other regions, the decline was smaller, and recovery took place more quickly.[27]

One way to view this depression is to examine the development of agricultural income. In figure 8.6, estimates of total wages (including the labor income of independent farmers) plus total rents (including the imputed rent of landowning farmers) are compared with independent estimates of value added in the agricultural sector. The difference consists primarily of the profit income

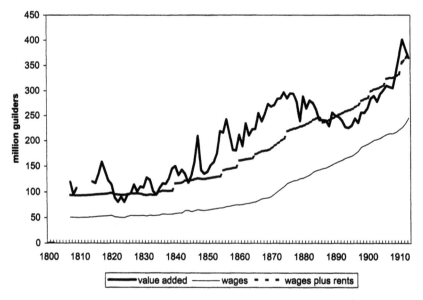

FIGURE 8.6. Estimates of total wages, the sum of wages and rents, and total value added in agriculture, 1800–1913 (at current prices and millions of guilders). Data from database national accounts.

of the farmers, including indirect taxes and interest and depreciation on working capital. In the years following 1840, this difference—that is, the profit income of farmers—increased to unprecedented heights. A famous description of the golden years before the "agricultural depression" states that the farmers became "rich in their sleep"; in view of the high profitability of farming in this period, this is not an entirely inaccurate reflection of the facts. In any case, they could indeed become wealthy, an opportunity that was given to few farmers in the past. The increase in wages and rents clearly lagged behind the spectacular growth of total agricultural income. But this surplus began a striking decline as far back as the 1870s: wages and rents increased sharply during these years, and value added began to decrease slowly but surely due to falling prices. During the beginning of the 1880s, the trends coincided; the net profit of farming became a net loss. This was certainly the case if one also takes account of depreciation and taxes, already mentioned. The worst years in this regard were those around 1890. Remarkably, the negative financial results continued until about 1910, although the extent of the losses began to decline after 1896.

During the years before 1880, there was a close correlation between farm profitability measured in this way and the growth of agricultural production in the medium to long term. Figure 8.7 illustrates this link, showing, for example, how the first agricultural crisis around 1823 led to a sharp decline in both

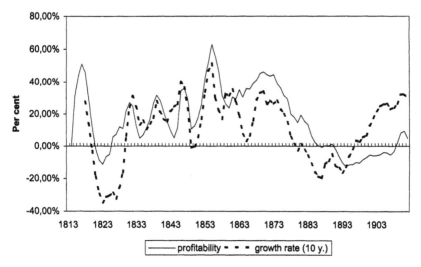

FIGURE 8.7. Long-term growth rate of agricultural production and the profitability of this sector, 1813–1913. Data from database national accounts. The long-term growth rate of agricultural production is defined as the average rate of growth during the previous ten years; profitability is defined as the ratio of the net income of farmers (therefore, value added minus the sum of wages and rents) divided by the sum of wages and rents.

profits and production growth. In addition, the recovery of profits that took place in the following decades appears to have always been followed by growth in agricultural production. This indicates that farmers responded very precisely to market signals; when things were going well, when the demand increased, and the prices were high, then production increased, whereas during periods of declining prices, production contracted. It is especially striking that this close correlation, which was still obviously present around 1880 (the increasing losses during the agricultural depression led to a deceleration of the growth of production), disappeared after 1890. At this point the growth of agricultural production suddenly accelerated, a growth spurt that continued until the start of the First World War, even though the financial result was still negative. This indicates that the determinates of growth during these years were changing.

The causes of this strong growth in production during a period of low farm profits or even losses can initially be found on the "input" side of the farm. The use of auxiliary inputs as a percentage of gross production remained virtually constant during the period up to about 1880. In 1807, for example, inputs amounted to 23 percent of gross production, while in 1880 this was 24 percent. Although the use of artificial fertilizers, feeds purchased outside the farm, and so forth had increased (guano and Chile saltpeter were widely used), the importance of such materials was still limited. But this changed radically after 1880; the share of inputs increased to 37 percent in 1900 and 45 percent in 1913.

Artificial fertilizers and purchased feed played a crucial role in this process. New insights from the agricultural sciences (the fertilization theory of Liebig) improved farmers' understanding of soil fertility. At the same time, technological changes in chemical and steel production (the latter generated basic slag, a fertilizer, as a by-product) resulted in enormous growth in the supply of artificial fertilizers. Between 1875–79 and 1900–1904, the price of nitrate, potassium, and phosphoric acid decreased by 44 percent, 40 percent and 64 percent, respectively, after which this price stabilized at the much lower level.[28] As a result, it became more and more attractive for farmers to purchase artificial fertilizers. The price developments in feed were comparable. As grain prices fell, the "wedge" between butter and meat prices, on one side, and the prices of feed, on the other, became larger and larger (a trend that had actually begun much earlier in the century). The transport of cheap maize and other new and traditional feeds from North America amplified this process.

These new options were especially attractive for farmers on the sandy soils of the eastern and southern regions of the Netherlands. These relatively poor soils previously required farmers to invest a great deal of labor in manure production, which could now be partially replaced by purchases of artificial fertilizer. Moreover, the purchase of feed accelerated the transition from arable to livestock farming. Through intensive pig and poultry farming it became possible for farmers to attempt to earn a reasonable income on small pieces of land.[29] However, farmers also encountered institutional problems—not only those who farmed the sandy soils but also those in other regions of the Netherlands where purchases of artificial fertilizer and feed increased greatly. These problems were the result of the "underdevelopment" of marketing networks. An initial problem was the quality of the purchased products. After 1870 there was a great deal of experimentation with new artificial fertilizers and new feeds. There were no guarantees that the purchased goods were not counterfeit or adulterated with worthless ingredients. A related problem concerned the magnitude of the transactions. Because new market channels had to be developed, purchasing a batch of artificial fertilizer for a single farmer was very expensive. Collective purchasing—by groups of farmers—could lead to significant savings, which could be as high as 50 percent of the purchase price. This also made it possible to have the purchased wares inspected by one of the agricultural experimental stations that were being established in the 1880s. A third issue was the increased dependence of farmers on local traders, retailers, and other middlemen, to whom the farmers often became indebted, especially during these depression years. Such middlemen often did not pass on lower prices for inputs to the farmer, thereby eliminating the stimulus to change.[30]

By establishing cooperative purchasing organizations that focused on the collective purchase of artificial fertilizer, feed, sowing seed, and similar items, farmers attempted to counteract this market failure. As a result, the middleman could be eliminated, and the benefits of high trade volumes—as well as quality guarantees—could be passed on directly to the farmer. Until 1890, however, the growth of this movement was very hesitant; middlemen were still influential, and farmers were still highly dependent on them. Many cooperative purchases took place only on an ad hoc basis, which did not benefit the continuity of the collective system. In 1893 approximately 4 percent of farmers in the Netherlands belonged to a cooperative purchasing association, a percentage that rose quickly to 30 percent in 1904 and 44 percent in 1910.[31] In certain areas these organizations had virtually no members because there was already a dense network of middlemen; this resulted in enough mutual competition to prevent excesses. For this reason, the "degree of organization" in Friesland, Holland, and Utrecht was much lower than average around 1910. Elsewhere, especially in regions with sandy soils and in Zeeland, the majority of the farmers became members of these new institutions.

These purchasing cooperatives, which were the first successful experiments with cooperative organizations in much of the country, were therefore a way for the small-scale family farm to benefit from the advantages of large-scale purchases of artificial fertilizer and feed. These economies of scale occurred at virtually all points where the farm came into contact with the market, including the processing of products such as milk, sugar beets, and industrial potatoes; farm financing; and the sale of horticultural products. The establishment of the cooperative movement during the last quarter of the nineteenth century was based on the following problem. In production, the optimal farm size was relatively small, and was becoming even smaller, whereas the economies of scale linked to purchasing, processing, sales, and financing were becoming increasingly important because market trading was being constantly intensified.[32] Prior to 1870 the economies of scale linked to commercialization were becoming increasingly important. In the regions where agriculture was particularly market oriented, this led to a tendency for farms to increase in size, thereby making wage labor in this sector more and more important. Commercialization and specialization had generally led to the establishment of large, capital-intensive farms that used a great deal of wage labor. In the Netherlands, the type of agriculture practiced in Zeeland functioned as a model for this system. Generally speaking, much more wage labor was encountered in the coastal provinces than the inland provinces, where farms had remained relatively small. In an international context, the tone was set by the large English farms, which were based almost entirely on wage labor in the eighteenth and nineteenth centuries.[33]

However, due to a range of developments, of which an increase in real wages was probably the most important, there was a tendency after 1870 for farms to become smaller; in other words, the optimal size began to be more and more in accordance with that of the family farm (which would become dominant in the twentieth century). On the other hand, the optimal size for processing milk, sugar beets, and potatoes increased sharply due to the arrival of modern industrial technologies. The most obvious solution for this problem was specialization: every part of the production process should be organized separately so that in different stages costs could be minimized. Due to high transport costs of unprocessed products (such as milk and sugar beets), however, farmers and the owners of processing plants became dependent on each other. The sugar manufacturer, for example, attempted to acquire a local monopoly on the processing of sugar beets providing credit to the farmers in the neighborhood of the factory. The fundamental problem that arose is that in these cases no objective market price for agricultural products could be determined. As a result, it was unclear which percentage of the sale price of the final product (butter or sugar) should go to the manufacturer and which should go to the farmer. In view of this uncertainty, which was expressed by the farmers as a fear of becoming dependent on the manufacturer, farmers hesitated to switch to new products and production technologies, and entrepreneurs hesitated to initiate new processing plants because they were unsure if they could conclude long-term contracts with farmers for the supply of the agricultural commodities. In short, the transaction costs of the rural markets of these commodities were too high.

The obvious solution, at least according to Oliver Williamson,[34] would be the formation of a single, integrated "governance structure" for both parts of the production process. In this way, the intractable conflicts over the market price of the agricultural product could be prevented.[35] In certain situations (e.g., the sugar industry on the island of Java), this problem resulted in the manufacturer actually taking over the production of the necessary raw materials and eliminating the farmer as an independent producer. In the Dutch situation, where there were major economies of small-scale production on the family farm, this solution was not pertinent. The optimal solution was often found in the formation of cooperatives that began to carry out these parts of the production process for a large group of farmers. In this way the farmers (who were actually the owners of the cooperative) were able to assure themselves of all the benefits of the integrated governance structure.

These problems became most acute in the dissemination of a crucial innovation, the factory-based production of barter.[36] Farmers feared becoming entirely dependent on the commercial manufacturers who set up dairy plants in their region. Factory-based butter production made it possible to realize large economies of scale in the processing of milk and the marketing of butter. Once again, farmers on the sandy soils of the eastern and southern regions of the Netherlands, where lower-quality butter was made on the farm, could benefit most from this innovation. But this was also an extremely profitable option for the farmers in Friesland, who were experiencing increasing competition from Danish butter and from Dutch surrogate butter (margarine). To take advantage of the new situation, however, the farmer had to close his own butter and cheese production, which meant that due to the high transport costs of milk he became dependent on the butter factory that was established locally. The first experiments with commercial butter production after 1878 resulted in sharp conflicts between the factories and the dairy farmers. Due to this problem, the initiatives of businessmen to take over dairy production lagged far behind the possibilities offered by new technologies.

In response to this incapacity of the market to organize factory-based dairy production, in 1886 the first cooperative dairy plant was established. In the years that followed, similar experiments took place elsewhere, which were sometimes accompanied by conflicts with butter traders who believed their position was threatened. The success of these initiatives is shown by the rapid growth of the amount of milk processed by cooperatives. In 1895 this was already 19 percent of total milk production, increasing to 48 percent in 1903 and 66 percent in 1910.[37]

The problem of one-sided dependency on local processors of agricultural products was also a factor in regions where new agricultural industries became established before 1880, that is, the sugar industry in North Brabant and Zeeland and the processing of potato flour and straw in Groningen. In the latter province the formation of a cartel of potato flour manufacturers in 1897 led to the establishment of a cooperative manufacturing plant.[38] In Brabant, farmers also responded to sugar beet processors who were joining forces; they had already formed a cartel in 1882. These farmers initially attempted to force the manufacturers to give them more reasonable conditions by forming a sales cartel, but this effort failed. The first cooperative sugar manufacturing plant was not established until 1899.[39] Cooperative factories in these regions gradually increased in importance, which limited the power of the commercial manufacturers. The cooperative factories could act as price setters, for example, which strengthened the position of farmers who were still dependent on commercial factories.

In horticultural regions, a different solution was found for a comparable problem: that is, the role of middlemen was threatening to become too great. In these areas, cooperative auctions, where members brought their products to be sold, were established to optimize market conditions. In this way, the transparency of the market was significantly increased.

These cooperative organizations played a major role in the restructuring of agriculture in the decades following 1880. These institutional innovations made it possible to make optimal use of new production technologies in the processing of agricultural products and corrected one-sided power and market relationships. Due to the actions of the purchasing cooperatives, the efficiency of the trade network increased, resulting in a sharp decrease in transaction costs. Regions with less well-developed markets were especially able to benefit from this.

For that matter, the cooperative movement cannot be seen separately from the process of "pillarization" that took place during these years (see chapter 7). Between 1834 and 1851 liberal agricultural organizations were established in all provinces, which played a modest role in initiating change on the farm. These organizations represented primarily the larger, wealthier farmers. They disseminated information by means of periodicals and meetings of "gentlemen" who were interested in agriculture, such as the annual Landhuishoudkundige Congressen, where many agronomic topics were discussed. The reach of these organizations was limited, however. For one thing, they did not have much of an eye for the specific problems of the small farm and expected the most important changes to come primarily from large, wealthy farmers. Their recommendations reflected this preoccupation; most of the attention was focused on relatively impractical innovations such as the steam plow or costly drainage techniques.[40]

At the local chapters of these agricultural organizations, local dignitaries sometimes took initiatives to establish cooperatives. The networks and organizational channels they created therefore played a role in reducing the costs of deciding to establish such cooperative forms. But the dominant liberal ideology of these provincial agricultural organizations also meant that they did not reach large groups of farmers.

In 1896 a number of Catholic gentlemen (including several clergy) established the Nederlandse Boerenbond (Catholic Farmers Union), which as a religious pressure group began to promote the spiritual and material interests of farmers.[41] In the years that followed, Catholic Farmers Unions were established in every province. They sometimes offered strong resistance to the liberal societies and actually tried to involve the smaller farmers in their work. They played a key role in establishing a range of agricultural cooperatives in the Catholic regions of the Netherlands. These organizations (which were dominated by the Catholic clergy) greatly stimulated the formation of purchase associations, cooperatives dairies, livestock insurance, and so forth. The problem with collective decision making—a cooperative can realize the economies of collective purchases (of fertilizer, for example) only if a large number of farmers decide to join—was solved by the influence of the clergy, who in turn were able to influence key figures in the village community. The Catholic Farmers Unions therefore became central nodes in the cooperative movement, especially in the predominantly Catholic southern part of the Netherlands, and were simultaneously taken up into the Catholic "pillar," where they promoted the interests of the farmers. A comparable Protestant organization was not established until 1918.

The role played by government in these changes deserves some attention. Initially, this role was entirely passive. In surrounding countries, especially France and Germany, governments reacted to the decline in grain prices with protectionist measures to keep the prices on the domestic market at a reasonable level. In the Netherlands, such political measures, which a few people had indeed called for, were hardly feasible, since the majority of agricultural production was exported. As a result, it was virtually impossible to stabilize the prices above the level of the world market. Moreover, livestock farmers were actually victimized by high grain prices, which would cause their competitive position on the international markets to be placed under even more pressure. After all, they used grain as feed.

This passive approach changed after 1890, following the publication of the report of the State Commission of 1886, which had investigated the situation in agriculture.[42] Responding to the problems identified in the report, the government began to pay more attention to and spend more money on agricultural education and research. It also began to establish experimental stations where new farming methods could be tested. The aim was to bring old and new generations of farmers in contact with new insights in agriculture. This led, for example, to new forms of education being established; following the example of German agricultural education, traveling teachers were hired to provide on-farm extension services.

At the same time, the links with the "organized business community" were intensified. The Agriculture Committee of the Netherlands, which was established in 1884 as the national umbrella organization of provincial agricultural societies, was acknowledged in 1893 as the official representative of agriculture.

In 1897 the Catholic Farmers Union was also admitted to the organization.[43] The rapid growth of the Catholic Farmers Union meant that there was a sharp increase in the collective organization of farmers after 1900. In 1913 the Agriculture Committee of the Netherlands represented 130,000 members, or about 65 percent of all farmers.[44] In this way a powerful lobby for the interests of the agricultural sector was established. Especially in the period after the 1920s, this lobby would begin to exert a strong influence on national politics.

The establishment of a professional system of agricultural research, education, and extension services resulted in a fundamental change in the way in which innovations were developed and disseminated in this sector. In the nineteenth century these innovations were frequently the result of trial and error of the individual farmer and were customarily disseminated from field to field, sometimes supported by information that was distributed through the provincial agricultural societies or through an agricultural press associated with these societies. In industry, a marriage between science and economics came about because large companies began to conduct independent technological research; the laboratories of Jurgens and Van den Bergh, Philips, and De Koninklijke are familiar examples of such research. The agricultural sector continued to be dominated by the family farm, but through political pressure farmers were able to convince the government to finance scientific research and to establish a system of education and extension. This new system, which would become very important in accelerating changes on the farm during the course of the twentieth century, is frequently seen as one of the keys to the success of Dutch agriculture during this period. A characteristic of this new system was that it focused on the problems of the family farm; most of the research focused on intensifying land use, while (at least for the time being) relatively little attention was placed on labor-saving technologies. As a result, the position of the small farm was strengthened even further.[45]

These institutional changes, which began after 1890, also made possible renewed growth in production and productivity (see figure 8.7 and table 8.3). This new growth was characterized by an optimal use of the new technologies that permitted rapid intensification of land use. For example, the use of artificial fertilizer increased to unprecedented heights in the Netherlands and was significantly greater than in the surrounding countries. Horticulture, which is characterized by exceptionally intensive land use, became one of the pillars of the agricultural sector. In livestock farming highly intensive pig and chicken farming especially increased rapidly in importance. At the same time, the significance of large, relatively extensive farms declined. The renewed growth after 1890 took place despite relatively low agricultural prices, which provided the farmers with little or no farm profits, a characteristic that distinguished it fundamentally from the growth that had been realized before 1880.

CASE STUDY: THE EMERGENCE OF THE COOPERATIVE BANKS

The changes experienced by Dutch agriculture during this period entailed a rapid increase in the magnitude and intensity of financial transactions in the rural area.[46] Especially on the farms on sandy soils in the eastern and southern parts of the Netherlands, the degree of commercialization continued to lag behind that in the western and northern regions of the country, which began to experience an accelerated development in the nineteenth century. However, the financing of this shift to greater market orientation and higher productivity remained a weak point. Nevertheless, farmers who owned their own farms could frequently obtain credit (with their land as collateral) through local notaries, among other methods. Due to the rise of specialized mortgage banks after 1860, this market became reasonably well organized in the coastal provinces. But for short-term credit, farmers usually had to appeal to the traders by offering their harvest as collateral. Retailers were another source of credit, which they supplied if the farmers agreed to buy all their goods from them. These forms of credit had a high effective interest rate, although the level of interest was often obscured by the complexity of the mutual transactions. Moreover, such credit often resulted in undesired dependence on middlemen.[47]

In Germany, where these problems were at least as serious as in the southern and eastern parts of the Netherlands, Friedrich Wilhelm Raiffeisen (1818–88) developed the concept of the cooperative bank. This bank collected the savings of rural residents with the aim of providing credit to farmers, thus allowing farmers to be freed from their dependency on external sources of credit. The idealistic character of the bank was heavily emphasized by its founder. Raiffeisen viewed the founding and administration of the bank as an act of Christian charity for which no compensation could be expected. According to this same principle, profits could not be distributed among the members but were to be deposited in a central fund and used to support farm credit. It was also essential to create reserves to cover the unlimited liability of the members of the cooperative as much as possible. Partly due to Raiffeisen's initiatives, the first cooperative banks were established in Germany as early as the 1860s. In 1876 the first central bank of this type (Landwirtschaftliche Zentral-Darlehnkasse) was established.[48]

The agricultural depression of 1882–96 greatly increased the severity of the rural credit problem. Due to low prices and shrinking incomes, the dependency on external creditors increased. At the same time the necessity to invest more in farm modernization, for example, in artificial fertilizers and animal feed, increased steadily. The State Commission for Agriculture of 1886 reported these problems in its final report, commenting that the rural credit situation was extremely unsatisfactory.[49]

During the years of crisis, however, this issue was hardly tackled. A handful of initiatives to develop cooperative rural banks based on shares—in accordance with the model of the Mutual Credit Societies, which were established beginning in 1853 to benefit urban retailers—never got off the ground.[50] The cause of this failure is evident: cooperative banks could only flourish if at least some of the farmers participating were capable of saving money. Up to the deepest point of the depression in 1896, only a very few farmers could save any money at all. Moreover, according to the State Commission for Agriculture of 1886, there was a lack of "the necessary individuals who are inclined to take the initiative or who have the required skills to administer and lead."[51] This meant that nothing happened. Cooperative purchasing associations and dairy plants were established in more and more villages beginning in about 1890, resulting in decreased dependence on suppliers and buyers. However, the purchasing associations required cash, and the smallest farmers simply had too little cash. As a result, it was exactly this group that threatened to fall behind. Starting capital was also required to establish dairy plants.[52]

Financing therefore remained a weak link in the development of agriculture. Why did urban bankers not make an attempt to fill this demand by providing farm credit? After all, the Netherlands was a wealthy country that exported large amounts of capital abroad during this period. Moreover, the high effective interest rates paid by farmers to shopkeepers and middlemen suggested that opportunities for a very profitable investment of domestic capital were being ignored. The actual problem, which was in fact acknowledged in the discussion on this topic at the end of the nineteenth century, was that urban bankers did not have access to the necessary *information* for selecting creditworthy farmers or the means to ensure that the farmers would pay off their loans. This creditworthiness was linked to the track record of the farmer, but the urban banker was unable to get reliable information on this. As a result, the risks of lending money to farmers were much too great for the urban banker unless solid collateral was available, but even then the banker could encounter problems if the farmer claimed he was unable to pay. Information about the track record of farmers was, however, available in the village itself. The local shopkeeper knew exactly how and when his customers paid their bills. The quality of every farm, of the cows, crops, and newly purchased implements, was inspected on a daily basis by the neighbors. Individuals such as the notary and the minister had access to all this "informal" information. One of the keys to the success of the credit cooperative was that this "informal" information was used to judge the creditworthiness of the farmers.

This helps to explain why urban bankers remained aloof from the problems of rural credit, but it does not entirely explain why many hundreds of cooperative banks were established after 1896. After all, banks are institutions that can exist only due to the trust of their clients, a trust that is usually the result of a long-term relationship between the bank and the client. The successful establishment of the cooperative farm credit banks can be explained initially by the role of the Catholic clergy, and to a lesser extent by the role of other local dignitaries. These were the groups from which individuals emerged, as called for by the State Commission for Agriculture of 1886, who took the initiative to establish the cooperative banks. Another important factor was the founding of the previously mentioned Catholic Farmers Union (NBB). This organization was almost immediately followed by a number of regional daughter organizations of which the North Brabant Christian Farmers Union (NCB) became the most important. The founders, primarily members of the Catholic elite, were inspired by the *Rerum Novarum* encyclical of 1891, in which cooperatives were praised as a means to improve the position of the working class.[53] The aim of the NBB was, following the example of comparable German and Belgian organizations, to improve the moral and social-economic situation of its members.

One of the first priorities of the new organizations was to improve rural credit. After 1896, Father Gerlacus van den Elsen, the dominant figure within the NCB, began to energetically establish local cooperative banks. During this process he made use of the "infrastructure" offered by the recently formed local chapters of the union. He viewed the cooperative farm credit banks as much more than pure financial institutions; he believed they were outstandingly suited as a means for improving the moral standing of the farming class: "To prevent usury, to help the farmer in need, but also to promote thrift, charity, industriousness and moderation . . . are the aims of the cooperative farm credit banks."[54]

Van den Elsen and other clergy used the trust they enjoyed among the rural Catholic population to establish cooperative banks. A few key figures—the village pastor, the notary, the schoolteacher, and leading farmers—were persuaded to support such an initiative. The "unlimited liability" of the members of the cooperative banks then meant that these pioneers supported the solidity of the bank with all their assets. In this way, trust could be established in the bank. In the north of the Netherlands, where the Catholic clergy customarily kept a lower profile, local dignitaries, frequently the members of the regional farming organizations, often took on this role.

During the following years, a fierce discussion began within the NBB and the NCB concerning the organizational form of the cooperative banks that were being established. In 1898 this discussion resulted in the founding of two distinct central banks, the Coöperatieve Centrale Raiffeisen-Bank, which took a neutral course and united primarily the credit banks in the north of the country, and the Coöperatieve Centrale Boerenleenbank in Eindhoven, which functioned as a central bank for the Catholic farm credit banks.[55]

Both central banks paid close attention to each other and appeared to compete in terms of establishing local banks. This competitive struggle, in a certain sense the result of the process of pillarization (where the Catholics established their own network of organizations as much as possible), was partly responsible for the extremely rapid growth of farm credit after 1900. Another very important factor was the powerful upswing in the agricultural economy after 1900. Due to the economic recovery, surplus savings increased rapidly. A significant part of these savings was deposited with the cooperative banks. If one looks at the development of the balance sheets of the cooperative banks, it is striking that much more was saved than was loaned out, especially in the south of the Netherlands.[56] Indeed, there was a great reluctance to borrow money, especially in the south. As a result, the new cooperatives in this region functioned primarily as savings banks. And most of the credit that was provided was loaned to the new agricultural cooperatives such as dairy plants and purchasing associations.[57] The success of these banks therefore rested initially on their ability to attract a rapidly increasing share of rural savings, which they did by offering an interest rate that was always at least half a percent above that of the Post Office Savings Bank, the most important competitor on the rural savings market.[58] The rural population therefore had a good reason to bring its money to the cooperative banks. In addition, due to the enormous growth in the number of such banks—from 46 at the end of 1899 to more than 1,000 in 1917 and 1,247 in 1925—a dense network was established, which greatly simplified saving.

The relatively high interest paid on deposits did not harm the primary aim of the banks, which was providing inexpensive credit to farmers. The average interest on loans fluctuated around 4.5 percent during the period before the First World War. This was below the 5 percent that was customarily charged by the mortgage banks, and the interest charged by the cooperative banks on supplier credit was even lower.[59] Due to the low interest on loans, the farmer got a much better deal at the cooperative bank.

This relatively low interest was made possible in part by the outstanding information available to the local bank managers, which they used to determine the creditworthiness of the farmers. The risk element of the loans could be minimized because the local banks had access to much better information than urban creditors.[60] The result of the extremely small interest margins and the limited risks on loans was a very strong competitive position. As a result, cooperative banks could significantly increase their share on the savings and credit markets. The small interest margin was in turn made possible by the very low costs of administration. The "zero-cost administration," which had previously been proposed by Raiffeisen, where there was minimum compensation for the cashier and the executive board was unpaid, made it possible to have the combination of a small interest margin and a financial policy focusing on creating reserves. Due to the convergence of idealistic motives and financial considerations, the cooperative banks became very attractive for farmers. To an important extent this explained their success in the following decades.

INDUSTRY: TWO PHASES OF GROWTH

During the fifty years that preceded the First World War, industry experienced two growth spurts that merged almost unnoticeably, separated only by a minor break around 1890. This break was, for that matter, significantly stronger in the capital goods sector than in the consumption goods sector and was closely related to the decline in investment during these same years (see table 8.11; cf. figure 8.2). In chapter 6 we extensively discussed the background of the industrial recovery that began in the mid-1860s and that actually signified the beginning of "modern" industrialization in the Netherlands. The most important factors behind the relatively sudden revival of industry were the accelerated integration of the domestic market, the revival of agriculture, and the shifting ratio between the costs of coal and steam-driven machinery and that of labor. In addition, a number of incidental factors played a role in the acceleration of industrial growth between 1865 and 1875. The elimination of the stamp duty on newspapers was an important stimulus for the printing industry (and, in its wake, the paper industry). The discovery of diamonds in the South African town of Kimberly led to an unprecedented boom in the diamond industry. The reduced excise on beer (and the sharply increased excise on gin) opened the way for important changes in beer brewing, where the industry began to focus on producing "Bavarian" beer (or lager). The import of superior Deli tobacco from Sumatra provided a stimulus not only to the tobacco trade but also to the tobacco processing industry. Finally, after the cotton famine that was caused by the American Civil War, the development of the cotton textile industry increased strikingly. These branches of industry—printing, diamonds, paper, textiles, brewing, and tobacco—dominated the first phase of the growth spurt after 1865 (table 8.10). It was primarily the growth of the domestic market and the accelerated integration of this market that resulted in strong growth impulses around 1870. Even the expansion of the cotton textile industry was largely dependent on these domestic market developments.[61] The increase in real wages and the decline of unemployment indirectly promoted the continuation of growth and industrial production (see figure 8.4).

After 1870 the economic revival was further strengthened by a rapidly expanding capital goods sector. The greatly increased investments in railroads and canals provided an initial stimulus for the construction industry. But perhaps even more important was the recovery of the urbanization process, which had virtually stopped in the Netherlands between about 1670 and 1860. As early as the 1860s, cities began to grow so rapidly that the Fortress Act was abolished in 1874. As a result, the walls of many fortified cities could be torn down, and the cities could expand on a much greater scale. Changes in the structure of the construction industry, such as the emergence of "jerry-building," took advantage

TABLE 8.10.
Growth of Industrial Production, 1860–1913 (average annual growth rates).

	1860–70	1870–80	1880–95	1895–1913	Share in Value Added
Consumption goods					
Food	2.57	2.64	4.37	1.77	30.7
Textiles	4.72	4.33	−0.03	3.38	11.5
Clothing	3.60	4.74	1.01	2.06	10.0
Leather	1.88	1.25	2.94	2.08	2.7
Pottery	3.43	4.10	1.92	4.63	3.3
Printing	13.53	8.64	4.14	3.62	2.2
Diamonds	6.81	9.99	4.77	−1.35	3.4
Paper	5.47	3.13	7.82	6.46	0.9
Utilities	3.36	6.44	2.99	3.84	3.6
Capital goods					
Construction	2.24	4.16	0.13	2.63	14.6
Metal	2.01	10.92	1.33	7.42	7.5
Shipbuilding	0.92	2.76	3.86	5.12	4.4
Industry Total	3.40	4.67	2.41	2.83	100

Source: Smits, Horlings, and Van Zanden, *Dutch GNP.*

of these new possibilities. At the same time, the metalworking industry was growing rapidly, stimulated by a large increase in investment after about 1865 (see figure 8.2). The mechanization of industry began across a broad front, while the market share of the Dutch metalworking industry, for example, in the production of steam machinery, increased significantly. The share of Dutch manufacturers in total "steam" capacity went up from 54 percent in 1876 to 59 percent in 1890, and to about 64 percent in the years following 1903.[62]

The boom in industry (and the services sector) lasted until the beginning of the 1880s. Although a severe international depression began after 1873 in nearby countries such as Germany, the Dutch economy appeared to be driven forward by a combination of beneficial internal developments. The "flywheel" of the rapidly growing construction sector played a primary role in this process. Consequently, the international crisis of 1882 was especially painful.

Excess capacity became apparent in the construction sector, which rapidly contracted as a result. Simultaneously (at least in the Netherlands), the "agricultural depression" began to spread, and trade with the Dutch East Indies—another source of dynamic change—also experienced severe problems due to the sugar crisis of 1884. However, a number of business sectors provided some balance. Due to the low grain prices and the continued rise in real wages (partly the result of low food prices), food consumption increased rapidly during these years. The food industry benefited greatly from this rise in consumption. In the 1890s this was by far the most important pillar supporting the continued expansion of industry (see table 8.10).

Perhaps more important was that structural changes in the organization of industry began to take shape behind this rise and fall in the growth of individual branches of industry. The first signs of the rise of large industrial companies can be identified in the decades before 1890. Virtually all the relatively large companies that were established during this phase were operated by a family or a group of partners held together by family ties. Coherent groups of companies that formed a single concern were not yet present during this period. The De Bruyn brothers, who in addition to a large Amsterdam sugar refinery and a gas plant also established a beet sugar factory in Zevenbergen, were to a certain extent the exception to this rule. However, their various businesses were still distinct units, each of which had its own group of shareholders, managers, and customers, although they of course preferred to do business with each other.[63]

The industrial empire that the Groningen industrialist W. A. Scholten built in the decades following 1842 had a somewhat comparable structure. As we have seen in chapter 6, his core activities were manufacturing potato flour and molasses. Beginning in the mid-1860s, when competition on the Dutch market increased, he started to establish similar factories in Germany, Russian Poland, and Austria, largely according to the formula that had been perfected in Foxhol. Besides this "chain" of potato flour factories, which was held together largely through Scholten's constant travel and the management skills of relatives and friends, he began manufacturing straw board and beet sugar. In 1870 Scholten even tried to extract crude oil in Galicia, but this attempt quickly failed. For the main, however, coherent groups of companies that formed a single concern would only be established much later.[64]

In another part of the periphery of the Netherlands, in North Brabant, the first conglomerate of international allure was established in the early 1870s. The butter trade in the town of Oss was the basis for the emergence of the margarine industry. In 1871 Henri Jurgens began producing margarine based on the original invention of this product by the Frenchman Mège Mouriés. Jurgens was one of the largest traders in cheap butter; he purchased large quantities of this product in the Netherlands and Germany and exported it to

England. He knew that there was a virtually unlimited demand for cheap butter—or something that appeared to be cheap butter. His largest competitor was the family company of Van den Bergh, who also became wealthy in the butter trade. Jurgen and Van den Bergh's success in reinventing margarine was made possible partly by the then recent (1869) repeal of patent legislation in the Netherlands. As a result, they were able to copy and improve the original process without experiencing legal difficulties.[65] In the 1870s there was tempestuous growth in the industry: more than seventy relatively small margarine factories had been established by 1880.[66] After 1880, however, a process of consolidation began, and Jurgens and Van den Bergh increasingly began to dominate the new industry. This was the result of a number of developments, such as improvements in production technology that allowed large-scale production at lower cost. In addition, the closure of the German margarine market in 1888, the result of Bismarck's protectionism, made it essential for both companies to establish new factories there. Nevertheless, around 1890 the two companies were not much more than a collection of factories—comparable with Scholten's industrial empire—and would start unifying only later on.

To improve our understanding of the qualitative changes in the industrial structure of the Netherlands in the decades following 1880 (which will be discussed in somewhat more detail later), we must briefly explore the background of that process as analyzed by Chandler. According to Chandler, the post-1880 transformation in the institutional structure of industry must be initially attributed to the second industrial revolution.[67] In the decades following 1880, a number of fundamental innovations in chemistry, electrical engineering, machinery (the internal combustion engine), and oil refining were introduced, which led to the establishment of entirely new industries that would ultimately dominate the structure of the economy in the twentieth century. Two important characteristics of these new technologies were their high capital intensity and their large economies of scale. Only by producing on a very large scale, for national or preferably international markets, could these economies of scale be optimally utilized. The entrepreneurs who began to dominate these new branches of industry therefore had to make extensive investments in three areas: production facilities, distribution networks, and management. The latter, which was essential to direct these large firms, led to the creation of a new type of company: the "managerial enterprise," which was characterized by a separation between management and ownership and by a complex, bureaucratic organizational structure.

The establishment of laboratories to conduct systematic research and development work was another characteristic of this development. The Second Industrial Revolution was based largely on insights derived from the natural sciences, which created the foundation for revolutionary developments in chemistry and electrical engineering. This meant close cooperation between science and engineering. Moreover, the large companies that were created during this process ultimately benefited from "economies of scope"; they were in an ideal position to diversify and to develop new products and production technologies. In the long term this led to the creation of the multidivisional company, the last phase in the emergence of the "managerial enterprise," according to Chandler.[68]

During the crucial decades after 1880, in most new sectors only a few entrepreneurs were capable of making the large investments necessary to establish these new companies. Chandler calls them the "first movers." Because they could optimally benefit from the economies of large-scale production, they were able to establish a strong position. This resulted in the creation of barriers to entry for new companies—"challengers," in Chandler's terminology—wanting to penetrate these branches of industry. The result of this process was that the ranking of the top one hundred industrial companies remained relatively stable. The "first movers" remained the largest companies in their branches of industry for a very long period.

In the decades after 1880, several Dutch companies began the transition toward becoming a "managerial enterprise." For the economy as a whole, these institutional changes were of little importance before 1913. Again, we are dealing the genesis of the new institutional structure that would dominate the Dutch economy after 1920. In the margarine industry, for example, the firm of Van den Bergh was in some ways the "prime mover" in the 1890s. This company began conducting a systematic, scientific study into the processes involved in the manufacture of margarine with the aim of making a product that was more like butter and had a better taste. Moreover, Van den Bergh—on the advice of the manager of the company's German subsidiary—began an innovative marketing program. The firm launched its own brands with expensive advertising campaigns, which also allowed it to eliminate the intermediary trade and construct its own sales organization.[69] After 1900 these innovations—which had first been applied on the German market—were also introduced elsewhere. This led to a very rapid increase in the profitability of the company. To finance these activities, the firm became a public limited company in 1895.

With some delay, the Jurgens family followed Van den Bergh's example. In 1902, for example, it also became a limited company. Further, in 1901 the firms began to cooperate on the German market; later, in 1908, they decided to share markets and profits in other countries.[70] But they experienced major problems with the implementation of this agreement, which, after many years of judicial quibbling, was converted into a complete merger (in 1927). Until the 1920s, the transition to the true "managerial enterprise" was incomplete because both families continued to control the company.

Two other companies, established around 1890, also closely fit the model identified by Chandler. During the 1880s, Aeilco Jansz. Zijlker began extracting oil on Sumatra after he had discovered an oil field while planting tobacco.

Due to a lack of capital and technical expertise, he made little progress during the first ten years. In 1890 Zijlker happened to meet the banker N. P. van den Bergh, who used his influence to convert the firm into a limited company under the name Koninklijke Maatschappij tot Exploitatie van Petroleumbronnen in Nederlandsch-Indië.[71] Due to its large capital base, it could rapidly expand and improve its activities. De Koninklijke created its own brand of lamp oil, which was sold almost exclusively on the Asian market and was the company's most important product during its first decade. Growth accelerated under the leadership of Henri Deterding, who became manager of the company in the Dutch East Indies in 1896. To ensure independence from middlemen, he started to build his own sales organization. Part of his new sales strategy was to ship kerosene by sea in newly built tankers—instead of in costly and difficult-to-handle barrels. Moreover, after 1900 the company benefited from the rapidly increasing demand for petrol in Europe. For the first time, it began to ship oil from the Dutch Indies to the European market. De Koninklijke built its first refinery in Rotterdam in 1902. In approximately ten years, it had become a fully integrated company with its own oil fields, refineries, tanker fleet, and sales organization.[72]

However, De Koninklijke was still dwarfed by the American company that dominated the oil industry, Standard Oil. Due to continuing expansion, the two businesses increasingly began to compete with each other. Deterding attempted to deal with this challenge by taking over smaller Dutch companies that exploited other oil fields in the Dutch East Indies and by working together with the largest British company in this sector, Shell Transport and Trading Company. With oil supplies from Russia, from Borneo, and in the United States, a very large tanker fleet, and a well-developed distribution system in Europe and Asia, Shell was an attractive partner for De Koninklijke. In 1902 the two companies signed an agreement to coordinate sales in the Far East. Then followed very profitable years for the Koninklijke—dividends averaged 60 percent between 1902 and 1907—but several very lean years for Shell, which suffered from "imperial overstretch" and a shortage of capital. In 1907 the two businesses therefore decided to amalgamate their activities on conditions that were favorable for De Koninklijke.[73]

The following years, during which Standard Oil was broken up into thirty-three separate organizations as a result of antitrust legislation in the American market, were exceptionally expansive for the new combination. In 1912 activities were expanded to include the United States, where the company built its own sales organization. The concern also invested in oil production in California. The American subsidiaries quickly became among the most dynamic parts of Koninklijke Shell. De Koninklijke had already established its own laboratory in Rotterdam in 1902, and in 1914 it opened a new, much larger laboratory in Amsterdam. As a result, the concern became a classical "managerial enterprise": it was led by managers (it had never been a family company) and was composed of a number of more or less independent divisions. The London headquarters focused on transport and marketing, while the Dutch operations, headquartered in The Hague, coordinated oil exploration, extraction, and refining activities.

The third Dutch industrial giant that emerged during these years was the incandescent lamp factory of Gerard Philips (founded in 1891). The absence of patent legislation (the result of the repeal of the Patent Act in 1869) gave the company an important advantage. For production for the domestic market, it did not have to worry about Edison's multiple patents on the manufacture of incandescent lamps. However, from the beginning this "challenger" had to take into account strong international competition, especially from German companies. But the lower production costs in Eindhoven—a location that was chosen especially for its low wages—gave the company an important competitive advantage. Philips came from a family of traders and bankers who were easily capable of providing the necessary capital for the company. During its initial period, the company strategy focused on the mass production of cheap but reliable incandescent lamps. During this phase, it paid much attention to improving existing production techniques.[74] This production strategy was combined with an aggressive campaign to increase market share, which enabled Philips to increase exports to major European markets.[75] By the end of the 1890s, the company dominated the Dutch lamp industry. In 1903 Philips supported the establishment of a European incandescent lamp cartel. As a result, he was acknowledged by the competitors as one of the "European players." During these negotiations, Philips insisted on a market share of 11.3 percent and consequently became the largest non-German participant in the cartel.[76] The company simultaneously shifted its attention to the development of an incandescent lamp with a metallic filament. The lack of patent legislation was again helpful in this process.[77] However, after several lawsuits, Philips had to pay large royalties to the German competitors who owned the European licenses on the original American patents. As a result, Philips was forced to invest in research and development on a much larger scale, which led to the establishment of his company's first professional laboratory.[78] In 1912 the firm was converted into a limited company, but the Philips family retained control.

Such impulses in the direction of the "managerial enterprise" were not limited to these three companies. Due to, among other things, changes in tax legislation, the limited company became an increasingly attractive option for family-run firms. This opened the way for the expansion of the circle of owners of the company. The number of industrial limited companies on the Amsterdam Exchange increased rapidly after 1890.[79]

After 1890 new structures also developed that supported the strong recovery of shipbuilding and certain branches of the machine industry (table 8.11). The modernization of the services sector in the previous years had resulted in the establishment of several large steamship lines and railway companies. Around

TABLE 8.11.
Occupations of Dutch Board Members in 1886 Compared with German Board Members in 1905.

	Netherlands	Germany
Services sector		
Financial (bankers/insurers)	25.9	30.9
Traders	22.8	12.4
Transport sector (shipowners/railwaymen)	8.1	—
Professions	12.2	10.9
Civil servants/politicians/judges	14.2	12.8
Industrialists	8.6	20.7
No profession/unknown	8.1	12.3
Total	99.9	100.0

Source: Schijf, *Netwerken,* 43–45.

1890 they began to acquire interests in suppliers such as shipbuilders and machinery manufacturers. The Stoomvaart Maatschappij Nederland had already established the Amsterdamsche Droogdok Maatschappij (a shipbuilding firm) in 1876. This would eventually develop into one of the largest shipyards in the country. In 1891 the Staatsspoorwegen and the Hollandsche IJzeren Spoorweg Maatschappij took over the bankrupt Koninklijke Fabriek van Stoom en andere werktuigen (a machinery manufacturer) in order to establish a new, greatly modernized machinery firm called Werkspoor. In 1893, on the location of the old shipyard of the Koninklijke Fabriek, the Nederlandsche Stoomboot Maatschappij established three steamship lines, which were active primarily in trade with the Dutch East Indies. Following these initiatives in Amsterdam, comparable new companies were established in Rotterdam. In 1902 the Rotterdamsche Droogdok Maatschappij was established by a consortium of Rotterdam shipping companies, with the support of several banks.[80]

In this way the large steamship lines and railway companies provided not only the capital for these new companies but also part of the essential expertise. Even more important, they offered a virtually guaranteed market for their products. As a result, the construction of large steamships only really became established after 1890. The relatively small-scale shipyards that existed before 1890 were not able to face the competition, especially from the British, on this market. For that matter, the steamship lines had good financial arguments for this vertical integration: due to German dumping practices, iron and steel prices were the lowest just outside the borders of the German Reich, which put Dutch companies in a competitive position. Another relevant factor was that wages in the Netherlands were significantly lower than in England or Germany. This combination of factors—a good competitive position and a more or less permanent market due to expansion of the steamship lines and railway companies—explains the rapid growth of heavy industry in the decades following 1890.

As shown by this example, many types of cooperation became more and more common after about 1890. In other contexts we have already encountered cartel formation in the potato starch and sugar industries, the diamond industry (due to the ANDB), margarine manufacturing, the oil industry, and the incandescent lamp industry. At the same time, the ties between business and banking became somewhat stronger, and the various sectors of the economy became more closely linked via interlocking networks of directors and members of supervisory boards. An analysis of these networks demonstrates this increased linkage. During this process, an important key role was often played in the Netherlands—much more so than in Germany, for example—by traders and shippers (owners of shipping companies and directors of railroad companies; see table 8.11). On the other hand, the role of bankers in the Netherlands was relatively modest, mirroring the smaller role played by banks in general economic life. It is striking that the industrial elite in the 1880s had hardly developed any institutional links with these centers of economic power. The Netherlands also differed greatly in this regard from its neighbors. Compared with surrounding countries, such as Belgium or Germany, these processes of linking and power concentration were still just beginning in the Netherlands. But here as well, the trend in the direction of a "cartel paradise in the Netherlands" (to refer to a typical twentieth-century development) began after about 1880.

The state began to play an increasingly prominent role in these new relationships, sometimes with some reluctance. This was shown, for example, in the decision to nationalize the exploitation of coal reserves in the province of Limburg, which led to enormous growth in coal production following the establishment and expansion of the state mines. But the relationship between the state and the economy became increasingly complex due to the emergence of the large companies. In 1898 J. Th. Cremer, the minister for the colonies, supported a drastic change in the organizational structure of De Koninklijke so that this company (which controlled virtually the entire oil production of the Dutch East Indies) could not be taken over by Standard Oil.[81] He helped to introduce one of the first examples of a "protective device" to create a certain buffer between shareholders and the board of directors of a firm; in this case the power of the shareholders in controlling the firm and appointing members of the board of directors was severely curtailed.

The accelerated expansion of industry after about 1895 was concentrated primarily in heavy industry, electrical engineering, food, and coal mining. It is striking how quickly Dutch entrepreneurs during this period were able to benefit from the fundamental innovations that formed the core of the second industrial revolution. This is even more the case when compared with the relatively delayed response to the British first industrial revolution after 1780. The greatly improved international competitive position, the result of the liberal reforms of 1840–70, and the fact that wages still lagged behind those in surrounding countries played important roles in this process. Of fundamental importance was the fact that, due to the new technologies that arose around the beginning of the 1880s, alternatives became available for the most important source of mechanical energy before 1880: the steam engine. Use of gas motors and electrical engines spread very quickly, while the progress of the steam engine slowed down. In 1913 the combined capacity of gas, electrical, and petrol engines was already more than 75 percent of the total capacity of steam engines (table 8.12).

One of the greatest advantages of the new generation of motors was that they could be used profitably on a relatively small scale because the fixed costs of the motors were low. Investments in costly steam engines, which also required a stoking room and a stoker, were often out of the question for small companies. By contrast, an electrical engine, which could be hooked up to a central electricity network, was relatively inexpensive and could be used very flexibly in the production process. Whereas the spread of the steam engine was accompanied by a concentration of production in increasingly larger units, gas and electrical motors provided advantages for smaller and midsize companies. This meant, on the one hand, that parts of industry that until then had remained dependent on manual power could now begin to mechanize as well. On the other hand, for companies that were already using steam power, this meant a redesign of the production process. The system of wheels and belts that was used to transfer

TABLE 8.12.
Energy Sources in Industry (horsepower per 1,000 laborers).

	1815	1830	1846	1873	1895	1913
Wind and water	29.3	23.8	21.7	20.2	14.2	7.3
Steam	0.1	0.9	4.2	48.8	122.0	174.9
Electricity	0.0	0.0	0.0	0.0	0.8	109.5
Gas	0.0	0.0	0.0	0.0	0.6	10.5
Oil/petrol	0.0	0.0	0.0	0.0	0.0	12.1

Source: Albers, *Machinery Investment,* appendix table A-6.3.

power from the central steam engine to the various machines (such as looms) could be dismantled. The machines were then equipped with independent electrical motors. This process increased labor productivity and led to very important labor-saving (and partly capital-saving) investments.[82] As Herman de Jong has shown, the electrical motor spread with remarkable speed throughout the Netherlands. The rate of this process is comparable with that in the United States, and it was even faster than that in the United Kingdom.[83]

Besides these successes, however, there were also gaps in the industrial structure. Attempts to establish a Dutch automobile industry were unsuccessful. The Dutch manufacturer of the *Spijker* stayed in business the longest (from 1898 to 1925), but like all the other automobile manufacturers in the country, it was unable to make the transition to cheap mass production.[84] Dutch participation in the new electrical industry consisted almost entirely of a single incandescent lamp factory, while the products of the rest of this new branch of industry (including generators) had to be imported from abroad. As noted previously, this caused a large deficit in the industrial trade balance. In this respect as well, the industrialization process had, in a certain sense, barely started.

SERVICES SECTOR GROWTH

During the period 1840–70, developments in the services sector, specifically in parts of trade, transport, the communications sector, and banking, led to an accelerated integration of the national economy. Over the long term, this integration resulted in rapid growth of production and income. In other words, the services sector, while interacting with changes in the institutional framework of the economy, was an important engine of economic change. However, beginning around 1865, industry gradually began to assume this role. Specifically, in the 1870s industry accounted for a disproportionately large share of economic growth (see table 8.3). But this did not mean that growth in the services sector weakened. After 1895 the tertiary sector even restored the balance and became the most important source of economic growth.

Generally speaking, three driving forces behind this growth can be distinguished: growth in income, the continuing integration of national and international markets, and exploitation of the Dutch East Indies. The latter became increasingly important after 1890.

The development of the services sector was initially characterized by the continuing growth of income and urbanization, which could be termed the "flywheel" effect. Smits has shown that income growth after 1860 provided important impulses for this sector. For example, demand for education increased greatly, and housing became a more important part of the family budget. The demand for banking services, insurance, and medical services also showed a strong link with income and urbanization.[85] In this way, the economic growth that exploded in the mid-1860s resulted in an almost continuous increase in demand for these services. In view of their labor-intensive character, this also resulted in an increased demand for specialized labor, which indirectly increased demand for many different kinds of education. Even more than industry, the services sector after 1870 became a source of new types of employment. The share of this sector in the national economy increased from 30 percent in 1870 to 35 percent in 1909; it became the largest contributor to GDP, even larger than agriculture (which over the same period was contracting, from 37 percent to 30 percent) and industry (which was growing more slowly over the same period, from 32 percent to 34 percent). The tertiary sector has maintained this position since.[86]

A special example of this effect is the development of the education system, in which the government began to play a decisive role. The educational reforms introduced by the liberals (including the regulation of secondary education in 1863 and major improvement for primary education in 1878) in particular led to a significant increase in investments in "human capital." However, also in primary education, the performance of the Dutch system was certainly equal to that in the surrounding countries (with the possible exception of Prussia). These reforms resulted in an accelerated increase in literacy, especially among women.[87] Between 1870 and 1890, the secondary education system in the Netherlands attained a level equivalent to that in surrounding countries, bringing with it comparable rates of participation. Moreover, the educational content offered in the Netherlands was relatively modern in the sense that less attention was paid to the classical languages than was the case elsewhere.[88] Furthermore, the much higher demands that were eventually placed on primary education resulted in a continuing professionalization of teachers, as is also evident from the rapid relative increase in their wages.[89] Over the long term, these increased investments in human capital must have been an important factor behind the continuing economic growth.[90]

The growing demand for services did not always lead to an increase in the quality of the work itself. The demand for domestic services also grew as a result of higher incomes, but work in this sector remained traditional. Its contribution to the growth of production and productivity was therefore modest. As shown in table 8.13, transport was the most dynamic part of the services sector. During the period before 1880, the growth of this sector was still slowed by the decline in sea transport, which was unable to deal with the international competition after the gradual elimination of protection by the NHM. Only after about 1880 did the competitive position of Dutch shipping improve somewhat, partly due to the accelerated transition from sail power to steam power. This sector gradually experienced greater prosperity, resulting from the activities of a few large shipping companies that were established around 1870 to benefit from the new opportunities offered by, among others, the opening of the Suez

TABLE 8.13.
Growth in Value Added of the Services Sector, 1860–1913
(annual average growth rates).

	1860–70	1870–80	1880–95	1895–1913	Share in Value Added
International trade	0.74	3.25	2.87	3.19	18.0
Domestic trade	5.52	−1.86	1.64	2.03	17.4
Ocean shipping	−1.12	−8.88	7.37	9.53	2.1
Rhine shipping	3.26	7.40	5.07	6.82	1.1
Railways	12.21	5.48	4.83	4.68	3.4
Inland waterways	0.86	0.31	1.79	4.76	4.3
Communications	9.12	7.13	3.90	5.25	1.0
Banking	2.83	2.76	3.99	3.00	2.8
Government	0.55	0.96	0.74	1.58	7.3
Housing	4.05	5.89	3.66	1.91	14.4
Domestic services	0.75	0.38	1.01	0.89	6.8

Source: Smits, Horlings, and Van Zanden, Dutch GNP.

Canal. The trade with the Dutch East Indies was one of the core activities of these new businesses (see later discussion).

While the market share of Dutch shipping was still declining during this period, the market share in international river shipping (e.g., Rhine trade) increased rapidly between 1870 (40–45 percent market share) and 1893 (approximately 70 percent market share). This, in combination with the enormous growth in transit shipping, the result of the rapid expansion of the German hinterland, made this branch one of the most dynamic in the business. It was linked specifically to the expansion of the economy of Rotterdam. Amsterdam played a diminishing role in the large trade flows on the rivers, despite a number of attempts to improve its links with the hinterland.[91]

Equally dynamic as the Rhine trade was the expansion of rail transport, which was followed after 1880 by the emergence of narrow-gauge railways. A growing concern at the time was how to maintain the competitive strength of various railway companies all using a single rail network. The liberal distaste for monopolies resulted in a situation where the staatsspoorwegen had to compete on various routes with several previously established rail companies: the Hollandsche Ijzeren Spoorweg Maatschappij (HIJSM) and the Nederlandsche Rhijnspoorweg Maatschappij (NRS). All companies used the rail network that was built and maintained by the state. There were also a number of smaller companies, such as the Nederlandsche Centraal-Spoorweg Maatschappij, that operated only on up to a few small lines. However, this structure led to many problems. Travelers often had to transfer from one company's lines to another, sometimes having to walk through a city to make the transfer because the stations in the networks did not link up with each other. Such travelers also had to buy separate tickets, which led to higher prices. Goods sometimes had to be transferred from one company to another, which resulted in higher transport costs. At times mutual competition resulted in one company refusing to ship goods from another company, causing the competitor to retaliate in identical fashion. Economies of scale, which could be attained in the purchase or maintenance of material, could not be exploited due to the relatively small size of the companies. With the arrival of many regional tramway companies, these problems became significantly worse. In short, many problems were caused by the various competitors operating on a single network.

As early as 1875, the state had acquired a number of competencies on its newly constructed network. For example, the minister was given the authority to establish transport regulations and minimum and maximum rates.[92] The problems cited earlier led to the establishment of a parliamentary commission in 1881, which was to make recommendations about the optimal exploitation of the railway system.[93] The commission's initial position was the desirability of competition. It also proposed merging several smaller railway companies with one of the three large companies and establishing stricter rules concerning competition. This issue became even more critical because the NRS experienced increasing problems beginning in 1881 as a result of the railway politics of Bismarck, which put transit traffic on the Dutch railways at a disadvantage. The sharply decreasing profits of the company resulted in pressure being placed on the government to take it over. The government gave in to this pressure in 1889, paying approximately 45 percent more for the shares than they were worth on the exchange.[94] The lines of the NRS were then transferred to the staatsspoorwegen; as compensation, HIJSM received several lines that had previously been exploited by the staatsspoorwegen. The railway agreement of 1890 resulted in a new distribution of the spheres of influence between the two remaining companies, the staatsspoorwegen and HIJSM. In addition, it stipulated that both companies could use each other's stations and lines. Finally, there was a provision that allowed the two railway companies to terminate the agreement; this would force the state to take over the private company for a previously determined price.

The result of this government intervention, which was forced upon the railways by one of the market parties, was that the sector began to be dominated much more than before by regulations imposed from above. Generally speaking, the cooperative use of lines and stations turned out to be expensive and not very efficient. The pressure on the two companies to publish beneficial profit figures resulted in cost-cutting measures, such as postponing maintenance and less beneficial terms of employment. The terms of employment on the railways had been relatively good, but they became increasingly poor compared with other sectors in the economy. This was one of the causes of the railway strikes of 1903, one result of which was that, in exchange for a no-strike agreement on the railroads, the minister of transport was authorized to stipulate the terms of employment of the personnel.[95] In this way the politics of "competition and concentration" (which began in 1890) led almost inevitably to the formation of a single state railway company, a step that was finally taken in 1917.

The last sector that we must explore somewhat further in this section is that of banking. In chapter 6 we analyzed why the growth of modern banking, which began in the 1860s, was relatively modest. The efficient on-call market, which brought together buyers and sellers of cash surpluses, made it very difficult for banks to attract deposits because investing money in the on-call market was usually more profitable. At the same time, the demand for business financing, due to the slow pace of economic growth in the Netherlands, did not appear to grow very rapidly. As a result, the "traditional" channels of financing—networks of relatives, informal contacts with banks, and other sources of capital—could continue to supply the need for business financing. The large Dutch banks that were established between 1863 and 1873 did not play a significant role in the financing of economic growth. Indeed, just like the trading houses of the eighteenth and nineteenth centuries, the banks continued to concentrate on providing short-term commercial credit.

It was only in the financing of the expansion of export agriculture in the Dutch East Indies that banking institutions played a more dynamic role. In the colonies there was large demand for capital, and consequently interest rates were relatively high. This financing was provided by several colonial banks (in Dutch the term *cultuurbanken* was used) and a few large trading firms. The result was actually a dual banking structure. The arrangements between the colonial banks and their clients can best be characterized as "relationship banking." The bank and the client developed a long-term relationship and shared important strategic information, and the banks provided a certain degree of supervision of the course of affairs at the *cultuurmaatschappijen* (holding companies of plantations), for example, by holding seats on their boards of directors. Outside the colonial sphere, the links between client and bank were much less intimate and can be characterized as "transaction banking," in which every transaction was individually evaluated on its own merits by the bank and the client, large companies frequently switched banks, and no strategic information was exchanged.[96] A typical example is that of the Van den Bergh margarine factory. It had conducted business with the Amsterdamsche Bank since 1885 and the Rotterdamsche Bank since 1891, but this relationship did not develop any further than providing a certain amount of credit at a reasonable interest rate. When the company wanted to issue shares as part of its ambitious expansion plans in 1895, it began doing business with a British bank, which arranged the emission, while Dutch banks—possibly due to a lack of relevant expertise—did not play a significant role. Moreover, the stock emission was placed on the London capital market. The role of Dutch banks was to be limited from now on to holding the current accounts of Van den Bergh.[97]

One can view these developments in two ways. On the one hand, it appears that the banking institutions responded adequately to a wide range of situations. In an economy with abundant capital, a highly developed financial infrastructure, and a slow process of industrialization, a totally different type of banking system was established than in a colonial economy, with great shortages of capital, an underdeveloped financial infrastructure, and a rapidly growing export sector. The comparison shows that the lack of close relationships between industry and the banking system in the Netherlands cannot be attributed to conservative entrepreneurship, as has sometimes been done in the past.[98] This is because it was often the same bankers, possessing the same mentality, who responded adequately in their relationships with Dutch East Indies companies regarding the great demand for long-term credit. On the other hand, this pattern had a downside, which was shown clearly by the banking arrangements for the stock emission of Van den Bergh. Due to their lack of long-term relationships with industry, Dutch banks had insufficient expertise and capital strength to serve these clients at strategic moments. The emergence of the "managerial enterprise" was accompanied with demand for new types of financial services. Dutch banks, due to their small scale, could not satisfy such needs, or could do so only with great difficulty. This was ultimately seen as a problem, and in response steps were taken toward increasing their scale. This began in 1911 with a merger between two large banks, the Rotterdamse Bank and the Deposito- en Administratiebank, which signaled a modest beginning of a process of consolidation that would continue to the end of the twentieth century.[99]

CASE STUDY: MODERN IMPERIALISM AND THE SERVICES SECTOR

After 1870, there was a drastic change in the way in which the Netherlands exploited its most valuable colony, the East Indies. The Cultivation System had been almost completely abolished, although compulsory coffee culture continued to exist to a certain degree throughout the period. Income from the colonies was replaced by payments from the Dutch treasury to finance the colonial budget, in particular to cover the costs of the various wars for the "pacification" of the colonial empire. From the perspective of the colony, however, the large income transfers to the national government were succeeded by comparably large private transfers of incomes to the Netherlands. After 1870 the East Indies was by far the most important destination for investments made abroad.

Income from these investments, especially after 1900, became substantial and covered a large part of the deficit on the balance of trade of the Netherlands.[100]

Following the complete elimination of restrictions on international trade with the colony in 1874, trade flows also began shifting to other destinations. In 1874 more than 60 percent of export from the colony was destined for the Netherlands. This declined to about 30 percent just before the First World War. Dutch exports to the East Indies remained more constant, comprising about 20 percent of the total export of the Netherlands, but also declined if measured as the share of total imports by the colony (from 55 percent in 1874 to 36 percent in 1913).[101] Their mutual trade had therefore become less important for both economies, but at the same time the flows of human and financial capital increased significantly in importance.

During this same period, the Netherlands was involved in dividing up the world between the western European powers. The Dutch were a relatively cautious player in the game of modern imperialism—the country lay in the shadow of the British, the superpower located just on the other side of the North Sea. Yet the Netherlands did contribute to the process of carving up the world, a fact that is sometimes neglected in the literature about political and economic developments during this period. This is, perhaps, because it did not fit the self-image that had been acquired during those years of a strictly neutral country that maintained a relatively passive—if not submissive—attitude toward the resurgence of nationalism and imperialism elsewhere. Nor did the active participation of the Netherlands in modern imperialism, which was expressed primarily in the consolidation and expansion of its authority in the East Indies Archipelago, fit very well with classic explanations of imperialism. Such theories emphasized the industrialization in western Europe, which led to the formation of surplus capital, which then sought an outlet in the colonies.[102] Because industrialization in the Netherlands began later than elsewhere—we understand now this was after 1865, but formerly the date proposed by J. A. de Jonge was used, which placed this event after 1890—the internal motivation for aggressive imperialism was thought to have been absent. A more recent formulation of the causes of modern imperialism, which emphasizes the dynamics of state formation in the periphery and stresses the problems the colonial authorities had to deal with in the border regions of the colonial sphere of influence, could consequently count on Dutch approval.[103] The most important conflicts fought by the Netherlands in the colonies, the "pacifications" of Lombok and Bali and especially the Atjeh War, appeared in various ways to fit this theory.

In the meantime, the tide has turned, and interest in the economic determinants of modern imperialism has grown once more. Emphasis is no longer placed so heavily on the relationship with the industrialization of countries because research has shown that industrial interest groups were not really involved in the process. It was especially groups in the services sector—wholesalers, bankers, shipping companies—that appeared to have played a decisive role in the drive toward imperialism, during which they entered into coalitions with the largely rural elite of England. This coalition of gentlemen from the city and the countryside was able to control politics. They aimed to expand the role of London as a central node in international trade and banking and used imperialistic politics as a powerful means to attain this goal.[104]

As emphasized by various authors, modern imperialism, including the Dutch case, is much easier to understand from this perspective. In the seventeenth and eighteenth centuries the merchant elite of Holland was the driving force behind powerful, early-modern imperialism (which supported the VOC and the WIC, for example); they were not at all hesitant to use the state for promoting mercantile expansion. Following the demise of these great trading organizations, the privilege to govern and exploit the colonies was transferred to the state of the Netherlands. As a result, Willem I, who bestowed upon himself this privilege, made grateful use of this competency to structure the East Indies as a district from which raw materials could be extracted. The role of the monarch weakened after 1840, and this ultimately led to the colonies being entirely opened up to private initiative. As a result, a new phase in colonial exploitation began around 1870, where the state was assigned the role of guardian of property rights of the various parties (ranging from Dutch businessmen to farmers in Java). In addition, the surplus that could be realized through the exploitation of the colony would from now on be appropriated primarily by the Dutch entrepreneurs.

As early as the 1850s and 1860s, companies and individuals were taking advantage of the new possibilities that had opened up. Beginning in 1855, for example, the NHM, which saw its role as a monopolist being threatened, rapidly began expanding its interest in various "free" cultures. As a result, it found a destination for the enormous capital it had acquired that was threatening to become idle due to the gradual contraction of the Cultivation System.[105] A serious financial crisis on Java in 1862–63 led to immediate reactions in the Netherlands. The intense capital scarcity in the colony led to the establishment of a number of financial institutions, which devoted themselves to productively investing their capital in the colony. The Rotterdamsche Bank and the Nederlandsch-Indische Handelsbank (a subsidiary of the failed Algemeene Maatschappij voor Handel en Nijverheid) were founded to satisfy the demand for trade financing on Java.[106] These organizations hoped to make their capital productive by financing new activities on Java and in the outer regions of the East Indies. New trading firms, which were also concerned with trade financing, were established at the same time. The most well known of these firms was the Internationale Crediet en Handelsvereniging "Rotterdam," abbreviated as Internatio (founded in 1863). The firm of Van Eeghen and Company played a comparable role in Amsterdam. It greatly expanded its activities and, like a traditional merchant house, combined trade in goods with banking, shipping, and financing the transactions of third parties. Therefore, even as early as 1870, parts of the commercial and financial world in Amsterdam and Rotterdam were anxious to expand their activities in the colony. This pressure, as we have seen in chapter 5, played a significant role in the decisive shift to liberal colonial politics in the 1860s. The liberal shift in colonial politics can therefore be understood from the driving force behind modern imperialism as analyzed by Hobson: the plain fact that entrepreneurs were looking for new possibilities for investing their capital.[107]

In all respects, these initiatives did not yield nearly as much as people had expected. For example, the Rotterdamsche Bank began focusing on domestic banking because its attempted penetration of the Dutch East Indies market quickly failed. There was substantial demand for capital from the colony, which would increase even further in the decades to follow, but to make successful use of this demand, good contacts and specialized information were essential. After 1870, large tracts of "wastelands" were passed off to unwary buyers to be converted into plantations. Families in the Indies with good contacts and excellent information were especially successful, although it was quite some time before their plans began to bear fruit.[108]

Enormous amounts of capital were required for establishing new plantations—in tea, coffee, or tobacco—and for the expansion of the highly capital-intensive sugar culture. But the growing numbers of entrepreneurs in the early 1860s who planned to make their fortunes "in tea" or other crops often had inadequate information about the quality of the land they had purchased, insufficient technical knowledge concerning the crops they wanted to introduce, and insufficient insight into the social-economic and cultural conditions of the regions in which they were active. As a result, only a few of these entrepreneurs succeeded in realizing their dreams. During the years of liberal economic politics between 1816 and 1826, these barriers had been so formidable that entrepreneurs from the Netherlands failed to play a significant role in export production. Many did not even try. The flourishing of export agriculture that began with the Cultivation System had led to an increase of information, trade networks, and entrepreneurship. As a result, the number of attempts that were made and the chance of success were greater than they were before 1830, but these were still extremely risky undertakings, especially where plantations were established in new regions or attempts were made to find new markets. However, some of these risks could be shared by the merchant houses that financed the operations of these entrepreneurs, with the harvest as security.

Some individuals were very successful, due to luck, skilled entrepreneurship, or a combination of both. The most spectacular example was the success of Deli tobacco. The Dutch planter Jacob Nienhuys, by means of a clever construction in the contract he had signed with the sultan of Deli, was able to rent

12,000 *bouw* (around 8,000 or 9,000 hectares), which would later turn out to be very valuable tobacco land, for a full ninety-nine years. He did not have to pay actual rent for this land, only import and export duties and a certain fee for each coolie he hired.[109] He was the first colonial to plant tobacco on these lands. He had to hire Chinese coolies on contract because locals refused to work on the plantations for the wages he offered. The tobacco he grew turned out to be of superior quality and fetched record prices in Amsterdam. This success led to the establishment of the Deli Maatschappij in 1869; during the first ten years of its existence it paid an average 50 percent dividend on its share capital. Of course, this outstanding success drew many other would-be planters. It also demonstrated the spectacular new possibilities of the "outer regions," that is, the islands outside Java that had previously been neglected by the colonial authorities.

However, the basis of this expansion—certainly before 1900—was relatively weak. The chronic lack of capital in export agriculture meant that the central "nerves" of this system—the merchant houses and cultuurbanken—became increasingly involved with financing the production. As a result, production and banking became closely interrelated. Even the merchant houses that were not directly involved with financing plantations still had to invest a great deal to maintain and increase their share in the affairs of the East Indies. The Chinese intermediaries, the essential links between the European wholesale trade and the rural population, worked exclusively on credit because they in turn gave credit to their buyers in the dessa. In this way Dutch capital, which for that matter was to a significant extent made up of profits originally earned in the East Indies, played an important role in the development of the colony.

This structure made gradual growth of export agriculture in the East Indies possible. However, it turned out to be extremely vulnerable during years of poor harvests and declining prices on the world market. When the plantations were unable to pay off their credit following the harvest, the trading houses and banks were also endangered, which threatened to paralyze the entire economy of the colony. Such a crisis indeed occurred in 1862, resulting in attempts to improve the availability of capital on Java. If this was dramatic, the sugar crisis of 1884 was significantly worse. Sugar prices and other raw material prices had been declining for several years, causing serious problems for sugar cultivation. The large trading firm Dorrepaal and Company, which was involved in no fewer than twenty-two sugar refineries, thirty-eight coffee plantations, and fifty-three other plantations, came into serious difficulties and almost took the Nederlandsch-Indische Handelsbank (NIHB) and the Koloniale Bank down with it as it fell. The NHM, which had taken timely precautions and had limited the amount of long-term credit it provided to plantations, escaped the crisis largely unscathed. During these years the trading firm was in the process of transforming itself into a pure banking firm, a transition that was accelerated by this crisis in the East Indies.[110]

The logical response of the merchant houses and the East Indies banks, which experienced serious problems during the crisis of 1884, was to change the way they provided credit for export agriculture. After 1884, under the leadership of the Van Eeghen merchant house and the NHM, they therefore began to establish limited companies (cultuurmaatschappijen) that owned these plantations and acquired long-term finance for them on the Dutch capital market. The number of limited companies increased quickly. By holding seats on the boards of these limited companies or by taking other subsidiary posts, the directors of Van Eeghen, the NHM, and the NIHB, among other firms and banks, made sure that their interests were protected. During the course of the 1880s and 1890s, a dense network of relationships developed between the cultuurbanken, the cultuurmaatschappijen, large steamship lines, and other businesses that were involved in the Dutch East Indies. Businessmen also began to organize themselves in the colony itself. In 1879 the Deli Planters Vereniging (tobacco planters) was established, which was quickly followed by the Algemeen Syndicaat van Suikerfabrikanten in Nederlandsch-Indië (sugar manufacturers). The latter was the most important business organization for a long period.[111] This colonial network reached the height of its influence when the former director of the Deli Maatschappij, J. T. Cremer, was minister of the colonies from 1897 to 1901.

From the preceding, one could perhaps acquire the impression that this expansion of the Dutch business community in the East Indies took place in a kind of political-economic vacuum. The Dutch government and therefore the colonial state had converted to liberalism and focused as much as possible on promoting private initiative. However, nothing could be further from the truth. After 1870 as well, the colonial government played a key role in the entire process. This of course concerned traditional activities such as providing new infrastructure (i.e., roads and railways), which was also built with some delay in the East Indies.

But entrepreneurs in the East Indies, both the indigenous and the expatriates, needed the government much more directly than did entrepreneurs in the Netherlands. State intervention played a large role in the making of new contracts and the enforcement of old ones. The expansion of plantation agriculture and mining on Java and Sumatra was often dependent on the contracts that Dutch entrepreneurs drew up with local monarchs, who claimed the property rights to these lands. These contracts had to be certified by the colonial government to make them enforceable. Due to the information advantage of Dutch entrepreneurs and their access to markets and power, such contracts were certainly not the result of negotiations between two equal parties. After all, the local elite frequently had no idea of the value of the potential tobacco lands or of the stinking mud (oil) that bubbled up out of the ground. For the sultan of Deli, such a contract meant that above all his own property rights, which were anything but clearly defined in his "feudal" society and were often only nominal, had been established and certified, and that he would be able to derive a certain income from those rights. The fact that this resulted in all kinds of other property rights being violated, for example, the rights of the local population or of competing elites, was not sufficiently acknowledged by the planters and the colonial state.[112] Similar problems arose during the expansion of sugar culture on Java, which used the best agricultural lands, that is, the *sawahs*. This was resented by Javanese farmers. During negotiations on compensation for these lands, the entrepreneurs took advantage of inequalities in the social and political power structures. Manipulation of the regent and the head of the dessa was often the cheapest way to acquire good land. Workers could be pressed into service in a similar fashion. In the unpopulated areas of Sumatra, where tobacco cultivation flourished, virtually no workers were available, and plantation owners had to import Chinese coolies, who were contracted for a specific period. After these laborers were transported to Sumatra, the plantation owners were allowed to force a coolie to work if he failed to follow the terms of his contract.[113] On many plantations, these practices verged on slavery—if they were not indeed slavery.

The essence of this problem was that the economy of the East Indies was only partially characterized by market transactions and private contracts drawn up between equal partners. Premodern forms of inequality were still very important, a fact that could not be ignored by Dutch entrepreneurs and one they frequently used to establish and maintain their privileged position and enhance their export production. Their information advantage and their better access to the centers of power in Batavia and the Netherlands also gave them a major advantage in drawing up these contracts. The local administration attempted to some extent to alleviate this inequality by aiming to protect the interests of the Javanese, but it only partially succeeded in this aim. Moreover, it could not get around the fact that it was required to support the Dutch entrepreneurs.

For these reasons, the Dutch business community needed a strong state to protect its interests. After 1870 the colonial government had to take on this role. The gradual consolidation of Dutch power in the outer regions of the East Indies was a second reason for entrepreneurs needing a strong colonial state. Until about 1870, colonial politics focused primarily on Java and Madura, and only modest attempts were made to delineate the sphere of influence. This changed after 1871 when the Netherlands, in exchange for relinquishing Elmina and several other supporting posts in Africa to Great Britain, was emphatically given a free hand on Sumatra, where Dutch authority had been virtually absent, even in a nominal sense.[114] This made it possible for the colonial state to take action against the sultan of Deli when he revolted against Dutch authority and ultimately led to the start of the first Atjeh War in 1873. The latter is customarily seen as the beginning of a renewed ambition for territorial expansion in the archipelago of the Dutch East Indies. Economic interests clearly played a role in this process, although Dutch historians have had some difficulty acknowledging this. The great interest in Sumatra was anything but accidental. This was where extremely profitable tobacco cultivation had begun and also where the production of crude oil started after 1890, which very quickly developed into one of the economic pillars of the Dutch East Indies. To a significant extent, the Atjeh War was fought to protect these economic interests.[115]

Between 1900 and 1913, colonial development accelerated. Prices on the world market were rising almost constantly, Atjeh was almost pacified, and the outer regions in particular profited from growing demand on world markets.[116] Returns on capital invested in the East Indies increased more rapidly during these years than did returns on capital invested in the Netherlands. This can be ascertained from data concerning the dividends of companies on the Amsterdam exchange. Dutch banks and industrial stocks paid a constant dividend of approximately 7 percent, but the dividend of businesses from the East Indies increased from an average of 6 percent in the 1890s (i.e., lower than the "normal" level of Dutch companies) to 9 percent in the following decade. It ultimately rose to around 11 percent in the years just prior to the First World War (table 8.14).[117] This favorable commercial development in the colony was also reflected in share prices. Very high prices of more than five times the nominal value were paid on the Amsterdam exchange only for shares in tobacco companies (those located in and around Deli) and for two oil companies. However, the spread around the average rates of East Indies stocks was much greater than that of Dutch stocks, with the exception of the railways, which generally performed weakly.

It is striking that, in comparison, the investments in the United States turned out to be much less profitable. More than 60 percent of American stocks in

TABLE 8.14.
Average Dividend on Stocks in the Netherlands and in the Dutch East Indies, 1880/89–1910/11 (percent).

	Dutch Industry	Dutch Banking	East Indies
1880–89	6.1	7.1	—
1890–99	6.7	6.3	6.0
1900–1909	6.7	7.2	9.1
1910–11	7.3	7.3	11.4
n	6–26	11–19	> 1000

Sources: Businesses in East Indies: Campo, "Strength": Businesses in the Netherlands: calculations based on *Van Oss' Effectenboek,* 1903–13.

1912 were at below parity, while the rate for Dutch stocks was 22 percent and for East Indies stocks 30 percent (table 8.15). In view of the large surplus of savings of the Dutch private sector, it was very logical to invest in a region such as the East Indies, where the Dutch held a major advantage in expertise over other investors. The example of the fate of the American stocks shows that if investors did not have access to the right information, the problem of adverse selection might occur, that is, only the less attractive investments were offered on the Dutch market. The great contrast between the "success" of the capital exported to the United States and that invested in the East Indies reflects the differing conditions—the lack of knowledge versus the knowledge advantage—under which this occurred.[118]

The economic boom after 1900 was accompanied by a significant shift in colonial politics. During the 1880s and 1890s, socialists, radical liberals, and supporters of the confessional parties argued that there was a "colonial question" (analogous to the "social question"), that is, that the colony was continu-

TABLE 8.15.
Highest Prices of Stocks on the Amsterdam Exchange in 1912
(percentage of nominal value).

	1[a]	2	3	4	5	6	7	8	9	Total
East Indies stocks										
Plantations	8	15	8	11	11	18	16	25	7	119
Mining	8	2	4	1	—	2	2	4	2	25
Other	1	4	2	5	1	3	4	7	—	27
Dutch stocks										
Banks	1	—	1	5	10	9	4	4	—	34
Steamships	2	—	1	2	5	6	6	—	—	22
Industry	4	2	2	6	8	12	9	4	—	47
Railroads	6	5	4	3	—	3	1	1	—	23
American stocks										
Railroads	13	5	1	2	6	7	3	2	—	39
Other	14	10	6	6	2	4	—	—	1	43

Source: Van Oss' Effectenboek, 1913.
[a] 1: <50 of nominal value; 2: 50–<80; 3: 80–<95; 4: 95–<105; 5: 105–<120; 6: 120–<150; 7: 150–<200; 8: 200–<500; 9: ≥ 500.

ously being exploited in a one-sided fashion by the homeland, and that the homeland had not established an active welfare policy to benefit the native population in return. Analogous to the shift in the policy regarding the Dutch agricultural sector, which was preceded in the 1880s by extensive surveys into the situation of those involved, after 1900 a major study was begun into the "lesser welfare" of the native population. This was one of the initiatives of the Kuyper cabinet that came into office in 1901. Through the Address from the Throne that opened the new Parliament, Kuyper announced that he was going to implement an "ethical policy" in the colony. This meant, among other things, that spending on education would be increased, that modern agricultural research and extension would be established, and that a development policy focusing more on the general welfare of the population would be implemented. During the first years of his cabinet, no strains could be discerned between this "ethical policy" (supported primarily by the confessional parties) and the interests of the Dutch business community. But this situation would eventually change.[119] Unlike similar initiatives that began hesitantly in the Netherlands around 1900 toward the formation of a welfare state—which were a direct reflection of changing political power relationships and were therefore also linked with the aspirations of the group of "new voters"—the ethical policy was not rooted in comparable changes in the social-political relationships in the colony. As a result, it did not progress beyond the stage of enlightened paternalism.

CASE STUDY: THE CHANGING ECONOMY OF THE HOUSEHOLD

Economists and economic historians have traditionally tended to emphasize the production side of the economy, that is, the role of companies, entrepreneurs, and workers. The argument is that this is where the most important decisions are made, for example, concerning investment, the level of output, and the technology of production. Due to this preoccupation, the role played by households in economic change is frequently underexposed. After all, how could these extremely modest units, each of which has no more than a few hundred guilders to spend, direct the course of economic development? Here we will attempt to demonstrate that this is a one-sided interpretation of the past. We believe that decision making in households and the family was also crucial to economic change in the nineteenth century.

On theoretical grounds—to begin with—this seems obvious. Most decisions about the magnitude and composition of consumption, the labor supply of men, women, and children, the amount of savings, and the magnitude of investment in human capital are made within the household. No less important were the demographic decisions that determined size and composition of the household. At what ages did people marry, and what were the consequences of different marriage patterns? Moreover, recent economic studies of the household have shown that these demographic decisions are closely interrelated. For example, there are links between marriage fertility and the degree to which (married) women participate in the labor market; similarly, there are links between fertility, child labor, and participation in education.[120]

In this case study we will attempt to map out a number of these links. To a significant extent this concerns the issue of how the household responded to three important changes in the period after 1870. The primary change was probably the increase in real wages, resulting in a higher standard of living. How did people deal with the new opportunities that were created by these changes? Did they respond to the greater demand for labor by working more to increase their real income? A second force that affected the behavior of households after 1870 was the "civilization offensive," where middle-class values were brought powerfully to the attention of workers. An important part of this campaign was the promotion of the "breadwinner model," that is, the idea that the married man must be able to earn the primary income for the household and that labor by children and women must be limited. Finally, economic development after 1870 led to the creation of new professional groups and a rapid increase in demand for educated workers—office clerks, bookkeepers, secretaries, teachers, and civil servants. As a result, opportunities for upward social mobility were created, and parents had to decide whether to take advantage of these new opportunities—which were often located far from home—by allowing their talented children to be educated for such new professions. Economic development led to an unequal distribution of the demand for these new types of labor. This was accompanied by rapid urbanization and loss of employment in the agricultural sector. To take advantage of these developments, households had to migrate as a unit or temporarily send one or more members to work in one of the centers of economic growth.

In the nineteenth century (and before), the establishment of a household was an important investment decision. This did not primarily concern the costs of the marriage itself; these were limited, especially for the poor, who could marry *pro deo*. But it did concern costs to be incurred when establishing one's own relatively independent economic unit. People had to buy or rent a house and have a prospect of one or more permanent incomes. According to this "European marriage pattern," where the spouses themselves made the decision to establish a new household, economic conditions therefore had a significant effect on marriage patterns. Moreover, there was a new link between marriage and reproduction: having children was probably the most important "profit" that resulted from the investment in a new household. To be certain beforehand of such "profit," premarital sex occurred on a relatively large scale, and a percentage of the marriages were "forced." After the marriage, the number of children people had was not far below the biological maximum.[121] However, people also married quite late; in the Netherlands the average age at marriage for women fluctuated between twenty-seven and twenty-eight, while men married on average one or two years later. These fluctuations were strongly influenced by economic changes that determined whether potential marriage partners could afford to finance their own household.[122] The recovery of the economy after 1815 was accompanied by a small decline in the age at marriage; it was only during the years of very low grain prices around 1820 that the average age at marriage of women fell below twenty-seven. Simultaneously, the number of births also increased, resulting in a significant rise in population growth due to natural increase (figure 8.8). By the same token, the economic crisis in the 1840s led to an increase in the age at marriage—especially among men—and a decline in demographic growth: in 1847 the number of deaths actually surpassed the number of births.

In contrast, the increase of real wages that began after about 1860 led to a decline in the age at marriage, which continued until about 1910. For that matter, it is striking that this decline proceeded much more slowly after 1890 than during the previous thirty years, which links up with the data about real wages in figure 8.4. At the same time, drastic changes in the mortality pattern

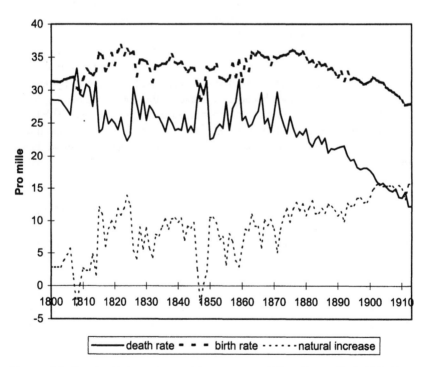

FIGURE 8.8. Deaths, births, and natural increase per 1,000 residents, 1800–1913. Data from Oomens, "Loop"; *Jaarciffers* 1901–14.

occurred during the thirty years that followed 1870. By international standards, the Netherlands had always been characterized by a high mortality rate, which resulted, among other things, from the very poor hygienic conditions in the overcrowded cities in Holland, Utrecht, and Zeeland. Infant mortality continued to rise until about 1870, from 164 deaths per 1,000 births in 1836–40 to 211 in 1871–75, an increase attributed by demographic experts to the decline in breast-feeding caused by industrialization.[123] However, this trend underwent a radical change after 1875. Infant deaths began to decline drastically and after 1900 stabilized at a relatively low level in a country that had suddenly become fairly clean. Between 1896 and 1900, infant mortality in the Netherlands declined for the first time to below that of Belgium—151 compared with 158 per 1,000—a difference that would continue to increase later on. In addition, total mortality in the Netherlands declined sharply (see figure 8.8). It fell by more than half over the forty years prior to the First World War, a decline that was also greater than in the surrounding countries.[124]

The rapid fall in mortality can probably be attributed to a combination of developments that will be discussed only briefly here. Improved nutrition and a rising standard of living, which led to increased resistance to infectious diseases, for example, certainly played an important role. Investments in cleaning up the environment, clean drinking water, and other public services in cities were also important. As a result of these measures, mortality declined more rapidly in the cities than on the countryside. Finally, the "civilization offensive," led to improvements associated with increased attention to hygiene. At the same time, more labor became available in the household for "reproductive" tasks; as a result, this campaign had an even greater effect.[125] For that matter, this increase in reproduction was made possible primarily due to increased household income (see later discussion). In the background, breakthroughs in biology and medical science also played an important role, allowing the causes of infectious diseases to be identified much more effectively (based on the work of Pasteur, Koch, and others).

The combination of a declining age at marriage and a sharp reduction in mortality—especially infant mortality—meant in the short term that after about 1860 population growth accelerated significantly. Due to the decline of age at marriage in the 1860s, the birthrate increased slightly, but after 1880 it began to fall steadily (see figure 8.8). This "demographic transition"—where the birthrate after 1880 began to follow the decline of mortality—appears at first glance to be in conflict with the European marriage pattern. Based on this pattern, "maximization" of the number of children within the marriage would be expected, as was customary before 1870. However, the decline in the birthrate indicates that men and women began to limit the number of children within marriage, a phenomenon that began on a national scale around 1880 but would only take effect in the Catholic south of the country (the provinces of Limburg and North Brabant) after 1900 or perhaps even later.[126]

This paradoxical development can be understood only by delving more deeply into the division of labor between men, women, and children. The "breadwinner model" had become relatively commonplace as a norm long before the nineteenth century. Whenever it could be afforded, there was "specialization" in the household; the wife concentrated on the reproductive activities, while the husband earned an income on the labor market (or from his own business).[127] In practice there were many exceptions to this trend, resulting from either need or professional pride. In the large cities there was a significant surplus of women. These widows and unmarried women attempted to earn a living as shopkeepers, laundresses, seamstresses, or prostitutes. Certain professions were dominated by women, such as the fish trade, cheese making, and domestic work (the innumerable servants were largely female). As the standard of living declined during the eighteenth century and at the beginning of the nineteenth century, the position of women in these professions came under increasing pressure, however, leading to even more women and children entering the labor market. The situation was summarized in 1850 by J. H. Beucker Andreae, a lawyer from Leeuwarden: "The material decline that goes hand in hand with moral neglect . . . may be assuredly and immediately attributed to overpopulation. . . . There are too many hands for the work that is available. . . . Where people used to earn a guilder for a day's wages, they are now earning no more than 70 cents. This causes the worker to send his wife and children into the field, where they work for much lower wages."[128]

The increase in real wages after about 1870 made it possible to bring ideals and reality more into line with each other. There are also many indications that the amount of labor performed by married women (and children younger than about fourteen years) decreased rapidly during these years. Unfortunately, the available census data and professional records do not provide unequivocal information on this point. For example, the following stipulation was included in the census of 1889: "Household activities are expected to comprise the main part of the activities of every married woman unless it is clearly shown that she has an independent profession or performs manual work apart from her husband."[129] More reliable information can be obtained by comparing sets of budgets that were kept between 1886 and 1891 and in 1910–11, which provide greater insight into the sources of income in households. The first series of budgets was recorded in or around the deep point of the agricultural depression of this period, when the urban economy also was struck by a crisis. The second series is from the period of rapid economic growth just before the First World War. A comparison of these two sets of budgets appears to allow us to obtain an impression of the effect of income growth on the structure of the labor supply.

The average income of the two sets of households, as shown in table 8.16, rose greatly, an increase of about of 50 percent in nominal terms, but when corrected for inflation it is about one-third. Around 1890 the husband contributed

TABLE 8.16.
Household Budgets of Various Income Classes, 1886–97 and 1910–11
(in guilders per year).

	1886–91			1910–11		
	All	<fl 584	>fl 584	All	<fl 888	>fl 888
Size of household	6.1	6.1	6.1	5.1	4.5	5.7
Total income	581.4	458.0	753.2	872.4	727.4	1025.9
Husband	430.2	382.0	497.9	723.5	658.0	791.0
Wife	41.9	27.9	61.0	29.8	31.0	28.5
Children	48.8	22.0	110.0	65.0	14.9	118.2
Working wives (%)	55	53	58	26	28	24
Working children (%)	39	29	50	24	11	38
Income share of						
Husband	74.0	83.4	66.1	82.9	90.5	77.1
Wife	7.2	6.1	8.1	3.4	4.3	2.8
Children	8.4	4.8	14.6	7.5	2.0	11.5
Other income	10.4	5.7	11.2	6.2	3.2	8.6
Total	100.0	100.0	100.0	100.0	100.0	100.0
N	38	22	16	70	36	34

Source: Database national accounts.

about 75 percent of the total income, a percentage that is approximately equal to that indicated by several more fragmentary records from the period before 1890. Women and children together provided approximately 15 percent of total household income, while income from the family's possessions—a piece of land on which vegetables and potatoes could be grown, rental income from their own house—provided the remaining 10 percent. It is striking that the poorer households around 1890 were more dependent on the income of the husband than were the wealthier ones. This difference probably can be attributed to the family cycle. In the poorer households, the labor participation of the wife was limited by the presence of young children, who were also too young to earn much money themselves. During the same period, successful, relatively "wealthy" households often had older children who contributed their own earnings. Moreover, the wife in these wealthier households also earned more than when her children were young.

This pattern, where the relative poverty or wealth of the household was strongly related to the phase in the life cycle of the family, changed drastically between 1890 and 1910. The share of income earned by the wife fell more than half, while that earned by the children declined slightly (from 7.2 percent to 3.4 percent and from 8.4 percent to 7.5 percent, respectively). The importance of other sources of income also declined, probably due to the steady proletarianization of the population. Due to these developments, the husband became more often the sole breadwinner, now earning approximately 83 percent of household income (in poorer households this was greater than 90 percent). It is striking not only that the income contributed by the wife declined but also that it no longer remained in step with income earned by the children (as was the case around 1890). In fact, the relative contribution of the wife decreased along with the income of the household. During the period around 1890, married women started looking for work as soon as their children were old enough to also contribute to the family income. This family life-cycle effect had disappeared by about 1910; when children were old enough to provide more income, the wife began to focus even more on household activities.

The backgrounds of these shifts in the labor supply of men, women, and children have been briefly illustrated earlier, that is, increasing household income and the civilization and denominalization campaigns that forcefully propagated the breadwinner model. Statutory measures, which were partly a reflection of these changes, made a modest contribution. Such measures included the Child Labor Act of 1874 and the Labor Act of 1889. Moreover, Catholics and orthodox Protestants lobbied for further statutory limitations on work by married women, but these efforts did not lead to actual legislation.[130]

These changes resulted in married women, whether they wanted to or not, being able to devote a greater portion of their time to household activities. Both the "civilization" and "pillarization" movements called for more attention to domestic life, better hygiene, better personal care, and improved nutrition and housing; in the eyes of these reformers, the married woman could satisfy an essential social and moral need by contributing in these areas.[131]

It is generally assumed that there is a negative relationship between paid work by married women and marriage fertility. In this regard, references are often made to the fact that marriage fertility in the Netherlands remained relatively high (compared with international standards) despite a striking decline after 1880. This probably was related to the low labor participation of married women and the influence of denominalized institutions on the decisions of households.[132] As a result of these factors, population growth in the Netherlands remained strikingly high after 1900—significantly higher than that of neighboring countries. In this way, a direct relationship can be assumed between the relatively successful "civilization" and "pillarization" movements after 1870, the changing position of married women, and population growth during the century after 1870.

However, this does not fully explain the decline of marriage fertility that actually did occur in the Netherlands (even though this was smaller than that in neighboring countries). It is likely that various factors were closely related to the position taken by young children in the household economy. The household budgets discussed previously probably underestimate the rapid decline of labor by young or very young children that took place in the decades after 1870. This underestimation could be the result, among other things, of lack of reliable data until after about 1890. Records of school attendance and literacy show that there was a virtually constant increase in school attendance during the nineteenth century, which accelerated especially in the decades after 1850. As a result, the participation of children between six and twelve years old in primary education became increasingly common. As early as the beginning of the 1860s, nearly three-fourths of the children in this age-group attended school at least occasionally, a percentage that increased to more than 90 percent by around 1900.[133] For an increasingly large percentage of the households, this meant not only that they lacked income from the labor of their children during the hours of school attendance but also that they had to (and were able to) pay for this education. At the beginning of the 1860s, about half of school-going children received free primary education, a percentage that declined to less than 30 percent after 1900. Before the implementation of compulsory education (in 1901), the great majority of households had already decided to invest a substantial percentage of their available means in their children's schooling.

During the second half of the nineteenth century, young children were therefore viewed less and less as a source of income (the "profit" of the marriage) and were increasingly seen as an "investment" that required a great deal of care (in the domestic sphere) and financial means to bring them to their full development.[134] The decline in infant mortality can be viewed from this same perspective. This development also made it possible to greatly limit the risk aspect of having children. As a result, rational family planning—"modern demographic behavior," in the eyes of demographic historians—came within the realm of possibility. The dissemination of knowledge concerning modern methods of contraception, as propagated by the Nieuw-Malthusiaanse Bond (established in 1881), possibly played a role in this process. For example, the number of abortions probably increased significantly.[135] In regions where these ideas were poorly received—in the strictly Catholic regions in the south and in the "Bible belt" of orthodox Protestants in the middle of the country—marriage fertility remained significantly higher than in the more "enlightened" west and north of the Netherlands. In these regions, professionals with a higher education and workers who had attended school first practiced deliberate birth control. Due to this development, the positive correlation that previously existed between welfare and the number of children disappeared.[136] Education also played an important role. People who could read, especially those from families who had been literate for two generations (where the parents were already literate) demonstrated this modern behavior (low marriage fertility and very low infant mortality) much earlier and to a greater extent than families that had not gone to school. In turn, these "modern" families were able to invest more in the fewer children they had. They were therefore able to take advantage of the opportunities for upward social mobility. In this way, these processes amplified each other significantly.

The rise in real wages had still other consequences for the labor supply. Workers, both male and female, wanted to convert part of their increased income into more free time. This "negative supply elasticity" of wage labor appears to be a fundamental phenomenon that was virtually unaffected by historical changes. The relatively high level of real wages during the late Middle Ages resulted in the expansion of the number of religious holidays. These extra holidays disappeared in the sixteenth century when real wages came under heavy pressure. According to Scholliers, between the fifteenth and nineteenth centuries the number of hours worked in Flanders increased from about 2,800 to between 3,500 and 4,000, a development that was probably typical for western Europe.[137] Workers traditionally responded to years with low prices and good earnings by letting go of the reins: they drank more, especially on Sunday, which caused increased absenteeism on Saint Monday. The rising wages after 1870 also stimulated the actions of trade unions for a shorter working week. Initially, they aimed for a working day of ten hours; later on, the eight-hour working day came into sight (this was statutorily implemented in 1919). This aim was in conflict with the interests of employers in modern industry, however, who wanted to achieve maximum utilization of their expensive capital goods. At the same time, and for the same reasons, they wanted a more disciplined workforce (by eliminating Monday absenteeism, for example). These factors, after all, made the workers unpredictable and threatened the organization of the production process. In this conflict, the trade unions were able to create "win-win" situations; by aiming for a combination of worker discipline and a shorter working week, the interest of both groups could be reconciled, at least to a certain extent. During the early labor movement, we therefore encounter a strong tendency toward the "moral edification" of workers.

The success of this struggle to shorten the working hours is shown from a comparison of estimates of the "normal" working times. Around 1870, people worked approximately eleven to twelve hours per day (scarce available records show that this was also a "normal" working day in the previous period). Two decades later—at the end of the 1880s—the working day had decreased to about 10.5 to 11 hours per day, while around 1910 a normal working day was about 10 hours (or slightly more). On balance, the length of the working day had therefore declined by about 15 percent during this forty-year period.[138]

Finally, as we have seen previously, "Engels's law"—the fact that households began to spend their extra income above a certain point primarily on industrial products and services instead of on food—played a fundamental role in the structural transformation that began after 1870. Similarly, migration processes were stimulated by factors such as the agricultural depression, and urbanization significantly accelerated economic development. Households, with their flexibility and market orientation, were as important to the process of modern economic growth after 1870 as were entrepreneurs and the government.

CONCLUSION

The fairly direct correlation that existed in the period up to 1870 between institutional changes and economic development became more disengaged after 1870. The establishment of the process of modern economic growth meant that the Netherlands could, in a certain sense, finally begin to benefit from the attempts at institutional reform that had been undertaken since around 1780. Ultimately, the liberalization and accelerated integration of the economy between 1840 and 1870 released forces that put it on a course of growth and urbanization. These were changes that, as we have already seen, amplified each other significantly, resulting in a cumulative process of expansion and modernization.

The dynamic social-political situation that was the central theme of chapter 7 was to a certain extent the result of this accelerated economic modernization. This was the case, for example, where it led to the establishment of relatively massive migration flows between the city and the countryside and where it undermined traditional labor relationships, thereby creating a breeding ground for the "social question." But these social-political changes also had their own dynamic. For example, the extension of the right to vote, one of the most important "destabilizing" developments, was, in a sense, already implied by the social-political relationships defined in 1848. To a certain extent, the state and the economy therefore went their own ways between 1870 and 1914. The relationships between state and economy became much less direct than they were, for example, during the economic experiments of Willem I or the implementation of the liberal program after 1840.

Of course, this is only part of the story. As in the previous periods, institutional changes played an important role in the growth process after 1870. This is most evident in agriculture, where an almost entirely new institutional infrastructure began to be established around 1890. This infrastructure was characterized by a dense network of cooperatives and by education, research, and extension institutions that focused on improving existing agricultural practices. It was also characterized by government policy that, to a significant extent, created the necessary conditions for such changes. This infrastructure played a prominent role in the resurgence of agriculture after 1890, when production and productivity began to rise once more. In fact, it defined the direction of agricultural development in the twentieth century.

In industry, however, the picture is less unequivocal. The rapid expansion during the period around 1870 was based largely on the institutions and technologies of the first industrial revolution in Britain, that is, the revolution of steel, coal, and steam-powered machinery. To a certain extent the Netherlands succeeded in eliminating its disadvantage in this regard, but beginning around 1890, other forces came into effect. The development of industry was, certainly in Germany and the United States, increasingly characterized by a second industrial revolution based on macro-innovations concerning the use of oil, electricity, and the internal combustion engine. In more or less the same way that the steam engine brought forth the large, mechanized company, this second acceleration in technological development led to further economies of scale that would result in the establishment of the "managerial enterprise," where management and ownership are separated and production and distribution are integrated. Consequently, multinational concerns were established with many production units and marketing departments in many countries. The impulses for these new institutional forms were already present in the Netherlands before 1913, as exemplified especially by the oil company De Koninklijke and to a lesser extent by the Philips incandescent lamp factory and the margarine companies of Jurgens and Van den Bergh. But it would still be several more decades before these new institutional forms would become dominant. In this regard as well, the institutional renewal of 1870–1914 was more of a prelude to the developments still to come in the twentieth century than a determinate force in this period.

The evolution of the services sector was characterized by renewed links between the state and the colonial interest groups. The gradually expanding colonial business community after 1870 could not have existed without the support of a powerful colonial state, but at the same time this segment of the business community exercised a relatively conservative, laissez-faire influence on economic policy. As a result, changes in the social-political sphere, caused by the expansion of the right to vote, were muted.

Between the growing economy and the cautiously operating state (which stabilized its share of expenditures in the national income at a low level), there was, however, a stormy process of institutional renewal where new organizations were established in virtually all areas of social life. These organizations promoted the interests of specific groups (such as trade unions, farmers unions, and the modern political parties) to edify and civilize the population and to control markets or avoid market failures (such as the cooperatives). In this chapter we have attempted to demonstrate the complexity of this wave of institutional renewal, that is, the problems that had to be solved through collective action and the extremely divergent aims of these new organizations. A common element that has not been sufficiently emphasized is that a new organizational form— the statutory form of the *vereniging* (association) which was established by law in 1855—was used on a wide scale. This organizational form had modern characteristics, such as a theoretically democratic structure with active participation by the members, and probably decreased the costs of establishing new organizations (trade unions, political parties). At the same time, the costs of distributing information decreased rapidly due to the emergence of the modern newspaper following the abolishment of the stamp duty on newspapers in 1871. In addition, the expansion of the rail network made it increasingly simple for people from different parts of the country to attend the essential meetings of the new organizations. Such changes may help to explain how a certain amount of the institutional renewal got started. Summarized in this way, these liberal reforms would have, ironically enough, indirectly provided the means by which the liberal establishment was ultimately undermined. With these changes in the institutional sphere, a path of social-political and institutional developments began that ended in the pillarized, pacified society of the mid–twentieth century.

Economic Development between Corporatism and Consociational Democracy

THE SPECIFIC economic and institutional development experienced by the Netherlands between 1780 and 1914 can be characterized in various ways. During a large part of this period, the country's *social-political development* was distinguished by the destruction of the corporatist structures that were inherited from the Republic. The Batavian reforms, the experiment of Willem I, and, as the final blow, the liberal wind that began to rise after 1840 all helped to break through the institutional sclerosis (Olson's term) that had burdened the Republic during the eighteenth century. But the most surprising aspect is that barely had this process been completed when people began establishing a new corporatist structure, a development that would ultimately lead to the consociational democracy of the strongly "pillarized" Netherlands of the first half of the twentieth century. This movement toward neocorporatism can be explained partly by the fact that liberalism was unable to formulate a response to the social issues that became the focus of political debate after 1870. Tension developed between the growing political rights of the working classes and the process of commodifying their labor. This tension could be resolved in practice only by the social movements that were able to establish a new future, a new institutional home (built by the socialists and the religious leaders of the pillarization) for workers and the middle classes. But the emergence of neocorporatism after 1870 was a much more complex process that cannot be easily reduced to a limited number of causes. In the countryside, for example, a powerful network of new organizations developed around the rapidly modernizing agricultural sector, which had not only economic functions (such as the cooperatives) but also social-political ones (such as the Farmers Unions, which also acted as political interest groups).

Of course, the question then arises about the continuity between corporatism and neocorporatism: Could neocorporatism build on the inheritance from the eighteenth century, and was the period of liberal reform only a brief intermezzo? It has previously been noted that the corporatism of the ancien régime was able to persist primarily along the "backbone" of Europe, the zone of urbanization that stretched from northern Italy through Germany to the Low Countries. Is it coincidental that the neocorporatism of the late nineteenth and twentieth centuries would also arise primarily in these areas? In these regions we encounter the most powerful forms of confessional denominalization, the welfare state acquires striking corporatist characteristics, and the relationships between government, the business community, and employee organizations still show characteristics that are common to the Rijnland model.[1] According to Esping-Andersen—perhaps the most important theoretician of the welfare state in recent decades—the corporatist welfare state that became established in these countries deviated fundamentally from the welfare state in Scandinavian countries or in the Anglo-Saxon world. This difference was caused by complex interactions between political relationships and social-economic developments at the end of the nineteenth century. The analysis presented in our book suggests that the historical roots of this type of welfare state go even further back in time.[2]

The unique *economic development* of the Netherlands—previously defined as the issue of the late and slow industrialization of this country—can, based on the preceding, be explained by three special conditions and developments: the institutional and economic inheritance of the Republic, the experiment of Willem I, and the specific response of the economy to the liberalization of international trade after 1842. As a highly developed and urbanized economy, the Netherlands was able to profit from the new technologies of the British industrial revolution only at a late stage. Similarly, given the modern features of the structure of its economy, the possibilities for growth based on structural transformation and the transition from agriculture to industry and services were relatively limited. The institutional structure of the Republic, that is, the inheritance of institutions such as high taxes and a sizable public debt (which were also interwoven with the social-political relationships), significantly slowed the transition to an economy that was more dependent on modern, large-scale industry. The interests of the pressure groups and these institutions were so closely interwoven that it would take several generations to untie this Gordian knot. Even Willem I, who briefly attempted to cut through the knot with support from the southern provinces of the Low Countries, quickly realized that he could not finance his kingdom without the support of the citizenry of the Province of Holland. Nevertheless, we also view the experiment of Willem I as a remarkably complex development that was partly responsible for the extraordinary evolution of the economy between 1820 and 1860. The negative consequences of his financial policy (for investment in railway construction, among other things) and the lack of trust between this autocratic monarch and interest groups had negative consequences for economic growth after 1830. Moreover, although his colonial policy yielded enormous benefits for the state and the economy, it also slowed the necessity for reforms, partly because it was linked with a high degree of protection for the most strategic sectors. The declining growth after 1840 can be attributed at least partly to this policy. But the specific response of the Dutch economy to the liberalization of trade after 1842 also played an important role in this process. The enormous growth of agricultural exports, the result of the relative advantage of this sector that had grown since the seventeenth century, indirectly hampered the continuing structural transformation of the economy, especially the growth of industry. The relatively slow industrialization up to the 1860s was therefore the result of a very complex interplay of factors and cannot be attributed simply to indicators such as excessively high wages or the lack of coal. This explains why the Netherlands incorporated the technology of the first industrial revolution at such a slow pace and why the dissemination of steam technology and all related innovations proceeded slowly.

In this book, the *state* is analyzed as one of the fundamental links between social-political and economic development. We have shown how important the rules established by the state were for economic life and how the series of constitutions, from the Union of Utrecht in 1579 to the constitutional change of 1887 (which expanded voting rights), were ultimately important in providing direction for the establishment of new frameworks for economic life. In this context the policy of Willem I, for example, has been given a great deal of attention because it shows the limits of autocratic experiment. This experiment failed for three fundamental reasons: first, the information flows about the condition of governmental finances were suppressed for a long period; second, it was impossible to replace failing decision makers (Willem I or his ministers); and, third, there was an increasing lack of control over those decision makers as a result.

This perhaps tells us more than simply another interesting case study. In his writing, North places a great deal of emphasis on the importance of efficient property rights for economic development. These property rights must ultimately be guaranteed by the constitution, because this defines the meta-rules of the political game, and these rules in turn determine how property rights (and changes in such rights) are established. Political rights and property rights are therefore closely related, and a constitution that fails to guarantee these essential political rights is also incapable of guaranteeing property rights. The changes in the Dutch constitution that began in 1840—which not only restarted information flows but also made it possible for the Parliament to exert effective control and replace incompetent ministers—had this double significance. After all, besides granting political rights, the constitution also offered new guarantees to the owners of the public debt, for example (in fact, it provided guarantees to everyone who paid tax; the poll tax was based on this principle). Ultimately, one might conclude, the quality of the political system had a major influence on the long-term development of the economy. The measures that were taken in the direction of continuing democratization, increased freedom of information, and civil rights (such as freedom of press and assembly) can also be viewed as measures that indirectly benefited the long-term development of the economy.

On the other hand, the accelerated expansion of voting rights that began after 1887 can also be viewed as a "shock" from which the political establishment was able to recover only with great difficulty. The emergence of the welfare state, it is argued, can be seen as one of the long-term consequences of this shock, or in any case the consequence of the aspiration to bind new groups of voters to the state. This aspiration was shaped primarily by new political entrepreneurs, who began to promote the interests of these groups of voters. During this process, property rights were "modified." For example, the right to dismiss workers, or to allow women and children to work, was limited, and new taxes and social security contributions were introduced. The original owners of these rights were not always happy with these changes, and they were especially displeased with the implementation of the Accidents Act of 1901, for example. But because these changes in property rights were implemented according to the rules of the game, following democratic procedures in which the interests of the stakeholders were taken into account, they were accepted, by and large, and were not seen as essential erosions of property rights. The relationship between political rights and property rights is again, therefore, very important to the question of whether the result of these processes is efficient. The most important conclusion is that liberal democracy, as it took shape during the second half of the nineteenth century, was an efficient way to implement changes in property rights and general changes in the rules of the game because the meta-rules appeared to be generally accepted. Consequently, the corporatism of the twentieth century was much more flexible and perhaps more efficient than the corporatism of the ancien régime. During the eighteenth century, the rules were largely based on tradition—*oude costumen en gebruyken*—and on a decentralized state structure that did not have meta-rules for changing the rules of the game. During the twentieth century, corporative institutions had to, and were able to, adapt themselves continually to social-political and economic changes. New constructions continually emerged (e.g., the guided wage policy after 1945 and the so-called polder model after 1982),[3] which provided relatively efficient solutions to the most urgent problems of that time. Therefore, the transition from the "stationary state" of the eighteenth century to "modern economic growth" took place in parallel with a complex transition from relatively static corporatism to a dynamic neocorporatism that was embedded in parliamentary democracy.

Notes

INTRODUCTION
INSTITUTIONAL CHANGE, NINETEENTH-CENTURY GROWTH,
AND THE EARLY MODERN LEGACY

1. King's (1648–1712) detailed social tables for England and Wales and accompanying crude estimates of per capita income in France and the Republic between the Glorious Revolution (1688) and 1695 originally appeared in 1696; cf. Barnett, *Two Tracts*.

2. See Israel, *Dutch Primacy*, 27ff.

3. See J. de Vries and Van der Woude, *Nederland*.

4. See Price, *Holland*, 211–13; on the role of the urban influence, 't Hart, "Dutch Republic," 57–98.

5. Price, *Holland*, 278–93.

6. Tracy, *Financial Revolution*.

7. Tilly, *Coercion;* see also 't Hart, *Making*.

8. For different views on the chronology and the extent of the economic decline, see Riley, "Dutch Economy"; J. de Vries, "Decline and Rise"; Van Zanden, "Economie"; Israel, *Dutch Primacy*, 377–404; and J. de Vries and Van der Woude, *Nederland*, 43, 498, 571. A critique of the lack of actual economic mechanisms specified in the latter view is given in Van Riel, "Rethinking," 223–29.

9. As, for instance, cited in Schama, *Patriots*, 2.

10. Brugmans, *Arbeidende Klasse;* De Jonge, *Industrialisatie;* a survey of the debate in Van Zanden, "Dutch Economic History."

11. Griffiths, *Industrial Retardation;* Bos, "Factorprijzen," 109–37; De Meere, *Economische ontwikkeling;* the effect of early modern wage changes on early nineteenth-century development was most notably stressed by Mokyr, *Industrialization*.

12. Note that the term was originally brought to the debate by De Jonge to stress the absence of industrial leading sectors within the Rostowian framework used; De Jonge, *Industrialisatie*, 346.

13. See ibid.; Griffiths, *Achterlijk;* Van Zanden, *Economische ontwikkeling;* Horlings, *Economic Development;* Smits, *Economische groei*.

14. See Kuznets, *Modern Economic Growth;* Kuznets, *Economic Growth*.

15. See North, *Institutions;* Hodgson (in *Economics*) provides another important summary of the new institutional economy.

16. See North and Thomas, *Rise*.

17. Kuznets, "Modern Economic Growth," 59.

18. Downs, *Economic Theory*.

19. Olson, *Rise*.

20. Van Zanden, *Een klein land*, 242–48; cf. Olson, *Rise*.

21. Kuznets, *Modern Economic Growth*.

22. See Tilly, *Coercion.*
23. See Van Sas, *Onze Natuurlijkste Bondgenoot.*
24. The classic reference is to David, "Clio."
25. For more information, refer to Smits, Horlings, and Van Zanden, *Dutch GNP;* this is also available on the Internet at http://.nationalaccounts.niwi.knaw.nl.

CHAPTER ONE
THE END OF THE REPUBLIC: ADAM SMITH'S "STATIONARY STATE"
AND THE ENLIGHTENED REVOLUTION

1. Smith, *Inquiry,* Chaps. 8–9 (page numbers differ between editions); Ricardo, *Principles.* A telling example of a later, changed use of this term can be found in John Stuart Mill, *Principles,* 178, in which he observes that "the mere fact that profits have to bear their share of a heavy general taxation, tends, in the same manner as a peculiar tax, to drive capital abroad, to discourage further accumulation and to accelerate the attainment of the stationary state. This is thought to have been the principal cause of the decline of Holland, or rather of her having ceased to make progress."
2. Smith, *Inquiry,* 697.
3. Klein, "Zeventiende eeuw," 108–10.
4. Neal, *Rise;* Riley, *International Government Finance.*
5. J. de Vries and Van der Woude, *Nederland,* 148ff.
6. Keuchenius, *Inkomsten en Uitgaven;* Metelerkamp, *Toestand van Nederland,* 61, which explicitly states that it modeled its tabulation of national sources of income and expenditure after the works by Beeke and Pitt.
7. Keuchenius, *Inkomsten en Uitgaven,* 16, 24, 31.
8. Ibid., 50–51.
9. Joh. de Vries, *Economische Achteruitgang,* 104–6.
10. These estimates are largely consistent with those published by De Vries ("Decline and Rise") and J. de Vries and Van der Woude, *Nederland,* 814.
11. Joh. de Vries, *Economische achteruitgang,* 40–41.
12. Keuchenius, *Inkomsten en Uitgaven,* 60, 79. Cf. De Bosch Kemper, *Geschiedkundig Onderzoek;* Van Leeuwen, *Bijstand,* 77–79; Pot, *Arm Leiden,* 188–92.
13. See Kooijmans, *Onder regenten,* 205–6; Prak, *Gezeten burgers,* 208ff; J. J. de Jong, *Fatsoen,* 185ff.
14. Harten, "Landschap," 43–44.
15. Wijsenbeek-Olthuis, *Achter de Gevels.*
16. See Faber, *Drie Eeuwen Friesland,* 243–50; Algemeen Rijksarchief (hereafter ARA), *Financiën van Holland,* 826–28, corrected for changes in excise rates; a doubling of revenues can be observed between 1700 and 1770.
17. J. de Vries and Van der Woude, *Nederland,* 156.
18. Riley, *International Government Finance,* 12.
19. Temple, *Observations,* 229.
20. Cited by J. de Vries and Van der Woude, *Nederland,* 158.
21. See Neal, *Rise;* Oppers, "Interest Rate Effect."
22. J. de Vries and Van der Woude, *Nederland,* 115–17.

23. Israel, *Dutch Primacy,* is the seminal study of relations between political, military, and economic developments.

24. Van Zanden and Horlings, "Rise."

25. Posthumus, *Geschiedenis,* 3, is the classic study of this topic; cf. Joh. de Vries, *Economische achteruitgang,* 83–85.

26. Cf. Hoffman and Norberg, *Fiscal Crisis,* 301.

27. Cf. J. de Vries, "Production"; Van Zanden, *Economische ontwikkeling,* 139–40.

28. Bruijn, "Personeelsbehoefte."

29. The classic study on this topic is by Hajnal, "European Marriage Pattern."

30. Van der Woude, "Demografische ontwikkeling."

31. Noordegraaf and Van Zanden, "Early Modern Economic Growth," 428–30; Faber, *Dure Tijden.*

32. J. de Vries and Van der Woude, *Nederland,* 814.

33. Cf. W. Bijker, "Sociale constructie," 10–13.

34. Cf., for example, the classic analysis of the British industrial revolution by Landes, *Unbound Prometheus,* 41–123; or Pieterson, *Technisch labyrint,* 25–65.

35. Landes, *Unbound Prometheus,* 231ff.; Pieterson, *Technische labyrint,* 135ff.

36. Cf. the contributions to McCloskey, *Essays.*

37. A recent overview is given in Davids, "Technische ontwikkeling," 9–38; also "Technological Change," 79–104.

38. Schmookler, *Invention.*

39. Davids, "Technological Change," 95.

40. Davids, "Technische ontwikkeling," 3–33, which, moreover, qualifies the slow technological development.

41. J. de Vries, "Barges," 245–50; Ames and Rosenberg, "Changing Technological Leadership," 13–31.

42. J. de Vries, "Barges," 245–48.

43. Cf. Aghion and Howitt, "Model," 323–51.

44. Griffiths, *Industrial Retardation;* Bos, "Factorprijzen."

45. Mokyr, *Industrialization.*

46. Israel, *Dutch Primacy;* Price, *Holland.*

47. Elbaum and Lazonick, *Decline.*

48. Chandler, *Scale and Scope,* 235–392.

49. Olson, *Rise.*

50. See for the madder industry: Schot, "Meekrapnijverheid," 42–62; Schot, "Meekrapbedrijf," 77–110; for deep-sea fishing, see the case study in chapter 4.

51. See Van Tijn, "Pieter de la Court," 304–70; Lucassen, "Welvaren," 13–49.

52. Van Zanden, *Rise,* 130–34.

53. Van Zanden, "Introductie," 63–80.

54. Griffiths, "Creation of a National Dutch Economy."

55. Prak, *Republikeinse veelheid.*

56. Gabriëls, *Heren,* contains the best analysis of the development of the political equilibrium in the second half of the eighteenth century.

57. Tracy, *Financial Revolution;* 't Hart, *Making.*

58. See North and Weingast, "Evolution," for a more theoretical development of this "financial revolution" in the English context.

59. Van Deursen, "Staatsinstellingen," 369ff.; Van der Meulen, *Studies*, 120ff.

60. Geikie and Montgomery, *Dutch Barrier*, 326.

61. A theoretical analysis of this problem has been published by Alesina and Drasen, "Why Are Stabilizations Delayed?"

62. *Gedenkstukken* 4:471–73; cf. Pfeil, *"Tot redding,"* 95–97.

63. Fritschy, *Gewestelijke Financiën*, 174; Sickenga, *Bijdrage*, 397–400.

64. Aalbers, "Machtsverval."

65. Wantje Fritschy (*Patriotten*, 57–74) has refuted criticisms of this "institutional inefficiency." Her approach was not so much through the effects of these institutions as such but rather through an analysis of the amount and distribution of tax income of Holland in the eighteenth century. She found (1) that these were significantly higher than in Great Britain and France and (2) that the system was less regressive than had been assumed; it was in the eighteenth century that all sorts of progressive direct taxation increased, simply because expenditure could no longer be deflected onto the shoulders of lower income groups. The supposition was that the degree to which financial institutions were able to generate high incomes was indicative of their success. Nevertheless, this argument ignores the considerable institutional problems confronting the Republic, cf. Pfeil, *"Tot redding,"* 11ff.

66. See Prak, *Republikeinse veelvoud;* Schama, *Patriots;* C.H.E. de Wit, *Strijd*. It is not possible here to treat the extensive literature on this matter, nor the interpretations of the Patriot movement discussed in it.

67. C.H.E. de Wit, *Strijd*, 49–54.

68. Pfeil, *"Tot redding,"* 33.

69. Ibid., 41.

70. White, "French Revolution."

71. Stuurman, *Staatsvorming*, 115–16.

72. Pfeil, *"Tot redding,"* 124ff. This entire section is based largely on his work and that of Fritschy, *Patriotten*.

73. ARA, Ministerie van Financiën 1795–1813, 877a.

74. Kossman, *Lage Landen*, 91.

75. Boels, *Binnenlandse zaken*, 266.

76. Van Genabeek, *Met Vereende Kracht*, 60.

77. Zappey, *Werkzaamheid*, 45ff.

78. Schama, "The Exigencies," cited by Pfeil, *"Tot redding,"* 130.

79. Pfeil, *"Tot redding,"* 202ff.; Fritschy, *Patriotten*, 177ff.

80. Fritschy, *Patriotten*, 75ff.

81. White, "French Revolution," 250–51.

82. *Gedenkstukken* 4:543, note 1.

83. For details see Pfeil, *"Tot redding,"* 309ff.

84. Publication (1806), 11, 60.

85. Pfeil, *"Tot redding,"* 445ff.

86. Ibid., 307.

87. See Fritschy, *Patriotten*, 171ff.

88. Sillem, *Gogel*.

CHAPTER TWO
A COMPLEX LEGACY TOSSED: THE DUTCH ECONOMY
DURING WAR AND REVOLUTION, 1780–1813

1. Joh. de Vries, *Economische achteruitgang,* 167–68.

2. J. de Vries and Van der Woude, *Nederland,* 786–88.

3. Buyst and Mokyr, "Dutch Manufacturing."

4. See, for example, Faber, "Scheepvaart"; Van Zanden, "Economie van Holland."

5. J. de Vries, *Rural Economy.*

6. Bieleman, "Productie," 156ff.; these agricultural structures have been analyzsed in more detail in Van Zanden, *Economische ontwikkeling;* and Bieleman, *Geschiedenis.*

7. See Priester, *Geschiedenis,* 322ff., for detailed information about this industry.

8. J. de Vries (*Rural Economy,* 172) estimated, for example, that grain imports fed more than half the population of the provinces of Holland and Utrecht; a detailed examination of this issue is found in Van Tielhof, "Grain Provision."

9. See Blanchard, "Continental Cattle Trades."

10. Priester, *Geschiedenis.*

11. Van Zanden, "Paradox."

12. The classic study on agriculture in this area is by Van Bieleman, *Boeren.*

13. Trompetter, *Agriculture.*

14. Harkx, *Helmondse textielnijverheid.*

15. Burger, "Dutch Patterns," 176.

16. Cf. J.P.H. Smits, "Size."

17. See J.P.H. Smits, *Economische groei,* for a more detailed analysis of these relationships.

18. Soltow, "Inequality," 135–38; cf. Burgers, *100 jaar,* 173.

19. Van Zanden, *Rise,* 138–41.

20. Lucassen, *Naar de kusten.*

21. Van Zanden, *Rise,* 137.

22. For more details on regional differences in wealth, see Noordegraaf and Van Zanden, "Early Modern Economic Growth," 417–20.

23. Soltow, "Inequality," 135–38.

24. Indeed, in his study of the traffic on Holland's towpaths in the seventeenth century, De Vries found a positive relation between economic activity and grain prices, one that in the eighteenth century, however, no longer existed; cf. J. de Vries, "Barges," 322–23.

25. Faber, *Dure Tijden;* Noordegraaf and Van Zanden, "Early Modern Economic Growth," 429.

26. J. de Vries, "Barges," 304ff.; Posthumus, *Geschiedenis,* 3:1124–44.

27. Joh. de Vries, *Economische achteruitgang.*

28. Wegener Sleeswijk, "Rendement."

29. Ibid. The average profits have been recalculated to take account of the ships that lost money; Wegener Sleeswijk left these out of the calculations, resulting in his figure of 10 percent average profit.

30. Details about this wage series have been published on the Internet at www. iisg.nl/hpw.

31. Faber, *Dure tijden.*
32. Trompetter, *Agriculture,* 132.
33. Harkx, *Helmondse textielnijverheid,* 126.
34. Van der Maas and Noordegraaf, "Smakelijk eten."
35. Roessingh, *Inlandse tabak,* 370.
36. Kops, "Betoog"; cf. the report of a commission that examined the trade politics of the Netherlands in 1815–16: ARA, *Collectie Goldberg,* 201.
37. Priester, *Economische ontwikkeling,* 532–34.
38. Van Leeuwen and Oeppen, "Reconstructing," 72.
39. Jonker, "The Alternative Road," 100.
40. Gaastra, *Bewind.*
41. Dillo, *Nadagen,* 200.
42. Steur, *Herstel,* 159–60.
43. Ibid., 109.
44. Cf. the activities of Cornelis van Foreest as a governor of the VOC; Kooijmans, *Onder regenten,* 96ff., 245.
45. Steur, *Herstel,* 75.
46. De Korte, *Verantwoording,* appendix 13A
47. Van Eyck van Heslinga, *Van compagnie.*
48. Riley, *International Government Finance.*
49. Dehing and 't Hart, "Linking the Fortunes," 45ff.
50. Van Dillen, "Ondergang," 417; our illustration of the decline of the Wisselbank is based largely on this publication.
51. Ibid., 420.
52. Ibid., 422.
53. Jonker, *Merchants,* 235–36.
54. Riley, *International Government Finance;* see table 1.3.
55. Ibid., 22.
56. Ibid., 48–49.
57. Jonker, *Merchants,* 237.
58. Ibid., 89, 97.
59. Pfeil, *"Tot redding."*
60. Calculated from Schwarzer, "Stellung"; cf. Horlings, *Economic Development,* 132.

CHAPTER THREE
UNIFICATION AND SECESSION: THE AUTOCRATIC EXPERIMENT
OF WILLEM I, 1813–1840

1. For a more detailed account of the genesis of the 1814–15 constitutions and their extensive legacy to the work of Van Hogendorp, see Kossmann, *Lage Landen,* 65ff.
2. The proposal was carried with 448 against 26 votes (with the opposing votes being cast predominantly by Catholic representatives) and in the absence of no less than 126 of the originally appointed provincial representatives. The next day Willem I was inaugurated as sovereign king, who subsequently (and independently) appointed the

first entire group of parliamentarians (which was to sit unchanged until 1817). Cf. Kossmann, *Lage Landen,* 68–69.

3. All citations from the articles of the 1814–15 constitutions taken from Bannier, *Grondwetten,* 304ff.

4. Kossmann, *Lage Landen,* 72–73.

5. On this period and its influence on Willem's outlook and his govermental experience as ruler of the bishopric Fulda, see Bornewasser, *Kirche,* 133ff.

6. M.S.C. Bakker, "Overheid," 96–99.

7. It is unfortunate that, in spite of initiating efforts by Bornewasser on this score, an adequate biography of Willem I is still lacking; cf. Bornewasser, "Koning Willem I."

8. Wels, "Stemmen," 326.

9. See Bornewasser, "Het Koninkrijk," 234–37.

10. See Buchanan and Tullock, *Calculus,* 63–84.

11. The case is that of a finitely repeated reputation game where asymmetric information (and hence uncertainty) on the relation between the opposing player's payoff and adopted policy stance causes the decision on acquiescence or conflict (through amendment) to be based on the accumulated information from the previous round (tit-for-tat reputation building). As, for instance, Hargreaves Heap and Varoufakis (*Game Theory,* 187–89) demonstrate, this is a game that is applicable to conflicts over the possible parliamentary amendment of legislation (or the budget) in a presidential system, with the game unraveling into a revealed behavioral identity of the executive. As argued in the main text, the fact that the alternative to the 1819 and 1829 attempted amendment of the budget and subsequent standoff was a constitutional crisis (given a lacking ministerial responsibility separated from that of the crown) added to this character of the conflict.

12. Pfeil, *"Tot redding,"* 452.

13. This, of course, is not to say that centralizing tendencies had been wholly absent from the political landscape of the old Republic. In certain ways, Willem I combined the style in which his father, the last stadtholder, Willem V, had ruled with the opportunities that the new form of government offered him. Even so, the political influence of the former stadtholders had largely worked through their right of appointment in numerous public offices (for instance, in city councils in turn participating in the appointment of delegates to the provincial states), which created the opportunity of influencing national policy. For an elaborate analysis of the patronage system under Willem V, see Gabriëls, *Heren.*

14. *Gedenkstukken,* 7:3, 72.

15. On these differences in "fiscal traditions" in the north and south, see H.R.C Wright, *Free Trade,* 71ff.

16. Ibid., 103, 118–21, 124.

17. Again, this is not to say that such debate had been absent, as discussion on an adopted trade policy stance can be traced to the late seventeenth century (cf. Faber, "Graanhandel"), and various eighteenth-century proposals (most notably those put forward 1751) caused serious political upheaval. Yet the fact remains that almost all of these were cast aside and, with some minor changes, the 1725 Placcaat remained in place. For a survey of tracts on the perceived relation between economic decline and trade performance (and proposed remedies), see Joh. de Vries, *Economische achteruitgang,* chapter 1.

18. *Handelingen Staten Generaal* 1814–1815, 132; letter, 17 November 1814.

19. Zappey, *Werkzaamheid*, 134ff.; details on the work of the committee and the secret letter of instruction to Goldberg cited can be found in ARA, *Collectie Goldberg*, 196–201.

20. H.R.C. Wright, *Free Trade*, 105–9.

21. Riemens, *Amortisatie-Syndicaat*, 41–43.

22. H.R.C. Wright, *Free Trade*, 118–24.

23. M.S.C. Bakker, "Overheid," 99.

24. Cf. Jonker, *Merchants;* more critical is the less recent (1935) work by Riemens, *Amortisatie-Syndicaat,* which actually was the first detailed study on the issue of post-Napoleonic fiscal policy since the likewise critical studies by Betz from the 1860s, over which the cloud of contemporary policy debate and the—then politically dominant—liberal appraisal of events looms prominently; cf. Betz, "Finantiële beschouwingen," papers I through VI.

25. Riemens, *Amortisatie-Syndicaat*, 25–26.

26. Betz, "Finantiële beschouwingen," 2:12.

27. Reconstructed national accounts of the Netherlands, 1807–1913; cf. Horlings and Van Zanden, "Enploitatie en Afooheiding"

28. Fritschy, "Staatsvorming," 229, reports that in 1818 British pressure was exerted on Willem in order to raise the defense budget, an effort with which he explicitly did not comply.

29. These technical reasons are set forth in detail in Van Zanden, "Development," 63–65.

30. Riemens, *Amortisatie-Syndicaat*, 44; what follows is based entirely on this early pathbreaking, yet by now largely forgotten, study.

31. Ibid., 72ff.

32. Ibid., 142; cf. M.S.C. Bakker, "Overheid," 99–100.

33. Riemens, *Amortisatie-Syndicaat*, 174–90.

34. Van Zanden, "Development," 69.

35. Ibid., 70.

36. Riemens, *Amortisatie-Syndicaat*, 195.

37. Mansvelt, *Geschiedenis* 1:344–442; A. M. de Jong, *Geschiedenis* I, 175–78.

38. Riemens, *Amortisatie-Syndicaat*, 217–23.

39. Van Popta, "Staatsschuld," 166.

40. Van Zanden, "Development," 62.

41. Jonker, *Merchants*, 89.

42. Compare the results of this journey as reported in ARA, *Collectie Goldberg*, 49.

43. Griffiths, *Industrial Retardation*, 69.

44. Ibid., 69–70; Van Zanden, *Economische ontwikkeling*, 148–49.

45. The following is to an important extent based on Filarski, *Kanalen;* for a more critical appraisal of these issues, see Van der Woud, *Lege Land*, 108–40.

46. Filarski, *Kanalen*, 348–56.

47. Cf. Groote, *Kapitaalvorming*, 74, 176.

48. Van der Woud, *Lege Land*, 133.

49. Filarski, *Kanalen*, 73ff.

50. Ibid., 231–32.

51. Ibid., 255–65; many more examples can be given in this respect, for instance,

that of the planning and construction of the Dedemsvaart, which was long held up by resistance on the part of Zwolle.

52. Cf. Zappey, "Fonds"; for a selection of detailed case studies on industrial policy in the case of the iron industry, see Gales and Fremdling, "IJzerfabrikanten."

53. Gales and Fremdling, "IJzerfabrikanten," 325 n. 81.

54. The financial accounts of the fund were reconstructed on the basis of ledger sheets of the Amortisatiesyndicaat as found in papers of the general auditor's office (*Algemene Rekenkamer*) within the national archives: ARA, 2.02.09.08, *Algemene Rekenkamer*, 640–706; and 2.08.16.01, *Amortisatie-Syndicaat*, 1849–53; cf. Griffiths, *Industrial Retardation*, 44–45.

55. The amounts suggested by our reconstruction are considerably larger than those cited from official sources by Griffiths (*Industrial Retardation*, 44–45) but appear consistent with those reported in Zappey, "Fonds," 34–35.

56. Cf. Gales and Fremdling, "IJzerfabrikanten," 323, who in overall terms are critical of the effectiveness of industrial policy but nevertheless concede to reasonable success in "picking the winners" as reflected in the characteristics and business achievements of the individual entrepreneurs described.

57. Jonker, "Lachspiegel," 5–23.

58. Trompetter, "Geld genoeg."

59. Zappey, "Fonds," 35.

60. Houtman–De Smedt, "Société Générale," 39.

61. Stevens, *Van der Capellen's*, 40–43; Schutte, *Nederlandse patriotten.*

62. Stevens, *Van der Capellen's*, 43–49.

63. Ibid., 54–55.

64. Mansvelt, *Geschiedenis*, 1:55.

65. Ibid., 59–60.

66. Ibid., 64–65, appendix 1.

67. Ibid., 65–67.

68. J. de Vries and Van der Woude, *Nederland*, 452.

69. Mansvelt, *Geschiedenis*, 1:173–78.

70. Ibid., 207–10.

71. Ibid., 201–2.

72. On the failure of Van der Capellen's "liberal" policy, see Stevens, *Van der Capellen's.*

73. Elson, *Village Java*, 40–45.

74. Mansvelt, *Geschiedenis*, 1:253–57.

75. Detailed analyses of the Cultivation System in Elson, *Village Java,* and Fasseur, *Kultuurstelsel.*

76. Figures taken from *Changing Economy in Indonesia.* Vol. 1.

77. Fasseur, *Kultuurstelsel*, 38.

78. Cf. De Jonge, *Industrialisatie*, 143–44; Horlings, *Economic Development*, 315.

79. Broeze, *Stad Schiedam*, 23ff., 208.

80. Mansvelt, *Geschiedenis*, 1:258–343, especially 335–40; Griffiths, *Industrial Retardation*, 141–49.

81. Broeze, *Stad Schiedam*, 60ff.

82. Cf. Mansvelt, *Geschiedenis*, 2:88ff., especially 101–2.

83. Ibid., 124–60, where, within the context of the debate on the abolition (in 1846)

of the turn-based assignment of freight in domestic navigation (the so-called *beurt-vaart*), Mansvelt observes that "the participants in the ship-owning companies after all were also mostly shareholders in the Trading Company [NHM] or even resided on its board of commissioners, people from whose influence there was no escape."

84. Smits, *Economische groei*, 98–102; De Jonge, *Industrialisatie*, 142–44.

CHAPTER FOUR
TROUBLED RECOVERY: SECESSION, POLICY ADJUSTMENT,
AND THE COLONIAL NEXUS, 1813–1840

1. Calculated from Schwarzer, "Stellung," and database national accounts; cf. Horlings, *Economic Development*, 128.
2. Cf. Williamson, "Impact," 124–25.
3. Brugmans, *Paardenkracht*, 144.
4. Jansen, *Industriële Ontwikkeling*, 101.
5. A review of the quality of these data in Griffiths, *Industrial Retardation*, 6–7.
6. The rapid growth during the 1020s has so far escaped attention of economic historians; De Meere, *Economische ontwikkeling*, comes closest to our conclusions but takes "1825–30" as a starting point of growth; see also Griffiths, *Retardation*.
7. Horlings, *Economic Development*, 409.
8. Van Nierop, "Amsterdams Scheepvaart."
9. Jonker, *Merchants*, 196, 219, 222.
10. Priester, *Economische ontwikkeling*, 294.
11. Ibid., 532.
12. Kramer, *Graanwet*, 39–43.
13. Van Zanden, *Economische ontwikkeling*, 208–14.
14. Kramer, *Graanwet*, 107–212.
15. Van Zanden, *Economische ontwikkeling*, 145–85.
16. Ibid., 238–45; Bieleman, *Geschiedenis*, 202–7.
17. Hoffman, *Growth;* Grantham, "Agricultural Supply."
18. Priester, *Geschiedenis*, 285–93.
19. Priester, *Economische ontwikkeling*, passim.
20. Demoed, *Mandegoed*, 26–44.
21. Ibid., 45–46.
22. Van Zanden, *Economische ontwikkeling*, 153.
23. Ibid., 154–55; Demoed, *Mandegoed*, 47–50.
24. Jansen and Trompetter, "Hoezo achterlijk," 150.
25. Van Zanden, *Economische ontwikkeling*, 155–56; Demoed, *Mandegoed*, 56.
26. Demoed, *Mandegoed*, 60–64.
27. Van Zanden, *Economische ontwikkeling*, 157–60.
28. Demoed, *Mandegoed*, 75–80.
29. With the notable exception of the commons in the province of Drenthe; cf. Van Zanden, *Economische ontwikkeling*, 163.
30. This case study is based largely on the study by Pons, *Bakens verzet*.
31. Pons, *Bakens verzet*, 19–23.
32. Ibid., 30.

33. Ibid., 31.

34. Ibid., 33, 114.

35. Potgieter, *Jan.*

36. Cf. Portielje, *Handel;* a brief summary of this debate in Griffiths, *Industrial Retardation,* 9–13, 40ff.

37. Van Dillen, *Omstandigheden;* Wieringa, *Economische heroriëntering.*

38. Brugmans, *Paardenkracht,* 84–86.

39. De Meere, *Economische ontwikkeling;* Griffiths, *Industrial Retardation.*

40. After 1870 the explanation becomes more complex: growth in industrial production pushed up the productivity of labor, thus increasing the margins for wage increases, which induce the substitution of capital for labor, etc.; see chapter 8.

41. Dil and Homburg, "Gas," 111.

42. Jansen, *Industriële ontwikkeling,* chapter 3.

43. Griffiths, *Industrial Retardation,* 118–20.

44. Ibid., 121–22.

45. Ibid., 136.

46. Van Hooff, *In het Rijk,* 187ff.

47. Griffiths, *Industrial Retardation,* 50–51.

48. Mansvelt, *Geschiedenis,* 1:54–58, 201–3.

49. Ibid., 258–340; Griffiths, *Industrial Retardation,* 145ff.

50. Mansvelt, *Geschiedenis,* 1:290–97.

51. Ibid., I, 300, 302ff.

52. Griffiths, *Industrial Retardation,* 164.

53. Mansvelt, *Geschiedenis,* 1:200–201.

54. Ibid., 159.

55. Mansvelt, *Geschiedenis,* 1:230.

56. Griffiths, *Industrial Retardation,* 88–89; Van Zanden, *Rise,* 154.

57. Westermann, *Kamer van Koophandel,* 196.

58. Mansvelt, *Geschiedenis,* 2:196–201.

59. Ibid., 32–42; Elson, *Village Java,* 99ff.

60. This case study is based largely on Van Zanden, "Introductie."

61. Cf. Lintsen, "Stoom in ontwikkeling."

62. See Van Zanden, *Rise,* 130–34.

63. The guild's moneys, a substantial amount, were converted into a burial and a widow's and orphan's fund; G A Amsterdam (Municipal Archive of Amsterdam), P.A. 366, Archief de Gilden en het Brouwercollege, no. 884.

64. Van Zanden, "Introductie," 70.

65. G A Amsterdam, P.A. 366, no. 884.

66. Van de Hoek Ostende, "Stoomkorenmolens," 370–72.

67. Lintsen, *Molenbedrijf,* 21.

68. G A Amsterdam, P.A. 347, Archief Het Werkhuis, no. 461; Van de Hoek Ostende, "Concurrentie," 87.

69. Van de Hoek Ostende, "Stoomkorenmolens," 373.

70. Ibid.

71. Ibid.

72. ARA, Archief Binnenlandse Zaken, Binnenlands Bestuur B, 1824–1831, no. 1366.

73. Van de Hoek Ostende, "Concurrentie."

74. Van Zanden, *Industrialisatie*, 43.

75. Lintsen, *Molenbedrijf*, 31; De Jonge, *Industrialisatie*, 218–19.

76. Van Zanden, *Industrialisatie*, 43–44.

77. Lintsen, *Molenbedrijf*, 31, 38.

78. Van Zanden, *Industrialisatie*, 44.

79. Horlings, *Economic Development*, 403, 411.

80. Nusteling, *Rijnvaart*, 5–7.

81. Ibid., 4.

82. Ibid., 14.

83. Horlings, *Economic Development*, 411.

84. Mansvelt, *Geschiedenis*, 1:216–17.

85. Westermann, *Kamer van Koophandel*, 1:170.

86. L., *Bijdragen*.

87. Westermann, *Kamer van Koophandel*, 1:170–72.

88. Ibid., 173; Mansvelt, *Geschiedenis*, 1:217.

89. Mansvelt, *Geschiedenis*, 1:92–93.

90. Van Malsen, *Geschiedenis*, 82.

91. Mansvelt, *Geschiedenis*, 1:256.

92. *Gedenkboek*, 456.

93. Van Malsen, *Geschiedenis*, 121ff.

94. De Boer, *Honderd Jaar*, 80.

95. Zwart, *Kamer van Koophandel*, 162–66.

96. Ibid., 83–84.

97. J. P. H. Smits, *Economische groei*, 143–44.

98. Mansvelt, *Geschiedenis*, 2:145.

99. Van der Woud, *Lege Land*, 132–35.

100. Horlings, *Economic Development*, 93, 447.

101. Van den Eerenbeemt, "Bedrijfskapitaal"; Klein, "Bankwezen"; Brugmans, *Paardenkracht*, 88.

102. Jonker, *Merchants*, 88–99; Jonker, "Lachspiegel."

103. Trompetter, "Burgers."

104. Cf. the analysis of interest rates by Jonker, *Merchants*, 96–98; in Van Zanden and Van Riel, *Nederland*, 421–23, we have tested an investment function that gives some clear evidence of the negative effects of high interest rates on investment during this period.

105. Fritschy, "Spoorwegaanleg," 197.

106. Ibid., 188–90.

107. Ibid., 189.

108. Mansvelt, *Geschiedenis*, 1:78.

109. Ibid., 64–78.

110. Ibid., 27.

111. Jonker, *Merchants*, 167–70; A. M. de Jong, *Geschiedenis*, 1:109–10.

112. A. M. de Jong, *Geschiedenis*, I, 179.

113. Ibid., 83.

114. Ibid., 281.

115. Ibid., 172–77.

116. Van Hogendorp, *Bijdragen,* 1:78.
117. Jonker, *Merchants,* 173.
118. Neal, *Rise,* 223–31.
119. Drieling, *Bijdragen,* 191.
120. Bogaerde van ter Brugge, *Essai,* 222.
121. Van der Boon Mesch, *Over het Nederlandsche Fabrijkwezen,* 15–16.

CHAPTER FIVE
THE LIBERAL OFFENSIVE, 1840–1870

1. Cf. Sillem, *Gogel;* Boschloo, *Productiemaatschappij,* 160–63.
2. Stuurman, *Wacht op onze Daden,* 112ff.
3. Riemens, *Amortisatie-Syndicaat,* 212–16.
4. Mansvelt, *Geschiedenis* 1:426.
5. As cited in Verberne, *Geschiedenis* 1:108.
6. Buys, *Nederlandseche staatsschuld,* 110–12; for a more elaborate description of these developments, see Boogman, *Rondom 1848.*
7. Buys, *Nederlandsche staatsschuld,* 148–49.
8. Ibid., 149–58; Brugmans, *Paardenkracht,* 187.
9. Again, this is a variation on the theme of a "war of attrition" delaying the stabilization of time-inconsistent fiscal policy as proposed by Alesina and Drazen, "Stabilizations."
10. Bornewasser, "Ministeriële verantwoordelijkheid."
11. Giele, *Pen,* 34ff.
12. Kossmann, *Lage Landen,* 131–36; Boogman, *Rondom.*
13. Van Tijn, "Party Structure."
14. Database national accounts.
15. Cf. Van der Voort, *Overheidsbeleid,* 109–13.
16. Ibid., 116.
17. Roovers, *Plaatselijke belastingen,* 33–34, 72; Griffiths, "Role of Taxation."
18. Griffiths, *Industrial Retardation,* 159–61.
19. Fasseur, *Kultuurstelsel;* Elson, *Village Java,* 99ff.
20. Fasseur, *Kultuurstelsel;* Elson, *Village Java,* 105ff.
21. *Handelingen,* 1848–49, 787–90.
22. Ibid., 788.
23. Mansvelt, *Geschiedenis,* 2:243–345.
24. This is not new information: Steijn Parvé's *Het koloniale monopoliestelsel* already attempts to assess the true magnitude and development of the Batig Slot; see also De Waal, *Aanteekeningen,* 7:145ff. Regrettably, this fact has not received the attention it deserves in the more recent Dutch literature, namely, the highly concise treatment of this issue in Fasseur's authoritative work on the Cultivation System (*Kultuurstelsel,* 41–42, 118).
25. Oud, *Honderd jaren,* 87.
26. Fasseur, *Kultuurstelsel,* 57ff.
27. Cf. Reinsma, *Verval;* and Fasseur, "Purse," for an eloquent critique of this assessment.

28. On the influence of the British example, cf. Brugmans, *Paardenkracht,* 214–18.

29. Nusteling, *Rijnvaart,* 1–10.

30. Ibid., 23.

31. Horlings, *Economic Development,* 195–96.

32. Jonckers Nieboer, *Geschiedenis,* 62.

33. Van der Voort, *Overheidsbeleid,* 158–60.

34. Horlings, *Economic Development,* 203.

35. Brugmans, *Paardenkracht,* 144–46.

36. On British politics in these years, see Ramsden, *Appetite,* 66–67; for an analysis of the macroeconomic and distributional effects of the Corn Laws, see J. G. Williamson, "Impact."

CHAPTER SIX
MARKET INTEGRATION AND RESTRUCTURING, 1840–1870

1. See Horlings and Smits, "Comparison."

2. Griffiths, *Achterlijk.*

3. Buyst and Van Meerten, "Generale Maatschappij"; Mokyr, *Industrialization* 27ff.

4. Attempts to measure the productivity of Dutch agriculture in international perspective: Van Zanden, "Experiment"; Van Zanden, "First Green Revolution."

5. Horlings and Smits, "Comparison," 92.

6. These effects are analyzed in much of the literature on agricultural growth in the early modern period; see Grantham, "Agricultural Supply"; Hoffman, *Growth.*

7. Horlings and Smits, "Comparison," 93.

8. Van Zanden, "Twee maal," 365.

9. Horlings and Smits, "Comparison," 93.

10. Ibid., 100.

11. De Jonge, *Industrialisatie,* 168–69.

12. Burger and Vermaas, "Dutch Industrial Wage Development," 114–15.

13. Bieleman, *Geschiedenis,* 151–52.

14. Van der Maas and Noordegraaf, "Smakelijk eten."

15. See De Beer, "Levensstandaard."

16. See Bergsma, "Potato Blight."

17. De Meere, *Economische ontwikkeling,* 98–110; De Beer, "Levensstandaard."

18. Hofstee, *Demografische ontwikkeling,* 212.

19. Van Tijn, *Twintig jaren,* 106, 127–28.

20. De Beer, *Voeding.*

21. Bieleman, *Boeren,* 381ff.; Bieleman, *Geschiedenis,* 306ff.; Van Zanden, *Economische ontwikkeling,* chap. 8.

22. Bieleman, *Geschiedenis,* 289ff.; Van Zanden, *Economische ontwikkeling,* 220–38; Knibbe, *Agriculture,* 128ff.

23. See the discussion by Van der Poel, *Honderd Jaar,* 185–200.

24. Ibid., 185–210.

25. Knotter, *Economische transformatie,* 230–31.

26. Veenendaal, *Slow Train,* 38–39.

27. Bos, *Brits-Nederlandse handel,* 242, 356.
28. Ibid., 226ff.
29. Boom and Saal, "Spoorwegaanleg."
30. Veenendaal, *IJzeren weg,* 26–34.
31. Cf. Dyos and Aldcroft, *British Transport,* 126–45, 172–75.
32. Jonckers Nieboer, *Geschiedenis,* 91.
33. De Jonge, *Industrialisatie,* 168–69.
34. J.P.H. Smits, *Economische groei,* 211ff.
35. Jonker, *Merchants,* chapter 19.
36. De Boer, *Honderd jaar,* 95-102.
37. Mokyr, *Lever.*
38. Bos, "Factorprijzen"; Lintsen, "Stoom"; Fischer, *Fabriqueurs,* 272–73.
39. Nusteling, *Rijnvaart,* 172.
40. Teijl, "Brandstofaccijns."
41. Gerding, *Vier eeuwen,* 337.
42. Muntjewerff, *Wolspinnerij,* 101–2.
43. Nusteling, *Rijnvaart,* 27ff.
44. Lintsen, "Een land," 191.
45. Cf. Polak, *Historiografie.*
46. Korthals Altes, *Van pond Hollands,* 143.
47. Ibid., 162.
48. Ibid., 163.
49. Ibid., 164.
50. Vrolik, *Verslag,* 188.
51. Ibid., table 1.
52. Ibid., 140, table 3.
53. Uittenbogaard, *Penningen.*
54. Jonker, "Alternative Road," 96.
55. A. M. de Jong, *Geschiedenis,* 1:280–88; Boele, "Komst," 259–64.
56. Boele, "Komst," 260–64.
57. Jonker, "Alternative Road," 109–10.
58. Jonker, *Merchants,* 92–93.
59. Ibid., 111.
60. Veenendaal, *Slow Train.*
61. Ibid., 22–24, 137–39.
62. Jonker, *Merchants,* 90ff., 253ff.; Jonker, "Alternative Road," 108–17.
63. Cf. Kymmel, *Geschiedenis*; Jonker, "Alternative Road," 110ff.
64. Kymmel, *Geschiedenis,* 1:143ff.
65. Jonker, *Merchants,* 259.
66. Jonker, "Alternative Road," 116.
67. Ibid., 115–16.
68. Cf. Ten Brink, *Geschiedenis,* 33.
69. Ibid., 41–43.
70. Ibid., 43.
71. O. de Wit, "Telegrafie," 277.
72. Ibid., 279.
73. Ibid., 280.

74. Ibid., 286–87.
75. This section is based on the yet unfinished doctoral research of Hans Simons (University of Utrecht).
76. Jonker, "Alternative Road."
77. Lindblad, "Handel."
78. Cf. Griffiths, *Industrial Retardation.*
79. Database national accounts.
80. Mansvelt, *Geschiedenis,* 2:95ff.
81. Ibid., 89ff.
82. Cf. Griffiths, *Industrial Retardation,* 177–78.
83. Ibid., 164–65.
84. Mansvelt, *Geschiedenis,* 2:316–20.
85. De Jonge, *Industrialisatie,* 132–36.
86. Van Hooff, *In het rijk,* 192ff.; Van Zanden, *Industrialisatie,* 37–41.
87. Cf. Burgers, *Honderd jaar.*
88. Cf. J.P.H. Smits, *Economische groei,* 145–51.
89. De Beer, "Levensstandaard," 30.
90. Cf. Priester, *Geschiedenis,* 342–63.
91. Schot, "Meekrapbedrijf."
92. Minderhoud, *Ontwikkeling,* 6.
93. Priester, *Economische ontwikkeling,* 373–76.
94. De Jonge, *Industrialisatie,* 41.
95. M.S.C. Bakker, *Ondernemerschap,* 72.
96. Ibid., 36.
97. De Jonge, *Industrialisatie,* 223.
98. B. W. de Vries, *Nederlandse papiernijverheid,* 386ff.
99. Van Tijn, *Twintig jaren,* 228–34.
100. Burger and Vermaas, "Dutch Industrial Wage Development."
101. Mandemakers, "Ontwikkeling," 110; De Jonge, *Industrialisatie,* 230.
102. Cf. Lintsen et al., *Registers.*
103. De Jonge, *Industrialisatie,* 168–69.
104. Ibid., 171.
105. Engels, *Condition,* 240.
106. De Jonge, *Industrialisatie.*
107. Lintsen, "Stoom."
108. Bos, "Factorprijzen"; Griffiths, *Industrial Retardation.*
109. Burgers, *Honderd jaar;* Griffiths, *Industrial Retardation* 182–83; Fischer, *Fabriqueurs,* 272–73.
110. Burgers, *Honderd jaar,* 171.
111. Ibid.; cf. Fischer, *Fabriqueurs,* 272–73.
112. Renssen, "Arbeid," 110.
113. Gorter and De Vries, "Gegevens."
114. Burgers, *Honderd jaar,* 82.
115. Ibid., 59.
116. Ibid., 116.
117. Fischer, Van Gerwen, and Winkelman, *Bestemming Semarang,* 52.
118. Fischer, *Fabriqueurs,* 84.

119. Knotter, *Economische transformatie,* 80.

120. Van Tijn, "Geschiedenis," 19.

121. Barents, *Diamantslijperij Maatschappij,* 26.

122. Ibid., 26–27.

123. Ibid., 28.

124. Ibid., 37–38.

125. Ibid., 48–52.

126. Schumpeter, *Capitalism,* 81–86.

127. J. de Vries, "How"; Noordegraaf, *Daglonen.*

128. Knotter, "De Amsterdamse bouwnijverheid," 131–32.

129. Ibid., 134.

130. Lucassen, *Naar de kusten.*

131. Van Zanden, *The Rise,* 167–69; Lucassen, *Naar de kusten,* 211–13.

132. Knotter, "Amsterdamse bouwnijverheid," 141; Knotter, *Economische transformatie,* 93ff.

133. Knotter, *Economische transformatie.*

134. Van Tijn, *Twintig jaren,* 237, 441.

135. Gooren and Heger, *Per mud,* 66, 81; Welcker, *Heren,* 368.

136. Marx, *Kapitaal,* vol. 1, chap. 19.

137. De Beer, "Voeding," 216–17.

138. Van Tijn, *Twintig jaren,* 237.

139. Vermaas, Verstegen, and Van Zanden, "Income Inequality," 160–61.

140. De Meere, *Economische ontwikkeling,* 96ff.

CHAPTER SEVEN
EMANCIPATION, PLURALISM, AND COMPROMISE: TOWARD THE
POLITICS OF ACCOMMODATION, 1870–1913

1. We use the terms "pillars" and "pillarization" here as equivalent to the Dutch words *zuilen* and *verzuiling,* which are the standard terms for these processes.

2. Cf. Blom, "Onderzoek."

3. C.H.E. de Wit, *Thorbecke,* 44.

4. Cf. Downs, *Economic Theory.*

5. Cf. Tamse, "Politieke ontwikkeling."

6. Harmsen and Reinalda, *Voor de bevrijding,* 40–44.

7. Boschloo, *Productiemaatschappij,* 204ff.; Roebroek and Hertogh, *"Beschavende invloed,"* 80–84.

8. Cf. Knotter, *Economische transformatie,* 133–38, 243.

9. Boonstra, *Waardij,* 20–32.

10. Cf. C.H.E. de Wit, *Thorbecke,* 31–33.

11. Lijphart, *Politics;* Schöffer; "Verzuiling," 121–27; Daalder, "Netherlands."

12. Andeweg and Irwin, *Dutch Government,* 38.

13. Mijnhardt, *Tot heil,* 264–65.

14. Van Genabeek, *Met vereende kracht,* 168.

15. Ibid., 171.

16. De Regt, *Arbeidersgezinnen,* 143ff.

17. Ibid., 148.
18. Van der Voort, *Overheidsbeleid,* 245.
19. According to yet unpublished research by Peter Lindert, no other European country spent that much on education between 1880 and 1900.
20. Van der Voort, *Overheidsbeleid,* 76ff.
21. Van der Bie, "Om het huiselijk geluk."
22. Stuurman, *Verzuiling,* 204ff.; Van Zanden, *Een klein land,* 25–31.
23. Righart, *Katholieke zuil.*
24. Olson, *Logic.*
25. Olson, *Rise,* 21–23.
26. Van Leeuwen, "Trade Unions."
27. Cf. Van Genabeek, *Met vereende kracht,* 65–71.
28. Ibid., 81.
29. Ibid., 123–27.
30. This points to the fact, not included in the analysis by Olson, that setting up an organization of laborers was to some extent a goal in itself, the benefits of which were social intercourse.
31. Van Tijn, "Voorlopige notitie"; Knotter, "Van 'defensieve standsreflex'"
32. Cf. Becker and Frieswijk, *Bedrijven.*
33. Knotter, "Van 'defensieve standsreflex,'" 80–86.
34. Van Tijn, "Algemeene Nederlandsche Diamantbewerkersbond"; Van Tijn, "Bijdrage."
35. See also Knotter, "Van 'defensieve standsreflex.'"
36. Van Tijn, "Bijdrage."
37. Noordam, "Sociale verzekeringen," 583.
38. The seminal study is Rüter, *Spoorwegstakingen.*
39. Harmsen and Reinalda, *Voor de bevrijding,* 74–77, 88–94.
40. A. M. de Jong, *Geschiedenis,* 2:224.
41. Flandreau, "French Crime," 884.
42. A. M. de Jong, *Geschiedenis,* 2:240.
43. Cf. ibid., 241ff.; it is typical that the Netherlands in 1867, at an international currency conference in Paris, voted against the introduction of the gold standard.
44. Ibid., 240–41.
45. Ibid., 241–311.
46. Williamson, "Globalization."
47. Bordo and Rockoff, "Gold Standard."
48. A. M. de Jong, *Geschiedenis,* 2:418–22.
49. Van der Voort, *Overheidsbeleid,* 209–12.
50. De Vrankrijker, *Belastingen.*
51. Lindert, "Rise."
52. Cf. De Meere, "Inkomensgroei."
53. Houwaart, *Hygiënisten,* 144–48, 254–55.
54. Van Zon, *Een zeer onfrisse geschiedenis.*
55. Van Poppel, "Stad en platteland."
56. Maas, *Gemeentepolitiek,* 22–24.
57. Knotter, *Economische transformatie,* 115–17.
58. Cf. Roebroek and Hertogh, *"Beschavende invloed,"* 132ff.

59. Van Zanden, *Economic History,* 4–5.
60. Roebroek and Hertogh, *"Beschavende invloed,"* 134ff.
61. Ibid., 161.
62. Cf. Van Zanden, *Economic History,* passim.

Chapter Eight
Modern Economic Growth and Structural Change, 1870–1913

1. J. P. H. Smits, *Economische groei,* 265; Horlings, *Economic Development,* 299; Van Zanden, *Economische ontwikkeling,* 349; Van Zanden, "Economische groei," 69.
2. Kuznets, *Modern Economic Growth,* 1.
3. Clark, *Conditions.*
4. Kuznets, *Modern Economic Growth,* 490–500.
5. Crafts, *British Economic Growth,* 50ff.; Burger, "Dutch Patterns."
6. Crafts, *British Economic Growth,* 55ff.
7. See Brugmans, *Paardenkracht,* 201ff.; De Jonge, *Industrialisatie,* 340–43; Griffiths, *Achterlijk* (who, on the one hand, adheres to the analysis by De Jonge but also stresses the balanced nature of growth during the nineteenth century.
8. De Jonge, *Industrialisatie,* 230–36.
9. Ibid., 341.
10. See Van Zanden and Van Riel, *Nederland,* 421–23 for details about this investment function.
11. Groote, *Kapitaalvorming,* 64.
12. Ibid., 60–71.
13. Groote, Jacobs, and Sturm, "Infrastructure."
14. Engberts, *Bouwactiviteiten;* De Jonge, *Industrialisatie,* 200–204.
15. Albers, *Machinery Investment.*
16. See the analysis of the relationship between inflation and interest rates in Van Zanden, "Historische ontwikkeling."
17. A more detailed analysis of the relationship between savings and investment in Albers, *Machinery Investment,* chapter 14.
18. Van Zanden, *Economische ontwikkeling,* 292–301.
19. H. de Vries, *Landbouw.*
20. Van Leeuwen and Oeppen, "Reconstructing," 87.
21 Horlings and Smits, "Private Consumer Expenditure."
22. See Lindblad and Van Zanden, "Buitenlandse handel."
23. Bosch, *Nederlandse beleggingen,* 73.
24. A. M. de Jong, *Geschiedenis,* 3:330, 591–95.
25. See J. G. Williamson, "Globalization."
26. See Van Zanden, *Economische ontwikkeling,* 248; the continuing prosperity of agriculture during the 1870s is also reflected in the lease and wage data collected by Priester, *Geschiedenis,* 86–104; Van Zanden, *Economische ontwikkeling,* 120, 198.
27. Van Zanden, *Economische ontwikkeling,* 121, 249.
28. Ibid., 260–62.
29. Bieleman, *Geschiedenis,* 306ff.
30. Van Zanden, *Economische ontwikkeling,* 261.

31. Ibid., 277.
32. Ibid., 331–37.
33. Cf. Koning, *Failure.*
34. O. E. Williamson, *Markets and Hierarchies, and Economic Institutions.*
35. Cf. Henriksen, "Avoiding Lock-In."
36. Cf. Van Zanden, *Economische ontwikkeling,* 263ff.
37. Ibid., 267.
38. Bieleman, *Geschiedenis,* 332.
39. Priester, *Geschiedenis,* 397–98.
40. Van der Poel, *Heren,* 5–57.
41. M. Smits, *Boeren,* 28ff.
42. Cf. Vermeulen, *Den Haag.*
43. M. Smits, *Boeren,* 58.
44. Bouman, "Landbouworganisaties," 244–45.
45. Cf. Hutten and Rutten, "Druk."
46. This section is derived largely from Sluyterman, Dankers, Van der Linden, and Van Zanden, *Coöperatieve Alternatief,* 20ff.
47. Cf. Van Zanden, *Economische ontwikkeling,* 273–81.
48. Van Haastert and Huysmans, *Veertig jaren,* 14.
49. *Uitkomsten van het onderzoek.*
50. Van Campen, Hollenberg, and Krielaars, *Landbouw en landbouwcrediet,* 34.
51. Ibid.
52. Van Zanden, *Economische ontwikkeling,* 279–81.
53. M. Smits, *Boeren,* 25ff.
54. Van Campen, Hollenberg, and Krielaars, *Landouw en landbouwcrediet,* 40.
55. Ibid.
56. Weststrate, *Gedenkboek,* 354–61; Van Campen, Hollenberg, and Krielaars, *Landbouw en landbouwcrediet,* 159–60, 555–60.
57. Jonker, "Welbegrepen eigenbelang."
58. Weststrate, *Gedenkboek,* 97, 283–85; Van Campen, Hollenberg, and Krielaars, *Landbouw en landbouwcrediet,* 562.
59. Weststrate, *Gedenkboek,* 287.
60. Cf. Sluyterman et al., *Coöperatief Alternatief,* 33.
61. De Jonge, *Industrialisatie,* 116.
62. Information collected and analyzed by A. Callewaert as part of the project of national accounts; cf. Van Hooff, *In het Rijk,* 192ff.
63. M. S. C. Bakker, *Ondernemerschap,* 29.
64. Cf. Wennekes, *Aartsvaders,* 45–78.
65. Wilson, *History,* 24ff, 55ff.
66. Ibid., 90.
67. Chandler, *Scale and Scope.*
68. Ibid.
69. Wilson, *History,* 72ff.
70. Schrover, *Vette,* 68; Wilson, *History,* 99.
71. Gerretson, *Geschiedenis,* 1:97–114.
72. Cf. ibid., 207ff; 2:passim.
73. Ibid., 2:179ff.

74. Heerding, *Onderneming,* 78.

75. Ibid., 63.

76. Ibid., 109.

77. Ibid., 175ff.

78. Schiff, *Industrialization,* 66.

79. De Jonge, *Industrialisatie,* 234–36; Bos, "Kapitaal," 104.

80. De Feyter, *Industrial Policy,* 207–11.

81. Gerretson, *Geschiedenis,* 2:71ff.

82. An extensive discussion of this can be found in H. J. de Jong, *Nederlandse industrie,* 184–90.

83. Ibid., 190.

84. Van Asten, "Spyker."

85. J. P. H. Smits, *Economische groei,* 85–86; cf. Horlings and Smits, "Private Consumer Expenditure."

86. Database of national accounts.

87. Boonstra, "Waardij," 21–22.

88. Mandemakers, *Gymnasiaal en Middelbaar Onderwijs,* 481.

89. Vermaas, Verstegen, and Van Zanden, "Income Inequality," 161.

90. Cf. Mandemakers, *Gymnasiaal en Middelbaar Onderwijs,* 137–42; Clemens, Groote, and Albers, "Contribution."

91. Nusteling, *Rijnvaart,* 201–17.

92. Van den Broeke, "Preludium," 63.

93. Veenendaal, *IJzeren Weg,* 75.

94. Ibid., 76.

95. Van den Broeke, "Preludium," 63.

96. This distinction is derived from Baker and Collins, "English Industrial Distress," 3.

97. Van Goor, *Banken.*

98. See the discussion by Jonker, "Lachspiegel."

99. Westerman, *Concentratie.*

100. For the magnitude of these transactions, see Smits, Horlings, and Van Zanden, *Dutch GNP;* Korthals Altes, *Betalingsbalans.*

101. Lindblad, "Handel," 280.

102. Cf. Kuitenbrouwer, *Nederland,* 9ff.

103. Ibid., 12 ff.; Kuitenbrouwer, "Drie omwentelingen."

104. The classic study is Cain and Hopkins, *British Imperialism;* cf. Kuitenbrouwer, "Drie omwentelingen."

105. Mansvelt, *Geschiedenis,* 2:357ff.

106. Kymmell, *Geschiedenis,* 1:143–49.

107. Hobson, *Imperialism.*

108. A wonderful example of this is given by Haasse, *Heren;* see also Van den Berge, *Karel Federik Holle.*

109. Breman, *Planters,* 17–20.

110. Cf. Mansvelt, *Geschiedenis,* 2:415ff.

111. Taselaar, *Nederlandse koloniale lobby,* 99.

112. Breman, *Koelies,* 20.

113. Cf. Langeveld, "Arbeidstoestanden," 296–98.

114. Kuitenbrouwer, *Nederland*, 43ff.

115. H. Bakker, "Economisch belang."

116. Cf. Lindblad, "Opkomst," 8.

117. A slightly different calculation carried out by Bosch for the Dutch East Indies arrived at 11.5 percent for 1900–1909 and no less than 18.4 percent for 1910–19; Bosch, *Nederlandse beleggingen*, 605.

118. Cf. ibid., 568ff., 604ff.

119. Cf. Van Doorn, *Laatste eeuw*, 149ff.; Booth, *Indonesian Economy*, 144ff.

120. See the pioneering work of Becker, *Treatise;* in the Netherlands: Pott-Buter, *Facts*.

121. Cf. Engelen, *Fertiliteit*, 35ff.; Kok, "Moral nation," 24.

122. Van Poppel, *Trouwen*, 117ff.

123. Vandenbroeke, Van Poppel; and Van der Woude, "De Zuigelingen en kinder-sterfte"; in comparison, infant mortality in Belgium declined almost constantly from 183 per 1,000 births in 1836–40 to 151 in 1871–75: Chesnais, *Demographic Transition*, 580.

124. In comparison, mortality in Belgium declined by less than 40 percent; Chesnais, *Demographic Transition*, 561–63.

125. De Regt, *Arbeidersgezinnen*, 50ff.

126. Engelen, *Fertiliteit*, 39.

127. Cf. De Regt, *Arbeidersgezinnen*, 50ff.

128. Beucker Andreae, "Rapport," 183.

129. For this census data and for estimates concerning the decline of agricultural labor by women, see Van Zanden, *Economische ontwikkeling*, 68–75.

130. Stuurman, *Verzuiling*, 232–34.

131. De Regt, *Arbeidersgezinnen*, 50–78.

132. Cf. Pott-Buter, *Facts*.

133. Van der Voort, *Overheidsbeleid*, 98.

134. See Engelen, *Fertiliteit*, 10–11, and the study cited in this work from Caldwell, "Toward."

135. De Regt, *Arbeidersgezinnen*, 87–90.

136. Ibid., 89; Engelen, *Fertiliteit*, 46ff.

137. Scholliers, "Werktijden."

138. Van der Veen, "Arbeidsduur."

EPILOGUE
ECONOMIC DEVELOPMENT BETWEEN CORPORATISM
AND CONSOCIATIONAL DEMOCRACY

1. Albert, *Kapitalisme*.

2. Esping-Andersen, *Three Worlds*.

3. Cf. Van Zanden, *Economic History*.

Bibliography

Note: Dutch rules for treatment of personal names are used throughout. For example, "De Vries" is under "Vries," and "van Hogendorp" is under "Hogendorp."

Aalbers, J. *De Republiek en de vrede van Europe*. Groningen 1980.

―――. "Het machtsverval van de Republiek der Verenigde Nederlanden 1713–1741." In J. Aalbers and A. P. van Goudoever, eds., *Machtsverval in de internationale context*. Groningen 1986, 7–36.

Albers, R. M. *Machinery Investment and Economic Growth: The Dynamics of Dutch Development, 1800–1913*. Groningen 1998.

Albert, M. *Kapitalisme contra kapitalisme*. Antwerpen/Amsterdam 1992.

Alesina, A., and A. Drazen. "Why Are Stabilizations Delayed?" *American Economic Review* 81 (1991): 1170–88.

Alphonse, F.J.B. D'. *Eenige hoofdstukken uit het "Aperçu sur la Hollande."* 's-Gravenhage 1900.

Ames, E., and N. Rosenberg. "Changing Technological Leadership and Industrial Growth." *Economic Journal* 73 (1963): 13–31.

Andeweg, R. B., and G. A. Irwin. *Dutch Government and Politics*. Basingstoke 1993.

Asten, H.A.M. van. "De Spyker van de weg gereden," *Economisch- en sociaal-historisch jaarboek* 33 (1971): 67–118.

Baars, C. *De geschiedenis van de landbouw in de Beijerlanden*. Wageningen 1973.

Baker, M., and M. Collins. "English Industrial Distress before 1914 and the Response of the Banks." *European Review of Economic History* 3 (1999): 1–24.

Bakker, H. "Het economisch belang van Noord-Sumatra tijdens de Atjehoorlog, 1873–1910." In A.H.P. Clemens and J. Th. Lindblad, eds., *Het belang van de Buitengewesten 1870–1942*. Amsterdam 1989, 41–66.

Bakker, M.S.C. *Ondernemerschap en vernieuwing, de Nederlandse bietsuikerindustrie 1858–1919*. Amsterdam 1989.

―――. "Overheid en techniek." In H. W. Lintsen et al., eds., *Geschiedenis van de Techniek in Nederland*. Vol. 6. Zutphen 1995, 91–139.

Bannier, G. W. *Grondwetten van Nederland. Teksten der Achtereenvolgende Staatsregelingen en Grondwetten Sedert 1795*. Zwolle 1936.

Barents, M. *De Diamantslijperij Maatschappij te Amsterdam 1845–15 april–1920*. Amsterdam 1920.

Barnett, G. E., ed., *Two Tracts by Gregory King*. Baltimore 1936.

Becker, F., and J. Frieswijk. *Bedrijven in eigen beheer*. Nijmegen 1975.

Becker, G. *A Treatise on the Family*. Cambridge, Mass. 1981.

Beer, J.J.A. de. "Levensstandaard in Nederland. Voeding en gezondheid in de eerste helft van de negentiende eeuw." *Tijdschrift voor sociale geschiedenis* 22 (1996): 24–52.

―――. "Voeding, fysieke arbeidscapaciteit en productiviteit in Nederland ca 1850–ca 1900." *Neha-jaarboek* 61 (1998): 196–225.

————. *Voeding, gezondheid en arbeid in Nederland tijdens de negentiende eeuw.* Amsterdam 2001.

Berge, T. van den. *Karel Frederik Holle.* Amsterdam 1998.

Bergsma, M. "The Potato Blight in the Netherlands and Its Social Consequences (1845–1847)." *International Review of Social History* 12 (1967): 390–441.

Betz, G. H. "Finantiële beschouwingen I." *Bijdragen tot de kennis van het Staats-, Provinciaal- en Gemeentebestuur in Nederland* 4 (1860): 212–49.

————. "Finantiële beschouwingen II." *Bijdragen tot de kennis van het Staats-, Provinciaal- en Gemeentebestuur in Nederland* 5 (1861): 1–47.

————. "Finantiële beschouwingen III." *Bijdragen tot de kennis van het Staats-, Provinciaal- en Gemeentebestuur in Nederland* 5 (1861): 269–94.

————. "Finantiële beschouwingen IV." *Bijdragen tot de kennis van het Staats-, Provinciaal- en Gemeentebestuur in Nederland* 6 (1862): 27–61.

————. "Finantiële beschouwingen V." *Bijdragen tot de kennis van het Staats-, Provinciaal- en Gemeentebestuur in Nederland* 6 (1862): 237–84.

————. "Finantiële beschouwingen VI." *Bijdragen tot de kennis van het Staats-, Provinciaal- en Gemeentebestuur in Nederland* 7 (1863): 89–146.

Beucker Andreae, J. H. "Rapport ingediend voor het vijfde Landhuishoudkundig Congres te Leyden, betreffende een onderzoek naar den zedelijken en materiëlen toestand der arbeidende bevolking ten platten lande en van de middelen om dien zoveel mogelijk te verbeeteren." *Tijdschrift voor Staathuishoudkunde en Statistiek* 6 (1851): 156–99.

Bie, R. van der. "Om het huiselijk geluk." In R. van der Bie and P. Dehing, eds., *Nationaal Goed. Feiten en cijfers over onze samenleving (ca.) 1800–1999.* Voorburg 1999, 201–18.

Bieleman, J. "De produktie en consumptie van akkerbouwgewassen in Drenthe in het begin van de 19e eeuw." *AAG Bijdragen* 28 (1986): 145–63.

————. *Boeren op het Drentse zand 1600–1910.* Wageningen 1987.

————. *Geschiedenis van de landbouw in Nederland 1500–1950.* Meppel 1992.

Bijblad De Economist. 1856–57.

Bijker, W. "De sociale constructie van netwerken en technische systemen; nieuwe perspectieven voor de techniekgeschiedenis." *Jaarboek voor de geschiedenis van bedrijf en techniek* 4 (1987): 7–24.

Biljlagen Handelingen der Staten-Generaal. 1844–45.

Blanchard, I. "The Continental Cattle Trades, 1400–1600." *Economic History Review* 39 (1986): 427–60.

Blom, J.C.H. "Onderzoek naar Verzuiling in Nederland. Status quaestionis en wenselijke ontwikkeling." In J.H.C. Blom and C. J. Misset, eds., *"Broeders sluit u aan." Aspecten van verzuiling in zeven Hollandse gemeenten.* Amsterdam 1985, 10–29.

Boele, C. "De komst van de Bijbank der Nederlandsche Bank in Rotterdam." *Rotterdams Jaarboekje,* 1997, 257–79.

Boels, H. *Binnenlandse Zaken. Ontstaan en ontwikkeling van een departement in de Bataafse Tijd, 1795–1806.* Den Haag 1993.

Boels, H., and Joh. de Vries. "De Thesaurier-Generaal in een Veranderende Wereld. De Tweede Helft van de Negentiende Eeuw, 1848–1905." In J. Th. de Smidt, R. Gradus, S. Katee, and Joh. de Vries, eds., *Van Tresorier tot Thesaurier-Generaal. Zes Eeuwen*

Financieel Beleid in Handen van een Hoge Nederlandse Ambstdrager. Hilversum 1996, 283–317.

Boer, M. G. de. *Honderd jaar Nederlandsche Scheepvaart.* Amsterdam 1939.

Bogaerde van ter Brugge, A.J.L. *Essai dur l'importance du commerce, de la navigation et de l'industrie dans les provinces formant le royaume des Pays-Bas jusqu'en 1830.* 's-Gravenhage 1844–45.

Boogman, J. C. *Rondom 1848, de politieke ontwikkeling van Nederland 1840–1858.* Bussum 1978.

Boom S., and P. Saal. "Spoorwegaanleg en het beeld van de eerste helft van de negentiende eeuw." *Economisch- en sociaal-historisch jaarboek* 46 (1983): 5–26.

Boon Mesch, A. H. van der. *Over het Nederlandsche Frabrijkwezen en de middelen om hetzelve te bevorderen.* Haarlem 1843.

Boonstra, O.W.A. *De waardij van eene vroege opleiding.* Wageningen 1993.

Booth, A. *The Indonesian Economy in the Nineteenth and Twentieth Centuries.* Basingstoke 1998.

Bordo, M., and H. Rockoff. "The Gold Standard as a 'Good-Housekeeping Seal of Approval.'" *Journal of Economic History* 56 (1996): 389–428.

Bornewasser, J. A. *Kirche und staat in Fulda unter Wilghelm Friedrich von Oranien 1802–6.* Fulda 1956.

———. "Ministeriële verantwoordelijkheid onder Koning Willem II." *Tijdschrift voor geschiedenis* 75 (1962): 436–58.

———. "Koning Willem I." In C. A. Tamse, ed., *Nassau en Oranje in de Nederlandse geschiedenis.* Alphen aan den Rijn 1979.

———. "Het Koninkrijk der Nederlanden 1815–1830." *Algemene Geschiedenis der Nederlanden* 11 (1983): 223–90.

Bos, R.W.J.M. *Brits-Nederlandse handel en scheepvaart, 1870–1914. Een analyse van machtsafbrokkeling op een markt.* Tilburg 1978.

———. "Factorprijzen, technologie en markstructuur: De groei van de Nederlandse volkshuishounding 1815–1914." AAG *Bijdragen* 22 (1979): 109–37.

———. "Kapitaal en industrialisatie in Nederland tijdens de negentiende eeuw." *AAG Bijdragen* 22 (1979): 89–107.

———. "Factorprijzen, technologie en markstructuur: de groei van de Nederlandse volkshuishounding 1815–1914. *A.A.G. Bijdragen,* XXII (1979): 109–37.

Bosch, K. D. *Nederlandse Beleggingen in de Verenigde Staten.* Amsterdam 1947.

Bosch Kemper, J. de. *Geschiedkundig Onderzoek naar de Armoede in Ons Vaderland, Hare Oorzaken en de Middelen die tot Hare Vermindering Zouden Kunnen Worden Aangewend.* Haarlem 1851.

Boschloo, T. J. *De productiemaatschappij.* Hilversum 1989.

Bouman, P. J. "Landbouworganisaties." In Z. W. Sneller, ed., *Geschiedenis van de Nederlandse Landbouw.* Groningen 1951, 234–51.

Breman, J. *Koelies, planters en koloniale politiek.* Dordrecht 1987.

Brink, E.A.B.J. ten. *De geschiedenis van het postvervoer.* Bussum 1969.

Brink, W.L.D. van den. *Bijdrage tot de Kennis van den Economischen Toestand in Nederland in de Jaren 1813–1816.* Amsterdam 1916.

Broeke, W. van den. "Preludium op een vijfsporenbeleid (1839–1939)." In J. A. Faber, ed., *Het Spoor. 150 jaar spoorwegen in Nederland.* Utrecht 1989, 52–87.

Broeze, F.J.A. *De Stad Schiedam.* 's-Gravenhage 1978.

Brugmans, I. J. *De arbeidende klasse in Nederland in de negentiende eeuw 1813–1870.* Utrecht 1958.

———. *Paardenkracht en Mensenmacht. Sociaal-economische geschiedenis van Nederland, 1795–1940.* Den Haag 1961.

Bruijn, J. R. "De personeelsbehoefte van de VOC overzee en aan boord, bezien in Aziatisch en Nederlands perspectief." *Bijdragen en mededelingen betreffende de geschiedenis der Nederlanden* 91 (1976): 218–48.

Bruyn Kops, G. F. de. *Statistiek van den handel en de scheepvaart op Java en Madura sedert 1825.* 2 vols. and supplement. Batavia 1858.

Buchanan, J. M., and G. Tullock. *The Calculus of Consent.* Ann Arbor 1974.

Buist, M. G. *At spes non fracta.* Den Haag 1974.

Bunk, W. *Staatkundige Geschiedenis van den Amsterdamschen Graanhandel.* Amsterdam 1856.

Burger, A. "Dutch Patterns of Development: Economic Growth and Structural Change in the Netherlands 1800–1910." *Economic and Social History in the Netherlands* 7 (1996): 161–80.

Burger, A., and A. Vermaas. "Dutch Industrial Wage Development in an International Perspective, 1850–1913." *Economic and Social History in the Netherlands* 7 (1996) 109–32.

Burgers, R. A. *100 jaar G. en H. Salomonson.* Leiden 1954.

Buys, J. T. *De Nederlandsche staatsschuld sedert 1814.* Haarlem 1857.

Buyst, E., and J. Mokyr. "Dutch Manufacturing and Trade during the French Period (1795–1814) in a Long Term Perspective." In E. Aerts and F. Crouzet, eds., *Economic Effects of the French Revolutionary and Napoleonic Wars.* Leuven 1990, 64–78.

Buyst, E., and M. van Meerten. "De Generale Maatschappij en de economische ontwikkeling van België." in E. Buyst et al., eds. *De Generale Bank 1822–1997.* Tielt 1997.

Cain, P. J., and A. G. Hopkins. *British Imperialism: Innovation and Expansion 1688–1914.* London 1993.

Caldwell, J. C. "Toward a restatement of demographic transition theory." *Population and Development Review* 2 (1976): 321–66.

Campbell, B. "Matching Supply and Demand in Crop Production and Disposal by English Demesnes in the Century of the Black Death." *Journal of Economic History* 57 (1997): 827–58.

Campen, Ph.C.M. van, P. Hollenberg, and F. Krielaars. *Landbouw en landbouwcrediet 1898–1948. Vijftig jaar geschiedenis van de Coöperatieve Centrale Boerenleenbank Eindhoven.* Eindhoven 1948.

Campo, J.N.F.M. á. "Strength, Survival, and Success: A Statistical Profile of Corporate Enterprise in Colonial Indonesia 1883–1913." *Jahrbuch für Wirtschaftsgeschichte* 1 (1995): 45–74.

Chandler, A. D. *Scale and Scope.* Cambridge 1990.

Changing Economy in Indonesia. Vol. 1, *Indonesia's export crops 1816–1940.* Den Haag 1975.

Chesnais, J.-C. *The Demographic Transition.* Oxford 1992.

Clark, C. *The Conditions of Economic Progress.* 3d ed. New York, 1957.

Clemens, A., P. Groote, and R. Albers. "The Contribution of Physical and Human Capital to Economic Growth in the Netherlands, 1850–1913." *Economic and Social History in the Netherlands* 7 (1996): 181–98.

Crafts, N.F.R. *British Economic Growth during the Industrial Revolution.* Oxford 1985.

Craig, L. A., and D. Fisher. *The Integration of the European Economy, 1850–1913.* London, 1997.

Daalder, H. "The Netherlands: Opposition in a Segmented Society." In R. A. Dahl, ed., *Political Oppositions in Western Democracies.* New Haven 1966, 188–237.

David, P. "Clio and the Economics of QWERTY." *American Economic Review* 75 (1985): 332–37.

Davids, C. A. "De technische ontwikkeling van Nederland in de vroeg-moderne tijd." *Jaarboek voor de geschiedenis van bedrijf en techniek* 8 (1991): 9–38.

———. "Technological Change and the Economic Expansion of the Dutch Republic 1580–1680." *Economic and Social History in the Netherlands* 4 (1992): 79–104.

Deane, Ph., and B. R. Mitchell. *Abstract of British Historical Statistics.* Cambridge 1962.

Dehing, P., and M.'t Hart. "Linking the Fortunes: Currency and Banking 1550–1800." In M.'t Hart, J. Jonker, and J. L. van Zanden, eds., *A Financial History of the Netherlands.* Cambridge 1997, 37–63.

Demoed, H. B. *Mandegoed schandegoed.* Zutphen 1987.

Deursen, A. Th. van. "Staatsinstellingen in de Noordelijke Nederlanden 1579–1780." *Algemene Geschiedenis der Nederlanden* 5 (1980): 350–87.

Dil, G., and E. Homburg. "Gas." In H. Lintsen et al., eds., *Geschiedenis van de techniek in Nederland.* Zutphen 1993, 3:107–34.

Dillen, J. G. van. *Omstandigheden en psychische factoren in de economische geschiedenis van Nederland.* Groningen 1949.

———. "Ondergang van de Amsterdamse Wisselbank 1782–1820." In J. G. van Dillen, ed., *Mensen en Achtergronden.* Groningen 1964, 416–47.

Dillo, I. G. *De nadagen van de Verenigde Oostindische Compagnie, 1783–1795.* Amsterdam 1992.

Doorman, G. *Octrooien Voor Uitvindingen in de Nederlanden Uit de 16e-18e Eeuw.* 's-Gravenhage 1940.

Doorn, J.A.A. van. *De laatste eeuw van Indië.* Amsterdam 1994.

Dormans, E. "De Economie en de Openbare Financien van de Republiek." In J. Th. de Smidt, R. Gradus, S. Kaatee, and Joh. de Vries, eds., *Van Tresorier tot Thesaurier-Generaal.* Hilversum, 1996.

Downs, A. *An Economic Theory of Democracy.* New York 1972.

Drieling, J. A. *Bijdragen tot een vergelijkend overzigt van Nederlands zeevaart en handel.* Den Haag 1829.

Dyos, H. J., and D. H. Aldcroft. *British Transport.* Leicester 1971.

Eerenbeemt, H. van den. "Bedrijfskapitaal en ondernemerschap in Nederland 1800–1850." In P.A.M. Geurts and F.A.M. Messing, eds., *Economische ontwikkeling en sociale emancipatie.* Den Haag 1977, 1–32.

Elbaum, B., and W. Lazonick, eds., *The Decline of the British Economy.* Oxford 1986.

Elson, R. E. *Village Java under the Cultivation System.* St. Leonards 1994.

———. "From 'States' to State: The Changing Regime of Peasant Export Production in Mid-Nineteenth Century Java." In J. Th. Lindblad, ed., *Historical Foundations of a National Economy in Indonesia, 1890s–1990s.* Amsterdam 1996, 123–36.

Engberts, G. E. *De Nederlandse en Amsterdamse bouwactiviteiten.* N.p., n.d.

Engelen, Th.L.M. *Fertiliteit, Arbeid, Mentaliteit.* Nijmegen 1987.

Engels, F. *The Condition of the Working Class in England.* Translated by W. O. Henderson and W. H. Chaloner. Oxford 1958.

Esping-Andersen, G. *Politics against Markets.* Princeton 1985.

———. *The Three Worlds of Welfare Capitalism.* Cambridge 1990.

Eyck van Heslinga, E. S. van. *Van compagnie naar koopvaardij.* Amsterdam 1988.

Faber, J. A. "Graanhandel, graanprijzen en tarievenpolitiek in Nederland gedurende de tweede helft der zeventiende eeuw." *Tijdschrift voor geschiedenis* 74 (1961): 533–39.

———. *Drie Eeuwen Friesland. Economische en sociale ontwikkelingen van 1500 tot 1800.* 2 vols Wageningen 1971.

———. *Dure Tijden en Hongersnoden in preïndustrieel Nederland.* Amsterdam 1976.

———. "Scheepvaart op Nederland in een woelige periode, 1784–1810." *Economisch- en sociaal-historisch jaarboek* 47 (1984): 67–78.

Fasseur, C. *Kultuurstelsel en koloniale baten: De Nederlandse exploitatie van Java 1840–1860.* Leiden 1975.

———. "Purse or Principle: Dutch Colonial Policy in the 1860s and the Decline of the Cultivation System." *Modern Asian Studies* 25 (1991). 33–52.

Feyter, C. A. de. *Industrial Policy and Shipbuilding.* Utrecht 1982.

Filarski, R. *Kanalen van de Koopman-Koning.* Amsterdam 1995.

Fischer, E. J. *Fabriqueurs en fabrikanten.* Utrecht 1983.

Fischer, E. J., J.L.J.M. van Gerwen, and H.J.M. Winkelman. *Bestemming Semarang.* Oldenzaal 1991.

Fisher, I. *The Theory of Interest.* New York 1961.

Flandreau, M. "The French Crime of 1873: An Essay in the Emergence of the International Gold Standard." *Journal of Economic History* 56 (1996): 862–97.

Flora, P., et al. *State, Economy, and Society in Western Europe 1815–1975.* Vol. 1. Frankfurt 1983.

Fritschy, W. *De patriotten en de financiën van de Bataafse Republiek.* Den Haag 1988.

———. "Spoorwegaanleg in Nederland van 1831 tot 1845 en de rol van de staat." *Economisch- en sociaal-historisch jaarboek* 46 (1983): 180–227.

———. "Staatsvorming en financieel beleid onder Willem I." In C. A. Tamse and E. Witte, eds., *Staats- en natievorming in Willem I's Koninkrijk (1815–1830).* Brussel 1992, 215–36.

———. *Gewestelijke financiën ten tijde van de Republiek der Verenigde Nederlanden.* Vol. 1, *Overijssel 1604–1795.* Den Haag 1995.

Gaastra, F. S. *Bewind en beleid bij de VOC.* Zutphen 1989.

Gabriëls, J. *De heren als dienaren en de dienaar als heer.* Den Haag 1990.

Gales, B., and R. Fremdling. "IJzerfabrikanten en industriepolitiek onder Willem I: De enquête van 1828." *Neha-jaarboek* 57 (1994): 287–347.

Gedenkboek van de Kamer van Koophandel en Fabrieken te Rotterdam, 1803–1928. Rotterdam 1928.

Gedenkstukken der algemeene geschiedenis van Nederland van 1795 tot 1840. 10 vols. Den Haag 1905–22.

Geikie, R., and I. A. Montgomery. *The Dutch Barrier, 1705-1719.* Cambridge 1930.

Genabeek, J. van. *Met vereende kracht risico's verzacht.* Amsterdam 1999.

Gerding, M.A.W. *Vier eeuwen turfwinning.* Wageningen 1995.

Gerwen, J. van, and E. J. Fischer. *Bestemming Semarang.* Oldenzaal 1991.

Gerretson, C., *Geschiedenis der "Koninklijke."* 3 vols. Utrecht 1939–42.

Giele, J. J. *De pen in aanslag: Revolutionairen rond 1848.* Bussum 1968.

Gogel, I.J.A. *Memoriën en Correspondentiën betrekkelijk den Staat van 's Rijks Geld-middelen in den Jare 1820.* Amsterdam 1844.

Goor, L. van. *Banken en industriefinanciering.* Amsterdam 1999.

Gooren, H., and H. Heger. *Per mud of bij de week gewonnen.* Groningen 1993.

Gorter, R. A., and C. W. de Vries. "Gegevens omtrent den kinderarbeid in Nederland volgens de enquêtes van 1841 en 1860." *Economisch-Historisch Jaarboek* 8 (1922): 1–261.

Grantham, G. W. "Agricultural Supply during the Industrial Revolution." *Journal of Economic History* 49 (1989): 43–72.

Griffiths, R. T. "The Role of Taxation in Wage Formulation in the Dutch Economy in the First Half of the Nineteenth Century." In Joh. de Vries et al., eds., *Ondernemende geschiedenis.* 's-Gravenhage 1977, 260–71.

———. *Industrial Retardation in the Netherlands 1830–1850.* Den Haag 1979.

———. *Achterlijk, achter of anders?* Amsterdam, 1980.

———. "The Creation of a National Dutch Economy: 1795–1909." *Tijdschrift voor geschiedenis* 95 (1982): 513–37.

Groote, P. *Kapitaalvorming in infrastructuur in Nederland 1800–1913.* Groningen 1995.

Groote, P., J. Jacobs, and J.-E. Sturm. "Infrastructure and Economic Development in the Netherlands, 1853–1913." *European Review of Economic History* 3 (1999): 233–52.

Haasse, H. *Heren van de thee.* Amsterdam 1992.

Haastert, H. van, and G.W.M. Huysmans. *Veertig jaren landbouwcrediet onder leiding der Coöperatieve Centrale Boerenleenbank te Eindhoven 1898–1938.* N.p., n.d.

Hajnal, L. "European Marriage Pattern in Perspective." In D. V. Glass and D.E.C. Eversley, eds., *Population in History* London 1965, 101–47.

Handelingen der Staten-Generaal. 1817–18, 1848–49.

Hargreaves Heap, S., and Y. Varoufakis. *Game Theory: A Critical Introduction.* New York 1995.

Harkx, W.A.J.M. *De Helmondse textielnijverheid in de loop der eeuwen.* Tilburg 1967.

Harmsen, G., and B. Reinalda. *Voor de bevrijding van de arbeid.* Nijmegen 1975.

Hart, M. C. 't. *The Making of a Bourgeois State.* Manchester 1993.

Harten, J.D.H. "Het landschap in beweging." *Algemene Geschiedenis der Nederlanden* 5 (1980): 38–77.

Heerding, E. *Een onderneming van vele markten thuis.* Leiden 1986.

Heeres, W. "Het Paalgeld: Een bijdrage tot de kennis van de Nederlandse handelssta-tistiek in het verleden." *Economisc- en sociaal-historisch jaarboek* 45 (1982): 1–17.

Henriksen, I. "Avoiding Lock-In: Cooperative Creameries in Denmark, 1882–1903." *European Review of Economic History* 3 (1999): 57–78.

Hobson, J. A. *Imperialism: A Study.* London 1948.

Hodgson, G. M. *Economics and Institutions.* Oxford 1989.

Hoek Ostende, J. H. van de. "Concurrentie tussen binnen- en buitenmolenaars." *Ons Amsterdam* 19 (1967): 87.

———. "Stoomkorenmolens in Amsterdam." *Ons Amsterdam* 19 (1967): 370–72.

Hoffman, Ph.T. *Growth in a Traditional Society.* Princeton 1996.

Hoffman, Ph. T., and K. Norberg. "Conclusion." In Ph. T. Hoffman and K. Norberg, eds.,

Fiscal Crisis Liberty and Representative Government, 1450-1789. Stanford 1994, 299–310.

Hofstee, E. W. *De demografische ontwikkeling van Nederland in de eerste helft van de negentiende eeuw.* Deventer 1978.

Hogendorp, G. K. van. *Bijdragen totde huishouding van staat in het Koninkrijk der Nederlanden verzameld ten dienste der Staten-Generaal.* 10 vols. Zaltbommel 1854–55.

Homer, S., and R. Sylla. *A History of Interest Rates.* New Brunswick 1991.

Hooff, W.P.H.M. van. *In het Rijk van de Nederlandse Vulcanus.* Amsterdam 1990.

Horlings, E. *The Economic Development of the Dutch Service Sector 1800–1850.* Amsterdam 1995.

Horlings, E., and J.-P. Smits. "Private Consumer Expenditure in the Netherlands, 1800–1913." *Economic and Social History in the Netherlands* 7 (1996): 15–40.

———. "A Comparison of the Pattern of Growth and Structural Change in the Netherlands and Belgium, 1800–1913." *Jahrbuch für Wirtschaftsgeschichte,* no. 2 (1997): 83–106.

Horlings, E., and J. L. van Zanden. "Exploitatie en Afscheiding. De Financiën van de Rijksoverheid in Nederland en België, 1814–1850." Mimeo project national accounts, University of Utrecht, November 1996.

Houtman–De Smedt, H. "De Société Générale tijdens de periode 1822–1848." In E. Buyst et al., eds., *De Generale Bank 1822–1997.* Tielt 1997, 13–68.

Houwaart, E. S. *De Hygiënisten. Artsen, staat & volksgezondheid in Nederland 1840–1890.* Groningen 1991.

Hutten, Th., and H. Rutten. "De druk der omstandigheden." In A.L.G.M. Bauwens et al., eds., *Agrarisch Bestaan.* Assen 1990, 125–45.

Israel, J. *Dutch Primacy in World Trade 1585–1740.* Oxford 1989.

Jaarcijfers voor het Koninkrijk der Nederlanden. 's-Gravenhage, 1881–1913.

Jacobs, A., and H. Richter. "Die Grobhandelspreise in Deutschland von 1792 bis 1934." *Sonderhefte des Instituts für Konjunkturforschung.* Berlin 1933.

Jansen, M. *De industriële ontwikkeling in Nederland, 1800–1850.* Utrecht 1998.

Jansen, M., and C. Trompetter, "Hoezo achterlijk?" *Textielhistorische bijdragen* 35 (1995): 101–20.

Jong, A. M. de. *Geschiedenis van de Nederlandsche Bank.* Vol. 1, 1814–64. Vols. 2–4, 1864–1914. Haarlem 1967.

Jong, H. J. de. *De Nederlandse industrie 1913–1965.* Amsterdam 1999.

Jong, J. J. de. *Met Goed Fatsoen. De elite in een Hollandse stad Gouda 1700-1800.* Amsterdam/Dieren 1985.

Jonge, J. A. de. *De industrialisatie in Nederland tussen 1850 en 1914.* Amsterdam, 1968.

———. "The Role of the Outer Provinces in the Process of Dutch Economic Growth in the Nineteenth Century." In J. S. Bromley and E. H. Kossmann, eds., *Britain and the Netherlands.* Vol. 4, 208–25.

Jonckers Nieboer, J. H. *Geschiedenis der Nederlandsche Spoorwegen 1832–1938.* Rotterdam 1938.

Jonker, J. "Welbegrepen eigenbelang; ontstaan en werkwijze van boerenleenbanken in Noord-Brabant, 1900–1920." *Jaarboek voor de geschiedenis van bedrijf en techniek* 5 (1988): 188–206.

———. "Lachspiegel van de vooruitgang." *Neha-bulletin* 5 (1991): 5–23.

———. *Merchants, Bankers, Middlemen: The Amsterdam Money Market during the First Half of the Nineteenth Century.* Amsterdam 1996.

———. "The Alternative Road to Modernity: Banking and Currency 1814–1914." In M.'t Hart, J. Jonker, and J. L. van Zanden, eds., *A Financial History of the Netherlands.* Cambridge 1997, 94–123.

Kampen, N. G. van. *Geschiedenis van den Vijftienjarigen Vrede.* Haarlem 1832.

Keuchenius, W. M. *De Inkomsten en Uitgaven der Bataafsche Republiek Voorgesteld in Eene Nationaale Balans.* Amsterdam 1803.

Kint, Ph., and R.L.W. van der Voort. "Economische groei en stagnatie in de Nederlanden, 1800–1850." *Economisch- en sociaal-historisch jaarboek* 43 (1980): 114–35.

Kirby, M. W. "Institutional Rigidities and Economic Decline: Reflections on the British Experience." *Economic History Review* 45 (1992): 637–60.

Klein, P. W. "Het bankwezen en modernisering van de Nederlandse volkshuishouding tijdens de tweede helft van de 19e eeuw." *Economisch- en sociaal-historisch jaarboek* 36 (1973): 102–30.

———. "De zeventiende eeuw." In J. H. van Stuijvenberg, ed., *De economische geschiedenis van Nederland.* Groningen 1979, 79–119.

Klovland, J. T. "Pitfalls in the Estimation of the Yield on British Consols, 1850–1914." *Journal of Economic History* 54 (1994): 164–87.

Knibbe, M. *Agriculture in the Netherlands 1851–1950.* Amsterdam 1993.

Knippenberg, H., and B. de Pater. *De eenwording van Nederland.* Nijmegen 1988.

Knoppers, J.V.Th., and F. Snapper. "De Nederlandse Scheepvaart op de Oostzee vanaf het Eind van de 17e Eeuw tot het Begin van de 19e Eeuw." *Eeconomisch- en sociaal-historisch jaarboek* 41 (1978): 115–54.

Knotter, A. "De Amsterdamse bouwnijverheid in de 19e eeuw tot ca. 1870. Loonstarheid en trekarbeid op een dubbele arbeidsmarkt." *Tijdschrift voor sociale geschiedenis* 10 (1984): 123–54.

———. *Economische transformatie en stedelijke arbeidsmarkt.* Amsterdam 1991.

———. "Van 'defensieve standsreflex' tot 'verkoopkartel van arbeidskracht." *Tijdschrift voor sociale geschiedenis* 19 (1993): 68–93.

Knotter, A., and H. Muskee. "Conjunctuur en levensstandaard in Amsterdam, 1815–1855." *Tijdschrift voor Sociale Geschiedenis* 12 (1986): 153–81.

Kok, J. "The Moral Nation: Illegitimacy and Bridal Pregnancy in the Netherlands from 1600 to the Present." *Economic and Social History in the Netherlands* 2 (1990): 7–36.

Koning, N. *The Failure of Agrarian Capitalism.* Routledge 1994.

Kooijmans, L. *Onder Regenten. De elite in een Hollandse stad Hoorn 1700–1800.* Amsterdam/Dieren 1985.

Kops, J. "Betoog wegens de kracht van Hollands Landbouw." *Magazijn van Vaderlandschen Landbouw* 6 (1810–14): 217–24.

Korte, J. P. de. *De Jaarlijkse Financiële Verantwoording in de Verenigde Oostindische Compagnie.* Leiden 1984.

Korthals Altes, W. L. *De betalingsbalans van Nederlandsch-Indië 1822–1939.* N.p., 1986.

———. *Van pond Hollands tot Nederlandse gulden.* Amsterdam 1996.

Kossmann, E. H. *De Lage Landen 1780–1940* (Amsterdam/Brussel 1976).

Kramer, E. L. *De Graanwet van 1835.* Rotterdam 1940.

Kuitenbrouwer, M. *Nederland en de opkomst van het moderne Imperialisme.* Amsterdam 1985.

———. "Drie omwentelingen in de historiografie van het imperialisme in Engeland en Nederland." *Tijdschrift voor geschiedenis* 107 (1994): 559–85.

Kuznets, S., *Secular Movements in Production and Prices.* New York 1967 [1930].

———. *Modern Economic Growth: Rate, Structure and Spread.* New Haven 1966.

———. *Economic Growth of Nations: Total Output and Production Structure.* Cambridge 1971.

———. "Modern Economic Growth and the Less Developed Countries." *Conference on Experiences and Lessons of Economic Development in Taiwan.* Taipei 1981.

Kymmel, J. *Geschiedenis van de Algemene Banken in Nederland 1860–1914.* 2 vols. Amsterdam 1992–96.

L., P. W. *Bijdragen tot bekendmaking van de voornaamste zaken van den handel der Nederlanden.* Utrecht 1837.

Landes, D. S. *The Unbound Prometheus.* Cambridge 1969.

Langeveld, H. "Arbeidstoestanden op de ondernemingen ter Oostkust van Sumatra tussen 1920 en 1940." *Economisch- en sociaal-historisch jaarboek* 41 (1978): 294–368.

Leeuwen, M.H.D. van. *Bijstand in Amsterdam, ca. 1880–1850. Armenzorg als Beheerings en Overlevingsstrategie.* Utrecht 1990.

———. "Trade Unions and the Provision of Welfare in the Netherlands, 1910–1960." *Economic History Review* 50 (1997): 764–91.

Leeuwen, M.H.D., and J. E. Oeppen. "Reconstructing the Demographic Regime of Amsterdam 1681–1920." *Economic and Social History in the Netherlands* 5 (1993): 61–102.

Lijphart, A. *The Politics of Accommodation: Pluralism and Democracy in the Netherlands.* Berkeley 1968.

Lindblad, J. Th. "De handel tussen Nederland en Nederlands-Indië, 1874–1939." *Economisch- en sociaal-historisch jaarboek* 51 (1988): 240–98.

———. "De opkomst van de buitengewesten." In A.H.P. Clemens and J. Th. Lindblad, eds., *Het belang van de Buitengewesten 1870–1942.* Amsterdam 1989, 1–39.

Lindblad, J. Th., and J. L. van Zanden. "De buitenlandse handel van Nederland, 1872–1913." *Economisch- en sociaal-historisch jaarboek* 52 (1989): 231–69.

Lindert, P. H. "The Rise of Social Spending, 1880–1930." *Explorations in Economic History* 31 (1994): 1–37.

Lintsen, H. W. "Stoom als symbool van de industriële revolutie." *Jaarboek voor de Geschiedenis van Bedrijf en Techniek* 5 (1988): 337–53.

———. *Molenbedrijf en meelfabriek in Nederland in de negentiende eeuw.* 's-Gravenhage 1989.

———. "Stoom in ontwikkeling." In H. W. Lintsen et al., eds., *Geschiedenis van de Techniek in Nederland.* Vol. 4. Zutphen 1993, 111–30.

———. "Een land met stoom." In H. W. Lintsen et al., eds., *Geschiedenis van de Techniek in Nederland.* VI Zutphen 1995, 191–216.

Lintsen, H. W., et al. *De registers van de dienst van het stoomwezen, 1856–1924.* 's-Gravenhage 1900.

Lintsen, H. W., et al., eds., *Geschiedenis van de techniek in Nederland.* 6 vols. Zutphen 1992–95.

Lootsma, S. *Historische studiën over de Zaanstreek.* 2 vols. Koog aan de Zaan 1939–50.

Lucassen, J. *Naar de kusten van de Noordzee.* Gouda 1984.

———. "Het Welvaren van Leiden (1659–1662): De wording van een economische theorie over gilden en ondernemerschap. In B. de Vries et al., eds., *De kracht der zwakken.* Amsterdam 1992, 13–49.

Maandelijksche Nederlandsche Mercurius. 1783–96.

Maas, P. F. *Sociaal-democratische gemeentepolitiek 1894–1929.* 's-Gravenhage 1985.

Maas, J. van der, and L. Noordegraaf. "Smakelijk eten. Aardappelconsumptie in Holland in de achttiende eeuw en het begin van de negentiende eeuw." *Tijdschrift voor sociale geschiedenis* 9 (1983): 188–220.

Maddison, A. *Dynamic Forces in Capitalist Development: A Long-Run Comparative View.* Oxford 1991.

Malsen, H. van. *Geschiedenis van het makelaarsgilde te Amsterdam 1578–1933.* Amsterdam 1933.

Mandemakers, C. A. "De ontwikkeling van de factor arbeid binnen de Nederlandse schoenindustrie: 1860–1910." *Jaarboek voor de geschiedenis van bedrijf en techniek* 2 (1985): 104–26.

———. *Gymnasiaal en Middelbaar Onderwijs.* Almere 1996.

Mansvelt, W.M.F. *Geschiedenis van de Nederlandsche Handel-maatschappij.* 2 vols. Haarlem 1924.

Marx, K. *Het kapitaal.* Translated by I. Lipschits. Bussum 1972.

McCloskey, D., ed. *Essays on a Mature Economy: Britain after 1840.* London 1971.

Meer, W. ter. "Patroonvarianten." Master's thesis, University of Utrecht, 1994.

Meere, J.M.M. de. "Inkomensgroei en -ongelijkheid in Amsterdam 1877–1940." *Tijdschrift voor sociale geschiedenis* 13 (1979): 3–46.

———. "Daglonen in België en Nederland in 1918 - een aanvulling." *Tijdschrift voor Sociale geschiedenis* 6 (1980): 357–85.

———. *Economische ontwikkeling en levensstandaard in Nederland gedurende de eerste helft van de negentiende eeuw.* 's-Gravenhage 1982.

Metelerkamp, R. *De Toestand van Nederland in Vergelijking Gebragt met die van Eenige Andere Landen in Europa.* Rotterdam 1804.

Meulen, A. J. van der. *Studies over het Ministerie van Van de Spiegel.* Leiden 1905.

Mijnhardt, W. W. *Tot heil van 't menschdom: Culturele genootschappen in Nederland, 1750–1815.* Amsterdam 1988.

Mill, J. S. *Principles of Political Economy.* Harmondsworth, 1985 [1848].

Minderhoud, G. *Ontwikkeling en beteekenis der landbouwindustrie in Groningen.* Groningen 1925.

Mitchell, B. R. *International Historical Statistics: Europe 1750–1988.* Basingstoke 1992.

Mokyr, J. *Industrialization in the Low Countries, 1795–1850.* New Haven 1976.

———. *The Lever of Riches: Technological Creativity and Economic Progress.* New York 1990.

Muller, S. *Een Rotterdams zeehandelaar: Hendrik Muller Szn. (1819–1898).* Schiedam 1977.

Muntjewerff, H. A. *Wolspinnerij Pieter van Dooren 1826–1975.* Tilburg 1993.

Neal, L. *The Rise of Financial Capitalism: Capital Markets in the Age of Reason.* Cambridge 1990.

Nierop, L. van. "Amsterdams Scheepvaart in de Fransche Tijd." *Jaarboek Amsteloda-mum* 21 (1970): 119–39.

Noordam, F. "Sociale verzekeringen 1890–1950." In J. van Gerwen and M.H.D. van Leeuwen, eds., *Studies over zekerheidsarrangementen.* Amsterdam/Den Haag 1998, 570–604.

Noordegraaf, L. "Armoede en bedeling. Enkele numerieke aspecten van de armenzorg in het zuidelijk deel van Holland in de Bataafse en Franse tijd." *Holland* 9 (1977): 1–24.

———. *Daglonen in Alkmaar, 1500–1850.* Haarlem 1980.

Noordegraaf, L., and J. L. van Zanden. "Early Modern Economic Growth and the Standard of Living: Did Labor Benefit from Holland's Golden Age?" In C. A. Davids and J. Lucassen, eds., *A Miracle Mirrored.* Cambridge 1995, 410–37.

North, D. C. *Institutions, Institutional Change and Economic Performance.* Cambridge 1990.

North, D. C., and R. P. Thomas. *The Rise of the Western World.* Cambridge 1973.

North, D. C., and B. W. Weingast. "The Evolution of Institutions Governing Public Choice in Seventeenth-Century England." *Journal of Economic History* 49 (1989): 803–32.

———. Constitutions and Commitment." In T. Persson and G. Tabellini, eds., *Monetary and Fiscal Policy.* Vol. 1, *Credibility.* Cambridge 1994.

Nusteling, H.P.H. *De Rijnvaart in het tijdperk van stoom en steenkool 1831–1914.* Amsterdam 1974.

———. "Periods and Caesura in Demographic and Economic History of the Netherlands, 1600–1900." *Economic and Social History in the Netherlands* 1 (1989): 87–111.

O'Brien, P. "Path Dependency, or Why Britain Became an Industrialized and Urbanized Economy Long before France." *Economic History Review* 49 (1996): 213–49.

Olson, M. *The Logic of Collective Action.* Cambridge, Mass., 1965.

———. *The Rise and Decline of Nations.* New Haven and London 1982.

Oomens, C. A. "De loop der bevolking in de negentiende eeuw." *CBS Statistische Berichten* M35. Den Haag 1989.

Oud, P. J. *Honderd jaren: Een eeuw staatkundige vormgeving in Nederland, 1840–1940.* Assen 1987.

Paping, R. *Voor een handvol stuivers.* Groningen 1995.

Pennings, P. "Verzuiling in Ontzuiling." In *Compendium voor Politiek en Samenleving.* Alphen aan den Rijn 1998, 3–43.

Pfeil, T. *"Tot redding van het vaderland." Het primaat van de Nederlandse overheidsfinanciën in de Bataafs-Franse Tijd 1795–1810.* Amsterdam 1998.

Pieterson, M., et al., eds. *Het technisch labyrint.* Meppel 1981.

Poel, J.M.G. van der. *Heren en Boeren. Een studie over de commissiën van landbouw (1805–1851).* Wageningen 1949.

———. *Honderd jaar landbouwmechanisatie in Nederland.* Wageningen 1967.

Polak, M. S. *Historiografie en economie van de "muntchaos."* 2 vols. Amsterdam 1998.

Pons, G. *De bakens verzet. Een analyse van de Hollandse pekelharingvisserij met kielschepen in de periode 1814–1885.* Utrecht 1996.

Poppel, F. van. *Trouwen in Nederland.* Wageningen 1992.

Poppel, F.W.A. "Stad en platteland in demografisch perspectief." *Holland* 17 (1985): 161–80.

Popta, K. B. van. "Staatsschuld en consolidatiebeleid in Nederland in de periode 1814–1994." *Neha-jaarboek* 57 (1994): 159–205.

Portielje, D. A. *De Handel van Nederland in 1844*. Amsterdam 1844.

Posthumus, N. W. *De geschiedenis van de Leidsche Lakenindustrie*. 3 vols. Den Haag 1908–39.

———. *Nederlandsche Prijsgeschiedenis*. 2 vols. Leiden 1946–64.

Pot, G.P.M. *Arm Leiden. Levensstandaard, Bedeling en Bedeelden, 1750–1854*. Hilversum 1994.

Potgieter, E. J. *Jan, Jannetje en hun kinderen*. Zwolle 1912.

Pott-Buter, H. A. *Facts and Fairy Tales about Female Labor, Family and Fertility*. Amsterdam 1993.

Prak, M. *Gezeten burgers. De elite in een Hollandse stad Leiden 1700–1800*. Amsterdam/Dieren 1985.

———. *Republikeinse veelheid, democratische enkelvoud*. Nijmegen 1999.

Price, J. L. *Holland and the Dutch Republic in the Seventeenth Century: The Politics of Particularism*. Oxford 1994.

Priester, P. *De economische ontwikkeling van de landbouw in Groningen 1800–1910*. Wageningen 1991.

———. *Geschiedenis van de Zeeuwse landbouw circa 1600–1910*. Wageningen 1998.

Prijscourant der Effecten. 1796–1811, 1815–45.

Provinciaal Blad van Noord-Braband. 1816–50.

Provinciaal Blad van Zeeland. 1830–55.

Publicatiën van de provisionele repraesentanten van het volk van Holland der Staaten Generaal sedert het begin der revolutie in 1795 tot 1807. Leiden 1807.

Ramsden, J. *An Appetite for Power: A History of the Conservative Power since 1830*. London 1998.

Regt, A. de. *Arbeidersgezinnen en beschavingsarbeid*. Meppel 1984.

Reinsma, R. *Het verval van het cultuurstelsel*. 's-Gravenhage 1955.

Renssen, G. G. "Arbeid en ondernemerschap in Nijverdal in de overgang van pre-industriële naar industriële maatschappij." *Economisch- en sociaal-historisch Jaarboek* 44 (1981): 103–10.

Ricardo, D. *The Principles of Political Economy and Taxation*. London 1821.

Riel, A. van. "Rethinking the Economic History of the Dutch Republic: The Rise and Decline of Economic Modernity before the Advent of Industrialized Growth. *Journal of Economic History* 56 (1996): 223–29.

———. *Postponed Conformity: Prices and Economic Development in the Netherlands, 1800–1913*. Forthcoming.

Riemens, H. *Het Amortisatie-Syndicaat*. Amsterdam 1935.

Righart, H. *De Katholieke zuil in Europa. Een Vergelijkend Onderzoek naar het Ontstaan van Verzuiling onder Katholieken in Oostenrijk, Zwitserland, België en Nederland*. Amsterdam, 1986.

Riley, J. C. *International Government Finance and the Amsterdam Capital Market, 1740–1815*. Cambridge 1980.

———. "The Dutch Economy after 1650: Decline or Growth?" *Journal of European Economic History* 13 (1984): 149–89.

Roebroek, J. M., and M. Hertogh. *"De beschavende invloed des tijds." Twee eeuwen sociale politiek, verzorgingsstaat en sociale zekerheid in Nederland.* 's-Gravenhage 1998.

Roessingh, H. K. *Inlandse Tabak, Expansie en contractie van een handelsgewas in de 17e en 18e eeuw in Nederland.* Wageningen 1976.

Roland-Holst, H. *Kapitaal en arbeid in Nederland.* Amsterdam 1902.

Roos, W.A.A.M. de. *Maatschappijeconomie.* Alphen aan de Rijn 1985.

Roovers, J. J. *De plaatselijke belastingen en financiën in den loop der tijden.* Alphen aan den Rijn 1932.

Rüter, A.J.C. *De spoorwegstakingen van 1903.* Leiden 1935.

Sas, N. van. *Onze Natuurlijkste Bondgenoot.* Groningen 1985.

Schama, S. "The Exigencies of War and the Politics of Taxation in the Netherlands 1795–1810." In J. M. Winter, ed., *War and Economic Development.* Cambridge 1975.

———. *Patriots and Liberators: Revolution in the Netherlands, 1780–1813.* New York 1992.

Schiff, E. *Industrialization without National Patents.* Princeton 1971.

Schijf, H. *Netwerken van een financieel-economische elite.* Amsterdam 1993.

Schmookler, J. *Invention and Economic Growth.* Cambridge, Mass , 1966

Schöffer, I. "Verzuiling, een specifiek Nederlands Probleem." *Sociologische Gids* 7 (1956): 121–27.

Scholliers, E. "Werktijden en arbeidsomstandigheden in de pre-industriële periode." In E. Scholliers and P. Scholliers, eds., *Werktijd en werktijdverkorting.* Brussel 1983, 11–18.

Schot, J. W. "De meekrapnijverheid: de ontwikkeling van de techniek als een proces van variatie en selectie." *Jaarboek voor de geschiedenis van bedrijf en techniek* 3 (1986): 42–62.

———. "Het meekrapbedrijf in Nederland in de negentiende eeuw opnieuw bezien in het licht van het industrialisatiedebat." *Economisch- en sociaal-historisch jaarboek* 50 (1987): 77–110.

Schrover, M. *Het vette, het zoete en het wederzijds profijt.* Hilversum 1991.

Schumpeter, J. A. *Capitalism, Socialism and Democracy.* London 1974 [1943].

Schutte, G. J. *De Nederlandse patriotten en de koloniën.* Groningen 1974.

Schwarzer, O. "Die Stellung 'Westeuropas' in der Weltwirtschaft, 1750–1950." In M. North, ed., *Nordwesteuropa in der Weltwirtschaft, 1750–1950.* Stuttgart 1993, 257–90.

Sickenga, F. N. *Bijdrage tot de geschiedenis der belastingen in Nederland. . . .* Leiden: P. Engels, 1864.

———. *Geschiedenis der Nederlandsche belastingen sedert het jaar 1810.* Utrecht 1883.

Sillem, J. A. *De politieke en staathuishoudkundige werkzaamheid van Isaac Jan Alexander Gogel.* Amsterdam 1864.

Sluyterman, K., J. Dankers, J. van der Linden, and J. L. van Zanden. *Het Coöperatieve Alternatief.* Den Haag 1998.

Smith, A. *An Inquiry into the Nature and Causes of the Wealth of Nations.* London 1910 [1776].

Smits, J.P.H. "The Size and Structure of the Dutch Service Sector in International Perspective." *Economic and Social History in the Netherlands* 2 (1990): 81–98.

————. *Economische groei en Structuurveranderingen in de Nederlandse dienstensector 1850–1913.* Amsterdam 1995.

Smits, J.P.H., E. Horlings, and J. L. van Zanden. "The Measurement of Gross National Product and Its Components: The Netherlands 1800–1913." Research memorandum, N. W. Posthumus Instituut no.1. Utrecht 1997.

————. "Sprekende cijfers! De historische nationale rekeningen van Nederland, 1807–1913." *Neha-jaarboek* 62 (1999): 51–111.

Smits, J.-P., E. Horlings, and J. L. van Zanden. *Dutch GNP and Its Components, 1800–1913.* Groningen 2000.

Smits, M. *Boeren met Beleid.* Nijmegen 1996.

Soltow, L. "Inequality of Income and Wealth at the Beginning of the Nineteenth Century." In L. Soltow and J. L. van Zanden, *Income and Wealth Inequality in the Netherlands 1500–1990.* Amsterdam 1998, 111–44.

Soltow, L., and J. L. van Zanden. *Income and Wealth Inequality in the Netherlands 1500–1990.* Amsterdam 1998.

Staatsblad. 1816–35.

Statistieken van de Nederlandse nijverheid uit de eerste helft van de 19e eeuw. 2 vols. Edited by I. J. Brugmans. 's-Gravenhage 1956.

Steijn Parve, D. C. *Het koloniale monopoliestelsel.* N.p., 1851.

Steininger, R. *Polarisierung und Integration.* Meisenheim 1975.

Steur, J. J. *Herstel of ondergang.* Utrecht 1984.

Stevens, Th. *Van der Capellen's koloniale ambitie op Java.* Amsterdam 1982.

Stuurman, S. *Verzuiling, kapitalisme en patriarchaat.* Nijmegen 1983.

————. *Wacht op onze daden.* Amsterdam 1992.

————. "James Watt en Jan Salie. Over de verhouding tusen politieke geschiedenis en techniekgeschiedenis." *Neha-jaarboek* 58 (1995): 63–71.

————. *Staatsvorming en politieke theorie.* Amsterdam 1995.

Tamse, C. A. "De Politieke Ontwikkeling in Nederland, 1874–1887." *Algemene Geschiedenis der Nederlanden* 13 (1978): 208–24.

Taselaar, A. *De Nederlandse koloniale lobby.* Leiden 1998.

Te Brake, W. *Regents and Rebels.* Cambridge, Mass., 1989.

————. "Provincial Histories and National Revolution in the Dutch Republic." In M. Jacob and W. Mijnhardt, eds., *The Dutch Republic in the Eighteenth Century.* New York 1992.

Teijl, J. "Brandstofaccijns en nijverheid in Nederland gedurende de periode 1834–1864." In J. van Herwaarden et al., eds., *Lof der Historie.* Rotterdam 1973, 153–84.

Temple, W. *Observations upon the United Provinces of the Netherlands.* Amsterdam 1673.

Thorbecke, J. R. "Verhandeling over den invloed der machines op het zamenstel der maatschappelijke en burgerlijke betrekkingen." *Bijdragen voor vaderlandse geschiedenis en oudheidkunde* 8 (1940): 145–60.

Tielhof, M. van. "Grain Provision in Holland, ca. 1490–1570." In P. Hoppenbrouwers and J. L. van Zanden, eds., *Peasants into Farmers? The Transformation of the Rural Economy in the Low Countries (Middle Ages–Nineteenth Century) in Light of the Brenner Debate.* Turnhout 2001, 202–20.

Tijn, Th. van. "Pieter de la Court. Zijn leven en zijn economische denkbeelden." *Tijdschrift voor geschiedenis* 69 (1956): 304–70.

———. "The Party Structure of Holland and the Outer Provinces in the Nineteenth Century." In J. S. Bromley and E. H. Kossmann, eds., *Britain and the Netherlands.* Vol. 4. Den Haag 1971, 176–207.

———. "De Algemeene Nederlandsche Diamantbewerkersbond (ANDB): Een succes en zijn verklaring." *Bijdragen en mededelingen betreffende de geschiedenis der Nederlanden* 88 (1973): 403–18.

———. "Geschiedenis van de Amsterdamse diamanthandel en -nijverheid, 1845–1897." *Tijdschrift voor geschiedenis* 87 (1974): 16–70, 160–201.

———. "Voorlopige notities over het ontstaan van het moderne klassebewustzijn in Nederland." *Mededelingenblad* 45 (1974): 33–38.

———. *Twintig jaren Amsterdam.* Amsterdam 1975.

———. "Bijdrage tot de wetenschappelijke studie van de vakbondsgeschiedenis." In P.A.M. Geurts and F.A.M. Messing, eds., *Theoretische en methodologische aspecten van de economische en sociale geschiedenis.* Vol. 2. Den Haag 1979, 159–87.

Tilly, C. *Coercion, Capital, and European States, AD 990–1990.* Oxford 1990.

Tracy, J. D. *A Financial Revolution in the Habsburg Netherlands.* London 1985.

Trompetter, C. *Agriculture, Proto-Industry and Mennonite Entrepreneurship.* Amsterdam 1997.

———. "Burgers en Boeren. Geld en Grond." *Neha-jaarboek* 60 (1997): 7–36.

———. "Geld genoeg. Ondernemersgedrag in de Twentse textielnijverheid in de achttiende en vroege negentiende eeuw." In C. Trompetter and J. L. van Zanden, eds., *Over de geschiedenis van het platteland in Overijssel.* Kampen 2001, 93–113.

Uitkomsten van het onderzoek naar den toestand van den landbouw in Nederland, ingesteld door de Landbouwcommissie, benoemd bij K. B. van 18 sept. 1886, nummer 28. 4 vols. Den Haag 1890.

Uittenbogaard, R. "Penningen en Papieren. Waarom de Republiek geen Centrale Bank had." Master's thesis, University of Utrecht, 1996.

Van Oss' effectenboek. Groningen 1903–13.

Vandenbroeke, C., F. van Poppel, and A. M. van der Woude. "De zuigelingen- en kindersterfte in België en Nederland in seculair perspectief." *Tijdschrift voor geschiedenis* 94 (1981): 461–91.

Veen, D. van der. "Arbeidsduur in Nederland vanaf ca. 1890 tot ca. 1925." In E. Scholliers and P. Scholliers, eds., *Werktijd en werktijdverkorting.* Brussel 1983, 40–59.

Veenendaal, A. J. *Slow Train to Paradise.* Stanford 1996.

———. *De IJzeren weg in een land vol water.* Amsterdam 1998.

Verberne, L.G.J. *Geschiedenis van Nederland in de jaren 1813–1850.* 2 vols. Utrecht and Antwerpen 1958.

Verheul, M. M. "Anderhalve eeuw Rijnvaart." Master's thesis, University of Utrecht 1994.

Vermaas, A., S. W. Verstegen, and J. L. van Zanden. "Income Inequality in the Nineteenth Century: Evidence for a Kuznets Curve?" In L. Soltow and J. L. van Zanden, eds., *Income and Wealth Inequality in the Netherlands 1500–1990.* Amsterdam 1998, 145–74.

Vermeulen, W. H. *Den Haag en de landbouw.* Assen 1966.

Voort, R. van der. *Overheidsbeleid en overheidsfinanciën in Nederland 1850–1913.* Amsterdam 1994.

Vrankrijker, A.C.J. de. *Belastingen in Nederland 1848–1893.* Haarlem 1967.

Vries, B. W. de. *De Nederlandse papiernijverheid in de negentiende eeuw.* 's-Gravenhage 1957.

Vries, H. de. *Landbouw en bevolking tijdens de agrarische depressie in Friesland (1878–1895).* Wageningen 1971.

Vries, J. de. *The Dutch Rural Economy in the Golden Age, 1500–1700.* New Haven 1974.

———. "Barges and Capitalism." *AAG Bijdragen* 21 (1978): 33–398.

———. "The Decline and Rise of the Dutch Economy, 1675–1900." In G. Saxonhouse and G. Wright, eds., *Technique, Spirit and Form in the Making of the Modern Economies.* Greenwich 1984.

———. "How Did Pre-industrial Labour Markets Function?" In G. Grantham and M. MacKinnon, eds., *Labour Market Evolution.* London 1994, 39–63.

———. "The Production and Consumption of Wheat in the Netherlands, with Special Reference to Zeeland in 1789." In H. A. Diederiks, J. H. Lindblad, and B. de Vries, eds., *Het Platteland in een Veranderende Wereld. Boeren en het Proces van Modernisering.* Hilversum 1994, 199–220.

Vries, J. de, and A. M. van der Woude. *Nederland 1500–1815.* Amsterdam 1995.

Vries, Joh. de. *De Economische achteruitgang der Republiek in de Achttiende Eeuw.* Leiden 1959.

———. "Het censuskiesrecht en de welvaart in Nederland 1850–1917." *Economisch-en sociaal-historisch jaarboek* 34 (1971): 178–231.

Vrolik, S. *Verslag van al het verrigte tot herstel van het Nederlandsche muntwezen.* Utrecht 1853.

Waal, E. de. *Aanteekeningen over koloniale onderwerpen.* Den Haag 1864–66.

Wegener Sleeswijk, R. S. "Rendement van 36 Friese partenrederijen (1740–1830)." *Fries Scheepvaart Museum en Oudheidkamer Jaarboek* 1986, 66–98.

Welcker, J. M. *Heren en Arbeiders in de vroege Nederlandse arbeidersbeweging 1870–1914.* Amsterdam 1978.

Wels, C. B. "Stemmen en Kiezen 1795–1922." *Tijdschrift voor Geschiedenis* 92 (1979): 313–32.

Wennekes, W. *De Aartsvaders. Grondleggers van het Nederlandse bedrijfsleven.* Antwerpen 1993.

Westerman, W. M. *De concentratie in het bankwezen.* 's-Gravenhage 1919.

Westermann, J. C. *Kamer van Koophandel en Fabrieken voor Amsterdam 1811–1922.* Amsterdam 1936.

Weststrate, C. *Gedenkboek uitgegeven ter gelegenheid van het vijftigjarig bestaan der Coöperatieve Centrale Raiffeisen-Bank te Utrecht, 1898–1948.* Utrecht 1948.

White, E. N. "The French Revolution and the Politics of Government Finance, 1770–1815." *Journal of Economic History* 55 (1995): 250–51.

Wieringa, W. J. *Economische heroriëntering in Nederland in de 19e eeuw.* Groningen 1955.

Wijnen-Sponselee, R. *Het Wit-Gele Kruis in Noord-Brabant 1916–1974.* Tilburg 1997.

Wijsenbeek-Olthuis, Th. *Achter de gevels van Delft.* Hilversum 1987.

Williamson, J. G. "The Impact of the Corn Laws Just Prior to Repeal." *Explorations in Economic History* 27 (1990): 123–56.

———. "Globalization, Convergence, and History." *Journal of Economic History* 56 (1996): 277–306.

Williamson, O. E. *Markets and Hierarchies: Analysis and Antitrust Implications*. New York 1975.

———. *The Economic Institutions of Capitalism*. New York 1985.

Wilson, C. *The History of Unilever*. 2 vols. London 1954.

Wit, C.H.E. de. *De strijd tussen aristocratie en democratie in Nederland 1780–1848*. Heerlen 1965.

———. *Thorbecke en de wording van de Nederlandse natie*. Nijmegen 1980.

Wit, O. de. "Telegrafie en telefonie." In H. W. Lintsen et al., eds., *Geschiedenis van de Techniek in Nederland. De wording van een moderne samenleving 1800–1890*. Vol. 4. Zutphen 1993, 271–98.

Witlox, H.J.M. *Schets van de Ontwikkeling van Welvaart en Bedrijvigheid in het Verenigd Koninkrijk der Nederlanden, 1815–1830*. Nijmegen, 1956.

Woud, A. van der. *Het Lege Land. De ruimtelijke orde van Nederland 1798–1848*. Amsterdam 1987.

Woude, A. M. van der. "Demografische ontwikkeling van de Noordelijke Nederlanden." *Algemene Geschiedenis der Nederlanden*. Vol. 5. Haarlem 1980.

Wright, H.R.C. *Free Trade and Protection in the Netherlands, 1816–1830*. Cambridge 1955.

Wright, J. F. "The Contribution of Overseas Savings to the Funded National Debt of Great Britain, 1750–1815." *EHR* 50 (1997): 657–74.

Zanden, J. L. van. *De economische ontwikkeling van de Nederlandse landbouw in de negentiende eeuw, 1800–1914*. Wageningen 1985.

———. "De economie van Holland in de periode 1650–1805: Groei of achteruitgang?" *Bijdragen en mededelingen betreffende de geschiedenis der Nederlanden* 102 (1987): 562–609.

———. "Economische groei in Nederland in de Negentiende Eeuw, Enkele Nieuwe Resultaten." *Economisch- en sociaal-historisch jaarboek* 50 (1987): 51–76.

———. *De industrialisatie in Amsterdam 1825–1914*. Bergen 1987.

———. "The First Green Revolution: The Growth of Production and Productivity in European Agriculture." *Economic History Review* 44 (1991): 215–39.

———. "Historische ontwikkeling van de nominale en de reële rente." In A. Knoester and H. Visser, eds., *De hoge reële rente en de Nederlandse economie. Preadviezen 1991 van de Koninklijke Vereniging voor Staathuishoudkunde*. Leiden 1991, 23–34.

———. "De introductie van stoom in de Amsterdamse meelfabricage 1828–1855." *Jaarboek voor de geschiedenis van bedrijf en techniek* 8 (1991): 63–80.

———. *Den zedelijken en materiëlen toestand der arbeidende bevolking ten platten lande*. Wageningen 1991.

———. "Economic Growth in the Golden Age: The Development of the Economy of Holland, 1500–1650." *Economic and Social History in the Netherlands* 4 (1993): 5–26.

———. *The Rise and Decline of Holland's Economy*. Manchester 1993.

———. "Regionale verschillen in landbouwproduktiviteit en loonpeil in de Lage Landen aan het begin van de negentiende eeuw." *Neha-jaarboek* 57 (1994): 271–86.

———. "The Development of Government Finances in a Chaotic Period, 1807–1850." *Economic and Social History in the Netherlands* 7 (1996): 57–72.

———. *Een klein land in de twintigste eeuw*. Utrecht 1997.

———. "Twee maal aan de top: Nederlandse landbouwproductiviteit in vergelijkend perspectief." *Tijdschrift voor sociaal wetenschappelijk onderzoek van de landbouw* 12 (1997): 357–66.

———. *The Economic History of the Netherlands 1914–1995.* London 1998.

———. "An Experiment in Measurement of the Wealth of Nations." In B. van Ark et al., eds., *Historical Benchmark Comparisons of Output and Productivity: Proceedings Twelfth International Economic History Congress.* Vol. B10. Madrid 1998, 49–60.

———. "The Paradox of the Marks." *Agricultural History Review* 47 (1999): 125–45.

Zanden, J. L. van, and E. Horlings. "The Rise of the European Economy." In: D. H. Aldcroft and A. Sutcliffe, eds., *Europe in the International Economy.* Cheltenham 1999, 16–50.

Zanden, J. L. van, and A. van Riel. *Nederland 1780–1914. Staat, instituties en economische ontwikkeling.* Amsterdam 2000.

Zappey, W. M. *De economische en politieke werkzaamheid van Johannes Goldberg (1763–1828).* Alphen aan de Rijn 1967.

———. "Het fonds voor de nationale nijverheid 1821–1846." In P. Boomgaard et al., eds., *Exercities in ons verleden.* Assen 1981, 27–42.

Zon, H. van. *Een zeer onfrisse geschiedenis.* Groningen 1986.

Zwart, B. C. *De Kamer van Koophandel en Fabrieken te Amsterdam 1811–1911.* Amsterdam n.d.

Index

Milton Keynes UK
Ingram Content Group UK Ltd.
UKHW020804020824
446340UK00001B/4/J

9 780691 114385